D1116115

THE
VOUCHER
PROMISE

THE VOUCHER PROMISE

"SECTION 8" AND THE FATE OF AN AMERICAN NEIGHBORHOOD

EVA ROSEN

PRINCETON UNIVERSITY PRESS

PRINCETON AND OXFORD

Published by Princeton University Press
41 William Street, Princeton, New Jersey 08540
6 Oxford Street, Woodstock, Oxfordshire OX20 1TR

press.princeton.edu

ISBN: 978-0-691-17256-9
ISBN (e-book): 978-0-691-18950-5

British Library Cataloging-in-Publication Data is available

Editorial: Meagan Levinson and Jacqueline Delaney
Production Editorial: Ellen Foos
Text Design: Leslie Flis
Production: Erin Suydam
Publicity: Maria Whelan and Kathryn Stevens

Jacket image courtesy of Baltimore Sun Media. All rights reserved.

This book has been composed in Arno Pro

Printed on acid-free paper. ∞

Printed in the United States of America

10 9 8 7 6 5 4 3 2 1

CONTENTS

Preface   vii

Introduction   1

Chapter 1. Park Heights: "A Ghost Town"   28

Chapter 2. Housing Insecurity and Survival Strategies   60

Chapter 3. "A Place to Call Home": The Promise of
       Housing Vouchers   91

Chapter 4. "No Vouchers Here": The Challenges of
       Using the Voucher   114

Chapter 5. "A Tenant for Every House": The Role of Landlords   130

Chapter 6. The Receiving Neighborhood: "Not in
       My Front Yard"   165

Chapter 7. Moving On   209

Chapter 8. Conclusion   234

Methodological Appendix   261
Acknowledgments   273
Notes   277
Works Cited   303
Index   323

PREFACE

In this country, growing up in the right neighborhood means you have a good chance of going to college, finding a job, settling down, and getting married. But if you grow up in the wrong neighborhood, you have a vastly lower chance of even living to see your twentieth birthday. In Baltimore, which neighborhood you grow up in has everything to do with the color of your skin. For many Americans in cities across the country, this is a simple fact of life.

A few years before I started the research for this book, I went to Baltimore for the first time to interview families who had participated in one of the largest social experiments this country has ever seen. In the late 1990s, a program called Moving to Opportunity, or MTO, offered nearly 5,000 families living in public housing in five cities across the country the chance to receive a voucher that could be used to rent a home in the private market. If where you live matters, then what would happen if policymakers offered families who lived in the most disadvantaged neighborhoods the chance to move somewhere with less crime, lower poverty, and better schools? The goal of this experiment was to definitively show whether and how the neighborhood environment shapes the lives of those who live within it. Social scientists followed participating families as they left public housing and watched to see where they moved, what kind of jobs they got, how their health fared, and how their kids did in school.

One afternoon, I set out with a list of addresses—my "cases"—on the seat next to me. I was to track down the MTO families who had participated in the housing study some ten years earlier and interview them about how things had changed in their lives. For the third time that week, I took a wrong turn down a small street in Park Heights, a neighborhood in the northwest part of the city. And for the third time, I came to the end of the short block where the road was barricaded with a big cement slab. Google Maps did not seem to understand that this road led nowhere. There were a few teenagers hanging out. They probably recognized me by now. One of the kids shook his head at me, smiling. I waved and turned the car around to try to get to the other end of the street.

Residents in Park Heights, as in many other neighborhoods to which voucher holders are flocking, face extraordinary poverty and violence. Life expectancy is almost fifteen years less than in affluent, white areas of the city.[1] One in four households lives under the federal poverty line, compared to only one in six nationwide. Unemployment is rampant. Despite the drastic drop in crime across the country, the crime spike of the 1980s and 1990s has only partially abated in neighborhoods like this one.[2] For the last several years, incidents of police brutality and ensuing unrest from Ferguson to Baltimore have brought America's attention to communities like Park Heights, and raised questions about underlying issues of poverty, unequal housing, and patterns of economic and racial apartheid in the U.S.

Policymakers hoped that with the ability afforded by the voucher to rent homes in new neighborhoods, poor families would spread out and access better schools, more job opportunities, and safer communities. But in a city of over 600,000 people, with only 636 MTO participants, why was I coming back to the same neighborhood over and over to find families on my case list? Were voucher holders moving disproportionately to this neighborhood?

The story of MTO is part of a bigger story of the way we provide housing for poor Americans today: housing vouchers. In 2011, I moved back to Baltimore to learn more about housing vouchers, and how they shape the lives of the over two million households who receive them. To begin my housing search, I called a number on a Craigslist ad for a one-bedroom in Park Heights. The landlord on the other end of the line asked me skeptically if I was sure I knew where Park Heights was. I convinced him to show me the converted row home later that afternoon. When I showed up, the landlord, an Air Force retiree with a head of thick, silvery hair, took one look at me and simply said, "Sweetheart, this is not a neighborhood for a girl like you." What he meant was, white people don't live in Park Heights.

A few weeks later I moved into a big apartment complex a few blocks down. Here too, I met some friendly resistance. Miss Betty, the friendly African American property manager for the complex, unnecessarily tried to assure me: "Don't worry, the folks on 'Housing' is all on the other side." Soon I learned that by "Housing," she meant the Housing Choice Voucher (HCV) program, also colloquially known as "Section 8." This federally funded program subsidizes the rent of many low-income households who rent homes in the private market. Over 17 percent of the homes occupied by renters in Park Heights were inhabited by voucher holders. But in my complex, these "Section 8" renters, as they are anachronistically known, occupied closer to half of the units, all of them located on the older side of the complex. The units on that side were smaller and hadn't been renovated as recently.

I spent more than a year in Park Heights, getting to know families and learning about why they moved to this neighborhood, accompanying them on housing searches and spending long hours sitting on front stoops chatting and people-watching in the neighborhood. I also got to know landlords who rented homes to families in the neighborhood. And I learned about the history of the neighborhood and the home-owners who had settled there decades ago.

Park Heights, like so many neighborhoods across the country, is part of a larger story of years of housing policy that confined black residents to poor areas of the city. After the Great Depression, federally backed mortgages made it easy for whites to buy homes, but nearly impossible for blacks to do so. Banks engaged in "redlining"—identifying predominantly black neighborhoods where the federal government declined to insure loans—in which they refused to lend or offer mortgages. White neighborhood associations enacted restrictive covenants to keep blacks out, and city zoning codes reinforced segregation.[3] In the 1960s, neighborhoods like Park Heights opened up to blacks for the first time, but through a process of "predatory inclusion," their access was on more expensive and unequal terms.[4] Real estate agents stoked fears of black incursion in Park Heights by flipping white-owned homes one at a time—a practice known as blockbusting. As whites fled in the subsequent decade, Park Heights transformed from 95 percent white and predominantly Jewish to 95 percent black.

It wasn't just Park Heights, and it wasn't just Baltimore. In 1967, Otto Kerner, then the governor of Illinois, led a commission that looked into the causes of urban unrest in cities like Detroit, Newark, Los Angeles, and Chicago. The Kerner Commission's final report revealed discrimination entrenched in federal housing policies. It pervaded every aspect of the system, ranging from how home loans were granted to where public housing was built. The commission warned of a nation "moving toward two societies, one black, one white—separate and unequal." As public housing stock aged and inner cities across the country declined, cities like Baltimore were living out this prophecy.

In the 1990s, facing levels of concentrated poverty never before seen, blighted high-rise towers were demolished across the country, and along with them began the dismantling of an entire system of publicly owned housing for the poor. Vouchers were used to transfer much of the burden of sheltering the poor to the private market: Out of the five million households across the country that receive some form of federal housing assistance, over half now live in privately owned properties.

Residents of public housing were "vouchered out," that is, they were kicked out of their homes in public housing and offered a ticket to live in their choice of private market housing with a significant subsidy. By making up the difference between what a needy household can afford and the market rent of the unit, the voucher can provide safe, affordable housing for the poor households who receive it. On these first counts, the program has done exceedingly well.

Beyond simply housing the poor, a secondary goal of the program has become to create choice for recipients, providing opportunities to move to safer neighborhoods with better schools and more jobs. It was hoped that by relying on the private market, the program could circumvent some of the pitfalls of public housing by allowing families a choice of where to live. But as I learned from the families in Park Heights, vouchers are harder to use than we might have expected. What's more, policymakers were fundamentally wrong in their assumption that "choice" alone would create widespread neighborhood mobility, let alone uproot existing patterns of segregation and concentrated poverty.

I started this research trying to understand the transition from public housing to housing vouchers, and to figure out why a program meant to provide choice results in so many voucher holders living in neighborhoods like Park Heights. What I found was that it was no accident that Park Heights is home to so many voucher holders. The history of the neighborhood plays a key role. Residential choice is highly constrained by the rules of the voucher program, limited by the supply and demand forces of the private housing market, and manipulated by landlords.

Yet vouchers remain one of the most powerful tools we have to help low-income households afford to put a roof over their heads. In focusing on the shortcomings of the program we sometimes miss the basic ways in which it provides shelter, security, stability, and flexibility. While vouchers fall prey to some of the same problems of the housing programs that came before them, they also have distinct advantages, and they have the potential to be more than just part of the problem; they have the potential to be part of the solution.

THE
VOUCHER
PROMISE

INTRODUCTION

A few months before I met Vivian Warner, she got the call she had been waiting for.[1] It had been so long that she'd forgotten to hope for it. After four years on the waiting list, Baltimore City Housing Authority (HABC)—the agency that oversees subsidized housing in the city—called to tell her that she had won the lottery entered by thousands of Baltimoreans. She would receive a housing voucher and could finally move off of her sister's couch and into her own home. A few weeks later, Vivian boarded a bus with the other lucky winners and drove around the city to visit eligible homes. At the last stop, the bus pulled up in front of a low-rise apartment complex. It was not quite what Vivian had imagined, but there was a two-bedroom available, and she would pay just $55 a month out of pocket from her part-time income. Vivian signed the lease that afternoon.

The housing voucher Vivian waited years to receive is part of the federal government's most recent effort to house the poor. Since the 1930s, it has employed housing assistance as a key tool in its war on urban blight and poverty. But these attempts have often failed to help all the people they were meant to protect, and at times they have re-created the very inequality they hoped to dismantle.

Vivian is among the over two million families whose rent is paid for—in large part—by the government. She belongs to a generation of poor urban dwellers who left the high-rise buildings of public housing en masse, enticed by the chance to break off their own piece of the American dream. More than white picket fences, they yearn for a home to call their own and a yard for their children to play in safely. Housing vouchers, which families can use to pay their rent in an affordable home, offer men and women like Vivian—many of whom were born in public housing—their very first chance to choose where to live.

By untethering federal housing aid from the disadvantaged neighborhoods to which it was attached in the past, this system was meant to offer the poor access to a new world: safe streets, good schools, and well-paying jobs. It marked a new housing regime, one built to create opportunity through choice. With vouchers in hand, policymakers promised, millions of poor Americans would be free to move to neighborhoods of their choosing. It was hoped that housing vouchers would be a ticket out of disadvantaged neighborhoods, and ultimately even be a tool in dismantling such neighborhoods. But what happened is more complicated.

———

Vivian has lived in Baltimore all her life. Once a bustling metropolis—America's sixth largest city in 1960—Baltimore was a classic "Rust Belt" urban center, built on industrial manufacturing, shipping, and transportation. But Baltimore experienced a dramatic decline beginning in the 1970s. The large steel plant located southeast of the city, Bethlehem Steel's "Sparrow's Point," began slowing production in the early seventies and was eventually closed in 1997. Many jobs were lost over this period, and with them 34 percent of the city's total population and almost 50 percent of the white population.[2] Baltimore remains a historically "black-white" city, with a black population share of 64 percent, a white share of 30 percent, and a Hispanic or Latino share of just 4 percent.[3]

Today the city is largely invisible to many Americans, who pass through with merely a glimpse from a passing Amtrak window. If they looked closer, they might see that inequality in Baltimore—like in so many cities across the country—is stark. There is a huge difference between the crumbling and vacant blocks of poor neighborhoods that fan out to the east and west sides of the city—and the serene, grassy lawns of the stately houses in Roland Park.

After visiting a number of homes around the city, Vivian moved to a neighborhood in the northwest, called Park Heights. Life expectancy for residents of Park Heights is fifteen years lower than in the white neighborhood of Roland Park, where people live to the ripe old age of eighty-four. While one quarter of Baltimoreans live under the poverty line, close to a third of residents in Park Heights are poor[4] and unemployment is rampant.[5] Even though crime has drastically declined across the country, Baltimore is still frequently named in the top ten most dangerous U.S. cities, and Park Heights one of its more violent neighborhoods. Residents in Park Heights face unimaginable poverty and violence. It is to these types of neighborhoods that voucher holders in Baltimore—and in many cities across the country—are moving. With a ticket to rent in a wide range of Baltimore neighborhoods, why did Vivian end up in this one?

Over the past twenty years, changes in American housing policy have transformed the landscape of urban poverty. In cities like Baltimore, much of the high-rise public housing has been dismantled, but the poor families it housed have not disappeared. This creates an important set of puzzles related to housing the poor: when low-income renters are given the opportunity in the form of a voucher to afford a home in a wide range of neighborhoods, where do they end up and how do these neighborhoods matter for their futures? While vouchers may not be providing the mobility that was hoped for, what advantages *do* they offer families? How does a housing voucher impact a family's residential experience? What role does the receiving neighborhood play in their lives?

To answer these questions, I moved to Park Heights in 2011.[6] I spent more than a year there getting to know residents and learning about the story of housing vouchers. Residents welcomed me into their homes to eat meals, help with chores, and celebrate holidays. I accompanied families in their daily lives, attended church with them, and saw loved ones buried. I sat for hours on homeowners' porches where they regaled me with stories of the well-kept, tree-lined streets that greeted them when they first moved in. I went on housing searches with renters, visiting home after home, witnessing inspections and evictions. I also spent time with landlords in the neighborhood, learning about their business practices, watching them do repairs, paint and repaint, unclog toilets, show units to prospective tenants, and deliver eviction notices.

Through stories of the renting families, the homeowners, and the landlords I came to know, I document the reality of a new era of housing policy, and how it operates within a particular neighborhood context. Policymakers hoped this policy might solve poverty by providing neighborhood opportunity in the form of jobs, social networks, education, and safety. Like their forebears, members of this generation of low-income families dream of living in their own homes, making their own choices, and raising children on their own terms. The reality is that no matter the shape of their desires and choices, the bounds of housing assistance shape their futures indelibly.

This book is the story of a housing policy, one that shows great potential as a key to addressing the affordable housing crisis, yet also faces critical limitations. In this newest chapter in America's housing history, the ghetto is not defined by walls or imposed with locks or gates. Instead, subsidized renters have been released from the confines of public housing and offered the choice of living in the private rental market. Vouchers offer a powerful tool to keep people from becoming homeless, as well as the flexibility to move when needed. But only a fraction of those who need a voucher get one. And of those who do receive one, many are unable to use it when and where they want to, if they are able to use it at all.

There has always been a tension within the voucher program. While its explicit goal is to provide relief from raw poverty by making housing more affordable, policymakers have increasingly embraced a broader agenda of providing families with more choice in where to live.[7] The voucher program has had much success in the first goal, but it has largely failed in the second.

Despite lofty hopes of uprooting patterns of racial segregation and poverty, this new approach to housing the poor has instead mirrored those same patterns. While families who receive assistance through a voucher in theory have more choice than they would have in public housing, much like their unsubsidized counterparts, they face severe barriers to finding a home of their choice in the private market. In some cases, the stigma of housing assistance makes finding a home even harder.

It might seem paradoxical that a federal program that some imagined would be a tool to dismantle concentrated poverty and segregation would end up mirroring the very same patterns. But perhaps we shouldn't be surprised. Given the policy decision to rely *by design* on the private production and management of rental housing to meet the housing needs of very low-income people, perhaps we might have expected that such a program would mirror the patterns of discrimination and segregation in the private market. And—without measures to counteract these private market forces—it will continue to do so.

A SHORT HISTORY OF HOUSING INEQUALITY

A roof over one's head. A place to call home. These are quintessential markers of the American dream. Housing is inextricably linked to a wide array of social goods like stable employment, quality education, health and well-being, and the accrual of wealth. And, just as there is so much good wrought by a safe, stable home, the lack of one can inflict much harm. It is impossible to understand inequality in this country without first understanding the ways in which housing and the policies that surround it have made, unmade, and remade patterns of concentrated poverty and racial segregation. Housing lies at the nexus of pervasive poverty, rapidly rising inequality, and pockets of stubbornly entrenched racial segregation.

There is a recent return to studying housing itself, not just as a physical entity, but as a structure that shapes social relationships in important ways.[8] In fact, this tradition in sociology goes way back. W.E.B. Du Bois studied housing in Philadelphia's Seventh Ward in *The Philadelphia Negro* (1899), and Louis Wirth set an agenda for "Housing as a Field of Sociological Research." In the sixties, seventies, and eighties, sociologists such as Lee Rainwater and Herbert Gans studied how the physical setting of the home shaped social relations in the public housing complex of the notorious Pruitt-Igoe in St. Louis and in the "slum" neighborhood of the West End in Boston before they were torn down.[9] Since then, sociologists have shifted to focusing their attention more on the neighborhood context than on the housing itself.[10]

William Julius Wilson's *The Truly Disadvantaged* brought attention to the plight of the urban poor in the inner cities of Rust-Belt urban areas like Chicago, where manufacturing jobs had departed, and with them,

the middle class.[11] Wilson's attention to this population inspired decades of ethnographic work: Elijah Anderson's *Code of the Street*, examining the social code of behavior in urban neighborhoods; Mary Pattillo's *Black Picket Fences*, considering the plight of a middle-class black
neighborhood; Sudhir Venkatesh's *American Project*, looking at public
housing residents as their homes were being torn down; and more recently, works such as Matthew Desmond's *Evicted*, looking at the process of eviction among poor tenants in Milwaukee, and Kathryn Edin
and Luke Shaefer's *$2.00 a Day*, documenting the survival tactics of the
extreme poor.[12] However, more than an ethnography of a place, a community, or a group of people—though it is these things too—this book
is an ethnography of a policy.

This book attempts to bring the physical nature of housing, the markets that govern it, and the social relationships to which housing structures give rise back into the study of neighborhoods in urban sociology.
We are embedded not merely in our neighborhoods, but also in our
homes. And the role of landlords—a key actor in the lives of poor
Americans—remains largely unexplored. In this way, housing conditions are not just an outcome of poverty, but also a cause.

Across the history of this country, the right to a home has never been
inalienable, and some Americans have always had more access to it than
others. In order to understand the landscape of housing in Park Heights,
it is important to understand the history of housing discrimination,
which has affected the life chances and well-being of poor minority
Americans throughout the history of this country. Even as the federal
government has employed housing assistance as a key tool in its war on
poverty and urban blight, and the legal system has been used to combat
entrenched discriminatory housing practices, housing discrimination
has remained deeply entrenched in both private and public practice, as
well as in the law itself.[13]

In the private domain, this country has a deep and ugly tradition of
excluding blacks from white neighborhoods. As black families migrated
from the South during the Great Migration, many white communities
reacted by enacting racially restrictive covenants, which were legally
binding agreements among homeowners dictating that their properties

could not be passed on to African Americans.[14] These agreements were enforced by homeowner and neighborhood associations.

In a 1917 case, *Buchanan v. Warley*, the Supreme Court declared explicit racial zoning—ordinances barring those of certain racial backgrounds in certain neighborhoods—to be unconstitutional, an important win for civil rights. However, the case only applied to *explicit* racial zoning, and so economic zoning—enlarging lot sizes and prohibiting multifamily dwellings—became more commonplace. Private racial covenants also became even more widespread in backlash to the ruling.[15] In 1926, the Supreme Court upheld private racial covenants in *Corrigan v. Buckley*. It wasn't until 1948 in *Shelley v. Kraemer* that the court decided that private covenants were unenforceable in a court of law; and in 1968, the Fair Housing Act made writing racial covenants into home deeds illegal. However, because private agreements are attached to land titles in perpetuity until they are manually removed, they remained widespread, effectively keeping black residents out of white communities across the country for years to come.[16]

Simultaneously, blacks were systematically unable to access mortgage capital.[17] The Federal Housing Administration (FHA)—created in 1934 to regulate home mortgages and make homeownership more widely available—underwrote home loans for millions of white Americans, while systematically denying them to black families. This process—called redlining, for the crimson lines drawn around the "risky" neighborhoods inhabited by African Americans—was a racially based color-coded mapping system that banks used to determine the provision of federally backed home loans. Excluding black neighborhoods from access to the home loans that were extended to large swathes of the rest of the country starved these communities of much needed mortgage capital. It asphyxiated development, limiting residents' access to adequate civil services, public transportation, and even fresh food.

Redlining was curbed by the Fair Housing Act of 1968 and the Community Reinvestment Act of 1977 and is no longer supported by federal underwriting of home loans. However, real estate agents, property owners, and loan officers continue to discriminate against black renters and homebuyers.[18] And policies to outlaw and remedy the discriminatory practices of racial covenants and redlining were not sufficient to undo decades of disinvestment, underdevelopment, landlord abandonment, and even arson: the damage was done.

In the domain of federally assisted rental housing as well, both de facto and de jure discrimination have shaped opportunities for low-income Americans, especially minority groups.[19] Since its inception in the 1930s, federal housing assistance has offered housing to many who need it, in the hopes that a clean and safe place to live will lift the destitute out of the trenches of poverty. But today only one-quarter of those in this country who need housing assistance get it.[20] And even for those lucky enough to receive assistance, federal programs have not always worked the way they were meant to.

Housing policy in the U.S. has cycled through a series of attempts at dismantling poverty. Tenement housing in neighborhoods like New York's Lower East Side and Chicago's South Side were America's first ghettos. As immigrants came to the cities for work, they were housed in old buildings divided into small apartments that soon were teeming with families—and tuberculosis.[21] The federal government's role in housing the poor developed in response.

In the 1930s, when modern industry, urbanization, and the ills of the Great Depression brought hardship for the working class to a fever pitch in America's cities, the U.S. government sought to alleviate the misery of slums overflowing with immigrants from overseas and migrants from the south. In the decades of the midcentury, these tenements were replaced with low-rise garden-style public housing. In other areas, state-of-the-art high-rise towers were erected, with public funding and great fanfare, across the country.

These tall towers were gleaming celebrations of modern technology. In a new approach to housing the poor, these buildings promised health, safety, and efficiency. This high-rise housing—typified by buildings such as the Pruitt-Igoe Homes in St. Louis and Cabrini-Green in Chicago—was intended as a temporary solution for families from all walks of life, to keep a roof over their heads when they fell on hard times.

For the early residents of public housing, the immediate improvement was dramatic. The hazardous slum dwellings from which they had moved were largely built in the nineteenth century and lacked basic services like electricity and running water. The new buildings, modeled after European designs, offered hot water and modern amenities such as washing machines, elevators, and large windows with good air circulation.

However, the gleam of the unblemished towers did not last long. Less than twenty years after Pruitt-Igoe opened, it was emptied out and demolished. In cities across the country, funding to maintain the buildings was hugely inadequate. The purported state-of-the-art design elements featured in many public housing complexes turned out to be urban nightmares in practice. Breezeways designed to provide airflow and access to the outdoors became wind tunnels in icy northern cities. Common spaces meant to foster community were instead monopolized by gangs. Buildings that faced inward rather than out, in order to foster a sense of community, instead walled off projects from their surroundings.

These problems were compounded in cities like Chicago, where the Department of Housing and Urban Development (HUD) withheld federal funding for maintenance in the face of gross local mismanagement. Buildings harbored long lists of unfinished repairs creating hazards such as lead paint, cockroach and rodent infestations, and un-repaired elevators, leaving residents to climb the poorly lit stairwells besieged by drug dealers. There were reports of children falling from windows lacking safety guards in high-rise buildings.[22]

The real problem was inadequate funding. As financial reserves dried up and maintenance flagged, the towers soon came to be seen as urban eyesores and created what historian Arnold Hirsch called the "second ghetto." Families who lived in high-rise public housing— disproportionately African American—had no choice but to live in the racially segregated and poverty-stricken neighborhoods where it was built.

In 1967, broader patterns of racial residential segregation were laid bare in the Kerner Commission's report. The commission was convened by the federal government to try to understand the riots of the 1960s in cities like Detroit, Newark, Los Angeles, and Chicago, and it famously warned of the pernicious effects of inequality. The report implicated federal housing policy as complicit in the creation and maintenance of the ghetto.[23] Families who relied on housing assistance had no choice in where they lived. They likened the concrete walls of many public housing buildings to those of a prison. These two factors—the concentration of poverty and the lack of choice in a place to live—would come to dominate the conversation around housing policy solutions.

Scholars of the city have long argued that the geographic unit of the neighborhood and everything that it encompasses—housing structures and the built environment, social networks, the spatial distribution of resources such as schools, job opportunities, and transportation—have an important influence on life outcomes above and beyond individual characteristics.[24] In his seminal book *The Truly Disadvantaged*, William Julius Wilson argued that with the decline in manufacturing and the departure of the black middle class from America's inner city, low-income black residents of the urban core experienced a new sort of social isolation that was at the root of many of the problems associated with concentrated poverty. He argued that this lack of contact with members of the middle class and the institutions that serve them has profound effects for social networks, employment opportunities, educational achievement, family management, behavioral development and delinquency among adolescents, and nonmarital childbirth.[25]

Research that followed demonstrated that the presence of housing projects in predominantly black neighborhoods had substantially increased the concentration of poverty in these areas.[26] Two features of public housing in particular shaped the deepening poverty in public housing.

The first took effect in 1969, after Congress passed the Brooke Amendment mandating that rental payments would be proportional to a family's income rather than a fixed sum.[27] The more a family earned, the higher their rent. While this may have been fairer to the poorest families, economists argued that the adaptive payment standard created perverse economic incentives, for example disincentivizing work and even potentially altering family structure. It could be advantageous for a working husband, father, or partner to live elsewhere, or to live in the home in secret.[28] A man working formally would have to report wages, affecting the amount rent owed to the housing authority. A man working informally in the drug trade, for example, risked putting his entire family at risk of eviction if he were to be caught, due to HUD's "one strike" rule, which went into effect in 1996 and was upheld by the Supreme Court in 2002.[29]

Meanwhile, a 1981 amendment to the U.S. Housing Act of 1937 gave the poorest households—those earning below 50 percent of the area median income—priority in assigning housing units. This effort to help the most needy did achieve the important goal of helping more families,[30] but due to the reduced rent collected it also had the effect of reducing operating budgets to unsustainable levels.[31] What's more, it resulted in concentrating the most disadvantaged families in federally assisted housing and contributed to neighborhood concentrations of poverty never before seen in American cities.[32]

Nor was concentrated poverty limited to the projects. The already poor and segregated surrounding neighborhoods only became poorer once public housing was erected.[33] A third of public housing units were located in neighborhoods where over 40 percent of residents lived under the poverty line, while less than 10 percent of public housing was located in "low-poverty" neighborhoods, or those where under 10 percent of the population was poor.[34] The location of much of public housing in blighted neighborhoods meant that jobs were scarce for tenants. Rates of unemployment and public assistance among residents were astronomical.

Families were structurally isolated from jobs, public services, quality schools, and adequate transportation to other areas of the city. With few prospects for upward mobility, and excluded from many homeownership opportunities, families ended up staying in public housing for generations rather than just temporarily. The neighborhoods surrounding public housing, which had been poor to begin with, deteriorated even further. Even though public housing only ever housed a fraction of the poor who might have qualified for housing assistance, its negative effect on the neighborhoods in which it was located reached well beyond those housed within it.

Even when the fair housing act outlawed segregation within federally funded housing, this would not eliminate the effect of the decisions made years earlier to erect public housing on inexpensive land located in neighborhoods that already suffered from segregation, underinvestment, and decline.[35] These neighborhoods were predominantly black—in many cases, deliberately so—and became even more segregated over time. Many federally owned buildings were segregated by race until well into the mid-1980s.[36] This would serve to simultaneously fuel the departure of middle-class whites to the suburbs and keep low-income black Americans in poor segregated neighborhoods.[37]

The legacy of this de jure segregation—segregation by law—led to several important fair housing lawsuits over the years: for example, Chicago's famous *Gautreaux* case in 1976, the *Walker* case in Dallas in 1985, and a lawsuit known as *Thompson v. HUD*, brought by the American Civil Liberties Union (ACLU) in 1995 against the HABC and HUD. In all three cases, the plaintiffs alleged that these housing agencies had failed to desegregate their public housing buildings, in violation of the Fair Housing Act (1968).[38] These lawsuits resulted in consent decrees that compelled housing authorities to desegregate their publicly funded housing programs. They also cemented the idea that racial segregation in federal housing programs was unacceptable, based on the principles of the Fair Housing Act.

Public housing policy faced a crisis. Across the country, it had become synonymous with the notoriously derelict Pruitt-Igoe, Cabrini-Green, and Lexington Terrace projects that towered over the skylines in cities like St. Louis, Chicago, and Baltimore. Sociological theories of concentrated poverty and social isolation made clear the dangers of isolating the poor from the rest of the city. Due to mismanagement and lack of adequate funding, much of the public housing stock had reached a deplorable state of physical deterioration, and many spoke of its failure.[39]

FROM CONCENTRATED POVERTY
TO HOUSING CHOICE VOUCHERS

By the 1990s, policymakers again began to take notice, setting the stage for a government inquiry examining the conditions in the nation's dilapidated public housing structures[40] and for an overhaul of federal housing assistance.[41] Congress established the National Commission on Severely Distressed Public Housing to assess the state of public housing and devise a new nationwide strategy and plan of action. The Commission's 1992 report documented extreme physical disrepair in the national stock of public housing: about 86,000, or around 6 percent, of the 1.3 million public housing units nationwide were in fact "severely distressed."[42] More than 80 percent of public housing residents lived in poverty, many earned under a fifth of what their unsubsidized neighbors earned, and there was an alarming increase in the proportion of the poorest families in public housing over the previous decade.

In response, the HUD secretary, Henry Cisneros, called for the "end of public housing as we know it," echoing the dismantling of welfare that Clinton had called for just a few years earlier in an attempt to squelch concern over dependence among the poor on government aid.[43] Cisneros identified "the concentration of very low-income families in dense, high rise housing" as the central problem with government-funded housing, and proposed reforms to convert all public housing subsidies into tenant-based vouchers. After receiving pessimistic projections from a case study in Baltimore, he backed down from this extreme solution.[44] But the idea of an overhaul of federal housing assistance that would make local public housing authorities (PHAs) learn to operate under market discipline stuck.

The acknowledgment that housing quality was deteriorating and an increased understanding of the perils of concentrated poverty spurred a dramatic change in housing policy. The commission recommended a comprehensive plan should unfold over the next decade, with two main components aimed at promoting the deconcentration of poverty. First, it entailed the demolition and redevelopment of large public housing complexes and their replacement with mixed-income developments through a program called HOPE VI.[45] Many public housing buildings across the country, including Lafayette Courts and Lexington Terrace in Baltimore—by then crumbling from the dual effects of poverty and neglect—were torn down. Second, with this substantial reduction in the amount of available public housing units, policymakers turned to an existing program to solve the problem of housing the poor: housing vouchers.[46]

In the wake of what many consider the "failure" of public housing, the federal government made an abrupt shift toward investing in housing vouchers. The voucher program was not new. The Section 8 Certificate Program, as it was originally known, was created under the Housing Act of 1974 and provided federally funded vouchers to make housing more affordable for low-income families. In the early years of the program, politicians and researchers touted it as an economically efficient way to provide housing aid.[47] Economic evaluations of voucher experiments showed that public funding would be more efficiently used by giving the poor money to find housing in the open market than by rebuilding existing housing stock.[48]

"Section 8" remained small for many years, but was expanded and renamed the Housing Choice Voucher (HCV) program in 1998. This moniker reflected a new attitude about the purpose of the program and the new goal of promoting geographic opportunity through residential choice.[49] Policymakers thought that given the choice, families would select a neighborhood environment with lower poverty concentration, spurring the deconcentration of poverty.[50]

By the end of the 1990s, vouchers would become the largest housing assistance program in the country. Over the past two decades, the federal government has closed many large public housing developments across the country in its quest to combat concentrated poverty. Since the height of public housing in the mid-1990s, over 250,000 of the 1.4 million units have been demolished (see figure 1).[51]

The demolition of public housing was especially pronounced in Baltimore, where almost all of the high-rise units were torn down in the 1990s and early 2000s. Many of them were replaced with HOPE VI mixed-income developments and scattered site housing, but there has not been one-for-one replacement—in which each unit of demolished housing is replaced with another hard unit.[52] Since the eighties, the total number of public housing units has decreased by almost half.[53] Baltimore is at one end of the spectrum in terms of the scale of demolition: cities like Chicago and Atlanta have had similarly large proportions of their public housing stock razed; however, this is less true of other cities, such as those in the Sunbelt.

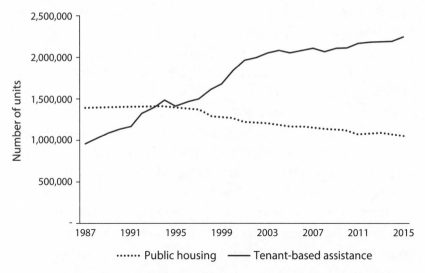

FIGURE 1: The Number of Units in Public Housing and the Housing Choice Voucher Program, 1987–2015. *Source:* Vale and Freemark (2012).

As public housing was torn down, many former residents were "vouchered out," or given a housing voucher to replace their public housing subsidy, and there soon was an unusually large voucher population in Baltimore City. Housing voucher subsidies increased from 5,966 vouchers in 1990[54] to over 17,000 in 2011,[55] and at over 14 percent of the rental market, the city's voucher rate is one of the highest in the country.[56] Even so, given its high poverty rate, there are many low-income families that qualify for housing assistance but do not receive it. It is estimated that there are over 16,000 families on the HCV waiting list, which has been mostly closed since 2003.[57]

Of course, public housing still exists; there are now approximately 1.2 million households living in public housing units.[58] In contrast, from 1993 to today, the number of voucher holders rose from 1.2 million to 2.4 million.[59] Today, 10.4 million people receive some form of federal rental assistance.[60] Alongside the Low-Income Housing Tax Credit (LIHTC)—which provides financial incentives for developers to invest in low-income housing—the expansion of these two programs means that the burden of housing the poor has been transferred to the private market:

out of the five million households across the country that receive some form of federal housing assistance, over half now live in privately owned properties.[61] HUD's programs reach a nontrivial portion of the American poor; however, the need far exceeds the supply: only one in four eligible households receives housing aid.[62]

The voucher makes up the difference between what a needy household can afford and the cost of a unit in the private market. The payment standard—the highest amount that a landlord can charge for a voucher property—is typically set at or around Fair Market Rent (FMR), a measure defined as the 40th to 50th percentile of the area rent, adjusted for number of bedrooms.[63] Families are responsible for paying 30 percent of their household income in rent.[64] The voucher covers the remaining portion of rent, and is paid directly to the landlord by the government.

This demolition and vouchering out of public housing is a significant feature of Baltimore. The city has a lot of vouchers compared to other similarly sized cities, and these vouchers are unevenly spread throughout the metropolitan area, concentrating in neighborhoods such as Park Heights and Belair-Edison.[65]

The country is now formally in a period of purportedly "race-blind" housing policies that no longer explicitly separate housing aid recipients on the basis of race. Nevertheless, there are countless policies—for example, zoning laws based on lot size or single-family dwellings—that have differential impacts on poor and minority residents and function to maintain segregation both intentionally and unintentionally.[66] Furthermore, federal housing programs do not operate in a vacuum. These programs rely, increasingly, on the private market to house the poor, which has a tendency to stratify housing voucher recipients. Instead of being race-blind, the scaffolding of the private housing market is reproducing decades-old patterns of racial segregation.

UNDERSTANDING MOBILITY:
MOVING TO OPPORTUNITY

Beyond the goal of making housing more affordable, policymakers and housing policy experts increasingly see vouchers as a tool to promote

residential mobility, allowing poor families to rent homes in more affluent neighborhoods.[67] Since vouchers are not tied to a particular building or housing project in the way that public housing subsidies were,
they can be used in any affordable rental unit that passes an inspection.
This offers—at least in theory—tremendous potential for poor families
to leave the disadvantaged neighborhoods to which they were tied
when public housing was the only game in town.[68] The possibility that
vouchers might be used more explicitly to promote residential mobility
raises an important question: What happens when a low-income family
moves out of a poor neighborhood and into a more affluent one?

In order to answer this question, scholars turn to several significant
mobility interventions in recent U.S. history. In one of the most notable
of these mobility interventions, the Gautreaux program, moved over
7,000 low-income families into subsidized private housing in more integrated, lower-poverty neighborhoods between the years of 1976 and
1998. Gautreaux was the result of a class-action lawsuit charging that the
Chicago Housing Authority (CHA) had contributed to racial segregation by building housing developments in predominantly African
American neighborhoods. *Gautreaux v. CHA* was initiated in Chicago
in 1966, and in 1976 the case went to the Supreme Court when HUD
was introduced into the suit.[69] While research on Gautreaux offered
promising findings for the advantages of moving to new neighborhoods,
conclusions were ultimately limited due to the nonexperimental design
of the intervention.[70]

In the 1990s, a team of researchers, supported by the federal government, embarked on an ambitious experiment. If where you live matters,
then what would happen if you offered families who lived in the most
disadvantaged neighborhoods the chance to move somewhere with better schools, a safer neighborhood environment, economic opportunities,
and services such as police, parks, libraries, sanitation?[71] The Moving to
Opportunity (MTO) experiment, authorized by the U.S. Congress in
1992, was a unique effort to understand how moving to a new neighborhood could improve the life chances of very poor families with children.

MTO was engineered with lessons from Gautreaux in mind: designed as an experiment, random assignment allowed for comparison

between the treatment and control groups. Across five U.S. cities—
Baltimore, Boston, Chicago, Los Angeles, and, New York—HUD offered
families living in public housing the chance to enroll in a special voucher
lottery. Those who enrolled were randomly sorted into one of three
groups. As in a medical experiment, there was a control, or "placebo,"
group who received nothing but kept their public housing subsidy. There
was also the Section 8 group who got a regular voucher. The third group,
the "experimental" group, got a special voucher, which could only be
used in a low-poverty neighborhood, where less than 10 percent of the
residents were poor. This group also received special mobility counseling
to help participants find a place to live in a low-poverty neighborhood.

Results from MTO have been mixed. On the one hand, results
showed that moving to lower-poverty neighborhoods had a positive
impact on physical health, mental health, and subjective well-being.[72]
There were some important gender differences: while girls benefitted
from moving, as measured by psychological well-being, boys showed no
difference in mental health and demonstrated negative outcomes in risk
behavior relative to those in the control group.[73]

When it comes to adult employment outcomes, for many years no
significant impacts were found. New research, though, shows something
different. Economist Raj Chetty and his team realized something that no
one had been able to consider with earlier data: What if the age at which
a child moved—and thus the child's exposure to the disadvantaged
environment—was a key factor? Indeed, he found that thirteen was the
magic number: children who leave disadvantaged contexts before the
age of thirteen experience tremendous benefits later in life, including
increased college attendance and earnings and decreased likelihood of
single parenthood.[74] The research offers support to the idea that longer
durations of exposure to disadvantaged neighborhood contexts may be
dangerous for children. However, Chetty's results also pose a conun-
drum for policy: policymakers need to think carefully about the negative
outcomes associated with moving families with adolescent children,
who—this research suggests—may be harmed by such a move.

Policymakers look to MTO for important lessons in how mobility
might work in the voucher program more broadly.[75] But as earlier

analyses from MTO made clear, even the families who received housing counseling and a special voucher that could only be used in a low-poverty neighborhood had trouble successfully doing so.

A SECONDARY GOAL

By implementing the shift toward vouchers, policymakers hoped that the government could rely on an existing supply of private housing stock and outsource some of the costs of maintenance that have plagued public housing. Perhaps the private market would be better able to provide homes free of lead paint, crumbling walls, mold, and vermin infestations, and could maintain better-quality homes for poor households.

In terms of the most basic goal of the program—providing adequate shelter by making a modest home more affordable to those with low incomes—much evidence suggests that the voucher program is succeeding. Vouchers offer a powerful tool to keep people off the streets and stably housed. Evaluations have consistently found that the program improves affordability, reduces homelessness, and alleviates over-crowding.[76] These successes should not be understated, especially in an era when many government programs for the poor are being cut. A housing voucher is one of the largest subsidies a poor household can be lucky enough to receive, often worth over $7,000 a year. Housing vouchers lift over a million people out of poverty every year.[77]

The question is, can the voucher program do more? Should it do more? Policymakers have come to hold a secondary hope for the program: social mobility "out-of-place" and "out of poverty." While this was not part of the explicit original intent of the program, the potential for the program to offer households "locational attainment," i.e., the chance to move to a higher-income neighborhood, has increasingly become an expectation.[78] By relying on the private market, policymakers hoped, the system would give recipients access to units in a wide range of neighborhoods, including many low-poverty, resource-rich neighborhoods. And by allowing families to make a choice about where to live, they hoped families would disperse to new homes in safer neighborhoods, go to better schools, and find better jobs, possibly providing a pathway out of poverty.[79] And they hoped it might even remedy the concentrated poverty and segregation that previous policies had helped to create.

On this secondary front, the program has been less successful. Unlike the subsidy attached to public housing, families with vouchers can take their vouchers to a new home across a range of neighborhoods. But where do they go? Many, in fact, don't go anywhere. A significant portion of new voucher holders—around one-quarter—lease in place.[80] Overall, voucher households are living in neighborhoods that are less poor than those where public housing was located, but they are subject to the same marginalizing forces that create disparity and segregation in the unassisted housing market. As public aid has become increasingly privatized, the mechanisms of residential segregation by race and income have extended from the private market to the publicly subsidized market.

In terms of the poverty level of neighborhoods in which voucher recipients reside, the story is mixed. As compared to the types of neighborhoods in which public housing was located, voucher holders live in less-poor neighborhoods overall.[81] This is in part because the numbers of neighborhoods of "extreme poverty" (over 40 percent poor)[82] were dramatically reduced during this time period, even given the reverse progress of the 2000s—many were artifices of high-rise public housing, and therefore disappeared with its demolition. Voucher holders are less likely to live in "extremely" poor neighborhoods than are their low-income counterparts without housing assistance, as well as compared to those who still live in public housing.[83] Voucher holders today are also less likely to live in "high-poverty" neighborhoods (over 30 percent poor) than they were at the beginning of the program in the 1970s.[84] However, voucher holders are *more* likely to live in "moderately" poor neighborhoods, or those that are 20 to 30 percent poor. While this is an improvement in pure numerical terms, anyone who's set foot in a neighborhood where a third of the residents live under the poverty line can see that this is still a very poor neighborhood indeed.[85]

There simply is not as much improvement in low-income families' neighborhood contexts as policymakers had hoped. In theory, the voucher allows recipients access to a wide range of neighborhoods, including many low-poverty, resource-rich communities. Yet voucher holders are underrepresented in such neighborhoods, and patterns of economic and racial segregation continue.

Many voucher holders have not been able to find places to rent in mixed-income neighborhoods, the kind of move shown to have long-term positive impacts on health and economic well-being.[86] Rather, a great many voucher holders are concentrating in poor neighborhoods. This is especially true for black voucher holders, whose neighborhoods are poorer and far more racially isolated than those of white voucher holders. Of particular concern, given the long history of socioeconomic and racial segregation in housing in the United States, housing vouchers seem to be mirroring long familiar patterns.[87] White voucher holder families are about twice as likely as black and Latino or Hispanic families to live in low-poverty neighborhoods.[88] Some research also suggests the emergence of voucher "hot spots" in certain metropolitan areas.[89] The location of affordable housing, renters' social networks, their access to information and resources, and landlords' influence all play a part.[90] Recent research clearly demonstrates that voucher holders are realizing far less locational attainment than their vouchers would, in theory, allow them to afford.

This concentration of vouchers in poor neighborhoods matters for a reason that social scientists like William Julius Wilson have long known to be true, but finally have the hard numbers to prove: where you live matters. It matters for your quality of life, for how much money you make in your lifetime, and for your children. Chetty's work shows that a child growing up in a city like Baltimore will make 14 percent less over his lifetime than one in a typical American county, even after accounting for individual factors like income and education.[91] Yet, we have so much more to learn about how and when neighborhoods matter, for whom, and what role housing vouchers can play.

What's more, these residential patterns raise an important puzzle that I will address in the coming chapters: Why do voucher holders like Vivian end up in moderately poor neighborhoods such as Park Heights, rather than in the neighborhoods with more resources that their voucher should give them access to? Researchers ask why families are not using the full value of their voucher by moving to the lowest-poverty neighborhood possible. Why don't they move to lower-poverty, less-segregated neighborhoods when the voucher would appear to provide the opportunity to do so?

A YEAR IN PARK HEIGHTS

To explore these puzzles, I needed to have a better picture of the history of Park Heights. I began by talking to older homeowners like Terrance Green, now seventy-eight, who settled in the neighborhood in the late sixties. Mr. Green was the first black homeowner on his block. During this time, when real estate in Park Heights first opened up to black families who had been previously confined to other areas of the city, existing white families left in droves. In the following decade, the entire neighborhood flipped: one by one, each of Terrance Green's white neighbors moved out, and African American families moved in.

At the same time, things were changing in Baltimore: manufacturing left the city, and with it, jobs. In the years after, the stable neighborhood that these working-class families had bought into began to decay around them. Many older residents on Mr. Green's block moved into nursing homes, or in with family, or passed away. Today, the Park Heights neighborhood remains predominantly African American, at around 96 percent, and its poverty is much higher than when the homeowners who live there now bought their homes. Mr. Green and his son are concerned about the renters getting closer and closer to his doorstep, who they fear bring with them crime and instability.

Many of these renters struggle to make ends meet with no housing assistance at all, and their experiences illustrate the extreme housing affordability and stability challenges that vouchers do seem able to address. Unassisted renters, many of whom had been on the voucher waiting list for years, lived in housing conditions that were generally much worse than those lucky enough to have gotten off the list. Destiny lived with her husband and two sons in one bedroom of a three-bedroom house, in which five adults and two children shared the same bathroom.

She hoped to get off the waiting list so she could have more space for her older daughter to come live with the family. Raven, who has been on the list for years, was facing eviction with her husband and nine kids, since her landlord's property was recently foreclosed on. Barbie grew up in a home that her parents owned, tried to buy a house of her own, but when she couldn't afford to fix the roof, had to give it up. These renters experienced residential instability in ways that affected their health, mental health, and employment opportunities in significant ways. And like three out of four poor renters in the U.S., they don't benefit from what the voucher has to offer, since they haven't gotten one yet.

What do vouchers offer families that the unassisted do not have? How does the voucher shape daily life at home? The stories of those who have won the voucher lottery illustrate the power of this policy. The lives of the voucher holders I met were indelibly changed when they received a housing voucher. Vivian was able to move off her sister's couch and get her twin boys back to live with her for good. For Tony Young, a fifty-five-year-old man with HIV, it meant getting out of a homeless shelter, or out from under the bridge where he slept when it wasn't too cold. Joann Jones, a young mother of two, started shopping at the natural foods store where she could get fresher fruits and vegetables for her seven-year-old. It is abundantly clear that access to housing subsidies improves lives, often dramatically. The families I got to know in Park Heights benefitted in tangible ways when they finally moved off the long waiting list and into subsidized housing.

But beyond the tremendous resources the voucher offered these families, I wondered, why weren't families using their vouchers in the kinds of well-resourced neighborhoods that policymakers expected them to? Why use the voucher in Park Heights? Finding a place to rent with a voucher, it turns out, is not as easy as it may seem. There are a number of barriers, including the availability of qualified homes, recipients' social networks, transportation to visit homes, access to information about properties, and landlord discrimination.

As I inquired about why and how voucher holders ended up in Park Heights, I learned that landlords played an important role in this process that not very many academics or policymakers were talking about.[92]

I learned that landlords have all kinds of incentives to keep voucher holders out of some neighborhoods, while enticing them to others. In predominantly white and affluent Baltimore neighborhoods like Federal Hill or Canton, landlords have plenty of eligible private market renters who are likely to pay their rent on time and whom neighbors won't object to because of their race. But in poor, minority neighborhoods, landlords are drawing from a pool of renters who have more unstable incomes and can't always pay their rent on time. In these areas, voucher holders offer landlords a viable solution to the volatility of the low-income housing market, because the majority of a voucher holder's rent is paid directly to the landlord by the HABC each month. I found landlords like David, who was so desperate for the reliability of voucher tenants that he waited outside the voucher office to catch new recipients on their way out the door, offering them a ride up to see his vacant property in Park Heights. These same landlords offered move-in incentives like new appliances, or even cash bonuses to move voucher tenants into their properties as quickly as possible. While these voucher tenants are able to find homes, they end up exercising very little choice in where they end up living. Landlords play an important role in shuttling voucher holders to neighborhoods like Park Heights, where there is the most profit to be made.

While policymakers have imagined vouchers to operate in an idealized market that provides information and choice to tenants, in fact, landlords and tenants alike scramble to stay afloat and make ends meet amidst chronic financial insecurity. In a complete reversal of the stated policy goals of the program, a program meant to provide a safety net to tenants ends up acting as one for landlords.

Once voucher holders move into Park Heights, what is their experience? While this isn't the type of higher income, integrated, "opportunity" neighborhood that policymakers might hope voucher holders could get into, the stable homeowners do have a strong community that could, in theory, make room for newcomers. Yet this is not what happens. Homeowners—who face their own challenges and precarity in the fragile neighborhood—are not always ready to welcome voucher holders with open arms.

Finally, how do low-income residents cope in poor and violent neighborhoods, and do vouchers provide a chance to exit these contexts? The evidence regarding the dramatic negative costs of living in poor and violent neighborhoods suggests that there is a role for vouchers as a stopgap measure to get poor families out of disadvantaged environments. Research clearly shows how life-altering it can be to move to a neighborhood where children are not dodging bullets and avoiding gang activity on their way to school, where women are not afraid to walk to the bus on their way to work, and where fathers are not arrested while walking down the street to the grocery store. Yet even when vouchers don't get recipients to more resourced neighborhoods, and even when they face heavy stigma from their new neighbors, housing vouchers do something quite powerful: they offer flexibility.

Vivian, Tony, and Joann are part of a generation of poor urban dwellers who left the concentrated poverty of high-rise public housing towers, which by the 1990s were crumbling from neglect. Housing vouchers now offer men and women like Vivian, Tony, and Joann their very first chance to choose where to live. This book highlights the deep value families place on feeling they have a choice in their own futures. These choices—while sometimes reproducing the poverty and disadvantaged neighborhood contexts that some hoped the voucher would help them escape—nevertheless have valuable meaning for the families who make them. Moving can solve problems—whether it is bullying at school, violence in the neighborhood, disruptions at work, or housing quality issues—and families need the flexibility to take their voucher and make a proactive change in their lives. These improvements do not always show up in the statistics, but they can leave indelible marks of positive change on the ground.

The simple economic relief that the voucher provides cannot be understated, but it also provides families with something more: a flexible solution in times of crisis. Unlike the rental assistance provided by public housing, which was attached to a fixed unit with little opportunity for neighborhood choice, vouchers can be used—at least in theory—in any affordable unit in the city. And they can be ported to other housing authorities. This allows families the flexibility to respond to the demands of their jobs, their children's needs, and even the whims of landlords. This is a flexibility that many middle-class families take for granted. What's more, vouchers offer residents a sense of control over their lives, the ability to realize their own dreams of a place to call home.

———

These dreams, though, are unmistakably circumscribed by the voucher program which, as it currently functions, does little to operate outside of the forces that regulate the private housing market. Where African Americans live in America is no accident. Market forces—catering to the underlying discriminatory impulses of those who hold the reins of power—have long shaped who can live where and for how much money. These forces are a thread linking together disparate housing practices and policies, and outlining the blueprint for who lives where in the urban environment.

African American residents of public housing were relegated to the poor neighborhoods in which it was built, absent many formal institutions and jobs. Middle-class black Baltimoreans were historically denied mortgages across the city, stifling their wealth, and kept out of neighborhoods like Park Heights through discrimination and racial covenants. These same forces undergirded the predatory blockbusting that later opened up Park Heights and sparked the flight of white residents as blacks moved in. These forces, too, are not unrelated to demographic shifts of the 1970s in response to deindustrialization and the shift of jobs to the suburbs, leaving neighborhoods like Park Heights bereft of resources and a tax base. With few jobs, drugs came to the neighborhood, crime rose, whites avoided the area, and housing prices plummeted. Residents who could leave, left, and their homes remained empty, leaving Park Heights with one of the highest vacancy rates in the city.

It is this confluence of historical factors of exclusion and predation that makes the neighborhood ripe for the entry of a voucher population: available housing stock, tenants desperate to find homes, and landlords made willing (even eager) with the right financial incentives. The forces that once undergirded redlining in home mortgages, racially restrictive covenants, and blockbusting are the same ones now pushing voucher holders into neighborhoods like Park Heights. And the same ones keeping them on the social margins of the neighborhood. Housing policy is part of social structure, and the voucher program is a function of these social processes over time. By relying on the private market to house the poor, we are throwing subsidized renters onto an uneven chessboard. Vouchers are a powerful tool to help people, but if we don't find a way to understand and unravel the forces that corrupt them, we risk recreating residential racial segregation in the very program policy-makers have tasked with unraveling it.

Chapter 1

PARK HEIGHTS: "A GHOST TOWN"

"Terrance?" Mr. Green incredulously repeated his given name back to me as I had just addressed him. "Young lady, is that what you're going to call me? *Terrance* is my son. You may call me *Mr.*," instructed Terrance Green, who alternately called me "Young Lady" or "Miss Eve." On a drizzly, cool June midday, I found myself alone in his dark basement. "The lights is on the wall, over on the left," Mr. Green called down to me, leaving aside the lesson in etiquette for now. "You find 'em?" At his age, the octogenarian didn't take the basement steps much anymore, but he had cajoled me into going down to see his handiwork, while he stayed seated in his arm chair, his legs clad in green knee-high socks, propped up on the ottoman. "You gotta see how I set it up down there," he'd said with pride, nearly pleading with me to go take a look. I fumbled around a bit, finally finding the switch. The lights flickered on and toward the back of the room a row of lights illuminated a dusty, fully stocked bar, with three stools carefully lined up in front of the gleaming Formica countertop.

On the faux-wood-paneled walls were photos of a life Mr. Green and I had spent the morning discussing. He had told me about his childhood in North Carolina, his first days in Baltimore as a young typesetter at the "Afro," the *Baltimore Afro-American Newspaper*, and buying his first home—this one—with his wife who was eight months pregnant at the time. They were one of the first African American families on the block. Mr. Green still lives in the same house, and his middle-aged son now lives down the street.

For Terrance Green, buying a home in Park Heights represented a once-in-a-lifetime opportunity. Having grown up in a small town in North Carolina, coming to Baltimore had been life-altering for him. "In a small southern town you could count the black men on your hand finished high school. But I did much better than most black fellows that come from that part of the country, 'cause I worked a skill. When I was twelve years old, the man that owned the newspaper liked me and I would work after school. He gave me a job, and I learned a trade."

Mr. Green came to Baltimore in 1960 to work at the *Afro*, where he worked until they stopped using the antiquated typesetting method of "stereotype." At that point he moved to the mailroom, and then stayed on as a security guard until retiring at the age of seventy-six. When he first arrived, Mr. Green lived in the YMCA on Druid Hill Avenue. Once he had saved a little money, he was able to bring his wife up from North Carolina, and they moved into the Georgia Apartments in Park Heights. Soon enough, his regular paycheck at the *Afro* allowed the couple to consider buying a home.

Like Mr. Green, many of Park Heights' older black homeowners came to Baltimore as young adults during the Great Migration, when massive numbers of African American men, women, and families moved from the south to take jobs in the expanding manufacturing industry. Once gainfully employed, buying a home was a step closer to the stable, middle-class life they dreamed of.

The Greens paid $10,000 for their home in 1962—Mr. Green's mother-in-law loaned them money for the down payment—which, he remarked, was "a hell of a lot of money then." The neighborhood had a different flavor at that time, as he remembers well: "Oh my goodness, Park Heights in 1960 was all Jewish. When I bought this house, then everybody, *everybody*, in this whole area was white. There were no black people nowhere."

For many decades, black residents in cities across the country were confined to mostly poor, mostly black neighborhoods.[1] After the Great Depression, federally backed mortgages made it easy for whites, but nearly impossible for blacks, to buy homes. Banks refused to lend to blacks in the "redlined" black neighborhoods where they were allowed to live, and white neighborhood associations used restrictive covenants to keep blacks out of white neighborhoods. Blacks were prohibited, whether by covenant or by custom, from most other nonblack neighborhoods. Due to this long history of racially discriminatory housing practices, African American families were not allowed to move just anywhere in Baltimore.

This changed in the 1960s as real estate agents "busted" into heretofore white neighborhoods like Park Heights, showing homes to black families like the Greens for the first time, and stoking fears of racial turnover. White families sold their homes at low prices and fled, giving black families access to neighborhoods they had never before been allowed to live in. This inclusion, though, was "predatory," in that blacks often had to pay more for their homes than they were worth.[2] But even at inflated prices, many black families bought homes, and as whites fled, entire blocks flipped one by one. When I asked Mr. Green about why things changed in the neighborhood so quickly, he said matter-of-factly: "Let me explain that to you, sweetheart. Any time a black person in those days would buy a house, all the Jewish people would leave." In Park Heights, most of the whites were Jewish, and so these two things were synonymous.

Patty Carlyle, a seventy-six-year-old homeowner who lives just a few blocks from Mr. Green's house, came to the neighborhood under exactly these circumstances. She moved to Park Heights in 1972 from Mosher Street near Pennsylvania Ave—a historic black neighborhood in Baltimore. She was then recently widowed and had three young children, but she had a good-paying steady job as a nurse. "I wanted something of my own," she explained to me. When she approached a real estate agency, they told her about the new opportunities in Park Heights and steered her there. Patty was proud of her purchase. She wanted to own a single-family home, and she wanted it to be quiet and family-oriented, which it was at the time. When Patty moved to Park Heights in 1972, it was well into its transformation to a black majority neighborhood; seven of the families who currently live on her block had moved in just before she arrived.

By 1970, Park Heights' white population had dropped from 95 percent to 18 percent. Ten years later in 1980, it was down to 5 percent. The mass exit of white homeowners in similarly transitioning neighborhoods across the country is called white flight. Such rapid racial upheaval was a complex product of racial fears and prejudices, a changing economy, as well as a set of concerted housing policies and real estate efforts.

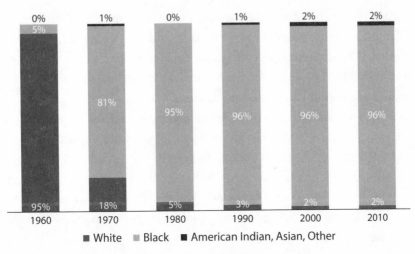

FIGURE 2: Racial Composition in Park Heights, 1960–2010.
Source: United States Census (1960–2010).

Mr. Green doesn't harbor animosity toward the white families who left. "They did what they felt they had to," he told me. "And you know something, they weren't wrong. They knew things were changing. 'Cause now we all stuck here with homes that ain't worth nothin'!" Blockbusting in places like Park Heights resulted in the transfer of substandard housing to black families who then assumed financial responsibility for an aging housing stock in a neighborhood that was already in decline.[3] Beyond the economic repercussions, there were social consequences as well: Edward Orser, a historian who documented blockbusting in nearby Edmonson Village, observed the psychological and social mark left by the "trauma of racial change" on neighborhoods that experienced such rapid upheaval.[4] Nearly half a century later, this is the kind of neighborhood to which many voucher holders have moved.

THE RECEIVING NEIGHBORHOOD

Policymakers and researchers hoped that providing assisted renters with the choice to use their voucher in a wide variety of homes and neighborhoods would help solve the problems of concentrated poverty.

Rather than being stuck in the disadvantaged blighted neighborhoods of public housing, abandoned by banks and supermarkets and businesses, they thought that voucher holders would take their vouchers and move to lower-poverty neighborhoods with more jobs, better schools, and safer streets.

For a good many reasons—the availability of qualified homes, social networks, transportation, information, and landlord factors—things did not turn out this way. Where, then, did families move? And what was waiting for them when they got there? The policy logic behind moving low-income renters out of the towers of public housing and into dispersed, voucher-based housing rests on a whole school of thought that suggests that where you live matters, that the neighborhood environment shapes your opportunities in life. If voucher holders moved to Park Heights, what, and who, was there to receive them?

In Baltimore, a city with an unusually high number of renters who receive housing assistance, many voucher holders have moved to Park Heights, a previously white, middle-class neighborhood. Between 1965 and 1975, the entire population of the neighborhood flipped as the predominantly Jewish population moved north of Northern Parkway, a main center-periphery dividing line in the city.

Today, the neighborhood remains predominantly black. Park Heights has moderate levels of poverty, around 31 percent, typical of the kinds of neighborhoods to which voucher holders move across the country.[5] Despite its poverty rate, Park Heights has a significant population of homeowners, many of whom were the pioneering working-class black families who bought homes in the neighborhood in the late 1960s and 1970s.[6] As voucher holders move in, homeowners feel there is a lot at stake for them: their reactions range from indifferent to hostile.

During my time in Park Heights, I spent many months getting to know longtime residents. I wanted to get a sense of who they were and what their neighborhood meant to them. One of those residents was Bob Marshall, who lived about ten blocks from Mr. Green's quiet homeowner street. Now sixty-two, Bob and his wife have lived in the neighborhood for over twenty-five years. A half-lifetime of manual labor shows itself in Bob's athletic body, only now beginning to soften with age. Bob never saw a dentist as a child, and his jaw, now entirely tooth-less, has the slack of a much older man who hasn't put in his dentures.

Bob worked many jobs, including working for an oil company, land-scaping, and truck-driving. But he never could save enough to buy a house. So, when he and his wife inherited a home in Park Heights from her aunt, it was like a dream come true: "Everybody's dream is to own your own home. And that was mines. I wanted the porch where I could sit out on, and everything. It was a nice neighborhood at that time." The neighborhood was showing minimal signs of decline when the Marshall family moved in in the mid-1980s. Although the house needed some work, Bob was up for the task: "You know, no matter where you live you gotta pay. I thought maybe it would be more better for us to go here and try to fix what we have, rather than try to pay some-body else. I mean you know, being that I was handy with my hands, I thought that I could do it well enough that we could live here and finish paying it off."

And pay it off they did. Bob and his wife and their two kids lived hap-pily in the neighborhood for several years before he remembers the change that began to creep in. On a rainy morning, Bob described to me how he remembered the neighborhood:

> You know when I think about the neighborhood I don't think about cloudy days like today, I think about nice sunny days with the trees out . . . there was a few more back then, that people done cut down since then. It was quiet and it was peaceful. It was like, you wanted to come home from work and put your feet up. During warm weather you could sit out there on the porch till late at night, and not be both-ered or anything, and relax you know, gather your thoughts.

This wasn't the scene Bob and I saw as we sat talking that day. On the end of his block there was a sandy-colored pit bull chained to the side of the house, huddled under the overhang of the porch to stay dry. Every few minutes it barked hoarsely, croaking with thirst and neglect. Bob just shook his head in dismay. To the right were two vacant homes, and in between them, a house in reasonable shape, with toys strewn about the lawn.

"Those people is Section 8," Bob told me.

"Oh really? How do you know?" I asked.

"Well they got little kids, for one." Many residents equate large families with voucher holders. "Plus, they got a black Lexus. No working person can afford a car like that," he scoffed. In my conversations with them, the homeowners of Park Heights frequently complained about voucher holders who they thought squandered away their extra money on fancy cars, TVs, and other so-called "bling."[7]

When Bob looked back on how the neighborhood has changed, he mentioned the more visible crises that might first come to mind: the drugs, the jobs, the schools. But for him, all this is in the background. In Bob's view, the "last nail in the coffin" that sealed the fate of the neighborhood was the arrival of voucher holders.

In fact, neighborhood decline began decades before the arrival of voucher holders—their recent presence is just the latest in a string of changes that have occurred in the neighborhood over the past fifty years. While the arrival of voucher holders correlates with certain other indicators of poverty, to some homeowners like Bob, it's a distinction without a difference.

A CHANGING COMMUNITY

Many old-timers lament the loss of the vibrant community life they remember in Park Heights. Older homeowners and longtime residents remember what it was like before things changed. There were renowned local delis and restaurants, a recreation center with activities for the kids, a pool, and a library. Mr. Green was not the only old-timer to tell me about the well-known deli in the center of town: "The Jewish man on the corner—Goldman—he had the best meat in Baltimore City."

Barbie McAdams grew up in the neighborhood in the 1970s. She recalled, "It was beautiful. Green grass, trees, it was real nice. Ms. Reiner lived next door. Mr. Roth lived over there. Mr. Roth had eight children. And they had a pool in the backyard. We had another neighbor that lived over there. He was a lawyer. He was real proper. They had a ground pool in their yard." Barbie told me all about the stores, amenities, and community services she remembers in the neighborhood growing up:

I had a great childhood living up here. We had everything right and convenient. We had a drug store, clothing shop, bakery, bowling alley, movies at the plaza. We had a Ponderosa on Ten Mile Lane, where we could go and eat. And then we had Cookies, which was a men's store. We had a Darnell's Ice Cream Parlor. . . . It was real nice when we first moved here. We had a recreation center out the back and a pool with a big diving board, swings, sandbox. We had the park. We used to go down there and picnic. . . . We had a library, too. There was a lot to do. Now, they don't have anything for the kids to do in the community.[8]

In those early years, Barbie's family had strong ties to the other families in the neighborhood, white and black. Her mother went door-to-door selling Avon cosmetics in the neighborhood, and she accompanied her mother on her rounds and wrote down all the orders. A few weeks later, she would deliver the products for her mother. Barbie got to know many Park Heights families this way, and often got hired to watch the children: "My sister and I, we did *all* the babysitting around here."

Barbie continued working for many of these families even when they moved north. "I used to clean a bunch of their houses," she told me. "I still see Miss Rachel, she always ask me how my children are." As a house cleaner, Barbie got to know the intimate details of the families whose kitchens she swept and scrubbed, whose trash she emptied, and whose sheets she washed, dried, and remade the beds with. Barbie smiled and sighed as she fondly remembered: "One thing I never understood, how they have all them children! They very religious. And even with all the kids they didn't have a TV in their whole house except in the basement there was a color TV. She had it for her husband's father, 'cause she said he liked to watch the sports." When Rachel's father-in-law got older, the family added on a room to the back of the house so he could have his own apartment which Barbie also cleaned. "It was real nice. Rachel said to me, 'We take care of our own.' I thought that was real considerate." Barbie's life was different in some ways from the families whose homes she cleaned. But she had a lot of respect for them.

Barbie could go on for hours telling stories. "Oh, and I have to tell you about Sarah! She had eight kids. And their bedroom, they had like, twin beds!" Barbie looked at me, her eyes wide. She had never seen an adult couple who slept in separate beds, except maybe in old sitcoms from the fifties. "'Y'all got twin beds?' In their room—the master bedroom. 'Y'all have twin beds and y'all had all these babies? I mean, y'all just need one bed.' She said, 'No, we have it like that so when we don't want to be bothered, we sleep in our own beds.' I said, 'How are y'all having sex?' She said, 'We move the beds together.' I said, 'Oh my god.'"

Soon enough most of the white families were gone. And with them, many of the stores, shops, and community resources. Barbie explained:

> It started changing. The house across the street, quite a few of the houses across the street was tore down. They done tore down a lot in this area. Even down on Park Heights where houses used to be, they tore all that down. . . . It's changed over the years. They tore down our recreation center, our movies gone, our Darnell's Ice Cream Parlor is gone, Mr. Goldman who had the market, he moved. Acme moved. . . . So really we don't have a market in the area. And we don't have a drug store. . . . And now they don't have anything for the kids to do in the community. . . . They closed the pool.

Over the years, as the population, the tax base, and the investment shifted, the neighborhood changed a great deal.

A TOUR OF THE NEIGHBORHOOD

Back at Mr. Green's, I heard the phone ring. Mr. Green called down to me, "Miss Eve, that's gonna be for you!"

I turned and hurried up the stairs from the basement. Out of breath and puzzled, I eyed Mr. Green. "For me? Why would anyone call me here?"

He sat back in his armchair, resting his spindly legs back up on the ottoman. "Hurry now, answer it, that'll be Terrance Jr. calling to check in."

I dutifully reached for the large yellow phone mounted on the wall in the kitchen.

Terrance Jr. grilled me on who I was, why I was talking to his father, and my intentions in the neighborhood. I did my best to explain, unsure if I was in trouble for not asking his permission to talk to his dad. Finally, he seemed satisfied that I wasn't there to sell anything or scam anyone.

"I just have to be careful, you know how it is these days. People come by pretending to sell things to the old folks, and the next thing you know, they stole your whole identity, credit cards, your social, everything! But look, if you wanna know about the neighborhood, you gotta get out *in* it. You can't just be sittin' in the living room talkin' to the old man. I'll pick you up tomorrow, we'll drive around. 10 a.m. okay?"

————

About two square miles, Park Heights has a population of 26,123.[9] It has an almost suburban feel, though it is within the city lines. In a few hours we covered much of it in Terrance Jr.'s old Buick, which had navy blue velvety seats and smelled faintly of tobacco. At fifty-six, Terrance has lived in the neighborhood his entire life. He knows it well. "I'm an old man," he said with a twinkle in his eye. While he may feel old, he's the young one in his family, keeping a close watch on his elderly father.

Terrance drove me up to the northern border by the Pimlico Race Course, over to the eastern edge of Park Heights by the Cylburn Arboretum, back to the western border of Wabash Avenue, and finally down to the southern border marked by the Park Heights traffic circle. The lower edge of the neighborhood is just above the Mondawmin Mall area, where the unrest broke out in April 2015 following the death of a young black man in police custody, Freddie Gray.

We then drove down the quiet street where Terrance Sr. lives, the same home where the family moved when Terrance was a kid. Just down the street is a public park and playground—so close it might as well have been his backyard. He was allowed to walk down the block and meet his friends. It was a place to let loose after school, spend time out of the house in the hot summers, and stay off the streets. There was a playground, a baseball field, and a basketball court. Looking back, Terrance said, "It was unbelievable," all the things they had to do back then. When we pulled over in the Buick, I saw what he wanted to show me.

What was once a park, playground, and sports field—a neighborhood resource and community institution—had since been partially walled off by a chain-link fence, now cut open, torn, and drooping in certain places. Wherever the baseball field had been, it had long since been overgrown with tall weeds, a basketball hoop lay fallen on its side in the mud, and puddles of standing water filled the court. Today, the surrounding pavement is torn up and littered with trash—it's hard to imagine playing, let alone skateboarding, which Terrance remembered doing, on such rough terrain.

There were few other cars on the road, so Terrance slowed to a crawl as he motored down the main artery that runs through the neighborhood, a wide two-lane street with a grassy median. On either side the land sloped upward and was lined with large overgrown trees and spacious detached homes. "Look here at these houses—you see how big those trees is? That means these folks had money. No more though," Terrance added. Most of the homes were empty now, with a porch or roof sagging, shutters askew, some windows patched over with plywood. Every now and then we saw a person sitting out front, or just a single potted plant that signaled life inside. It was clear that the street was once beautiful, even regal. It was still impressive, but in a weathered, unkempt sort of way.

As we wove down smaller streets branching off Park Heights Avenue, there were shorter blocks with more modest homes that varied in up-keep. Over two-thirds of the housing stock in Park Heights is old, built before 1960,[10] and much of it comprised of two-family semi-attached, extra-wide row homes separated from adjacent units by narrow pas-sageways, which lead into small backyards. The homes have covered front porches, modest front lawns, and backyards or parking spots, ac-cessible by an alleyway that runs behind the block. Some homes have toys strewn about the chain-linked front yards, grills in the back, and dogs chained in the alleys. Some yards have meticulously trimmed grass and carefully potted flowers, while others are empty.

We drove on to blocks of attached row homes, narrow, just two win-dows wide, with shallower lawns. On any given street, more homes are vacant than occupied. Reasonably well-kept homes stand next to those with caved-in roofs or porches with trees growing through them. Empty lots overgrown with weeds sit like rotted-out teeth between the homes still standing.

One striking block was almost entirely emptied of residents, the ply-wood used to cover glassless windows long gone—pulled off by a storm

FIGURE 3: Boarded-up Home.

FIGURE 4: Vacant Homes.

or by someone trying to get inside for shelter. But in a single house at the end of the block, an air-conditioning unit was humming in a second-story window. Drapes covered the lower windows, and a few flowerpots graced the railing of the front porch, glimmering red and yellow in the morning sun. Who was this single tenant on a block of vacants?

Many homes on this block were branded with a bright red "X" nailed to the façade by the city housing inspector to let the fire department know that the home should be left to burn if doing so would not endanger surrounding buildings. Our route took us by several memorials where residents had left flowers, notes, candles, or teddy bears and balloons to commemorate the loss of a loved one in a shooting or violent altercation.

A bit further down, we drove down a street bounded on one side by an open, serene field of grass. I never would have known or guessed what had once stood in the field if Terrance had not told me: "This here was The Ranch," he told me. "The O.K. Corral" they used to call it, for the wooden fence that once encircled it and the "mayhem" that it was

FIGURE 5: Teddy bear memorial.

known for inside. Pall Mall Apartments, aka "The Ranch," was legend-
ary for its drugs and violence.

The block where Pall Mall used to stand is quieter now. The city revoked the privately owned facility's license in 2005, citing it as a "drug
nuisance." In 2006 the housing authority issued residents housing
vouchers to move elsewhere, and in 2007 the city purchased the property. Mayor Sheila Dixon presided over its demolition in 2008. People
in the neighborhood still refer to it as "Section 8 Housing" even though
it was privately owned.[11]

Pall Mall's reputation lives on: the stigma attached to a place sometimes
outlives the people who occupy it. Terrance pointed out that we were not
alone. "Look how many police cars right there, look. Just count, just count."
I counted two police cars stationed at different points along the block, and
a third cruiser parked next to a police van at the end of the block. Their
lights were not flashing; it was not clear what they were doing, but their
presence was obvious. This was a common sight in the neighborhood.

Terrance turned down Park Heights Avenue and through the neighborhood's busiest intersection. On one corner was a Rite Aid pharmacy, housed in a dour, concrete structure the color of wet mud. Across the street was a competing Beauty Berry, a brighter red and white dollar-store full of beauty supply products for a fraction of Rite Aid's price. The entrance to Beauty Berry offered a sanctuary to a wide array of peddlers hawking various informal goods. You could pick up a used book or magazine; a loosie, if you didn't have the cash for a whole box of cigarettes inside the store; and other black-market items, if you knew how to ask. A woman tugged her child's hand and she shooed him into the store, past all the people hanging around outside. Several yards away, three older women sat huddled under the bus shelter, chatting as they waited for the bus.

A two-story building occupied the northeast corner of the intersection. A liquor store occupied the ground floor space, with the upper level boarded up with painted plywood. To the left was a fenced-in empty lot. On the last corner was In and Out Bail Bonds, a full-service bail bond shop, with dirty white vinyl paneling that was missing in patches. Grass pushed up through the cracks in the sidewalk out front. Along the two main intersecting streets alone, the *Baltimore Sun* reports, there were at least forty liquor stores in the neighborhood.[12]

Physical evidence of the neighborhood's steep decline was everywhere. But when Terrance looked out, his mind's eye overlaid a different picture, one from his memory of the way things used to be. "You've got to understand, this was the suburbs." What he meant is that it *felt* like the suburbs, even though it was within the city limits:

This area was prominent. It was very nice, very nice single-family homes all like this. . . . You had people working at the General Motors, some of those old postal workers, stuff like that, teachers. . . . Right at the corner of Reisterstown and Cold Spring was Howard Johnsons, which was an upscale restaurant.

We drove up Park Heights Avenue until we turned the corner onto Belvedere, where the vast empty expanse of a parking lot the size of many football fields revealed itself. The white stands of Pimlico Race Course, weathered by age and disinvestment, rise up in the distance like the

FIGURE 6: Pimlico Racetrack.

tattered sails of a ship abandoned at sea. For three days a year, the 140-acre-area comes alive with tourists driving in to see the famed Preakness Stakes. The lot fills with expensive cars. Ladies in heels and fascinators and men in seersucker suits with ascots knotted around their necks, most of them entirely unaware of the challenges faced by the surrounding community, stream into the area.

For this brief annual event, the Preakness provides seasonal employment for residents. They are hired as ushers and janitors. People who live in the surrounding streets earn money selling parking spots, cold drinks, and snacks to tourists from their front porches. The racetrack also hosts concerts and a carnival a few times a year, and on Wednesdays a small farmer's market occupies a fraction of the vast lot. But for most of the year it sits abandoned and underutilized.

Of course, Terrance remembered a different time:

This area was so important, the world renowned. You have Pimlico Race Track right there, and horseracing was year-round. On the

corner of Belvedere and Park Heights there was bookies and newspaper stands and stuff like that, unbelievable. Delis, delicatessens,
corned beef was big back then. Corn beef with those really good hotdogs. Not just regular hotdogs but kosher hotdogs.

As we drove west on Belvedere, the concrete Bel Park Towers loomed
ahead. Bel Park is one of the two public housing complexes in Park
Heights. With 276 units, it is one of the few mixed-population (for families and seniors) high-rises left in the city. Bel Park used to be exclusively
for seniors, and is made up of predominantly studio and one-bedroom
apartments. In 2014 Bel Park became part of Baltimore's Rental Assistance Demonstration (RAD) program, allowing public housing authorities to lease public housing to private developers who invest the capital
to renovate and manage these buildings.[13] Under RAD, residents' public
housing subsidies are typically converted into fixed Section 8 vouchers
that are attached to the complex rather than the tenant. The deals offer
developers tax credits and finance much needed renovations. Housing
authorities across the country have been relying on RAD to deal with
underfunding and enormous repair backlogs, such as for HVAC systems,
windows, roofs, flooring, security, laundry facilities, bedbug infestations,
and upgrades to apartments including appliances, cabinets, plumbing,
lighting, and doors. But the conversion to project-based vouchers comes
with some downsides for tenants, including weakened tenant protections and diminished support for the most-low-income families.

The second public housing complex in Park Heights is Oswego Mall,
with 35 two, three, and four-bedroom units. Lots of people erroneously
told me that Oswego Mall was "Section 8" housing, perhaps because it
is a series of low-rise, town-home-style units. In reality, like Bel Park,
Oswego Mall is a public housing development for families. Today, "Section 8" carries much of the stigma that public housing did, if not more,
which may also account for the reason that community members assumed the complex was for vouchers.

A block north of the racetrack on Northern Parkway we came upon
a large brick complex that looked like a school, save for the field out

FIGURE 7: Oswego Mall.

back that resembled a military boot camp training facility. From my vantage point on the street, I could see an obstacle course and fences of different heights placed at regular intervals. Terrance confirmed: "It's not a school anymore. That's the training place for the Baltimore City Police. They have the rope climbing, they do climbing rocks and stuff. Everything is out back there."

The site used to be Pimlico Middle School, where Terrance was a student. He pointed to the track: "We used to have to run that. That was the gym right there." When Pimlico Middle School (then Pimlico Junior High) opened in 1956, the *Baltimore Sun* described it as "big, expansive and sparkling, with shiny new desks and chairs, practice ranges, gym equipment, polished corridors and pastel walls." It was set to enroll 1,925 students that year. But fifty years later, by 2007, it was closed due to dwindling enrollment.[14] With white flight came the loss of a tax base and a simultaneous decline in population.

FOLK THEORIES OF DECLINE:
WHITE FLIGHT, BLIGHT, AND SLUMLORDS

Earlier that morning, before we got in the car, Terrance had pulled a thick leather-bound yearbook with the number 1969 printed in bold gold letters from his shelf. "Now this is Pimlico Junior high in '69." He opened the page to a photo of several young men on the basketball team: "That's me right there. That's me. I was number 38," Terrance beamed. "But here's what I wanted to show you." He flipped the page to the section with the photos of the graduating class. "That's what it looks like. Now you've got to understand that in 1969 the school—" Terrance stopped speaking to show rather than tell me. He put his finger to trace the rows of photos—a sea of mostly pale faces—as he read the names: "Goldberg, Goldberg, Goldstein . . . that's all white. See that?" He put it down and pulled out the yearbook from 1970. The faces here were a mix of black and white together. "Just keep looking at the difference of it." Terrance looked stunned himself that he found such a clear illustration of how quickly the change took place. "Then, see it starts to turn all black. See that? Just one day, real fast like that. I guarantee you two or three years before this, that book was all white."

White flight continued apace until there were no white people left to leave. Terrence explained: "The most amazing thing about this area is the exodus of the Jews; how they did it overnight like that. I think within three or four years the neighborhood turned completely 100 percent black. In 1960 we were the second [black] family in the neighborhood. From '59 to '64. Right in front of your eyes, just vanished, disappeared. . . . It was so crazy. Before you knew it, they were gone."

White flight is by no means a "Jewish" phenomenon. In the nearby Edmonson village, real estate blockbusting led to the flight of the white, predominantly Protestant, population.[15] But in Park Heights, the white residents who lived in the neighborhood before the seventies were almost entirely Jewish. Not unlike the African American families after them, Baltimoreans of Jewish descent were confined to certain areas of the city. Barred from elite neighborhoods such as Roland Park, they settled along the northwest corridor in Liberty Heights, Park Heights, and Pikesville.[16] At first, I wondered about Terrance's habit of referring to the prior residents as "the Jews." But over time I came to realize that in the context of the neighborhood, it was a simple description. Many residents now use "Jewish" interchangeably with "white," because they were virtually synonymous at this particular time in this particular place.

"Everything changed, everything, changed," Terrance sighed as he took in the magnitude of it. Narratives of change and decline are complicated and multilayered. Residents have a wide variety of folk theories to explain what happened over the years: white flight, the arrival of drugs, the loss of jobs. Terrance's explanation goes all the way back to the 1970s and the war in Vietnam, in which so many of his older friends in the neighborhood had served.

> It's all because of the war, the Vietnam War. When those guys that came back from the war, a lot of those men were hooked, they were messed up. . . . [The Draft was] something that you had no choice in. They take you and just put you in the war because you are of age. You've got to do two and a half, three years. So, a lot of them guys became addicted to heroin and marijuana and hash.

Communities such as Park Heights were hit hard by the Vietnam war, sending a disproportionate number of young men off to war, and welcoming those who returned home back into the community a few years later. For Terrance, this was not benign:

> When they came back to the United States they infiltrated the area that they came from. That was in the '70s. And in the '80s all of a sudden crack cocaine comes into the same neighborhoods. . . . This area right here, became notorious for crack cocaine, and always heroin. Heroin is still big in this area. Then the "high" becomes priority, then the whole lifestyle starts—prostitution, hustling, stealing, boosting, stuff like that. A whole society of people. Education does not become priority. Decency does not become priority. Work does not become priority. Drugs destroyed the nucleus of the family.

Terrance blames the drugs that came in after the war for the neighborhood's decline. Echoing the rhetoric of the era's conservative politicians, he noted how the drug epidemic affected and destroyed the families living in the neighborhood, struggling to explain what happened and who was to blame.

> When blacks move into a neighborhood it brings the property value down. For some strange reason, I don't know why they do that, but you can just look in the area. There is trash that's there. The maintenance of the yard is not there. There is something going on, I can't figure it out but something is not right. I don't know how to put it. I do think in my heart that all men are created equal, but in some cases when you have an area and it's infiltrated by black Americans it goes down immediately.

It is easy for Terrance and other residents to see the trash, the people hanging around during the day. These things are visible. It is harder for residents to pinpoint the underlying root causes: the city's disinvestment in poor minority neighborhoods, a social group hit hard by the loss of manufacturing jobs, a neighborhood beset by neglect and underinvestment.

For Terrance, as for many of the long-term residents I got to know, the decline of the neighborhood was deeply linked to racial change. But despite Terrance's condemnation of the racial change in the neighborhood, many residents would agree that the decline was not caused by the racial change itself, but rather by the loss of institutions, wealth, and jobs that went with it. Working-class blacks, who tended to be concentrated in neighborhoods like Park Heights, were hit especially hard by the decline in manufacturing and the loss of factory jobs. Sociological accounts suggest that similar processes were occurring in poor minority neighborhoods in cities across the country.[17]

While few residents expressed an understanding of these broader forces contributing to the decline of neighborhoods like Park Heights, some did shift the blame away from the residents and onto outside forces. Barbie pointed to the landlords. "Some of those white families, they didn't sell their homes when they left. They became slumlords. They moved away and stopped keeping up those houses, but they sure made money off them." Many residents noted the shift from owners to renters. Not only do absentee landlords sometimes neglect maintenance on the home, but they may also leave properties vacant for long periods of time.

Residents' sense of when things really started to look different is borne out in the numbers. Between the 1970s and 2011, the poverty rate in Park Heights spiked from 16 percent to 31 percent, well above the city average, which was at 22 percent.[18] The median household income was $29,062, as compared to Baltimore City's median household income of $40,100, and the U.S. median of $52,762.[19] The unemployment rate was 21.8 percent, compared to Baltimore City at 12.6 percent, and the U.S. at 8.6 percent.[20] Between 1970 and 2000, the overall vacancy rate rose steadily in tandem with the city of Baltimore, but in the following decade, vacancies in Park Heights pulled ahead, jumping to a full 25.2 percent, as compared to 19.1 percent in the city of Baltimore as a whole.[21] In other words, a quarter of the housing stock in Park Heights was unoccupied during the time I was living there—one of the highest vacancy rates in the city.

By the early nineties, the neighborhood's racial transformation was complete. Those few whites who had not sold their homes in the earlier wave—those who had stayed rooted in their community—now began to leave. Barbie remembered each of her neighbors on the block and when and why they moved out.

> Miss Reiner stayed here a long time even after her husband died. Miss Carter, down the street, and Miss Epstein stayed. A lot of the whites still stayed around here. But in the early 90s a lot of them started to move. You know, 'cause they husbands had died, they really didn't have anybody to come in the house and I guess they start to get scared.

The last twenty years brought vacancies and residential turmoil into the neighborhood. Many homes changed hands or were abandoned. Barbie said that change had been gradual, until she noticed an abrupt shift on her block: "I think after about '98, it really started to change. Quite a few of the houses across the street was tore down. They done tore down a lot in this area." Patty too remembers that "Park Heights was a beautiful place. But then it came a point in time that it wasn't. People were just moving out, and they weren't fixing up the houses, and the houses were boarded up. And I do not like to be in a community where the homes are not being taken care of."

Mae, a fifty-four-year-old resident of Park Heights, had moved to the neighborhood when she was four years old and remembered it as a nice place. She pointed out a home on the block with trees growing up through the front porch, with leafy vines wrapping around the front posts of the house, obscuring the entryway. Baltimore has long humid summers where vegetation grows quickly, especially in areas that are not carefully maintained. "All these houses, they weren't like *that* [pointing across the street], they were beautiful houses, nice beautiful gardens." Mae explained that the owners of the home don't live too far away, just a "hop, skip and a jump from the Hill," in Washington, D.C., but don't do anything to maintain the vacant homes.

> I guess they figure mine is in a drug area and don't nobody have money like that to buy them. They just let it go, and that's how the rats will come. Like this house right here next door, I was on the porch the other night, and I kept hearing something over there. It was two opossums! He was showing his teeth at me, I said, "I am not going to bother you." He came right out that hole right there. Cats be over there too. And I seen a fox down there. There is a lot of animals around here. They just come on up here because there's a lot of trees and grass.

Even when derelict homes are torn down by the city, empty lots remain in their stead, and the city is not always vigilant about cutting back the vegetation that sprouts so quickly in Baltimore's balmy climate. The overgrown vacant lots have become refuge for wild animals.

Residents spread blame for the decline in all directions. Was it the government, whose policies closed off many neighborhoods to black homebuyers for so long? Or perhaps the real estate agents who stoked racial fears and sparked a mass white exodus? Or was it the white residents, who held those fears in the first place? Some blamed the black residents themselves, embracing a familiar popular narrative of welfare queens and absent fathers who lost their jobs and became addicted to drugs. Others pointed to the greedy landlords who bought up the properties and then fled, leaving the homes to abandonment and decay.

I heard variations on each of these theories. These are old, tired debates, and there is little lingering animosity toward the government or the former white residents. Instead, several residents blamed the newest, least familiar arrival: "Section 8" voucher holders. While the other explanations are hard to pin down, as Bob pointed out, you can *see* voucher holders.

As Terrance and I turned back onto his father's street at the end of our drive, it felt like a quiet refuge compared to the bustle of the rest of the neighborhood. Terrance said he and his father are far enough from the center of the neighborhood that they are buffered from the crime of the more "lively" areas. But he's warned his father: If the crime moves further back, he will have to sell the house. Terrance pointed to a few houses at the end of the block, one with a For Sale sign, the other vacant. "These are going to turn out to be Section 8," he sighed. "Yeah, my neighborhood is going downhill."

THE RENTAL MARKET

Barbie, who grew up in the neighborhood, keeps tabs on all the homes on the block. On a late afternoon in October, she and I stepped into her front yard to survey the surrounding homes. We looked out past the chain-link fence that encloses her small plot of grass to the small side street lined with large, somewhat dilapidated, single-family homes. Many were visibly vacant. With some dismay in her voice, Barbie told me: "Ms. Tracy moved out, so that's empty," pointing to the house across the street. "Somebody just moved in this corner house right there. Let's go say hi."

We walked across the street and three houses down and knocked on the door. Though we could hear children laughing and yelling inside, it took some time before anyone came to the door. Barbie turned her head to glance sideways at me over the rim of her glasses and murmured "Mmm-hmm," as if to say, "see, just as I thought." I was not sure yet what suspicion of hers had been confirmed, but I kept quiet and waited. Finally, a young woman opened the door a few inches to peer out, a bandana holding her hair back, a toddler on her hip, and a small child trailing at her feet. She looked tired and disgruntled to be bothered with the door. Luckily, Barbie—who had met the young woman, Penny, before—was with me. She turned on the charm, flashing a genuine toothy smile that seems to work on everyone, and said "You hear that racket last night out here? How you and the kids holding up?"

Penny's face relaxed, and she welcomed us in to sit at the kitchen table, the only piece of furniture that I could see on the entire first floor aside from the TV. The children were quieted with a snack, and Penny told us all about her family and her move to the neighborhood. "Yeah, but how much is your *rent*?" Barbie got straight to the point. When she told us that the rent was $1,200 a month, Barbie's jaw dropped and she burst out, "Where you think we be at? . . . You crazy? Girl, you must be on Section 8!" Barbie didn't mean it as a jab at Penny—residents knew all too well that landlords in the neighborhood were getting way more for the voucher properties than they could for the market ones. Still, she was incredulous. Most of the rented homes on the block were going for around $700 a month, maybe $900 for the really big ones.

After we left, Barbie told me about another landlord she knows, Tony: "He own Miss Lorraine's house and he owns another house down here. The house he got down here is empty, the people moved out. I think he trying to rent it for $700. That ain't bad . . . and I think that Louise pays $700 or $650," Barbie said, pointing to another home on the block. Penny's place was fixed up a little to pass inspection. But even so, Barbie was shocked to hear that the landlord charges almost $500 per month more than the neighboring homes. "She could have gone to the county with that kind of money!" Barbie remarked. Many of the neighborhoods in the counties surrounding Baltimore City are known to be safe areas with good-quality homes, but prices in these desirable neighborhoods can be higher. The lack of public transportation and a fear that landlords will not want to rent to voucher holders keep many voucher families from moving out to these areas.[22]

While the unassisted renters in Park Heights can barely afford their $700 per month rents, new voucher holders are moving in, and the landlords are charging $1,000 to $1,300 for the same-sized homes. These units are renovated to varying degrees, and have to pass more stringent quality inspections to qualify for the voucher program, but Barbie and others don't think they are worth that much more.[23]

WHERE ARE ALL THE VOUCHERS?

While some voucher holders lived peppered around the neighborhood on blocks like Barbie's, I soon realized that I wasn't meeting as many on these small blocks as I would have expected given the sheer number of vouchers in the neighborhood. So, where were they? I soon realized that—despite hopes for deconcentration—many weren't living in row homes spread throughout the neighborhood, but instead lived clustered together in big apartment buildings.

One of these buildings, I soon learned, was Oakland Terrace. The first time I found it was by accident. I was leaving an elderly homeowner's house who lived on a quiet residential block. Looking for a shortcut, I took a turn down a small street where nearly all of the homes were vacant. I reached the end of the block and turned left onto what looked like a back alley. It was overgrown with trees, the asphalt was all torn up and there were huge potholes, and off to the right I saw a ramshackle series of shacks in what looked to be someone's backyard, but had overgrown into a dense, wooded area. When I saw the speed limit sign ahead, I realized that despite all appearances, it was an official street. Just then, four of the low-rise units of Oakland Terrace came into view, and I saw the outer building of a housing complex of over one hundred units hidden on this backroad that bisected two different areas of the neighborhood.

Over the next months I spent many hours visiting with the residents of Oakland Terrace, sitting with them at the picnic tables in the parking lot, having a cold drink in their dimly lit apartments, where they draped sheets over the windows to keep out the hot sun in the summer and the drafty air in winter.

People in the neighborhood used to call the complex "The Pool," for the in-ground swimming pool that attracted young families to the development in the late sixties and early seventies. "The Terrace," as others called it, offered the suburban-like comforts of a pool, play area, and designated parking, all within city lines. But as the neighborhood swiftly changed in the seventies, so did Oakland Terrace. The owner had trouble keeping the place at full occupancy, and there were disputes over who was allowed in the pool and when. And as drug selling took hold all over the neighborhood, community spaces shut down and residents spent more time indoors. Soon after the complex opened, the gates to the pool were locked shut, and a few years after that the pool was filled in with dirt.

The demise of the Oakland Terrace's private pool brings to mind a parallel history of public pools in Baltimore and across the country. For decades, Baltimore City offered access to just one public pool for the city's 100,000 black residents: Druid Hill Park's "Pool No. 2," built in 1921. White residents enjoyed access to six pools across the city, including the Druid Hill Park Pool No. 1—the "white pool"—which was twice the size of Pool No. 2, deemed the "colored pool." Pool No. 2 was so crowded in the summer heat that pool-goers were allowed entry in waves. When the city's pools were desegregated in 1956 and blacks were allowed access to the spacious and renovated "white" Pool No. 1, white attendance dropped off sharply and Pool No. 2 soon closed altogether.[24]

Today, Pool No. 1 is mostly frequented by black residents. Pool No. 2 stands as a memorial to Baltimore's segregated past—in the nineties, the old ladders and diving board were painted a bright (though now rusty) blue, leading down not to water, but to a field of lush green grass filling the depth of the pool.

The old pool at Oakland Terrace—while also filled in with dirt—serves a different function. The curved edge of the cement is just visible through the scraggly weeds that now nearly cover it, and the lot is filled with discarded furniture and appliances—rusty old refrigerators that could be repaired for tenants if necessary, soggy mattresses, broken plates, and discarded toys—pillaged from the units of evicted tenants in the complex.

Today, Oakland Terrace is home to about fifty voucher households, which makes up about 43 percent of the units in the complex.

FIGURE 8: Pool #2, Druid Hill Park, Baltimore, photograph by Paul Henderson, 1948.

FIGURE 9: Memorial Pool, 1999, by Joyce J. Scott. Photo by Graham Coreil-Allen.

FIGURE 10: Old Pool at Oakland Terrace.

AN OUTSIDER'S VIEW

As I got to know the neighborhood better over the time that I spent there, I learned how residents saw the space in different ways, and my understanding shifted as well. Many different social groups live in Park Heights, and the longtime homeowners don't have a monopoly on describing it. Even among homeowners there is quite a bit of variation. While low-income, unassisted renters generally saw the neighborhood as a "rough" kind of place—never knowing it to be otherwise—voucher holders often see it as a step up from the neighborhoods they've been living in.

As an outsider looking in, I sometimes saw a different order to the neighborhood than the residents did. For Terrance, for example, there were just two areas: his block and then everything beyond that. But to me, it was clear that the feel of the neighborhood changed block by block. The longtime homeowners tended to live in certain pockets, while many of the voucher holders lived in others. The areas in between were transitional. Park Heights has three distinct ecological areas or "microneighborhoods," characterized by different patterns of residential status, length of residency, and geographic boundaries.

In the *homeowner havens*, where blocks of longtime homeowners have remained largely intact and sheltered from the changes affecting the rest of the neighborhood, few renters have moved in.[25] Like Mr. Green and Ms. Patty, most of these African American homeowners moved into the area in the late 1960s and early 1970s as the white population was moving out. They were often working class and bought homes with the aspiration of building wealth and joining the ranks of the middle class. Many were children of migrants from the south, and they were among the first black families to be offered mortgages in the neighborhood.

Most of these original settlers have remained in the neighborhood, and those who have died often passed on their homes to their children and grandchildren. Their family and social networks are deeply embedded in Park Heights, as are their most significant financial investments: their homes. They have a lot invested in their neighborhood, and many are reluctant to leave, not just for sentimental reasons, but also because their homes are not worth much.

Mr. Green lives in the same house that he and his wife moved into in 1962. He has no desire to leave. When his neighbors don't see his car move for a few days they stop by to make sure he is okay, and when he comes home with groceries, Mr. or Mrs. Peabody, who live next door, come running out to help him carry them inside. But Mr. Green knows that his son worries about the changes in the neighborhood inching closer to his doorstep. He is holding his breath that the neighborhood will hold: at his age, starting over somewhere new would be hard. And he is well aware that the house is worth much more to him than to the real estate market. From what he's seen of local home prices, he'd be lucky to break even on what he paid back in the 1960s.

These homeowners have been in the neighborhood for years, developing and relying on a network of stable social relations. This network could be, in theory, a valuable resource to incoming renters. However, as we will see in the coming chapters, these systems are not always able to support and absorb newcomers. The homeowners' position is precarious: their financial worth is vested entirely in this one asset. And it is this very home that is most threatened by the influx of renters.

A few blocks away from Mr. Green's homeowner haven is Maple Avenue, which is a *transitional area,* where Bob and his wife live. Here there aren't a lot of homeowners left, and renters are beginning to come in. Many of Maple Avenue's homeowners have died or have sold their homes to investors who turned them into rental units. The street is occupied by a mix of dwindling homeowners and newer renters. In the past ten years there has been a decline in homeownership for the first time.[26] These areas tend to have a high number of vacant and abandoned units, some of which are occupied illegally. There are row homes with small covered porches on either side of the block, and the street is peppered with holes where homes once stood, now empty lots filled with weeds. Vibrant, occupied homes are interspersed with vacant ones, some of them in very bad shape, falling down with rotting frames, caved-in roofs, and broken windows. There are few trees and just small scraggly patches of grass in front of the houses. There are often people hanging out in front of houses and on porches.

Other areas are now completely bereft of the homeowners who settled the neighborhood years earlier. *Voucher enclaves* such as Oakland Terrace have huge portions of voucher holders, as well as many unassisted renters.[27] These renters often reside in complexes or large buildings and so they are "bounded" in the sense that much of their social organization and community norms and rules are defined within and by the space of the complex.

In these parts of Park Heights, landlords have turned to recruiting voucher holders because it can be hard to find market rate renters who are interested in living in these areas, especially renters who are capable of paying their rent on time. Voucher holders often make up as much as a quarter to a half of residents in areas like Oakland Terrace.[28] Renters tend to churn in and out of these residences more frequently than homeowners, making them transitory spaces.

———

The neighborhood no longer looks the ways so many residents remember it from their early days in the community. The accounts of abundant stores, shopping, and open community relations stand in stark contrast to the way things look in Park Heights today. There is a bustle and a vibrancy, but also a sense of isolation and abandonment. For better or worse, *this* is the neighborhood that voucher holders have flocked to. One that is still reeling from the shock of white flight in the seventies, the loss of jobs, the rise in drugs and crime, and the blight of vacancies.

In Park Heights, the stigma of vouchers looms large. Voucher holders are a visible representation of a slew of changes that have hit the neighborhood in recent decades. Whether or not they are actually to blame—and I will argue that they are not—many residents hold them responsible for the many ills that have beset the neighborhood. But for many voucher holders, Park Heights is a chance for a new home.

Chapter 2

HOUSING INSECURITY AND SURVIVAL STRATEGIES

Several times a day Destiny carries her own roll of Save-A-Lot White Sheets, off-brand toilet paper, into the one bathroom she shares with her husband, her two kids, and the three other adults who live in the house. According to house rules, each renter must provide their own toilet paper. Every night she and her family squeeze into their "room-for-rent" in this home on a quiet street in Park Heights.

A few blocks away, Tina lives with her thirteen-year-old daughter. Several years ago, she ran out of money to fix the leak in the roof and pay for an exterminator in the home she had inherited in East Baltimore. She adopted a cat to try to keep the rats under control, but it wasn't enough. She eventually abandoned the house and moved with her daughter into Oakland Terrace, the first place she could find that would accept her.

Marlena lives with her boyfriend Derrick in a ramshackle third-floor walk-up owned by a notorious Baltimore drug kingpin. They boil pots of water on the stove to heat the apartment and keep their infant daughter warm. While Derrick works regular hours at KFC, Marlena tries to make some extra cash for the family by advertising escort services online.

Unlike the fortunate recipients of a housing voucher, these renters don't get any help from the government to pay their rent even though their housing situations are clearly precarious. They are like the vast majority of the poor, who don't receive any housing assistance, simply because the U.S. government doesn't budget enough to provide housing aid to everyone who needs it. "Housing insecurity" is a blanket term that refers to any number of housing-related issues: it can mean being unable to afford rent, experiencing frequent moves, living in an overcrowded space, or experiencing homelessness. Housing insecurity also refers to problems of safety and quality within the home or in the neighborhood surrounding the home.[1] A person who experiences any one of these problems is also likely to experience others, including poverty, unemployment, alternative employment, even health problems. Yet only one in four households experiencing housing insecurity—by some estimates as few as one in five—receive the federal housing assistance they qualify for.[2]

Baltimore, like many cities across the country, is experiencing an affordable housing crisis.[3] A long-held rule of thumb suggests that families should spend no more than 30 percent of their income on rent or mortgage.[4] But households typically spend far more than that today. In Baltimore, for example, 57 percent of all renters are "rent-burdened," meaning that more than a third of their income goes to rent.[5] Across the country, a majority of poor families who rent spend over half of their income on housing, while one in four spend over 70 percent. Writing such a large check to your landlord means having less money for essentials like food, transportation, and childcare.

This problem is not limited to the extremely poor. While individuals below the poverty line have struggled for decades to afford housing, more and more renters are joining the ranks of the rent-burdened. In 1998, 44 percent of Baltimore renters earning between $20,000 and $40,000 per year paid more than a third of their income in rent.[6] By 2013, this number had jumped to over 70 percent. Researchers disagree on whether rents have outpaced income or incomes have lagged behind rents, but either way, the need for housing assistance is the highest it's been for decades.

The problem of finding affordable housing is of particular importance for renters who don't receive any housing assistance. That fact that rents in Park Heights remain somewhat more affordable compared to the rest of the city draws some renters to the area. Park Heights' average monthly rent of $792 is significantly lower than the Baltimore City average of $889.[7] But because renters in Park Heights tend to have lower paying jobs, many still spend more than a third of their income on rent. A substantial number of renters in Park Heights—over three out of ten—pay over half of their income in rent. And even given the significant numbers of voucher holders, only 40 percent of renter households pay under 30 percent of their income in rent.[8]

In recent years unassisted renters have been moving to the area. Multiple factors draw them to the neighborhood. For instance, landlords, recognizing Park Heights' declining reputation, offer incentives such as waiving the security deposit or skipping the credit check to attract tenants. For many low-income unassisted renters, this "perk" is a necessity. The neighborhood is full of signs offering "rooms-for-rent," in which a landlord furnishes an apartment and rents out each room individually. Other residents come seeking access to the drug and alcohol rehabilitation centers and halfway homes that dot the neighborhood.[9]

These unassisted renters, and those who depend on them, live in a constant state of uncertainty. They are more likely to be evicted and are more likely to experience periods of homelessness or "doubling up" by staying with a family member or friend.[10] They frequently experience pressured housing decisions, or may be in the midst of active crisis. And because they are perpetually short on cash, unassisted renters often work long hours or accept informal work with poor pay and unsafe working conditions. Sometimes they turn to illicit activity in an attempt to keep a roof over their heads. The story of those who receive no housing assistance offers an important counterpoint to the voucher story, highlighting the relief that vouchers can provide to those lucky enough to receive them.

DESTINY, RAVEN: ALTERNATIVE HOUSING SOLUTIONS

People living in poverty avoid homelessness by staying with family, friends, or loved ones, at times putting up with overcrowding, dangerous and substandard living conditions, or even abusive situations because they have nowhere else to go.

Destiny Stevens is twenty-seven. She, her fiancé James, and her two little boys, five months and five years old, all share one rented room in a three-bedroom house. They pay $600 per month for the room, which is about ten feet by twelve feet. The space contains a full-size bed, a small cot and a crib for the two little ones, and all the family's possessions. One of the other bedrooms is occupied by a couple in their thirties, and the third room is occupied by a fifty-year-old single man.

Like a growing number of Baltimoreans, they live in a modern-day rooming house. The room is theirs, but Destiny and her family share the kitchen and bathroom with other renters. Landlords sometimes pay the electricity, provide furniture for the common areas, and generally keep up the property. Destiny's landlord provides extra amenities like a library of DVDs, a TV, and an extra fridge to make sure there is enough room for everyone's food; it's right outside the kitchen, in the dining room. These arrangements are quite profitable for landlords. At $600 a room, Destiny's landlord is bringing in $1,800 a month for a house that would he would be hard-pressed to rent for more than $1,000 to a single family.[11] Even after paying for electricity, water, and cable, the landlord is making a significant profit.[12]

This arrangement is also attractive to tenants who have little savings and move frequently enough that they may not own a mattress, a coffeemaker, or a TV. This was exactly Destiny's situation when she found the house through an ad on Craigslist for a room-for-rent less than a year earlier. At the time, her fiancé was in jail, she was pregnant with her youngest, and she needed to get off her brother's couch. She wanted to live somewhere where her kids could play outside, without a lot of drug activity. She also wanted the house and its other residents to be clean and neat. She gets along very well with her housemates, who have only been in the house for a few months.

Given the opportunity, Destiny would prefer to have her own place instead of sharing common areas with four other adults and carrying her own roll of toilet paper into a bathroom used by seven people. But this was the most affordable option she could find on short notice. Destiny has been on the housing voucher waiting list for over six years, since well before the housing authority stopped adding new names to the list. In the meantime, she's been saving money to rent her own apartment so that she will have room to take custody of her nine-year-old daughter, currently living with Destiny's mother three-and-half hours away in

Virginia. While Destiny's living situation is far from ideal, she considers herself lucky to have a roof over her head.

Less than ten blocks from Destiny's room-for-rent, I met Raven Greeley. Raven is on the taller side, around 5'9", and has the lean muscles of a runner. The afternoon I met her she was sitting on her front porch with a friend, discussing a recent mugging on the block. They've been there for three years, and she talks about the neighborhood as if it were her own. But unlike the majority of her neighbors, Raven has neither a lease nor a mortgage. She squats.

Raven and her husband live in a three-bedroom row house with her nine kids, who range between the ages of four and eighteen. The house is in bad shape. Inside, the entire first floor has no lights due to an electrical short circuit from a leak during the last storm. The wall that runs the length of the living room is stained with dark streaks from water damage; when it rains, water streams down the wall and Raven's four-year-old asks: "Mommy, why does the wall rain?" The front room is covered in a dingy wall-to-wall shag carpet. There is no furniture except for a glass dining room table with plastic lawn chairs where we often sat when I would visit.

The house is located directly next to a vacant home that is literally falling to pieces. The boards over the windows and doors do little to cover up the huge holes in the outer structure and porch. From Raven's porch, you can see down to the piles of trash and debris under the neighboring house. Not too long ago, Raven said, one of the local crews used it as a stash house. They'd stage shootouts from down there.

Growing up in the projects, Raven cared for her mother, who had sickle cell disease. Living in the projects made her illness worse. The damp hallways, reeking of urine and feces. The mold in the walls. The windows that often stayed stuck shut in the summer and leaked precious heat in the winter. Raven remembers the violence as well as the humanity of the place. "People took care of each other," she told me.

Raven has an illness that appears to be similar to her mother's—fatigue, joint pain, headaches. This keeps her from working. But with nine kids, there is more than enough to do at home. Her husband works for a company that lays asphalt, but the work is seasonal so he picks up odd jobs when he can.

A few months ago, Raven's landlord went into foreclosure. She and her family decided to stay, landlord or no. They could be evicted by the bank or a new buyer at any time.[13]

TINA, BARBIE: HOMEOWNERSHIP AND HOUSING INSECURITY

For some renters, like Destiny, and for squatters, like Raven, even precarious housing is a step up. In contrast, some of the renters I met in Park Heights had known what it was to own their own home. Owning a home, especially an older home, is expensive, and sometimes people can't keep up. These renters knew exactly what they were missing.

The first time I met her, Tina Jackson was waiting for me outside of her apartment building: "I just wanted to make sure you got in OK," she said, escorting me upstairs and straight into her apartment, which was a vision of calm and order in an otherwise run-down complex. While heavy blankets were draped over the two windows in the living room that looked out on the parking lot to keep out noise from the neighbors who liked to congregate below, the living room was neatly furnished with worn, well-oiled furniture that used to belong to her grandmother.

Tina is thirty-four years old. She has a thirteen-year-old daughter, and is expecting another child in a few months. She was raised by her grandmother on her father's side in the Lafayette projects in Baltimore after her mother passed away when she was eleven. In that neighborhood, all the kids played together and knew each other's families. Tina still keeps in touch with many of these old friends. When she first left home, she moved to a subsidized apartment complex nearby. Though affordable, Tina was not comfortable there; she was mugged several times. She said her neighbors thought she was "uppity." They always wanted to borrow things but rarely returned them.

After a few years, she was relieved to move into a house left to her by her great-grandmother in East Baltimore, in a quiet homeowner neighborhood. She hoped to raise her daughter in a similar environment to the one in which she had grown up. Tina and her daughter loved the home, and the fact that her grandmother had lived there made her feel safe. Pointing to a photograph on the wall, Tina told me:

> That's my great-grandmom. She passed away a couple of years ago but I maintained her home for three years until I moved here. The roof and everything caved all in. I didn't have enough money to fix it and my family, we didn't have the money. So I ended up leaving . . . and moved in here until my grandma and my uncle and the rest of them can try to fix it up. . . . The house was old. I wish I could show you these pictures. My bedroom wall there was rocks, stone, that's how my wall was in my bedroom. . . . The antique man said to me he would come in and give me $3,000 just for my walls. . . . They were so old. And my rocking chair is still there, my grandmother's rocking chair that's sitting on the porch, he even wanted that. . . . I said "No, you're not getting that." I said "No, indeedy!"

Although the house was paid off and the property taxes weren't too high, the house had structural problems. Things started going wrong, and the bills began to pile up. First the roof caved in. Then a pipe burst in the basement and started leaking into the neighbor's house. The electrical sockets were not working properly.

Tina also inherited unpaid utility bills dating back to when her uncles were living in the house. While she managed to pay off some of the water bill and the taxes, she found it difficult to keep up. She tried to get grants to help pay for the electric bills, but she had had a falling out with her aunt, whose name was on the deed to the house. Her aunt refused to put her name on the grant applications.

Then Tina started seeing rats. She thought they were coming in through a hole in the basement wall, but she couldn't pay to hire an exterminator. She got a cat, but it wasn't enough: one day, she came down the stairs to see the cat fighting with a rat of about the same size. The cat-sized rat was the straw that broke the camel's back. Tina abandoned the house and moved with her daughter into the first place she could find. This turned out to be Oakland Terrace. As an unassisted renter, Tina is surrounded by voucher holders, who make 43 percent of residents there.

While homeownership is thought to offer stability, it is not always a permanent condition. Housing insecurity is relevant for homeowners too. As the Park Heights neighborhood has declined because of its aging housing stock, drugs, and disinvestment, many homeowners have experienced downward mobility, sometimes, like Tina, even losing their homes and being forced to join the renter class. Five of the renters I got to know in Park Heights fell off the path to homeownership.

Like Tina, Barbie McAdams had experienced the loss of a home that she owned. At fifty-three, Barbie is both a mother to her daughter and a grandmother to her three-year-old granddaughter, who live with her. Her partner Roman lives with her too, and her son stays with them intermittently when he's not with his girlfriend. Barbie used to own a home but lost it, and at one point she even had a voucher, which she also lost. Now, she rents the home she grew up in from her parents, who bought a smaller place to retire to in Northern Park Heights. They bought the home Barbie lives in now back when it looked like it would be a good investment.

After Barbie's first two kids were born, she and her husband were living in a small apartment in Forest Park. They were on a safe, quiet street, but there was barely enough room for one kid, let alone two, in their one-bedroom apartment. Barbie's friend, who worked for North Community League, told Barbie about an opportunity: "Barb, we have a program for the area where you can buy these houses for $500 down." The only hitch was, "you have to be working." Barbie had worked her whole life—this wouldn't be a problem. At $25,000, with only $500 down, it was a steal.

Her husband was not as convinced. "I ain't moving down there to no ghetto," he told Barbie when she first proposed the idea. Georgia Avenue, which is mostly a large empty field today, was full of dilapidated, abandoned homes in the 1980s, some occupied by crack addicts. But the area was changing. The city was tearing down the worst homes and the real estate group promised that the neighborhood would be completely turned around within a few years. Barbie was ready to take a risk and make the investment, with or without her husband. "You ain't got to come," she told him. But in the end, he did come, seduced by the chance to get in early on the up-and-coming neighborhood.

They moved the two kids in, and everyone had their own room. But soon after, Barbie and her husband split up. A few years after that, Barbie said, "everything started going wrong" in the house. First it was the heat. The repairman told her it would cost $5,000 to fix it. Barbie didn't have the money—a fifth of the cost of the entire house. For a few months they bundled up. Sometimes the kids left their own rooms at night and slept with Barbie to keep warm.

Then the roof leaked. When it snowed, the snow and ice would freeze on the outside of the house. When it melted, it would leak into her son's bedroom, damaging the walls and the carpet, and growing discolored, mushroom-smelling mold.

On top of it all, Barbie's car broke down. At the time, Barbie was working out in Owings Mills. For a while she tried taking the bus, but the trip was long and complicated. Her commute was sometimes nearly two hours door-to-door each way. By now, she had also had two more children. She eventually left the job and signed up for social services so that she could take care of the kids until she could find work closer to home. But it wasn't enough. "I lost it. I lost it because I wasn't working and I was trying to pay the mortgage." The money from social services couldn't possibly keep the lights on, keep the kids fed, and pay the mortgage.

Barbie finally found a job and tried to get the house back, but she still needed to come up with $1,000 in mortgage payments. "I came up with the money. So, I paid, and tried to get it back, but the lawyer told me I had to come up with *another* $1,000, and I told him I couldn't do that. So I just let it go. I just started taking my stuff and I moved in with my cousin." It was a simple problem really: "I couldn't afford to fix it up, so that's when I left." And just like that, Barbie had lost the home she had worked so hard to hold on to.

Barbie's cousin lived a few streets over. With four kids in tow, it was more than a mild imposition. Her cousin suggested she sign up for "Section 8." Incredibly, she ended up getting a voucher. But the house she moved into had structural problems that were even worse than in the home she had owned on Georgia Avenue. When it rained, the roof leaked and water trickled down to pool in the ceilings. The water damaged the back door, which swelled and broke off its hinges. To use the entrance, Barbie had to lift the door out of the frame and then pop it back in. Anyone else who wanted to get in could do the same.

The voucher program has mechanisms in place that are meant to protect renters. All homes must pass an initial inspection, and pass it again annually. When the housing inspector came, Barbie showed him the problems and told him she couldn't live there. He walked around the house, slowly and skeptically, looking things over. In the end, he agreed with Barbie that the landlord was obligated to make repairs. If the owner didn't do so, Barbie would have to find another house to use with her voucher, one that would pass inspection.

The landlord told Barbie she would fix the roof and the door, but weeks passed and she did nothing. So Barbie left. She knew the landlord was breaking HCV rules, and she figured that once the inspector returned, they could get the paperwork together and she could transfer her voucher to a new house. She found a new little home with a landlord who said he would accept her voucher. But when she followed up with the housing authority to transfer the voucher, they told her it had been terminated. She had been kicked out of the program for leaving without giving her landlord notice, even though the landlord had failed to make the repairs. Barbie told me, "I was working, so I didn't fight it."

Barbie has worked many different jobs to stay afloat. She worked at the Solo Cup factory off of Wilkins Avenue. She packed lightbulbs at General Electric. For eight years, she picked orders and packed boxes at the Armory, where they sold war-themed games with tiny silver men and wizards and knights. For a few years she cooked lunch in the kitchen of a boarding school until their budget was cut and they downsized. She even worked at the Laurel Park racetrack, an hour-long shuttle bus ride away. She has always done whatever it took to keep a roof over her kids' heads.

Now, Barbie does home care. She started working for Home Services Healthcare a few years ago. She has three patients. Two of them live right on her block. "The lady that I grew up with, Miss Wilson. . . . And Miss Lyman, she lives right across through here. I do them." Barbie means she takes care of them; they are patients of hers. "I gets up 6:00 every morning . . . I go down to Jolene's and I do what I gotta do for her. I leave there about 8:00–8:30 and back up this way. I go over there for a couple of hours. I leave there and I go down to Miss Wilson's for a couple hours."

Before Barbie started getting paid to do home care, she used to go and check on Ms. Wilson a few times a week. "Because you know, they don't really have that much company. So, I would go down there and ask Miss Wilson if she want me to help do anything." Roman would rake the yard for her in the fall, or shovel the snow in winter. Ms. Wilson had a homecare worker from Home Services Healthcare, but she wasn't fond of the people the company sent. "She didn't want them going in her closet, touching the things on her dresser." One day Ms. Wilson asked Barbie if she might want to work for the company and take over, since she was coming to help her anyway. "Would you come down here and help me with eating, if you don't mind?" So, Ms. Wilson put Barbie in contact with Mary, the manager. Barbie went up to Reisterstown to be finger-printed, have a background check, and apply for the position formally.

In two weeks, she was approved for five days a week of care. She asked for more patients in her area, and now she has two more. But payment is shady. "Mary cheap." Barbie explained. "She only pays $10 per case. . . . I told her, I said, 'I'm only staying an hour because you paying $10. I'm making $10 per hour. That's it." But sometimes Barbie needs to stay longer to help Ms. Wilson with a bath, or with the cleaning. If she stays for two hours, that adds up to only $5 an hour. If she stays for longer, it's even less.

Barbie works hard to pay the bills, but it's barely enough to pay the rent she owes her parents. Luckily, they are understanding and give her a break whenever they can. Barbie knows that if her parents weren't supporting her, she might be out on the street. As would her daughter, and her granddaughter.

DERRICK AND MARLENA: MAKING ENDS MEET

Derrick Thomas knew firsthand that without a place to live, it would be even harder to get the job he so desperately needed in order to pay rent. When you don't have a home base from which to search the internet for job listings or to take a shower and wash your clothes, it becomes very tricky to look for work and show up for job interviews. Like Barbie, Derrick was willing to do a lot to cobble together the money each month to maintain the stability afforded by a roof over his head. For those who are poor and don't receive housing assistance, maintaining a steady place to live requires some ingenuity.

When I met Derrick, he was on his way from a job interview, dressed in a smart gray and white pinstriped suit. He gave me his address and told me to come by the next week. The following Monday, I knocked on the door at the address Derrick had given me. No one came, and there was no doorbell. I decided to wait for a bit, leaning against the side of the building. After a few minutes, a young woman came strolling up, pushing a baby carriage with an infant inside and toddler struggling to keep up alongside. "You must be Miss Eve." She smiled matter-of-factly and offered a firm handshake, "I'm Marlena, come on up, Derrick not home yet."

Marlena had smooth, coffee-colored skin, her movements precise but graceful, like a gymnast. She opened the door with her key to reveal a narrow stairway stretching up into a dark corridor. I offered to help with the stroller, but she declined. "I had the baby seven weeks ago. Well eight, come Monday. But the doctor said to get back on my feet as quick as possible. And this guy doesn't give me much choice," she said, pointing to the quiet, runny-nosed toddler holding tightly to the side of the stroller. Marlena talked fast, and I got the sense her mind was moving even faster.

I watched as she deftly lifted the stroller up what seemed like two-and-a-half flights of dimly lit stairs. The little boy climbed behind her, peering back at me shyly every few steps. Long ago, the walls had been covered with vinyl, now browning with age and peeling from water damage. Musty, plush dark carpet covered the stairs. As we climbed from one floor to the next, we passed by several closed, locked doors, but Marlena said no one except the landlord lived there.

At the top of the stairs the apartment door opened up into a small windowless entryway. It was likely a corner of what used to be a big dining room, but was now partitioned off, too small and dark to serve much of any purpose. Double doors led out into a multi-function bedroom/living room area. A full-size bed with a mattress cover, but no sheets, was pushed against the opposite wall. A bassinet occupied a corner, and a convertible couch draped in a blanket sat in front of the window facing the street. An electric heater sat on top of the coffee table. Marlena left the stroller in the middle of the room, next to the heater, while she rushed around to straighten up, shifting the convertible back into the "couch" position and tidying up some of the baby things lying around.

The baby, Rose, was Marlena's first child. Amhad, the two-and-a-half-year-old, was her godson, whom she watched a few days a week. His face was dirty and his hands sticky. Wordlessly, Amhad showed me his one toy, an electronic game with a pen and keyboard that no longer turned on. His face lit up when he asked me to pretend-draw with him. But when Marlena popped a kids' movie, *The Fox and the Hound*, into a DVD player attached to an old 12- by 12-inch TV, Amhad quickly forgot about the broken toy.

"Derrick shoulda been home by now," Marlena remarked. She pulled out her Android phone. "Lemme see if I can remember which number he has this week." Marlena had a monthly plan, so her number doesn't change the way Derrick's does every time he buys a new card for his flip phone or a new burner from the Rite Aid. Quickly forgetting why she pulled out the phone, Marlena enthusiastically showed me the games on it: Bejeweled, Farmville. Then she suddenly remembered, "Oh! I was gonna call Derrick." But we couldn't reach him on either of the two burners he'd been using for the past few weeks.

Before living here, Derrick and Marlena lived in a room-for-rent. They tried to rent the whole three-bedroom house to have some privacy, but the landlord wanted $1,200. "In the Park Heights area, that's definitely not right." When the electricity got cut off in the middle of the winter, the landlord moved them into a place nearby. "That's where we messed up," Marlena told me. It was one of the only houses on the block that wasn't vacant. They didn't realize that the new lease they signed was month-to-month, so the landlord could end their stay whenever he wanted.

Derrick has this habit when I give him the money to pay the rent, he said, "Oh, the landlord said such and such about me" [in other words, they got in an argument]. "I don't want to give him the money." I said, "Okay, that man can say whatever he wants about you. You still pay him! He can put us out in the street today or tomorrow. He don't care. He don't have to do anything for you." Well, he so proud, he didn't pay the man the rent. And we got put out.

After they got kicked out, the couple moved around a lot. "We lived in so many places that year, it's hard to even remember them all," Marlena explained. From there, they went to stay with her mom while they looked for something more permanent. They found out about their current apartment from Derrick's friend Marlowe, who played chess in the park every day with a guy who had an apartment available in his townhouse. The owner didn't normally rent it out, but he was willing to help a chess buddy since the apartment was just sitting there, empty. It was cheap, and cheap was what Derrick and Marlena needed.

Instead of just having a room in a shared house, they now have an entryway for extra storage, and they have the kitchen all to themselves. The couple has lived here for about a year, though Marlena stayed with her aunt for a few months last summer when Derrick was in jail. Since the landlord hadn't rented it out while they were gone, they went back when Derrick got out. "The same way I left it was the same when I came back," Marlena told me. "He never had any problems with us, so he doesn't mind us staying here. He lives downstairs, so he doesn't want just anybody up here."

"Didn't he need the money while you were gone?" I asked.

"Let me tell you about them people down there," Marlena pointed downward toward the floor below and leaned in as she said this: "He's rich." I asked her how she knew. She sat back, "It's on the video he showed us. He's in the *American Gangsters* movies. He is sittin' on billions of dollars."

One of the episodes of BET's true crime series *American Gangster* features "Little Melvin" Williams,[14] whom Marlena named as her landlord. A notorious Baltimore crap shooter and high-rolling gambler, he became a drug and gang kingpin and one of the most important figures in the city's heroin business in the 1960s and 1970s. But despite his alleged responsibility for hundreds of unsolved gang-related murders, he is beloved for stepping in during the riots that followed Martin Luther King's death in 1968. According to legend, he single-handedly put an end to the violence simply by asking. He is also known for being the object of police misconduct, sent to jail for years on charges of drug possession—drugs that were planted on him *by* the police. "They wanted to get him for anything," Marlena explained. All this seems to have cemented his reputation as a beloved symbol of the plight of the low-income black community in Baltimore.

"Mr. Melvin," as Marlena called him, is well-liked by his accidental tenants as well. Rent is $600 a month, Marlena told me, "everything included!" Except of course the heat, which isn't currently working. But Marlena said he has been good to them. Even though the landlord pays for gas and electric himself, he signs the couple's LIHEAP (Low Income Home Energy Assistance Program) form saying that they pay it, in order to get them the $50 a month reimbursement. It was her landlord's idea—a small way for him to help out the struggling couple. To Marlena, this isn't cheating the system, it is survival.

With the baby being so little, Marlena isn't working. She gets $674 in Supplemental Security Income (SSI)—she has been diagnosed with bipolar disorder and ADHD. Marlena scoffed, "$600. I can pay rent, but then it's like, what am I gonna to do? I was in the Social Security Office when they told me they were raisin' it to $694 or $698, whatever it is. I said, "Wow, $98 for me to play with." Marlena remarked sarcastically. Her rent is $600, so it doesn't leave much left over to pay other bills and stock the kitchen.

As a kid, Marlena's two loves were babies and animals. She always wanted to be a veterinarian. "I've loved animals since I was little. I used to run around Park Heights catching cats, feeding them, saving them. Let me see, I think my father had some cats I can show you at least. I've saved quite a few of them." She scrolled through photos of cats on her phone.

Marlena had a rough childhood. "I think I've had twenty different foster families. And I'm only twenty-three, so that's a lot of movin.' I used to throw temper tantrums; I wanted my mother and I thought she was a saint—I didn't know. I didn't know until I actually met her that she was not."

Things got harder as Marlena got older. The foster mom she was closest to eventually became wary of her: "She was afraid of what I was into. She didn't know what I was doin'. She didn't know if I was on drugs. I wasn't, but she didn't know. She didn't know who I was; the person she'd met was gone, because I had learned a new system. I learned how to work the streets and I'd learned how to be around the streets."

Marlena transitioned to independent living, and that's when she met Derrick. But their relationship was hot and cold, and when she found out that Derrick had cheated on her and had possibly fathered a child by someone else, she left him and needed somewhere to go. She remembered a woman, Miss Lacy, who had shared her number when they met on the bus one day and said, "Call me if you need me." And that day Marlena needed her.

Marlena went to stay with her in the northwest. In exchange for a room, Marlena would babysit Lacy's kids. Marlena soon learned that Lacy was turning tricks for money, with her boyfriend Dante running the show. "That girl was a beast, and when I say she was a beast, she was a moneymaker. . . . She rode the right man and come home with $400 and shoppin' bags," Marlena told me.

Lacy offered to show Marlena how it worked. "At first it was me, Lacy, and her boyfriend. He started taking me downtown. And that's when I learned a new trade, and you know what that was." Marlena winked at me. "I could walk around and make money and get it and hop in the car." Marlena realized she could make money faster than she ever had before: "Lacy got me hooked on it."

Dante acted as security for the girls. "He was our ride back and forth. That was your protection. He followed you to make sure you're alright. He made sure you get your money and he'll hold the money, because he don't want you walkin' around with a whole bunch of money." But one day Marlena went downtown without him and realized it was a better deal. "Whenever I went down with Dante I had to give him half. That's when I said, 'Nah.'" Marlena realized that if she took the men's phone numbers, she could arrange to meet them again without Dante.

She wouldn't need him at all. "That's why he didn't want me to get them [phone] numbers. . . . The first time I made $100 down there [on my own] was the last time I needed him. I took this man's number and I started gettin' money from him all the time. I would go there and come home with $300 and I didn't have to break it with nobody."

All the while, Marlena and Derrick were trying to patch things up. Derrick did not know about Marlena's new scheme, and she didn't know how to tell him. "Derrick didn't find out until I brought him $86 one day. And I told him the truth, finally. It took a while for it to come out, but I told him. I thought he really needed the money, so I did it." Turned out, Derrick wasn't mad. He thought it was clever.

She stopped for a while once they got back together. "I was baby-sitting, if there's anything I'm good at, it's babysitting. I never let my personal life get in the way of my babysitting work." But when they needed extra money, Marlena started going back downtown. When it got tiresome to be out on the streets, she learned how to market herself online. "Me and D figured out I didn't have to do downtown any-more. . . . We got a computer. We found something called Tagged. I was on Tagged a lot. I'd post stuff like this." Marlena took out her phone to show me the social networking website. She pulled up some photos of herself posing on a satin sheet, dressed in lacy lingerie. There was noth-ing too racy, since nude or overtly sexual photos would be flagged and removed.

"Soon as my pictures go up, I start getting messages," Marlena ex-plained. "Derrick talks to 'em first, 'cause he know how to talk like the men are lookin' for to hear. He has to talk in code so as not to get deleted off of Tagged. Like I can talk, but I don't know what to say. Derrick will get on there and have me lined up with five different people in one night."

There's another site, Groove, that she plans to try as well. She ex-plained by saying, "You can sit in your house and make porn and get paid for it." She and Derrick had other tricks to make money. They would host "stripper parties": $15 in advance and $20 at the door, and the strippers get the tips.

Marlena has done other kinds of work as well. She has worked for a number of different childcare businesses. For a while she worked at a daycare place downtown, but she quit over the filthy conditions—mice, roaches, three-month-old bologna. Working at places like this doesn't make Marlena eager to go back to the formal economy. And for now, she wants to be there for her daughter while she's young. When she does go back to work, though, Marlena would prefer daycare because the "other stuff," she said, takes a toll on her relationship.

Marlena has other ways of procuring the things she and her family need. She interrupted our conversation remembering something she had forgotten to do: "What's today?"

"Thursday," I told her.

"Damn, I forgot. I knew I was supposed to be doin' somethin' today. Oh well I'll do it next week." I raised my eyebrow wondering what Marlena meant: "Wednesdays and Thursdays they give furniture vouchers. You have to be down there at 10 a.m., so I gotta go next Wednesday. It's not really furniture, it's really just household supplies, but it never hurts to have more. If it's free you might as well get it. You never know what you might get that you don't already have. 'Cause we need a can opener. I'm tired of them knives we're usin' to open cans. I don't do it 'cause I'm scared that I might cut myself. Derrick, he's a professional, so let him do it. He's good with his hands. He fixed that box in there," pointing to the DVD player, "that's how we were able to watch TV."

The fix did not hold. Soon after she said this, the DVD froze. And since they had lost the remote, Marlena could not fast forward past the glitch. The only choice was to restart the movie from the beginning, previews and all. Unperturbed, Ahmad happily settled in to re-watch.

By the time Derrick came home, the sun was setting, and the room had developed a winter chill. Marlena explained that the heat had been off for five days, so she's been doing her best to warm the place—that explained the three pots on the stove filled with simmering water. "It's not so bad," she declared, "It stays pretty warm up here most times. And it's not just us, the whole building's out. The landlord don't have no heat neither, so it's not like he cheatin' us or anything, it just don't work. Anyway, it's much safer to use the boiling water then to just open the oven door. Anybody can boil water. See how it's making the windows foggy? Which means it's getting hot."

Marlena and Derrick had gotten their food stamps that week, so the kitchen was fully stocked with snacks and meal staples. Derrick invited me into the kitchen to offer me something to eat. "What you want Miss Eva?" He read off my list of options: "We got Fritos, fruit cocktail, and apple sauce, you want a apple sauce?" He didn't wait for my answer, tossing me the kid-sized carton of off-brand apple sauce from across the room. I barely caught it, distracted by what I saw that I hadn't noticed before: opposite from the first stove being used to heat the house was a *second* stove. Derrick saw the perplexed look on my face. "Oh yeah," he said, "We use that one," gesturing at the second stove, "to store the food so the mices don't get it. You would not believe how fast those things will eat through your snacks!"

"Yeah—" I stammered, "but, why are there two stoves?"

Derrick smiled, "Oh yeah, well this one don't work no more! So our landlord got us the other one. And now we have more cabinet space!" he proclaimed triumphantly.

Each month, Derrick and Marlena cobble together money from Derrick's pay from whatever job he is working with Marlena's SSI allowance and the food stamps they each get. They pay $600 to their landlord, and on a good month, they have about the same amount from Derrick's earnings to stock up on additional groceries, buy clothes and diapers for the baby, pay for their phones and transportation, and purchase whatever else they need for the month. On a bad month—when Derrick is out of work—things get dicey. Together they face multiple barriers to steady employment: Marlena has been diagnosed with mental illness and Derrick has a criminal record. He is capable of working and wants to work, but needs help finding a good job. The couple works creatively to make extra money when they need it. But this resourceful job seeking comes with risks, and now that they have a baby, these risks are harder to take. They may need long-term support when it comes to housing, but currently they aren't getting it.

When I went outside to drive home, I saw a glaring scratch running the length of my car: it had been keyed. Derrick and Marlena know their neighborhood isn't the safest. But they would probably have to pay more for less space if they moved. What's more, Mr. Melvin is lenient when they are late on rent. This is essential because some months, they don't have the money.

MARILYN: BREAKING THE CYCLE

I waited outside of a massive high-rise apartment building to meet Marilyn. A middle-aged woman who once had a housing voucher but had lost it, she was now living at Green Acres, where the apartments are subsidized through the Low-Income Housing Tax Credit (LIHTC). In this type of building, the investor receives a tax credit to offer units at reduced rent to low-income residents.[15] Everyone's rent is subsidized, but the subsidy is attached to the unit, not the renter, like it is with Housing Choice Vouchers. The building was not only tall, but also long, curving to wrap through the wooded area up on the hill, away from the bustle of daily life in Park Heights. Every few minutes an MTA transport bus came to pick up and drop off elderly and disabled residents. The grounds were well kept, the driveway newly paved, clean cut grass, no trash. It was quiet and peaceful.

When I called up on the intercom to Apartment 902, Marilyn answered and told me that her buzzer system was broken, so she would have to come down to sign me in. An older man let me in through the locked door so I could wait indoors. Inside, the lobby was humming—people entering and exiting, chatting with Miss Tabitha at the desk. As I stood waiting, two different security guards kindly asked me if I wanted to go upstairs. I stayed put, as I didn't want to miss Marilyn by taking one of the two elevators up while she was on her way down—they were old and slow and, as she had warned me on the phone earlier, could take as many as ten or fifteen minutes to get up or down from the ninth floor where she lived. Eventually, Marilyn appeared. On her way over, she stopped to chat with an elderly lady in a colorful Muumuu, who was leaning heavily on a grocery cart full of clothes, on her way out of the laundry room.

Marilyn and I rode the elevator up what felt like fifty floors to get off on the ninth. We then walked down to the end of the long hallway, sticky with stale heat. The doors to all of the apartments had a rectangular floor-to-ceiling vertical window, like ones you might see in a hospital or office building, covered by a built-in curtain.

Marilyn's apartment was spacious, neat, and clean. "When we moved in here two-and-a-half months ago, we had a bed, no, we had a box spring, a mattress, a little tiny flat-screen TV, our clothes. My son bought me a fork, spoon, dish, and pot set." Now she and her husband had a couch with a matching armchair, some throw pillows, a coffee table, a large TV, and a small kitchen table and chair set. They had made the most of a small budget: there were a few decorations, including some stock photos of flowers on the walls. Everything was placed just so. The blinds were partially drawn on the large windows overlooking the parking lot. A light gray wall-to-wall carpet, old but not dingy, covered the floor.

At fifty-six, Marilyn is tall and healthy looking. She has gold rimming the edges of two of her front teeth. Her hair, pulled back into a low ponytail, highlights her dark skin. On the day that we met, she wore a lot of jewelry—a chunky necklace, four large bracelets, and several glittering rings on each hand. She was wearing a tight-fitted, colorful button-down shirt and coordinating pants. Clothes shopping is a passion of hers, and she knows where to get the deals.

Marilyn is warm and chatty. She seems remarkably unworn by the struggles life has brought her. We sat angled toward each other on the couch, and as she spoke, Marilyn looked out the window at the trees and glanced at me from time to time. She was eager to tell me her story and launched right away into what she called her "testimony."

Marilyn and her husband George have been married for thirty-nine years. They have been through a lot together, including drug addiction and rehabilitation, since they had their first child when she was sixteen and he nineteen. When her aunt tried to take the baby from her, afraid she was too young to care for the child herself, Marilyn left with George. "While my aunt was at work I moved out and left her a nice note saying, 'It was a nice place to live but I don't want to be here anymore.'" The two got married just after her eighteenth birthday. "I was eight months pregnant with my second child when I got married. I was young, but I wasn't dumb." Nearly four decades later, they're still together.

When Marilyn was ten, her mother died of a drug overdose. Her mother, sister, and brother were all active drug users. Her mother and mother's friends would shoot up right in front of her. The day her mother died, Marilyn remembers being asked to hold the rubber band around her mother's arm while she inserted the needle. Marilyn spent the rest of her childhood bouncing between the homes of different relatives, where she was often mistreated. Twice, she was molested by a relative.

Marilyn grew up in Park Heights. As an adult she lived in a number of different neighborhoods around the city: Penn North, Walbrook Junction, Forest Park. When she and her husband got married, she put her name on the Section 8 list. In the meantime, they moved to North Avenue, near Pulaski, where they lived in a small cramped apartment. They got off the voucher waitlist after just six months, shortly after she gave birth to a son. In the early 1980s, that short wait time was not as rare as it is today.

Marilyn and George used their voucher to move back to their old neighborhood in Forest Park, and Marilyn had a third child, a boy. "It was a semi-detached house. We only had one neighbor and the rest of it was just a big yard. Everything was good, everything was awesome. I had the little picket white fence. The lady next door gave my daughter a poodle. I had a Irish Setter–Labrador Retriever [mix] for my boys. We had the car in the front. We even had a pool in the back." Her husband had a "state of Maryland job" at the hospital. "And every two weeks when he got paid from the state we would go out as a family to eat and we would go to the park and have picnics. And we raised our kids really well."

Still, the family didn't have much money, and so, from time to time, Marilyn's brother would give them money from his business selling marijuana. "All his $1 bills he would bring just to help out, you know. He would just say, 'Here.'" Marilyn slapped her hand down on the table the way her brother would with the bills. With the young kids at home, it was hard for Marilyn to get out of the house to work. "I did try to work but it didn't work out. . . . Having two kids still at home and not having anybody available to watch them." But as the kids got older Marilyn was able to go back to work. She worked part-time at the elementary school, "the same little school my kids went to." In the afternoon, she went to school to become a nursing assistant.

Things changed when a series of deaths in the family sent Marilyn into a downward spiral. "When my dad died it was really hard for me. He had cancer. Then my brother died real suddenly. He was sick in the hospital. Went in there for tests and never came out. . . . They said a blood clot came from his foot and busted his heart. That destroyed me. That destroyed me because he was my rock."

"After that," Marilyn said, "things started just going so wrong. I was going out on the weekends and just trying to not think about what I been going through about my brother and father gone. And then my sister died." Marilyn didn't know that her sister had died from AIDS until the funeral home called asking for another $500 for the funeral in order to take "special sterilization precautions because of the complication." Marilyn asked, "What complication? What are you talking about?" He said, "Oh you don't know? She died of AIDS."

"I just dropped to the floor." There was so much stigma at the time that she never told her nephew what caused his mother's death. "Back then AIDS was just coming out. I'm like, 'Oh my God, what is going on?' I knew she was a IV user but it never—you know, you don't think that'd happen to you. I done had enough happen."

Marilyn fell into a depression with the loss of her father, her brother, and her sister, and with the kids growing up and about to graduate. "I didn't have no desire into doing nothing. My kids were getting big. I thought they didn't need me anymore. And I was like okay, so I need to do something. Just do me." That's how she got into drugs: "And things went from bad to worse kind of real fast. First, I was just smoking dope, then I started smoking crack."

Unlike her own mother, Marilyn always took care to use in private. Her kids never saw her. "My kids don't even smoke cigarettes today. They never did drugs or never smoked cigarettes and I thank God for that. They broke the cycle, you know. Because it was a cycle with my family and my sister and brothers and then me." Marilyn reflected: "I think I turned to drugs because that's what I seen coming up. I seen a lot of drug usage. I seen if something, a problem, would occur in my family, they would get high, you know. And they would sit there and do that in front of me."

Then Marilyn allowed an acquaintance to use her home as a stash house, "just for two days," she explained. But in those two days, the police raided the home and arrested Marilyn on distribution charges. "They gave me a $50,000 bail, they thought I was a big wheel in this organization that they was looking for."

"Were you?" I asked.

"Of course not!" Marilyn laughed. "I was just trying to make it day by day." She was locked up for the first time in her life, spent six months in prison, and then got out with five years of parole. But after the house raid, Marilyn lost her voucher.

With about two years left on her probation, Marilyn found herself in a bind. Her husband had just had an aneurism and had lost his job. They were facing a stack of medical bills and both of them were battling drug habits. Her daughter was pregnant. And to top it all, the electricity had been cut off because they didn't pay the bill on time. "I needed a solution," Marilyn sighed. Marilyn thought hard about what to do for her family. She wanted to buy the baby a crib for the nursery. She wanted so much to give her daughter and her granddaughter what they needed for a stable and healthy life, one unlike the life she had known as a child.

As she was walking down to the store thinking about what to do, one of the dealers she knew, Carlos, drove by. "How you doing?" he asked her.

Marilyn knew many of the dealers around there, and they had a certain respect for her, she said. "I always kept myself clean and neat. There's a difference between a addict and a junkie. I am a recovering addict now, but I've never been a junkie." Carlos had often tried to sweet talk her in the past, so she kept on walking as she responded: "Fine. How are you?"

He leaned out the window, "Marilyn come here." He said, "I need um, I need to make some money." Marilyn was immediately offended, thinking he was suggesting some sort of sex scheme.

"I'm about to cuss him out because I'm thinking he trying to proposition me, right, because I don't get down like that. I do a lot of things but not *that*."

Carlos quickly followed up, "No, no, no, not like that." He said, "I got this deal going on. Make some good money."

Marilyn paused to think, "What you call 'good money'? And what do you need done?" Marilyn remembered how hard up she was at the time and explained her thinking to me: "I'm broke as hell, my lights off. I'm about to have a grandchild in another four months. My daughter was five months pregnant. This is my first grandchild."

Marilyn couldn't believe how much he was offering: "What? $7,000? What are you talking about?" she asked Carlos in disbelief. "He broke it down to me. He's like, 'I need a package taken to Columbia. I provide everything.'"

In Baltimore, when you hear "Columbia," as Marilyn did, you hear Columbia, Maryland, a city just twenty miles from Baltimore. The job sounded easy, almost too good to be true. Marilyn reflected as she told me the story on the couch. "Oh dumb me, 'Yeah. I'll do it.' I told him. Got suckered in too quick. Because, I'm thinking, Columbia, *Maryland.*"

"Wait." I interjected in disbelief, "Did he mean—did he mean Colombia . . . the *country*?"

Marilyn nodded affirmatively, her eyes widening with the same fear and despair as she remembered the realization. "But by this time, he done gave me a big old down payment and I'm getting my passport and everything like he told me to. But all the while I was thinking, why do I need a passport?" Marilyn had never been outside of the state, let alone the country. By the time she realized she had signed up to be an international drug mule, it was too late. She thought "I can't back out now because I done spent the money trying to get my lights on and all this stuff. So, I'm like, 'Okay, I'm in it.'"

The plan was for Marilyn to fly to Bogota and pick up the package. She would spend the night, and then "tape it in my underwear" and fly home. She remembered:

I didn't tell my husband the truth—I didn't tell nobody. The first bit of money, I said I hit the numbers. I used to be a telemarketer, so when it was time to go, I said one of my old bosses called me back and they want me to go to different cities and train telemarketing people. That was my way out. So, I said, "They gonna give me some money. I'mma leave y'all some money and I'mma do this for a couple days or a week or whatever and then I'mma be back." He was like, "I don't want you to go." I'm like, "Baby you know I gotta do something." I talked him into it. Talked to my kids, and they was like, "Okay Ma." They were proud of me now.

Marilyn had tears glistening in the corners of her eyes as she remembered how uncomfortable she felt deceiving her family into thinking she was earning money through licit means. Ironically, this whole endeavor was so emotionally demanding that Marilyn stopped getting high so that she could think more clearly. "I stopped because, I can't think and take care of this and do that. So, I bought some meth [methadone] off the street, weaned myself off. My husband and I both, we got clean."

This was November, and Marilyn remembered, "I had to go get my little summer clothes, because I'm going to a whole other side where it's hot at. I borrowed my cousin's suitcase." Marilyn steeled herself for the trip that she could no longer back out of, telling herself, "I can do this, this is a one-time deal and I'm not gonna do it anymore." When Marilyn got to Bogota, she had a few days to kill before returning, and they put her in a nice hotel: "The best of everything. I got my little room service. And I walked around to do little things. I would get little tokens to bring home to my kids and stuff." Marilyn was not a savvy traveler, she didn't speak the language, and she didn't even know what the exchange rate was. "I probably paid them people five times the amount that was due because I didn't know. Give 'em $20 bills, 'Is this enough?'" she'd say. "As dumb as grits," Marilyn laughed at her own lack of worldliness. It was the only funny part of the story.

When the time came, Marilyn made a call, and a man came to tape the drugs to her body. "This man brought this stuff and told me how to put it in my girdle and whatnot." She put on loose-fitting pants. "I was smaller then!" she told me, so it was really impossible to tell she was carrying. Marilyn got her things together and went back to the airport. The trip home was long, and she had to make a connecting flight. On the second plane she started to get really nervous. "I felt something. Something was not right. I mean I don't know if I felt somebody looking at me or I just got paranoid. So, I went to the bathroom. Something told me to get rid of it; you need to get rid of it now. But I was pulling and pulling and I couldn't. I just couldn't. I panicked and then they said, 'All passengers put their seatbelts on.' So, I go back to the seat, and I am terrified now."

When the plane landed, Marilyn got off and went to the baggage claim. She was so nervous she started making conversation with another lady who was also waiting. "You know, trying to hold decent conversation with people so I wouldn't look so [suspicious]. 'I'm so glad to be off that flight. This is my first time flying,'" said Marilyn to the woman next to her.

Just then a man came up and tapped her shoulder. "Miss, do you know her?" he asked. Marilyn shook her head no and he said, "You need to come with me."

"Me?" Marilyn froze.

"Yes."

"Okay," she said, following the man, who looked like some kind of police officer. Inside, she was panicked. "I said, 'What's the problem?' Trying to act like they disturbing me," Marilyn remembered.

"We need you to get your luggage," the man said.

"What is wrong with my luggage?" Marilyn asked. "I'm trying to play stupid now," she explained to me.

"We got a tip that you were transporting drugs."

"I'm like, 'What? Me?'" Marilyn repeated it just the way she'd said it to the officer, her tone lifting in incredulity to indicate her innocence: "Me? Transporting? Are you serious?' Well they got the wrong tip!"

"Well, we gonna have to bring the dogs."

The dogs came and sniffed Marilyn and her bags, and miraculously, they didn't find anything. Marilyn explained: "They had [the drugs] wrapped so good, you know, I mean my circulation was kinda—because I was taped to the gill. So, I'm like, 'Well are you finished?'" Marilyn said to them, trying to hide her relief.

"No, we need to search you."

Marilyn thought to herself: "'Okay, I'm busted now. I'm busted.' So, they take me in the bathroom and they was like, 'You need to strip.'" Marilyn continued with her story: "I couldn't talk my way out of that one. The police lady stood there and I started pulling my clothes off." Marilyn knew the jig was up. "I said, 'Okay, okay. Alright, okay, okay, I'm done. I'm done. I will tell you the truth.' I told them the truth."

The officers asked her to explain everything. "I couldn't tell 'em any names, I didn't know no names. I knew the people that gave me the money and that was it. And they talking about forty years, forty years! No baby, for me trying to look out for my family? Oh no, no, no, no." Marilyn was willing to do anything to get back to her family. After initially threatening her with the long sentence, Marilyn was able to work out a deal: she wore a wire and helped the federal authorities catch Carlos and his crew. Marilyn ended up doing just three years.

Marilyn kept a remarkably positive attitude throughout all this. "I had to go to federal prison in West Virginia." It was her first time in West Virginia, and from the way she spoke about it, you'd think it was just a brief sojourn out of state: "It was a journey. I met some of the nicest people from all over the world. I was at the place where, what's that woman's name?" Marilyn thought for a second. "Martha, Martha Stewart. The place where Martha Stewart was at, that's the same place!" Indeed, Marilyn was at Federal Prison Camp, Alderson, in West Virginia. "And then," she said, "God got me outta there."

When Marilyn got out, she immediately got a job at a clothing store in Mondawmin Mall. She and her husband found a nice place to live, with an understanding landlord who gave them a break on the security deposit in exchange for her husband doing some work on the house. Marilyn was staying clean. But then the landlord was killed in a car crash, and they had to move.

Around that same time, tragedy struck. Marilyn still doesn't know if it was a stray bullet or a gang-related shooting, but either way, someone shot and killed her younger son. Marilyn spiraled down and started doing drugs again. "We just lost everything. We lost our apartment and we were homeless." They would often stay with their older son or daughter, but they didn't want to burden them with their addiction. "My kids have beautiful homes and I don't wanna bring my problems to there." Both of them continued working as much as they could for a cleaning service, but "the money went to our addiction. That was the worst time in my life," Marilyn remembered.

Finally, Marilyn's sister-in-law's illness pulled them out of their troubles. "We went up there to help her, and wound up staying. It was a good thing for us. She had a nice home. . . . I cleaned her floors, I done cooked the food, I done did everything while she was down." On top of taking care of her, Marilyn and her husband paid his sister a few hundred dollars in rent. It was affordable, and they were happy to do it. The change of scenery and the stability of having somewhere to live provided them the foundation they needed to deal with their addictions.

The couple got on a Suboxone program, which treats opioid drug addiction with a combination of Buprenorphine for the withdrawal symptoms, and Naloxone to counteract the effects of opioids and deter misuse of the medication. Suboxone has been a miracle drug for many people, and it did wonders for Marilyn and her husband. Having a stable place to live was life-altering: "The treatment just made me not care about getting high. But the truth is, I never would have signed up if I had been worrying about where I was gonna sleep at night." They have been clean ever since.

Eventually, when Marylin's sister-in-law was feeling better, she asked them to find their own place. Her head clear, Marilyn knew she needed two things: a phone and some information. First, she went for the phone. She knew a place where they gave them out for free: "They give 'em around here in Baltimore like water. If you get food stamps you can get a free phone." Marilyn went down to the housing office and got a list of low-income apartments. That's how they found their current apartment where their rent is heavily subsidized. The rules are less stringent for LIHTC—she's allowed to benefit from the subsidy even though her felony conviction disqualifies her from receiving a voucher again. Things have been very stable for Marilyn since moving into Green Acres.

Marilyn and her husband experienced years of housing instability: homelessness, eviction, doubling up, losing the voucher. You name it, they've known it. As for so many people, their housing instability was inextricably linked to mental health, drug addiction, unemployment, and alternative employment. For Marilyn, the instability began at an early age. She grew up poor and in a family where drugs were rampant. Her mother's death from a drug overdose left her vulnerable to abuse, depression, and drug abuse. Her addiction and related social networks made her even more vulnerable: when someone she knew brought drugs into the home, her home was raided and she lost the one thing providing stability: her voucher. Desperate to turn on the electricity and buy a crib for her grandchild, she naively and unwittingly agreed to become an international drug mule, thinking she was doing something far less serious. This says a lot about what it means to grow up and live in a context where drugs are everywhere and where it's easier to make money in the informal economy than the formal one.[16] Eventually, stable housing played a key role in her ultimate recovery. It was not until she and her husband benefitted from secure and affordable housing that she was able to find and successfully commit to a drug treatment program.

———

In this chapter we see a range of housing instabilities. Destiny lives in an overcrowded room-for-rent where she shares one room with her husband and two kids. Raven and her husband and nine kids squat in a home from which they could be evicted any day. Tina loses the home she inherited from her grandmother and moves to Oakland Terrace, a run-down apartment complex where many voucher holders live. Barbie loses her home, then gets a voucher and loses the voucher, and is now doubled up with her children and granddaughter, paying rent to her elderly parents and trying to make ends meet as a home care worker. Derrick and Marlena live in a home with no heat, turn to the informal economy to make ends meet, and appear to have a notorious but benevolent drug dealer as a landlord, whose rent forgiveness is the only thing that keeps them stably housed. Marilyn loses her voucher too, ends up in the illicit economy, and finally gets help with her drug addiction only once she finds stable housing in a subsidized building.

All of these stories highlight the key link between housing instability and a range of important life outcomes, such as health and mental health, and the ability to work a steady job. These unassisted renters face a number of challenges that vouchers buffer against: they are more likely to "double up," moving in with family or friends, and more likely to be evicted. Resource-poor renters without housing assistance are more likely to work double shifts or two or three jobs in order to cobble together enough money to pay rent. The unassisted also experience diminished housing quality relative to their assisted counterparts. As the stories of all these households show, housing insecurity has direct links to a multitude of negative life outcomes. Though we cannot be certain that vouchers would have solved all of these problems, the larger issue that vouchers help address—housing insecurity—is clearly a powerful force in the lives of those who experience it. Federal housing policy cannot provide help to everyone who needs it, leaving many renters out in the cold.

Chapter 3

"A PLACE TO CALL HOME": THE PROMISE OF HOUSING VOUCHERS

When Vivian Warner got the keys to her first apartment at forty-nine, she was so excited she tried to use them in her neighbor's door. She drove back to her sister's house—where she had been sleeping on the couch for months—before she realized she had been at the wrong door. Vivian had waited her whole life to have her own home—what was an extra few hours? The voucher would provide Vivian with the stability that she had sought through all her years of homelessness and bouts of staying with friends, relatives, and abusive relationship partners.

For Vivian, moving to Park Heights was a homecoming of sorts, although the memories were not entirely fond. Things were not easy for Vivian when she was growing up in Park Heights. Her parents started out as homeowners in the neighborhood, and with seven brothers and two sisters, the house was crowded. Vivian remembered, "There wasn't enough love to go around. I had a very unhappy childhood. My friends, their parents could afford to buy them nice things and nice clothes and cars. I never got to have any of that."

Vivian and I sat down one day on her semi-circle couch, which was covered in a scarlet drop cloth that hid the stains underneath, to talk about her childhood. Vivian was tall and lanky, with thinning gray hair. She sat with her shoulders hunched forward, as if she were protecting herself. But she was excited to tell me about growing up.

When Vivian was eight, the family moved out of her favorite home: "That was my mother's dream house. But daddy wasn't coming home with his money, so we lost the house." Vivian's mom moved the family over to the eastern edge of Park Heights, where there were more trees and space, but the homes were in worse shape. Her mother didn't know it when they moved into the new place on Marlboro Road, but the home was condemned. "That's why there was so many rats in there." The landlord had taken advantage of her mother by allowing the family to move in and pay rent on a house that was slated to be torn down.

Even though the family struggled with money, there was always food on the table. "Mom always made sure we ate," Vivian said. The electricity, though, was a different story. Vivian remembers sometimes coming home days to a cold, dark home when her mom didn't have the money to pay the bill. But when this happened, her brother knew how to rig it from the neighbors. "My brother would hook it up, he just born with the gifts to know how to fix anything. He was nine years old turning the gas and electric back on, fixing the TV." Vivian also remembered how her brother Dante partitioned off the rooms in the basement, "He put up walls so there were rooms, so we all had somewhere to sleep. . . . But we enjoyed sleeping with one another." It became a bit of a game for the kids to "watch the rats running around on the floor while we in the beds."

Despite the hardships growing up, Vivian said she came away with some important lessons:

> I learned the most important thing about the struggle is that you learn to appreciate life more when you get older. If you have never had any struggles then you don't know how to go after something that you want because you're so used to it being given to you. I always tried to have my own place, my own car.

The housing voucher wasn't a handout in Vivian's eyes, but something for which she had worked hard and waited long. It symbolized independence and the ability to care for her two younger children. Vivian's oldest two girls are grown, but the younger two boys are still in their teens. Kayla, the oldest, was born when Vivian was in eleventh grade and her sister Leticia was born fourteen years later. Vivian fears that—just barely out of childhood herself when she gave birth to her first daughter—she wasn't the best mom to Kayla. Being older when her Leticia was born meant that Vivian was able to be more present for her.

As a teenager, Vivian didn't relate to men her age. She turned instead to older men, not realizing at first that, as she put it, "some of the older ones is just as worse than the younger ones!" Her first husband was sixteen years older than she was. Their marriage meant that Vivian could suddenly afford things she had always wanted, but never had. "He gave me everything I wanted. He bought me my first car. I was 22." But there was a darker side to their relationship too: "He wanted to fight from time to time, so that wasn't a good start from the beginning." Vivian knew she had to protect herself. "I just thinking ahead. Thinking about my future and thinking about the possibilities. If he decided he wanna run around or whatever there's nothing I could do because I didn't even have any skills to get a job." So, Vivian asked him to pay for nursing school. "I was determined that I wasn't gonna be solely dependent on him and if anything start going wrong I'd have a leg to lean on."

Vivian worked for twenty-seven years as a nurse. She said, "I loved taking care of old people. 'Cause seeing me means somebody was there to do good. Somebody to make them have a nice day. They used to say to me 'Why are you so nice to me? Everybody else they mean, they nasty to me.' I said, 'Because my mother or my father will be in the same predicament that you're in and I wouldn't nobody to mistreat them.'"

Vivian was thirty-one when she got pregnant the second time. She harbored hope that the new baby might smooth things over with her husband.

> I thought that everything could go back to the way it should have been, but it didn't change nothing . . . 'cause that was years had went by. And people change. People change and you hopin' that—I was lookin' for that husband that I married, just tryin' to hold on to the husband that I married but I could never get that husband back. He was still, he still provided for me, he still took care of me but still wasn't the relationship that we had in the beginnin'.

Vivian made the difficult decision to leave her husband. With the new baby in tow, she went home to live with her mother, where Kayla was already living. But doubling up in her mom's home was hard on her. She and her husband tried again, but "there was still abuses from time to time mentally and physically and so I left and went into a shelter." I asked Vivian what it was like at the shelter. "It was okay," she told me:

A little scary in the beginning 'cause you don't know what to expect. But there were other women there that was in the same predicament that I was in. It wasn't as bad as I thought it was gonna to be. . . . I had a room with two other girls that had one child. All three of us had a child so we helped each other out with things we might have need and I would say "Watch the baby, watch my baby I'm going to the store" or they might have somewhere to go and I watch theirs. So that worked out pretty good.

Over the next ten years, Vivian lived in and out of shelters and on and off of friends' sofas. Most recently, she had been staying on her sister Charice's couch. She experienced bouts of depression, which made holding a steady job difficult. At the beginning, she just had her younger daughter with her; the twin boys arrived a few years later.

Vivian had never really thought about applying for housing assistance, but then she attended an information session during one of the shelter stints. "Everybody was talkin' about goin' to the housing department, so we went right around the corner. There really was no excuse not to go in there and put in a application." It took about four years—in that time her boys went from elementary school to high school—but Vivian did get off the list. "I guess I been on there long enough," she told me.

VIVIAN: "A LEG TO LEAN ON"

The receipt of a housing voucher can be transformative. Like a winning lottery ticket, a housing voucher radically changes lives, solving problems that can be intractable for unassisted renters. Housing vouchers have the power to end homelessness and can stabilize living arrangements, for example, allowing recipients to stop living doubled up, and to reunite with their children.[1] Sometimes the change is more marginal, making it easier to buy fresh fruits and vegetables or to work fewer double shifts. For Vivian, a voucher was all of these things, and more. For the first time in more than twenty years, Vivian felt in control of her own life.

Now Vivian could move off of her sister's couch. She could petition for custody of her teenage twin boys, who had been living with her older daughter, Kayla, who was eighteen years older than her brothers. She was married with her own kids. The boys had only recently moved in with her, having previously stayed with Vivian's aunt. Vivian immediately started the process to get them back. "I went and got them just as soon as I could."

Vivian thought perhaps she could move to the home she had always wanted. She knew she wanted to be in Northwest Baltimore. "I don't know [why]. Roots, I guess." I asked Vivian "How did you make the decision to move here?" She gave a straightforward answer, "Well, I came and applied and I didn't have a problem with it."

The voucher makes up the difference between what a needy household can afford and the cost of a unit in the private market. In theory, this system should give recipients access to units in a wide range of neighborhoods, including many low-poverty, safe neighborhoods, with good schools and, of course, jobs. But frequently, recipients end up in low-income neighborhoods that might not, at least on paper, seem to offer much opportunity. Yet many voucher holders nonetheless feel empowered by their vouchers, as they are all too aware of the alternative. For Vivian, the alternative had been having nowhere to live at all.

Over time, Vivian told me a longer, and more complicated, story of how she ended up back in Park Heights. Vivian's depression qualified her for disability status, which entitled her to certain "extra" services, such as a seat on a bus tour offered to recipients who may need help finding a place to live. A few weeks after receiving her voucher, Vivian boarded a bus with other new voucher holders. They spent the afternoon driving around the city, stopping at a handful of apartment complexes. They didn't see any single-family row homes, like the one she had lived in as a young girl. They did see some places out in the county, but, Vivian explained, "It was nice, but you need a shuttle bus to go to the store, and everywhere. It was just too far." The tour also stopped at a big complex near the downtown area, in the city. Vivian did not feel too comfortable there; "It looked like sure-enough ghetto!" she told me. Eventually, the bus pulled up in front of Oakland Terrace, in Park Heights not too far from where she grew up.

There was a two-bedroom available, and from there, it would be only a short walk for her boys to get to school. Although the voucher would cover rent up to $900, the apartment was listed for only $550. And with her small income, her portion of the rent would be just $55 a month. Vivian signed the lease that afternoon.

Vivian remembered the low-rise complex from growing up nearby. But back then it was a very different place:

> It was awful. . . . I came one time to a best girlfriend house here, and I never went back. . . . There were three bullet holes in the wall when you come to the front door. I said, "Is those bullet holes in the wall?" "Yeah girl they done shot the place up." And he had paneling all on the wall, that's where the roaches would hide.

This unit she remembered was in the same building as she lives now, just three doors down from her current unit. Vivian heard it had changed, though, and in some ways, it had.

> They got cameras all over the place, so there's less crime. And it's not infested with drugs. But this building is still infested with roaches, I gotta get a gallon of roach spray. See people they movin' in and out downstairs, they come in with kids and they not very clean down there, and they bring 'em from wherever they move. You know roaches move with you. . . . In your pockets, they'd be in everything. And then when they come around to spray, people are not home and nobody's gonna take off of work to be here for them to spray! So they're not goin' anywhere and their little minds they go through the pipes from one apartment to the next.

She stopped her story suddenly. "Lemme show you something." Vivian grabbed my arm and steered me into the kitchen. "I don't put nothing in here 'cause of this." She pulled open the drawer next to the sink, empty save for the swarming colony of adolescent-sized roaches.

I told Vivian about the mouse infestation I'd discovered in my apartment earlier that week upon opening my cabinet: a box of oatmeal chewed open and spewed across the shelf, spaghetti strewn like pick-up sticks, and mouse turds everywhere. Vivian laughed, "Oh girl, yeah they crawl. That's right. Where I use to live the mices they used to climb up the cord on the refrigerator and be sittin' up on there, just looking at me. . . . I don't care where you live, you gonna have field mice—I mean you can live in Beverly Hills."

Vivian hasn't had too much of a problem with mice lately, but she does wish management would keep the common areas cleaner than they do. "They don't have a lot of help—the rental office don't have but one person. From time to time I go out there and scrub my own hall because the rental office might do that once a month, and so to me, it's up to the tenants. When it gets too nasty out there in the hall I go out there and scrub it." Vivian said she doesn't mind this, or at least, doesn't mind it too much. For her, dealing with the roaches and the dirty hallways are part of what it means to have a home.

Vivian acknowledges that Park Heights isn't the safest neighborhood in Baltimore. Just a week before she moved in, she heard about a shooting in the area. Vivian's sister Charice couldn't believe she moved back to their childhood neighborhood. "Why she wanna go back? It's wild up there," she told me. That summer there had been a spate of murders in the neighborhood, and Charice had followed it all on TV and through old friends who still lived nearby. She was worried for her sister, but she also knew how badly Vivian needed somewhere to live so she could get custody of her kids. "I guess Viv just happy to have a door to lock," she remarked, "And room for those boys." This was, of course, the most—maybe the only—important thing to Vivian.

Having a voucher made all the difference in her ability to show that she had a suitable place for her children to live. With the stability of the voucher, Vivian has found work and has established a household of her own. While she finds it hard to keep a steady nursing job because of her mental health, she has established an informal housecleaning business. She also receives SSI for her clinical depression and receives around $150 in food stamps, but, she said, "It's not enough. That little $100 and something don't go nowhere."

Her husband, Roland, also pitches in for household expenses. The two met one night when they were both working an event at the

University of Baltimore. She was waitressing and he was cooking. "She kept coming back in the kitchen," Roland told me with a wink.

Roland is from Delaware but has lived in a lot of different places. "A lot of people in Delaware itself came from the bottoms of Georgia and the Carolinas and Virginia and all that. So, it's like a tradition. Basically, everywhere I went north they do the same, everybody came from the south." Roland has always found travel exciting, "You know it's different lands and different ball teams everywhere you go."

Roland has a degree in culinary arts, from a community college. "Certified safe food handler with the state of Maryland. I worked for Frank Perdue. They make chicken." Roland worked for a long time in restaurant kitchens, as far as Howard Johnsons in Cape May, New Jersey, and as close as the Sheraton and the Marriott in downtown Baltimore City. "You go where the money is," he told me. Roland stays active: "I'm not one that needs to be sitting down 24/7. I can't do that." The last time he had that kind of job was at Tyrone Chicken off of North Avenue. Now he has a landscaping business. "I plant rose bushes and cactus, and things of that nature. Gives me a pretty good business." In fact, Roland is so busy that he works over forty hours a week. He has a regular gig doing landscaping with a funeral home in Liberty Heights. "I work in the house and on the ground." For the landscaping he gets paid by the job. Sometimes they need extra work inside to prepare for a health inspection: "Cleaning up, flushing the blood out of the bodies. Just push them on their side. It's not frightening, it's nothing but a shell"—for this, he gets paid $15 an hour, all under the table.

Now that Roland lives with Vivian, he doesn't have to commute downtown to the cooking jobs. He can focus on his landscaping business and take as much or as little work as the family needs to make ends meet. Plus, he can be home when the boys come home from school. The income he brings in makes a huge difference in their lives. While the rent is mostly paid for, Vivian needs money for groceries, household expenses, and medical bills. And the teenage twin boys need so much—they eat her out of house and home, plus they need school supplies and sports equipment. It all adds up.

Roland is great with Vivian's boys. Often when I came to visit, Roland would be preparing food—one day it was pancakes with cherry jam from a jar; another day it was collard greens, cooked with maple syrup until they were soft and all the bitterness had been boiled away. "I like to cook each day," Roland told me. He is teaching the twins to cook too. They are starting with the basics: rice is the most recent food they have mastered. The three of them went to the store to buy big bags of long grain rice—the first batch stuck to the bottom and had a burnt flavor, but the second was white, fluffy, and seasoned just right.

Learning how to cook—such a simple, mundane activity—nonetheless requires access to a kitchen, a place to store your staple goods, a set of pots, pans, and utensils, and the heat of a functional stove. In the context of a precarious residential past—living in abusive situations, shelters, or in friends' homes—this simple thing that a home provides is quite important. For Vivian, Oakland Terrace is the home that she did not have for so long.

EDIE: THE WAIT

Today, housing vouchers—like the one Vivian received—house more people than the high-rise towers most people associate with "public housing."[2] Voucher recipients pay a third of their income in rent, and live in a home of their choosing. Unlike in public housing, where a family has to take whatever apartment is offered to them, the voucher system allows a family to pick a home in the private market, much like any other renter, albeit with some limitations in which units qualify: the home must rent for under the local Fair Market Rent, and it has to pass a yearly inspection. Nearly two-and-a-half million households across the country receive federal housing assistance in the form of rental housing vouchers.[3] Even so, the demand for housing vouchers greatly exceeds the supply. Only one in four eligible renters receives assistance of any kind.[4]

Who, then, receives a housing voucher? Despite the relative scarcity of aid, research suggests housing assistance primarily goes to some of the people who need it most: extremely low-income households, the elderly, households with children, and people with disabilities.[5] The income limits to qualify for a voucher in Baltimore in 2015 were $52,650 for a two-person family and $65,800 for a family of four.[6] But qualifying for a voucher is different than receiving one: 87 percent of households holding vouchers have incomes of less than $20,000. Over a quarter of voucher recipient households include at least one member with a disability. Nearly half—43 percent—of voucher households have children. Despite their poverty, 68 percent of voucher recipients who could work (the nonelderly, nondisabled) *were* working or *had* worked recently.[7] Voucher recipients are not the jobless welfare queens of racist stereotypes.

Voucher households—like poor households more broadly—are more likely to be headed by women: 83 percent of voucher-holding households are headed by women, and 44 percent by single mothers.[8] There are key patterns by race too. African American households represent about 45 percent of recipients, followed by white households at 35 percent, and Hispanic or Latino at 16 percent.[9]

Edith Baxter was born in the Flag Homes. As a kid, she had mixed feelings about public housing. On the one hand, it represented everything she wanted to get away from: the broken elevators, urine in the stairway, drugs sold in the courtyard and down the hall. At the same time—and much to my surprise—Edie told me that it was a safe haven. She was raised not just by her mom, but also by her aunt, who lived two floors down, and by her grandmother, who would trek up and down between the two apartments to keep an eye on whichever kids needed her most that day. There was always a hot plate of food in one of the two apartments. When Edie needed boy advice she could walk over to her mom's friend's place for a listening ear, so her whole family wouldn't hear about her love life. When the sink needed fixing or her brother punched a hole in the wall, she could call over for her neighbor Andy to come take a look. No need to get management involved—they were slow if they came at all—and Andy was happy to do odd jobs for a few bucks. But Edie always had a dream of getting out.

Edie is in her early fifties but looks about fifteen years younger. She wears her thinning dark hair parted elegantly on the side, pulled back into a low bun, and slicked tight against her temples with a slight wave that gives her the air of a 1930s movie star. She never leaves the house before doing her eyes and applying lipstick the color of deep eggplant. The neighborhood kids call her Aunt Edie.

When Edie's mother remarried, the family moved out of public housing to their own home in Park Heights. But Edie did not get along well with her stepfather, who was abusive. As soon as she was old enough, Edie moved out. She had a young daughter and the only place she could afford was in the nearby Pall Mall apartments, which, Edie reminded me, was called the Ranch: "It started out nice. Then the guys started hanging in the hallway at all times of day, at all times of night. Doing whatever, shooting dice, running money and stuff, selling drugs. And I was like, I can't stay down here. . . . They was so terrible they tore those apartments down."

Edie applied for a housing voucher in 2002 when she was pregnant with her second daughter. Edie was in her early forties, the baby was unplanned, and she had nowhere to go. She had no idea how long it would take to get off Baltimore's waiting list. She moved in with her mom, who had received a housing voucher of her own after leaving her abusive husband.

"You know how mothers is." Edie smiled a half-smile as she reflected on the years spent living with her mom. "Until you get your own house, 'You can't do this you can't do that.' Years and years of headaches. You know, some older people they still set back in their ways. Even now, I be telling her, 'You got to come on up, it's 2012, don't nobody do that no more.'" When Edie would have a male visitor, her mother would walk into the room and make a big show of looking at the clock to let them know it was time to wrap up. Edie felt it was impossible to carry on a social life under her mother's roof, especially at a time she was trying to find a father for her daughter. Edie sighed, "Who knows, that could have been the one on the white horse, to take me off my feet, me and my kid," she remarked, only half joking.

It wasn't just hard to live with her mom: it was illegal. According to voucher rules, all adults living in the home must be on the lease, and their incomes must be reported to adjust the family's share of the rent.[10] This makes it hard for families to support relatives experiencing housing instability without breaking the voucher rules.

During the time she lived with her mom, Edie was waiting. Once a year, she would make the trip on the bus down to the housing voucher office on West Pratt Street to update her information and check her place in line. Each year she was told there was no new information, and that she was still on the list. "The lady at the office told me that sometimes it takes up to five, six, even eight years. I said 'for just a piece of paper?' She told me, 'It's that many people.' I am thinking, why is it so hard when you see all these empty houses? It shouldn't be that long."

This is a fair question in a neighborhood like Park Heights where there are so many vacant homes. But of course, the number of vouchers does not depend on the number of available homes, it depends on federal funding, which is not always evenly disbursed. And of course, any home rented through the voucher program must pass an inspection to qualify. Finally, there is no guarantee that the landlord will accept a voucher holder. In some places, landlords are legally obligated to accept the voucher as payment; but in most cities, such as Baltimore at the time of this study, it is perfectly within landlords' rights to refuse a voucher holder.[11] These two facts—a shortage of quality homes on the one hand and a shortage of landlords willing to accept voucher holders on the other—account for much of the trouble that voucher holders have finding a place to use the subsidy, as I will discuss in more depth in the next chapter.

In 2010, more than eight years after she applied, Edie got the news that she was off the waiting list. She felt as if she had won the lottery. Edie called her mom and they cried tears of joy.

––––––

In Baltimore, as in many major cities, the housing voucher wait list effectively operates as a lottery. Local public housing authorities (PHAs) manage waitlists and select recipients quasi-randomly. PHAs have some discretion in how to operate the waitlist for their jurisdictions. Before 1998, it was mandated that local public housing authorities offer preference to certain categories of voucher applicants, including people who had been forcibly displaced, those experiencing homelessness, and those who were severely cost-burdened (i.e., people spending over

50 percent of their income on rent). This set of preferential requirements was repealed in 1998 by the Quality Housing and Work Responsibility Act, and PHAs are now permitted to develop preferences based
on the needs of the local population.[12] Typically, PHAs give priority to
the same sorts of categories of people as before, for example, persons
experiencing homelessness or victims of domestic abuse.[13]

Mismanagement of waitlists is rampant among local PHAs across the
country, and the Housing Authority of Baltimore City (HABC) is no exception. The sheer magnitude of names on the list poses a logistical nightmare. Over the past twenty years, many have criticized HABC for letting
the list get too long, failing to update contact information, and spending
undue resources on maintaining the names on the list—many of whom
would likely never receive a voucher—rather than on housing itself.[14]

By the early 2000s, Baltimore's list was a mess. It included people
who had died, moved, and no longer needed aid. At any given time, the
housing authority could only locate one out of every ten families on the
list.[15] The city shut down the list entirely in 2003 when it swelled to over
18,000 names and kept it closed for more than a decade, so no one could
apply for a voucher.[16]

Then, for just nine days in 2014—from October 22nd to 30th—the
city reopened the list. Those wishing to apply for a housing voucher
could sign up via a new website: www.JoinTheListBaltimore.org. The
Baltimore Sun reported that 10,000 people applied in the first few hours,
and 58,000 in the first few days. Through a process the HABC described
as "random representative selection," the housing authority selected
25,000 applicants from four priority groups for the waitlist: the elderly,
families with children, the disabled, and other families. The contact for
each of these 25,000 households received a yellow piece of paper in the
mail indicating their household's place on the waitlist. Despite its obvious inadequacies, the city described this as an improvement over the
previous first-come, first-serve system, in which in-person applicants
received a time-stamped paper as evidence of their place in the queue.

Only a fraction of the 25,000 households would ever receive a voucher.
The housing authority distributes around 100 new vouchers a month, or
1,000 to 1,500 vouchers a year.[17] The website's FAQ explains: "When

your name nears the top of the Waiting List, you will be contacted by HABC to complete the 'full application' to determine program eligibility. You will be notified by U.S. mail and email (if you provided an email address)." The FAQ also explains that "it is difficult to estimate the length of time an applicant may be on the Waiting List before being scheduled for an eligibility interview. Long waiting periods are common." This is perhaps an understatement.

The situation in Baltimore is not atypical. In many cities, the wait for a housing voucher is over ten years.[18] Nationally, 44 percent of applicants spend over a year on a waiting list, and one-fifth wait more than three years.[19] Nor was Baltimore's decision to close its waiting list at all unusual. A recent study of eighty-three cities with declining populations finds that over 80 percent of them had closed their voucher waiting lists.[20] Across all cities, 59 percent of housing authorities have closed lists.[21] Low-income residents who approach the housing authority in cities as diverse as New Orleans, Scranton, and Chicago receive the same answer: the list is closed.

KELLEY, RAY, AND SANDRA:
"SOMEWHERE TO CALL HOME"

Kelley wears her hair straightened and neatly combed into a high ponytail. At thirty, Kelley has four kids: an infant, a four-year-old daughter, and two boys, ages five and fifteen. She lives with her kids and fiancé, Jeremy, who is a janitor at a school nearby. While Jeremy brings in a steady income each month, it's not enough to support the four kids. The family receives $700 a month in Temporary Cash Assistance (TCA) and around $250 in food stamps. But, "That stuff is temporary," Kelley said. "I'm trying to find a job. But I need to have to try to get my hens in a row, you know?" In the meantime, Kelley is home with her two-month-old. She is grateful for the voucher which covers $1,300 a month, a big chunk of their rent on the three-bedroom house.

While technically in the city, Kelley and Jeremy's home is in a more remote area of Park Heights, where there is a bit of respite from the hubbub and traffic of the neighborhood center. The home itself is beautifully renovated and very well maintained, freshly painted with shiny hardwood floors. While there is not a dust bunny in sight, with four kids in the house it's often a total mess—clothes and toys strewn everywhere. As for the house, Kelley declared emphatically: "I love the house."

> It's quiet. I go sit out on my front and have peace and quiet. The only thing that might break my peace is the ambulance going to the hospital. But I know it's an emergency, it could be life threatening so it don't bother me, because somebody probably going to get their life saved. It's the best place that I ever lived.

Out back is a wooded area that you can see through the sliding glass door. Kelley told me that once they had seen "a wild rabbit hopping through the backyard. It was black, white, and brown. The kids tried to catch it to keep, as a pet, you know? And we've seen possums over there too, all kinds of wild animals." One icy winter afternoon as we sat at the table I thought I saw some movement flicker outside the window. Kelley's five-year-old, with the eyes of a hawk, was a step ahead of me: "Miss Eva, look, a wolf!" he shrieked with mix of fear and delight. Kelley got up to look. "Oh my god. Baby, that's a fox!" Terrified, Kelley rounded up all the kids and we moved into the other room. "I grew up in the city," Kelley explained to me—"we don't have foxes over in West Baltimore!"

Kelley has had her housing voucher for four years. She was six months pregnant with her third child when the family's rented home caught on fire and she had to climb out the second story window with her eleven-year-old a few steps ahead and her thirteen-month-old on her hip, using one of those fold up ladders her mother had given her "in case of emergency." She never thought she would have to use it. After the fire—which all but destroyed the home—she and the kids moved into a two-bedroom house in West Baltimore with her sister, her sister's husband, and their two kids. Needless to say, it was crowded.

Then Kelley learned about Transitions, a local transitional housing program. One afternoon she left the kids with her brother-in-law to go see if they could help. The young woman who did her intake form told her something she did not know: Kelley was homeless. "A lot of people don't classify themselves as homeless, but they really are." Kelley told me it wasn't like she imagined homelessness would be. Even though she had a roof over her head, she was "doubling up" at her sister's, which meant she was technically "homeless." Kelley got signed up to receive a voucher through the Transitions program, which helps families in need with rapid rehousing, and within a few weeks, she was able to look for a home.

The housing program offered to help her find a place to live, but Kelley had her own plans: "Sometimes they like to place you where *they* want to place you. So, I found a house on my own. Actually, I found three different houses. I was on a mission. I wanted to be somewhere comfortable, I want to be somewhere that we could call home."

Kelley hadn't had what she would call a "real" home since her childhood. Her parents rented their two-story row house near Mondawmin, right across from Druid Hill Park. It was "kinda rough" at the time— there were drugs and some violence, but Kelley said "that's to be expected" in some neighborhoods. Overall Kelley said she felt lucky to have had such a good childhood, and to have grown up in a stable household with two parents present. She spent a lot of time outside, went to the park with her father, and played with other kids in the neighborhood. Both Kelley's parents worked—her dad worked mostly on the weekends as a musician so he was often home during the week, and her mom worked in retail at a department store.

But things got complicated for Kelley during her freshman year of high school. "I went to a dance that my momma didn't want me to go to. I met his father [pointing to her son] and well, stuff happened." When Kelley missed a period, she knew she was pregnant. But she did not tell her mom until just before she gave birth. "I was scared," Kelley admitted to me. "I told one person, my sister. Nobody else knew. I hid it until two weeks before I had him."

I wondered out loud, "Didn't your mom *notice*?"

Kelley laughed and shook her head: "I mean, I looked small, my stomach was real small. I don't know how, but my mother just didn't really see. Finally, I told her and she had a fit of course, because I was fifteen. And she couldn't do nothing but accept it, because I was so far along."

Even though Kelley's pregnancy had barely shown, in the middle of her ninth-grade year the baby was born weighing in at a healthy six pounds. The baby's father had gone off to military school several hours away, so she didn't tell him he was a father until two weeks after the birth. He was thrilled, and he and his family came to care for the baby every weekend, so Kelley had a chance to "be a teenager." Kelley's father watched the baby during the week while she went back to school.

Kelley worked hard to try to finish high school as a young mom. Before having the baby, she had begun her freshman year at Western High School—a prestigious merit-based application-only public school for girls. English was her strong suit, and after school Kelley was a majorette in the marching band and a member of the youth leadership program. But after she had the baby, Kelley found it hard to keep up, even with her parents' help. Kelley dropped out and got her first job at the Dairy Queen.

Within a few months she missed school. Yearning to be back in the classroom, she decided to re-enroll at the nearby Douglass High School. That whole first semester of classes from her freshman year didn't transfer over, so she had to attend classes at night and on the weekend to make up the credits and graduate. After she graduated, her parents wanted her to move out and be more self-sufficient. Since then, things have been rocky.

Kelley lived in at least ten different homes in the eleven years before she got the voucher. She tried over and over to create a stable home for her kids, but it was one thing after another: the landlord wouldn't fix the broken heat, the street was too dangerous, the house was foreclosed on—culminating in the fire that left her and her kids homeless.

After all this, the house Kelley lives in now feels too good to be true. Kelley has never had this kind of stability as an adult. The house sits by itself at the top of a hill. Most of Kelley's neighbors are homeowners, except for a big apartment building just down the street where a number of voucher holders live. "Everybody looks out for each other," Kelley told me.

In the winter of 2010 there was a big snowstorm, dubbed "Snowmaggedon" by the media. Kelley had never seen that much snow in her life. "It was really high. *Really* high. It had to been about up to my knees or even past it." In fact, the storm dumped over 25 inches of snow on the Balti-more region—probably well above her knees. When after two days the city had still not come to plow out the street, Kelley and her neighbors cleared out the entire block with hand shovels. "Oh my goodness. We dug that street out. We helped each other."

Kelley defied stereotypes of teen pregnancy and single motherhood by going back to high school to finish her degree. Her husband works a low-wage job, and she plans to go back to work as soon as the baby is a few months older. Despite a number of challenges, Kelley has perse-vered to create a real home for her kids. But she was not able to create it until she could count on having a roof over her head.

For others, the voucher isn't as life changing, but offers an important leg up. I first visited Ray and Sandra on a 102-degree summer day. When I entered the house I was blasted by a burst of cool air. Their brand-new AC had no trouble keeping up with the heat, while most people in the neighborhood didn't have AC at all. Ray and Sandra are a middle-aged couple with a housing voucher. They live with their eight-year-old daughter, and Sandra's adult daughter is also living with them temporar-ily. Ray got his voucher in 2009. He had applied for it in 2000 just before the waiting list closed and before he and Sandra got married.

The voucher has made things so much easier for Ray and Sandra. Rent on their house is $1,109, of which their portion is $262. Ray has worked on and off throughout his life. One of his favorite jobs was as a janitor at Johnny Cochran's law firm when it was in Baltimore. But he's had a "bad leg" since his stint in Vietnam and that makes it hard to keep up the physical labor.

Sandra is a certified nursing assistant and works at a long-term care facility for the elderly. She used to pick up extra shifts in order to pro-vide some extra cash for the family. "And they pay me more now than they used to!" Sandra declared with a hearty smile, pride in her voice. "But it ain't enough." At $13 an hour, Sandra does well compared to many people she knows, but she's not bringing in enough to live on. Before meeting Ray and benefitting from the voucher, Sandra was work-ing forty or fifty hours a week and still barely making ends meet. In the past few years she's been able to cut back so she can have more quality time at home with her family. There's no way they could afford anything like the house where they live now without the voucher.

BENEFITS OF RECEIVING A VOUCHER

"So," I asked Vivian, "what's different now that you have a voucher?" She told me, "It's different 'cause I have my own place. That's the most significant part about it."

Vivian's unstable childhood instilled in her the desire to find a home where she could be independent and care for her children. As a young woman, she strived to get an education to open a door out of an abusive relationship. She worked long and hard, but she struggled under the weight of depression, poverty, and housing instability. She was in and out of homeless shelters and friends' couches for years. She was unable to maintain her independence and hold on to her kids. Getting the voucher provided a solution to all this. To Vivian, the voucher symbolizes independence and self-sufficiency.

The families I got to know in Park Heights benefitted in tremendous and tangible ways when they moved off the waiting list and into their homes. While policymakers discuss a number of potential benefits from vouchers, it is difficult to overstate the simple power of providing a home. Both Kelley and Vivian had been living with family when they got their vouchers. Vivian had been on and off the streets for years; the voucher meant she got her kids back. For Kelley, the voucher provided much-needed stability after a period of living in low-quality homes and narrowly escaping a catastrophic fire. Across the range of positive changes voucher holders experience individually, four aggregate patterns stand out. Vouchers increase access to shelter, decrease poverty, don't seem to deter employment, and may provide opportunities for residential mobility.

Studies conducted with experimental designs and large sample sizes corroborate residents' lived experiences. In one study, low-income families with children were randomly selected to receive a voucher and compared to families in a control group without vouchers over a period of five years.[22] Wood and colleagues found that vouchers had a number of important effects on homelessness, doubling up, overcrowding, and frequent moves.[23] Vouchers reduced the proportion of families living in shelters and on the streets by three-quarters (from 13 percent to 3 percent) among the experimental group. The number of families without their own home—including those who were doubled up as well as those in shelters or on the streets—was reduced by nearly 80 percent. The number of families living in crowded conditions went down by more than half. Housing instability was reduced significantly as well: the number of times that families moved over a five-year period was reduced by close to 40 percent.[24]

A second study, the Family Options Study, compares families with children who were issued vouchers with families randomly assigned to one of two other housing interventions and a control group who received no special treatment.[25] Results from both the interim and final evaluations show that vouchers reduced homelessness (defined as having spent at least one night in a shelter, outside, or doubled up in the past six months) by more than half. Results from this study also show that vouchers reduce crowding and instability *more* effectively than the other interventions that were examined. The study demonstrates a number of other positive effects linked to housing stability including foster care placements, school instability, alcohol dependence, psychological distress, and domestic violence.

Large-scale data can also help us to understand how vouchers affect broader patterns of poverty—that is, the number of people who live above or below the federal poverty line. Federal rental assistance was responsible for helping 2.8 million people move out of poverty in 2012—vouchers may be responsible for more than half of this effect.[26]

The voucher quite obviously provides recipients with an extra chunk of change—disposable income they might otherwise have spent on rent. In the Wood study, voucher users spent on average $211 less each month on rent and utilities than those without vouchers.[27] For some, the voucher makes an even bigger dent: for a mother of two working thirty hours a week at minimum wage, whose pre-voucher rent is $700 a month, a voucher is worth about $440 a month. This is a significant amount for a low-income family. So, what do people do with the extra money?

The Wood study finds that voucher holders spend that "extra" money on their children and household expenses and needs. Beyond the cash benefits, added financial security also allowed recipients to take financial risk they might not otherwise, such as changing jobs or paying for extra schooling that might improve their financial well-being over time. The research shows that voucher families often spend more on food than nonvoucher families by an average of about $39 per month, which is about a 40 percent increase. This allows families to avoid skipping meals and to eat healthier food.

In addition to providing shelter and alleviating poverty, the voucher may have an effect on how much people work. Researchers have considered whether having a voucher might disincentivize recipients from working or from earning higher wages, or on the flip side, whether it might provide the stability that would allow someone to hold a steady job. Large-scale data offering robust empirical evidence on the effect of a voucher on employment and earnings is scarce, and the research that exists finds conflicting answers to this important question. While some analyses find little effect of voucher receipt on employment and earnings,[28] others find small to moderate negative effects.[29] Following low-income families for six years after voucher receipt, Carlson and colleagues find little effect on employment, but a negative effect on earnings, largest in the first few years. They also find that earnings responses to voucher receipt differ substantially across demographic subgroups.[30] Other work supports the idea that getting a voucher reduces employment in the short term only marginally.[31] Using experimental data, Wood et al. find that after two years of receiving housing assistance, voucher holders did not work any more or less than those in the control group.[32] While this is encouraging for those who worry vouchers may deter work, these findings also suggest that the voucher alone may not be an appropriate intervention for promoting work and additional self-sufficiency.

Other research finds benefits to stable housing for employment. One study shows a range of positive effects for children in households receiving either public housing or vouchers (compared to siblings who did not benefit from assisted housing), including positive and significant impacts on young-adult earnings for nearly all demographic groups, especially women from non-Hispanic black households, as well as a reduction in the likelihood of incarceration.[33]

While the verdict on how vouchers promote housing stability is strong and clear, we are still learning about exactly how vouchers may be related to employment outcomes, with mixed results in the research so far. Yet, the stories of the families I studied offer a very clear picture. For these families, the question that plagues many economists— whether the voucher acts as a disincentive to working in the formal labor market—is completely moot. Ray and Sandra were working overtime just to pay rent and continued to work after receiving their voucher. After the fire and new baby, Kelley needed some help to get resettled and take care of the kids while she interviewed for jobs. Vivian's struggles with mental health made it hard for her to keep a steady job. Nevertheless she does as much informal cleaning work as she can, and she was homeless until she received her voucher. For the families I studied, receiving a voucher was a tool for survival in times of crisis and was by no means a disincentive to working.

———

Housing vouchers are tools for combatting poverty. They increase access to shelter, decrease poverty, and provide opportunities for residential stability, and even mobility. Vouchers help people get back on their feet and provide for their families in times of need.

Vivian was homeless and took the first place she could find with her voucher. Once she moved into Oakland Terrace, she was able to get her boys back to live with her for good. The kids were relieved and happy to be home with their mom, and Vivian was happy to have a roof over her head.

With four children at home, Kelley and her husband rely on the voucher to keep a roof over her kids' heads and put food on the table while she looks for work and he earns minimum wage as a janitor. Now that she's not worried about leaks or fires or having to move again, Kelley is ready to start looking for work to supplement her fiancé's income. They probably won't have the voucher forever, but it's been a key transitional tool after the fire.

Ray and Sandra were doing okay, but they needed a leg up. Ray's injury from combat meant that Sandra was working overtime to take care of the family. Getting the voucher allowed Sandra to work more reasonable hours. More importantly, it gave them both stability, making it easier for Sandra to get to work and keep her job.

For all of these families, housing vouchers have solved problems—whether big or small—that the unassisted renters in the previous chapter had few tools to tackle. Vouchers end crises and provide stability where there was precarity. They can offer people a sense of control over their lives, validate their narratives of independence, and allow them to realize their own dreams of a place to call home. Yet, for many, using the voucher is anything but simple.

Chapter 4

"NO VOUCHERS HERE": THE CHALLENGES OF USING THE VOUCHER

Housing vouchers make a tangible difference in people's lives, but getting off the waiting list is only the first step. Very little about the voucher process is straightforward. Voucher recipients are living in poverty, and many are juggling multiple jobs, children, and even illness and disability. Many lack their own transportation. And yet they are instructed to find a new place to live—what is for some the first housing search they have done in their lives—in just sixty days.[1]

Policymakers have increasingly come to hope that expanding the voucher program might solve some of the problems of the concentrated poverty that was entrenched in public housing. By offering families the opportunity to move to a home of their choosing, they thought, people would end up in better quality homes in more affluent neighborhoods, with higher-performing schools, more jobs, and less crime. By relying on the private market, they hoped to leverage an existing housing stock—maintained by a fleet of private landlords—that was in much better physical condition than the public stock. But with choice comes complications. In practice, the choices that policymakers so wanted to provide families are in fact constrained by the same forces that constrain housing searches in general: scarcity of time, not enough money, disability, and both structural racism and overt discrimination.

EDIE: "ANYWHERE YOU WANT TO LIVE"

Edie was on her own as she walked out of her first appointment at the voucher office after learning she'd gotten off the list. She was elated, but also terrified. "They tell you, you got this amount of time to find an apartment or a house before the voucher expires," "they" being the Housing Authority of Baltimore City, or HABC. In Baltimore, new voucher holders have sixty days to find a place to live, with a thirty-day extension available by application. But other than making sure you know the deadline, "they don't help you do nothing," Edie told me.

Edie didn't know where to begin. Landlords anticipate this. "At the time where you go and pick [the voucher] up, there is some homeowners that stand right there in front of the program showing how they houses is and how many bedrooms and how many bathrooms, what street and everything, and so on." One of these landlords (whom she calls "homeowners"), David, approached her and offered to drive her up to see one of his properties. Edie shrugged, grateful for the ride back uptown, and got into the passenger's seat of his bright blue Camry.

When we sat at her kitchen table many months later, Edie recalled the tour David gave her of his properties. The first house he took her to was on a run-down block in Southern Park Heights. As soon as they turned the corner, Edie sighed. She had seen blocks like this before. "How many of these homes still has people in them?" she asked David skeptically. Edie recognized signs of life—a stray toy in the front yard, a sheet nailed up inside a window as a curtain, a well-watered plant out front—in only a few out of about twenty houses on the block. But judging from the dilapidated facades and missing roofs, it was hard to imagine anyone lived in the rest. One house had a porch that had caved in entirely, like a bomb had gone off, leaving what looked like a sinkhole with just a pile of rubble at the bottom. Two homes across the street had no roof—you could see clear to the alleyway behind them, save for the tree that had sprung up through the living room and was now peeking up over the top of the structure. Three of the lots were vacant. The empty fields were overgrown with weeds, ghosts of the homes that once occupied them.[2]

David pulled up in front of what was clearly the nicest home on the block. It had a silvery new chain-link fence, in stark contrast to the rusty, gaping one on the adjacent patch of grass next door. The walkway and stairs leading up to the front porch had been freshly poured with smooth concrete. New, pale yellow siding covered the exterior. The sturdy new windows fit snugly in their sills, double-paned to insulate the newly rigged central heating and cooling system. The inside was spotless. The wood floors downstairs had been refinished, and plush gray carpet covered the stairway and the entire second floor. The kitchen had salt and pepper granite countertops and all new appliances. Out back was a small fenced-in yard.

"What did you think of the house?" I asked Edie. "The house was good. It was just, the *area*," pronouncing it "Uh-rea" with a thick Baltimore accent. Edie told David the house was perfect. "But," she added, "I need more than two neighbors on my street. It's just not safe with all those vacants. Plus those weeds! Them rats love to hide out in there. It's no good," Edie sighed. David wasn't exactly surprised. But "it was worth a shot," he told me later. "You'd be surprised how often that works," he said with a wink.

Next, he drove her to an apartment building, Fairway Gardens, just a few blocks away. The complex had around forty units, a combination of low-rise apartments and more recently renovated semi-detached townhomes. David took Edie to the apartment side, where the complex accepted voucher holders. The townhomes were priced above the maximum payment standard allowed for a voucher, so she couldn't use it on that side of the complex.[3] The apartment was a dirty brown color, on the ground floor, with small dark windows lined with iron bars. David didn't own the unit he showed her, but he helped out the owner sometimes as a tenant placement agent. If Edie signed the lease David would get her first month's rent as commission.

The apartment obviously hadn't been updated in years—that was evident from the midcentury appliances—but it was mostly clean and quiet. And Edie thought the street seemed safe. The rest of the block was calm, and the homes old but well cared for. "It's mostly homeowners over here," David told Edie. Unlike the house on the street with all the vacants, the apartment building at least felt doable to Edie. But she wasn't excited about either of the options.

Edie knew she had a choice about where to move, even to the county if she wanted to. "You can move anywhere you want to go. Hell, you can go all the way to California if you want! That's what I heard," she told me. Voucher program rules do allow recipients to "port" their voucher to other jurisdictions, though it's a complicated bureaucratic process.[4] Edie reads insatiably about all the rules and regulations of the voucher program. "I go on the internet a lot. I be on there two or three o'clock in the morning. That's how I found out about how to go about getting it [the voucher]. What you need. The dos and don'ts."

Edie had always wanted to live in the suburbs. Maybe Owings Mills, she thought. "God knows where I got that idea in my head. I just thought it always seemed like a nice place to live. All them trees." Edie did not sign a lease with David that day. Instead, she powered up the old Compaq Presario PC she inherited from her neighbor and typed "Owings Mills" into Craigslist. There were so many options. Edie knew her voucher would pay up to about $1,200. She was approved for a two-bedroom so she and her daughter would each have their own room.

Many of the ads said very clearly "No Section 8" or "Vouchers Not Accepted." Edie just skipped these ads. Then she began making phone calls. She decided she wouldn't explain the voucher situation on the phone; it seemed too complicated. "I just need to meet the landlord," she thought. Edie was confident she could assuage whatever worries they might have with an in-person meeting. So, the next day, she went out to see the place at the top of her list, a house in Owings Mills.

It was a large, beige home with what seemed to Edie to be an enormous front lawn and an even bigger backyard. "I don't even know how I would take care of that much grass," she worried. "The whole time I was out there, I didn't see nothing but deer. I could get used to being out here . . . if I had my way and things would be like how I want them to be, hopefully in the county. It's really quiet in the county."

Everything went well, until Edie brought up the matter of the voucher. "Section 8?" the man sighed heavily. "You should have told me that on the phone, ma'am. I can't accept no voucher." "You *could* accept them," Edie thought to herself, but didn't say it, "You just *won't*." In her recollection, he wasn't mean about it, but he also wasn't willing to budge.

Mounting evidence suggests that this kind of discrimination, especially against minority housing voucher recipients, is all too common.[5]

While some landlords avoid voucher holders because of cumbersome inspections, others turn down vouchers for more insidious reasons. Edie was disheartened. The idea of going out to see more places, only to be turned down when the voucher came up, felt impossible. Still, she needed a place to live. She continued her search, but from then on, she mostly avoided the county.

After a few more misses, Edie remembers thinking to herself, "Why make this so complicated?" Even though she suspected she was being manipulated in some way, Edie called up David, who had shown her the two homes a few weeks back. She ended up renting an apartment in the large complex he showed her, just down the block from where her mother lives.

DISCRIMINATION

In Baltimore, as in its suburbs and most of the way to D.C., it was perfectly legal for landlords to refuse to accept voucher holders at the time of my fieldwork.[6] "That don't sound legal to me," Edie told me. But in most places in the country, it is. While Source of Income (SOI) discrimination protection laws exist in thirteen states and a number of cities and counties across the U.S., there is no federal SOI law, and no such law existed in Baltimore until 2019.[7] Landlords could simply say, "No Section 8."

In jurisdictions with SOI discrimination protection, the money that a voucher holder uses to pay rent is treated like income (even though it never passes through their hands), and voucher holders cannot legally be rejected by a landlord on this basis. Of course, recalcitrant landlords find ways to work around SOI laws where they exist by setting the rent just above market rates, for example, or by citing some other reason, such as credit score, for renting to another qualified applicant. Most of the time, the rejection happens early on in the process: the landlord simply turns the tenant away with or without an explanation, legally or illegally.[8]

Once a landlord makes a verbal agreement with a tenant to accept his or her voucher, they negotiate the exact contract rent with the local housing authority. Then the landlord signs a Housing Assistance

Payment, or HAP, contract, a three-way agreement between the housing authority, the landlord, and the tenant.[9] And finally, the landlord and housing authority set up an inspection. Any unit being paid for with a housing voucher must pass an inspection before being cleared for rental through the program. These Housing Quality Standards (HQS) inspections are performed by licensed inspectors employed by the housing authority. They check all kinds of things in a house, ranging from important safety issues, such as the security of stairway railings and the condition of the paint job, to more mundane (but still important) things like the proper working condition of doors and windows, light switches, and appliances.

The inspection process provides another avenue for landlords who don't want to rent to voucher holders in general, or to an individual voucher holder in particular, to exclude tenants. This could be for any number of reasons: perhaps a landlord wants to avoid tenants with children, or perhaps the landlord harbors more explicitly racist attitudes. In areas subject to SOI protections, a failed inspection provides legal cover for discrimination. The law prohibits landlords from discriminating on the basis of gender, age, race, or family status. But it's easy to fail inspection. Perhaps the oven isn't working that particular day, or the sink leaks. Maybe a door is missing a hinge. Any of these would be grounds for a provisional failed inspection, and if the problems aren't fixed, a legal reason to prohibit voucher holders from the property—even in areas governed by SOI laws.

In Baltimore, 94 percent of voucher holders are black, which means that race and voucher status often become conflated, and a landlord's refusal to accept housing vouchers is effectively racial discrimination.[10] Landlords with properties in predominantly white neighborhoods such as Canton and Federal Hill frequently report being unwilling to rent to voucher holders.[11] "It's not me," one white landlord in his forties with six properties in Canton told me. "I have nothing against those people. But the neighbors—they would all move out." To anyone familiar with the history of residential discrimination patterns in this country, the echoes of the racist logic underpinning blockbusting and white flight are unmistakable.

RAY AND SANDRA: FINDING A QUALIFIED UNIT

Ray and Sandra are doing well with their voucher. But finding a place was not straightforward. The couple was determined to find a unit that matched their needs. When Ray got together with Sandra, his monthly rental payment went up because of her income. At that time, they also qualified for another bedroom, because of their daughter.

The couple decided to start their search at www.gosection8.com, a privately administered website to which, like many housing authorities, HABC now directs voucher holders. Sandra explained how it works: "You put in what you want." Ray interrupted her to clarify for me: "*Amenities* that you want." Sandra gave him a sideways glance, and then looked back at me as she continued patiently:

> Say you looking for a house. We went there [to the website] and then we got a virtual tour of the house on the computer and everything, and we even mapped different houses out or whatever. The website is great. . . . You can see what you want to see. You can check for different ones. . . . That's what we did. We made a list of houses we was interested in and that's the houses that we called. Oh man, they have a lot of houses.

With all this choice, Ray and Sandra started to envision their ideal home: It would be a standalone house with its own entrance and yard. Ray has always dreamt of having a garden where he can grow tomatoes and hot peppers. "I always said if I had some kids I wanted them to grow up with some grass and trees, not concrete," he said.

Sandra and Ray's search process was an unusually informed one, in that they made a list of criteria that were important to them, conducted an online search to find homes that fit their needs, and then drove around to visit these units before making a choice.[12] It exemplifies the principles of informed choice that the architects of the voucher expansion envisioned.

The gosection8.com website is an improvement over the three-ring binders of listings that local public housing authorities used to keep on hand. In theory, an online search engine that allows tenants to search for a unit that best fits their needs would seem to be a powerful tool. In practice, though, the online search process has some important limitations. In a city with SOI protection, there would be no need for a special registry—in theory, tenants could approach any landlord offering a unit within the payment standard and apply to rent it. But in places without SOI protections, many landlords who are willing to rent to vouchers list their properties on sites like gosection8.com. Landlords have to make an active choice to put themselves on the registry, and so the website represents a particular selection of landlords. At any given time, the available properties listed on the site are those that landlords *have not been able to rent* to tenants on the open market, or those for which landlords would for some reason *prefer* a voucher tenant. Thus, more often than not, these listings are for properties in disadvantaged neighborhoods.

Ray and Sandra had more resources than many who undertake this process—a car, a computer—and they needed those resources to work their way around multiple obstacles. As soon as they were issued the voucher, the sixty-day clock started. The couple first settled on the neighborhood of Forest Park, near where both Ray and Sandra grew up. The first home they found was a two-bedroom on a small street off Liberty Heights Avenue. It was a lovely old home, with original features, including a porcelain claw-foot tub and the original unpainted wood moldings in the doorframes and windows. Ray and Sandra found it charming. But while the landlord had advertised on gosection8.com, he had never actually rented through the voucher program. When it came time for the inspection, the list of things needing to be fixed seemed endless.

The landlord called a few days later to tell Ray and Sandra it wasn't going to work out. He didn't want to make the changes the inspector required; the whole process was much more of a hassle than he had anticipated. Ray and Sandra had no way of knowing whether this was true, or whether perhaps the landlord preferred white tenants, or tenants with no kids, or tenants who earned more money or had a higher credit score. They were frustrated—they knew the clock was ticking—but they tried to stay positive. "In the end, we was probably better off,"

Sandra remarked. "We could have ended up stuck in a house with a broken refrigerator and a toilet that don't work."

The couple went back on the website and found another place, this one even more convenient for Sandra's work commute. This house was newly renovated—the landlord had been renting to voucher holders for years, and had just bought this home in hopes of expanding his voucher portfolio. But again, when it came time for the inspection, the home failed. On re-inspection, it failed again. The house was old—like much of the Baltimore housing stock—and every time the inspector returned he found a new problem. "It came down to it where Section 8 just told us 'You're not moving in there.'"

Ray and Sandra's difficulty finding a viable unit is common. In fact, a significant portion of voucher recipients do not end up successfully using their voucher. The most recent data available, from 2000, shows that only about two out of three voucher holders, or 69 percent, nationally were able to find a unit with their voucher.[13] In other words, nearly a third of households issued vouchers simply couldn't find a place to live with their voucher. Only 18 percent of voucher holders found a home in under a month. The study finds that on average, it took nearly three months (eighty-three days) to lease up. Almost 40 percent of voucher holders took more than ninety days to find their unit, suggesting that they applied for extensions.[14]

While there are discernable patterns in the struggle to lease-up, they don't necessarily fall along lines of race or gender. Large families (those with five or more members) were about 7 percentage points less likely to successfully use their voucher, compared to others. The elderly were about 14 percentage points less likely to use their voucher. Nonelderly, single men without children—a population that includes many people coming from homelessness—were about 11 percentage points less likely to succeed. Perhaps unsurprisingly, a well-run public housing authority helps. Success rates go up when voucher holders receive individual briefings from their local public housing authority as well as when the program is actively recruiting new landlords.[15]

One big reason that it can be hard to find a home with a voucher is simple availability: there isn't a lot of affordable housing available, and where it is available, it tends to be in poor, segregated neighborhoods.[16] A 2007 study finds that there are only about 79 available affordable units per 100 eligible households, and when quality is taken into account, there are only 69 per 100.[17] Voucher recipients sometimes have so much trouble finding a landlord to accept their voucher and pass inspection that they end up using it in units that already benefit from subsidies, such as the Low-Income Housing Tax Credit. Recent work estimates that 30 percent of voucher holders end up "cross-subsidizing" in this way.[18]

As Ray and Sandra neared the end of the sixty-day window in which they had to move, they decided to cut their losses by not waiting around to see if the second home would pass on re-inspection. They had already given notice to their current landlord, so they had to find somewhere to live, one way or another. That's when they found Jim.

When the couple went to the housing office, Sandra noticed a card table in the waiting room covered with ads for available homes. She picked up a business card, nestled among the fliers, that read, "Jim Lewis, Tenant Placement Agent." Maybe we need an expert to help, Sandra thought. She put one of the cards in her purse and called Jim later that day.

Jim took Ray and Sandra to Park Heights, which was *not* on their list of preferred neighborhoods. As a kid, Ray would visit his aunt and uncle and cousins who lived in Park Heights. Over the years, he watched as the neighborhood deteriorated around their home: "So many blocks is like ghost towns, like on TV on the old westerns." Indeed, vacancies in Park Heights are quite high. But Jim convinced them to see a beautifully renovated home where he promised they wouldn't have any of the inspection problems they had had with the other two places.

When they pulled up to the house, Ray and Sandra were pleasantly surprised: the whole street had been recently paved, it was quiet, and some homeowners sat on their porches. Sandra remarked, "To be honest, we were kind of impressed with the neighborhood. You don't see no rodents running around. This neighborhood used to have a lot of rats. Further up Park Heights up by Forest Avenue, that's infested up there."

Ray agreed: "You don't see trash lying around. People's grass is cut. Their yards are clean." I recalled that as I walked down the block to their house, I saw several fences that had plastic shopping bags tied into the chain link.

I asked Sandra about this and she confirmed: "You see little trash bags tied up on people's fences so if you have any trash you just put it in there. The owners, they would take them up and dispose of them. Even the alleys on both sides are pretty clean." Sandra was careful to clarify that she could not speak for neighboring blocks. "But this block here, is more families. Everybody has been here for a long time and they know each other."

The home is on Central Avenue, which is just off the main thoroughfare in Park Heights. Though the street has recently been paved and is outfitted with camera surveillance, the couple remains less than thrilled with the location. The street is still notorious for the now-demolished housing complex known as "The Ranch," which Terrance Jr. told me about when he drove me around the neighborhood, and where Edie had lived for a while. While the Ranch is now gone, its reputation for drug trafficking and violent shoot-outs earned its nickname, the "O.K. Corral," by residents and police. After years of violence, the city revoked the owner's multi-family dwelling license in 2005, and apportioned housing vouchers to all the residents. In 2008 the complex was demolished. But Ray and Sandra explained that its legacy is durable: "I'm going to tell you something. I was real apprehensive in moving into this house because of that. 'Cause I know what that was. I know what this whole area was saturated with drugs, saturated. And each place you've got saturated with drugs, you've got problems. I was real apprehensive."

But the house has almost everything they had hoped for: refinished hardwood floors, central air, a newly renovated bathroom and kitchen, a bedroom for their young daughter, and a finished basement with a second bathroom that allows their adult daughter to stay in the house (although this is against the rules of the lease). And time was running out. Ray and Sandra took the house.

There are, of course, trade-offs. For example, they do not have a dishwasher, but, Sandra said, "this is an amenity I can do without." It's more important to her to have a washer and dryer because it allows her to do laundry from the safety of her own house rather than lugging an enormous bag down the street to the laundromat. The ability to get things like laundry done without going outdoors feels safer and more manageable.

Ray and Sandra are rational, pragmatic housing consumers. Before committing to moving their family into this home, they researched their options, surveyed the possibilities, and did their best to make an informed decision about where to live. The couple had a car, enabling them to scout out the neighborhood to get a feel for it. Sandra explained: "We had even drove around here different times of the day before we even moved in the house. You know it would be nighttime. We had went out and then about two o'clock in the morning we would drive around just to see if we could see any activity. Eleven o'clock in the evening time, just to check it out." To their relief, they found the street mostly quiet at night, and what they saw during the day didn't seem much different from other streets on which they had lived in the past, so they felt they could handle it. Most voucher holders don't have cars and aren't able to do this type of scouting to make sure they feel safe in a neighborhood. Even with this advantage, Ray and Sandra encountered significant roadblocks and delays that nearly cost them their voucher altogether. In the end, they count themselves lucky to have found the place they did. And so far, they haven't had any problems in their new neighborhood.

Nevertheless, they don't plan to stay in Park Heights forever. Ray has plans for the future:

> We'll stay here for a while and then we will move up, because everyone wants to grow and stuff. Me, I'm a patient person and in time we will grow. I want a single-family home, the grass—because we're family orientated. At different times we have friends and we do like to have cookouts. We like doing the family thing, you know what I mean? So there is room for us to entertain our family.

Living where they do represents a significant compromise for Ray and Sandra. While they love their house and feel safer on their block than they expected to, the neighborhood raises a number of concerns for them. To Ray, "moving up" means moving to a quieter neighborhood, with less crime, better schools, and a bigger yard.

THE MOBILITY PUZZLE

It is clear from these stories that there are many barriers to using a housing voucher, and especially to using it to move to a low-poverty neighborhood. By offering housing choice to people—who, in another era,
might have had little—policymakers hoped that vouchers would provide an opportunity for families to move to neighborhoods with more
resources. A number of positive life outcomes—including health improvements, higher educational attainment, and higher earnings—are
associated with living in a low-poverty area, integrated area.[19]

In practice, however, housing voucher recipients do not, by and large,
move to the mixed-income, diverse communities that policymakers
envisioned as a key outcome of the program. Only about one-quarter,
or 26 percent, of voucher holders live in low-poverty census tracts,
where less than 10 percent of residents are poor.[20] One recent study
shows that, of voucher families with children, only one in eight live in
low-poverty neighborhoods.[21] In 2013, almost half of voucher holders
lived in areas with 20 percent poverty or more.[22]

The voucher program's failure to move families to better neighborhoods is especially stark for minority renters.[23] While voucher holders
live in less-poor neighborhoods than residents of public housing, there
are key disparities by race and ethnicity across all types of subsidized
housing. Black and Hispanic voucher holders are significantly more likely
than white voucher holders to live in neighborhoods with extreme poverty.[24] About 12 percent of black voucher holders and 11 percent of Hispanic voucher holders live in extremely poor neighborhoods (where over
40 percent of households live in poverty), compared to just 4 percent of
white voucher holders who live in such neighborhoods.[25] On the flip side,
while 68 percent of white voucher holders live in neighborhoods with low
or moderate poverty (up to 20 percent), only 35 percent of blacks and
45 percent of Hispanics do.[26] Another way to think about this is that only
a small share of voucher holders have been successful in using their vouchers to move to low-poverty areas, and those that have tend to be white:
white voucher holder families are about twice as likely as black and Hispanic families to live in low-poverty neighborhoods.

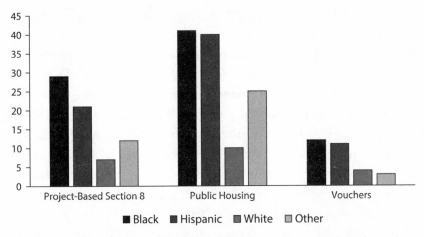

FIGURE 11: Households Living in High Poverty Neighborhoods (40%+),
By Race, Across Housing Programs. *Source:* NLIHC, "Who Lives in
Federally Assisted Housing?"

Vouchers are more spread out than most housing subsidies. Research shows that vouchers make up less than 2 percent of the occupied housing stock in the nation's fifty largest metropolitan statistical areas (MSA). And in almost 90 percent of all neighborhoods with voucher units, the program represents less than 5 percent of the occupied housing stock. The HCV program utilizes over 10 percent of the occupied stock in only a tenth of areas that have any subsidized housing, and it uses 25 percent or more of the occupied stock in an even smaller proportion, less than 1 percent. But, there is some evidence that voucher use is clustering in certain areas.[27] In one-fifth of neighborhoods with *any* affordable housing, voucher holders are overrepresented.[28] In Baltimore, vouchers occupy 14 percent of the rental stock, over twice the average for other large MSAs, and one of the highest rates for large cities in the country.[29]

Let's say you were a voucher holder in Baltimore, and you went on gosection8.com to find a home to rent. You would find very few listings in white, affluent neighborhoods like Roland Park, Federal Hill, or Canton. Many of the listings would be concentrated in neighborhoods like Park Heights and Belair-Edison. In Park Heights, about 17 percent of the rental stock is occupied by voucher holders.[30]

It's not that there aren't good reasons for families to move to Park Heights. Many voucher holders grew up in the neighborhood, or they have relatives nearby. Located within walking distance to the subway, and also at the crux of several major bus lines that run both downtown and out to the suburbs, Park Heights is a reasonable choice for people who need access to public transportation.[31] Additionally, Park Heights has a high concentration of single-family homes, many of them detached from neighboring units. This makes it attractive to low-income families who aspire to live in a single-family home.[32] But Park Heights isn't the only neighborhood in Baltimore that has these characteristics, and, even by Baltimore standards, Park Heights is poor and crime-ridden. As Raven put it: "Why would you come to Park Heights if you have a voucher you can use somewhere else?"

The complex search process is part of the answer. Voucher holders face myriad obstacles to leasing up, from tight rental markets, bureaucratic delays, limited time windows, lack of education about the program, and problems with landlords. On paper, housing discrimination laws protect renters from discrimination on the basis of race, gender, disability, and family status, but in reality, landlords find ways to work around these laws. And in Baltimore—as in most cities—there were no laws barring landlords from turning voucher holders away due to their voucher for many years. Some landlords do this out of concern for their neighboring tenants who they believe will not want to stay if voucher tenants come in. Others are motivated by more overt racial animus: while excluding voucher holders can't guarantee that a landlord won't end up with a black renter, it does exclude a lot of black renters from the market.[33] In all too many cases, voucher discrimination is effectively synonymous with racial discrimination.

These barriers lead to two distinct outcomes: Many voucher holders—around 30 percent based on the most recent data—are unable to lease up at all.[34] The rest do find a home to use with their voucher, but their choice of where to use it is severely circumscribed.

The housing voucher market replicates the same forces of discrimination and racial and socioeconomic stratification that affect renters in the private housing market more broadly. This is not entirely surprising since the housing voucher market is not in fact a separate market. Part of the appeal of vouchers was their reliance on the advantages of the private housing market to solve some of the problems that besieged public housing (inadequate funding, maintenance backlogs, geographic immobility); yet, without adequately addressing the private market's shortcomings, we are seeing them mirrored within the voucher program.

Chapter 5

"A TENANT FOR EVERY HOUSE": THE ROLE OF LANDLORDS

I waited with David in the shade offered by the two-story HABC "Section 8" office. The sun beat down and waves of heat reflected off the pavement, bouncing off the brick walls and back up onto our bodies. "Three-bedroom with central AC. Vouchers welcome," David chanted over and over as he pushed a flyer into the hands of anyone exiting through the double doors. A middle-aged man put his arm around the shoulders of the woman next to him, shook his head, and steered her away without taking a flyer. An older woman reached out for one. "Thank you young man," she said slowly with a big smile. "Three beds is just what I need for my grandkids."

"They would love it," he responded. "There is a fenced-in area out back and a finished basement for them to play. I can show it to you right now if you like, Miss . . . ?" He leaned down at her deferentially, his eyebrows raised, waiting for her name.

"Miss Hayworth, but you can call me Louise."

"Well Miss Louise, what do you say? My car is just around the corner." He turned to show her the way. The woman paused and concern rolled over her wrinkled and worn face.

"Well just a minute young man, where is this apartment?"

"Oh, it's just a short drive, it's up near the race track, beautiful area," he responded without missing a beat.

"Oh no, up near Pimlico? But that's up in Park Heights. No, no, I won't go up there." She turned away as she spoke, shaking her head and waving the paper for emphasis. "Oh no, no, too much of that drug activity up there." She muttered as she walked away, her smile wiped from her face.

David was unperturbed. For the rest of the afternoon, he continued to hand out flyers and give his spiel to anyone who would listen.

Eventually he found someone to come take a look at the apartment. David told me he comes down to look for potential renters in front of the voucher office anytime he has a unit open. David wants voucher holders in his units in Park Heights, because he knows he'll get most of the rent on time every month from the housing authority. He has to do a little extra work to recruit the voucher tenants, but it's worth it, he said.

Other landlords I got to know echoed David's sentiment. Oscar, for example, is a white landlord who also works as a property manager for other owners, helping them to fill vacant units. "The thing is," he explained, "you don't need a lot of help when it's a good area. But in the bad area, that's when it's hard." To many landlords, Park Heights has a reputation as one of the "bad" areas, where some people don't want to move because of the high number of vacant and boarded-up homes, high crime rates, and drug traffic. But Oscar has a more entrepreneurial way of thinking about this. "The key is, you got to understand that everyone needs somewhere to live," he told me. "There's a tenant for every house. You've just got to find the right tenant." There is a hierarchy of tenants, in other words, just as there is a hierarchy of homes.

The voucher program in Baltimore used to be—and in many places still is—deeply maligned. In the past, stereotypes of "Section 8" tenants as loud, discourteous, and messy were rampant. Larry, an older white landlord who has owned about ninety properties in Baltimore City for nearly half a century, told me that voucher tenants come with certain risks: "As far as their housecleaning, housekeeping habits. A lot of them come from poor families, uneducated families." For instance, he explained, "they still cook a lot with grease. You go in there and you will find a frying pan on the stove with that much grease all hardened in there." Larry held up his fingers to mime about an inch of grease. "They take the grease and pour it down the drains. The drains get stopped up. Their arteries get stopped up. That's where Obamacare comes in." Larry admitted, "You have some that are really really clean too." Larry attempted to answer a question I hadn't exactly asked, as to which tenants are better, market tenants or voucher tenants: "Are the percentages more weighted?" he asked himself out loud. "I can't say if they are or not." One thing Larry knows for sure:

Most of the people in the city that are Section 8 are African American. As we well know, African Americans, the structures of their families and the black male . . . they are not real good developed family structures. They move in, and then here comes someone else moving in their family with [another] kid. They have a kid sleeping in the basement. Probably the typical Section 8 tenant is a mother, and one, two, three, four, or five children. The man is nowhere to be found, or he is found and he's sleeping on the sofa or he comes and goes. A lot of times—take their lease application—they have four children, and each of the four children have a different last name. That's what you are dealing with. Those people need a place to live too—those children need a place to live. They need to grow up in a better manner than the previous generation.

Larry has some clear racial prejudices about his voucher tenants, and draws on old tropes of the *culture of poverty* dating back to the Moynihan report and earlier.[1] But, Larry said, "We put our pants on the same way in the morning. You've got your good ones and your bad ones. I like the idea of getting my check in the mail. Most of it, not all of it, every month." This financial incentive has motived many landlords to put aside their prejudices and open up their properties to voucher holders.

WHAT'S IN IT FOR THE LANDLORDS?

Most of this book focuses on the voucher experience from the perspective of the *tenant*, but they are not the only actors in this story. Landlords play an integral role in how, whether, and where voucher holders use their vouchers.[2] The involvement of private landlords marks a major departure from older forms of housing assistance, such as public housing, where public housing authorities (PHAs) provided housing directly to tenants with no middleman. Landlords play a powerful role in the rental economy. While a recent book, *Evicted*, by sociologist Matthew Desmond, demonstrates how landlords play a role in selecting tenants *out* through eviction, we know little about how landlords select tenants *in*—how they make decisions about desirable tenant characteristics and sort renters into neighborhoods across the city. They are a missing piece of the housing assistance conversation.

The time I spent at the Housing Authority of Baltimore City left me convinced that to fully understand the voucher system, I needed to learn more about the landlords' perspective. Specifically, I needed to know how the real estate market was functioning *as a market*.

Nearly all of Baltimore's high-rise public housing was torn down in the 1990s. Now, with one in four households living under the federal poverty line, the city also has one of the country's highest voucher rates. Baltimore landlords face a common set of challenges within this local housing landscape: vacancies, turnover, early lease termination, late or sporadic rent payments, and property damage. The financial crisis of 2008 also left many landlords with properties on their hands that they had intended to sell. In these circumstances, Baltimore landlords find that the stability of the voucher program offers a set of solutions to these challenges. Simultaneously, recent changes in the local voucher program rules have reduced financial risk for landlords around the program.[3] This has, in turn, increased the competition to attract and retain voucher tenants in Balitmore.

Filling all of their vacancies requires that landlords play a complicated game of matching tenant characteristics—such as family size, race, voucher status, and financial risk—to property characteristics like size, condition, and location. As landlords manage their portfolio of properties across different types of neighborhoods, they cherry-pick the tenants they want and match them to the units they most need to fill. This has important consequences for tenants, and partially explains why so many voucher holders often stay in, or even move to, disadvantaged neighborhoods.

If the landlord plays the matching game right, "there's a tenant for every house." This means that from the landlord's perspective, some homes are better for voucher tenants, and others are better for market tenants. The voucher homes occupy a certain sweet spot: on the one hand, they're nice enough to pass inspection, so they tend to be in better condition than some of the worst rentals on the block. On the other hand, because these homes are often located on rough blocks in poor neighborhoods, they're often hard to rent to tenants with enough money to pay for something on the open market. The way voucher payment standards are set provides a financial incentive for landlords to find voucher holders to fill their properties in disadvantaged neighborhoods.

Many voucher landlords employ tactics of targeted recruitment, offering enticements to sweeten the deal for these hard-to-rent units: recruiting tenants directly in front of the voucher office as David does, offering a new kitchen appliance, or a move-in cash bonus. These practices shape the voucher experience in two key ways: on the positive side, some voucher tenants whom landlords deem to be most desirable may benefit from the higher-quality units they are offered. These units have to pass yearly inspections and so—in theory—they should be up to quality standards.[4] On the other hand, landlords are often working to attract and keep voucher tenants trapped in units that deliver the biggest profits, which happen to be in some of the very neighborhoods from which the voucher might afford families the opportunity to escape. This perverse incentive structure has important implications for inequality: the tenants at the bottom of the social ladder are being matched to homes in some of the worst neighborhoods.[5]

Landlords who operate in poor neighborhoods face a perpetual challenge in collecting rent.[6] Renters in Baltimore have a high rent burden. The median household income for renters is $25,000 and a quarter of all renters earn $9,600 or less. This means that an affordable monthly rent (30 percent of income) for the median renter would be $694. And for renters in the lowest income quartile, it would be just $240 per month.[7] Yet the average gross rent in Baltimore at the time of this study was $889 per month, and it has climbed since then. In Park Heights, where the average gross rent is $792, almost three in ten renters pay more than 50 percent of their income in rent.[8] It is not surprising that landlords cannot always collect rent from their tenants: many low-income renters in Baltimore simply cannot afford to pay.

Many landlords go so far as to say that they simply cannot make a living renting to low-income market-rate tenants. The costs (in time and money) of collecting rent, taking tenants to rent court, and processing evictions for nonpayment are simply too high. Landlords have a strong incentive to find ways to make rental payments more reliable. Oscar articulated this clearly: "Everybody prefers Section 8, it's tough times now. If the tenant doesn't pay the mortgage, you have to. Section 8 ensures that you going to get your money." The predictability of the program appeals to a certain segment of landlords who have now oriented their businesses toward attracting and retaining voucher holders.

The landlords I got to know expressed a strong preference for voucher tenants. They recognized the economic advantages reaped from a tenant whose rental payments are mostly issued directly and dependably from the housing authority. As one landlord, Tyrone, said: "A lot of owners like voucher tenants because the rent is guaranteed. It's going to be in your account between the first and the fifth. You don't have to worry about chasing any money."

In their quest to attract voucher holders, many landlords have become "specialists," converting their businesses *specifically* to attract them.[9] Mark, a white landlord in his midthirties who is part-owner of one of the bigger real estate companies in the city, told me how his company got into the voucher business. In 2007, his company Reservoir Properties completed an analysis of its rental portfolio and realized that their voucher properties were outperforming their market-rate properties. Market rate tenants were defaulting on rental payments at much higher rates than units rented to voucher tenants. The company decided to make a change. In the span of a year, it went from 15 percent voucher-occupied units to 85 percent: "We literally just vacated everyone and . . . we just said 'Hey, we're not renewing your lease and it's time to get out,' and we just did like fifteen to twenty houses a month . . . turned the whole portfolio over and then marketed exclusively to Section 8."

Smaller independent landlords also changed their strategies around the same time. Noah is a white landlord in his late forties who comes from a conservative, religious Jewish family. He took over the family real estate business from his uncle and cousin, who had about thirty properties and never accepted voucher tenants. Against his family's advice, Noah began accepting vouchers in 2006. Within a year he had converted almost half of his units to rent through the voucher program, and was having enormous success.

Landlords report that the voucher program offers them a set of powerful tools to combat some of these persistent problems of rent collection and turnover. For this reason, many landlords have a strong preference for renting to voucher holders, leading them to convert their business toward targeting voucher holders, and implementing the program in strategic ways. In Alex's words: "Everybody is chasing them now, everybody. It's what everybody wants."

FINDING TENANTS WHO PAY AND STAY

Landlords have properties located across a range of neighborhoods. Finding and attracting tenants who are able to pay their rent reliably in disadvantaged neighborhoods is no easy task. So, to find tenants, they look for "fit," matching tenants with rentals based on the characteristics of the property, such as its size and location. Voucher status is one trait that they consider.

Although the Fair Housing Act explicitly forbids discrimination and preference based on gender and family size, it is surprisingly common among landlords. For example, some readily admit that they prefer male tenants. Oscar explained:

> I'd rather have a man living in my property than a woman. Because a man—you wouldn't think they would take care of the property better but—a woman a lot of times they get into a little something with somebody, or different guys may come over and there's a big dispute. Not only that, but a man can take care of his apartment a little better than a woman, you know, they're more handymen.

What Oscar implies, but does not say overtly, is that women are more likely to come with children.[10] Noah articulated the same preferences, but made the underlying issue explicit: "It's been my experience that the younger single mothers with multiple children aren't quite as focused on what they need to do to maintain the property." A full 83 percent of households in the voucher program are female headed, but many of these households are elderly, and only about 40 percent are single mothers with kids.[11]

Landlords' preference for childless families shapes their inventory. At first glance, a large house might seem to be a better investment, since the more bedrooms, the larger the payment from the housing authority. Oscar set me straight: smaller units come with less headaches. Similarly, Ryan explained: "When I first started, we were always looking for the [families with] bigger vouchers and [homes with more] bedrooms, because, more money. But the house was destroyed. . . . Now, I want a single person to walk through the door that has a one-bedroom [voucher] and no children and no family. They're not going to wreck your house." But at the end of the day, a landlord's preferences all depend on what kinds of properties he has.

Different kinds of tenants will be ideal for different kinds of properties. When Noah had an open one-bedroom unit in what he called a "rough" area of the neighborhood, I observed him interview three potential tenants before finally settling on a thirty-two-year-old man with schizophrenia. I asked him why, and he told me: "The perfect tenant depends on the property. . . . If it's a lower-level one-bedroom then I'm looking for a NED, a nonelderly disabled person." Jim Lewis, the tenant placement agent who helped Ray and Sandra find their home, expressed this to me as a general rule of thumb: "The ideal tenant is this: the fewest amount of people in the house, with the highest amount of yield." This process of matching tenant to unit is key to understanding how landlords' strategies sort tenants.

Credit history, residential references, and criminal history are three criteria upon which landlords sometimes rely to screen tenants during the rental process. Of the three criteria, landlords are most interested in two aspects of their residential history: (1) how long a tenant stayed at the previous home and (2) their relationship with the previous landlord. David explained:

How many years have they been in a property, how often they change and why? In our experience if they had an issue in the last property after a year, they're going to have an issue with me. It's not so much the landlord, it's the tenant. If they have mice everywhere they go, that were just too bad to treat, clearly it's *them*. So rental history is definitely a big one and we speak to the landlord. The landlord says "Yeah, we got along fine. I'm sorry they had to leave." I'm more open to that. If the landlord is like "Yeah, they were horrible to deal with," and the tenant is like, "The landlord is horrible to deal with," I'm going to shy away.

Many landlords don't even run credit and background checks for voucher tenants. They use the voucher status as a proxy for the check. They know that they will receive at least a portion of the rent on time every month from the housing authority. As the selection criteria suggest, landlords are trying to find tenants who will give them little trouble, but who are also likely to stay in the unit for as long as possible. The latter is often more important than the former, and landlords use screening criteria strategically to select for tenants who are most likely to pay, and stay.

THE VOUCHER PREMIUM

Beyond the reliable payment portion from the housing authority, landlords have an obvious motivation to accept housing vouchers. Depending on the location, they may be able to charge a premium above the local market rate for voucher units.

The voucher program's rent ceilings, or "payment standards," are based at or around Fair Market Rent (FMR), which is set at either the 40th or 50th percentile of rent across the entire metropolitan area.[12] For Baltimore City, this zone includes a huge geographical area encompassing the much wealthier suburbs that reach nearly all the way to Washington, D.C. These are some of the wealthiest counties in the country. So, depending on where a property is located, local rents might be significantly below the payment standard. This is the case in Baltimore City, which is much poorer than its surrounding counties.[13] And in neighborhoods like Park Heights, the discrepancy is quite large. While the payment standard for a two-bedroom in Baltimore was about $1,200 per month in 2012, typical rents in Park Heights for a three-bedroom house were usually around $800 or $900.[14] This amounts to a huge premium for landlords who can pass inspection, find a voucher tenant, and convince the housing authority to set the rent as close to the payment standard as possible.

Within this payment standard, the PHA also considers "rent reasonableness," that is, what the unit is worth based on size, amenities, and other comparable units nearby.[15] Though many of these criteria are based on fixed characteristics, landlords find ways to manipulate the rent reasonableness determination. They can add amenities like new appliances, air conditioning, or a finished basement. They can also alter seemingly fixed characteristics, such as the number of bedrooms, through renovating or counting a den as a bedroom. Rent reasonableness is supposed to ensure that properties are not rented for more than comparable homes nearby, but PHAs have wide discretion in how to implement it, and the system does not always work as intended.

Ryan, a forty-five-year-old white landlord, is a self-proclaimed voucher "specialist," who owns over 150 units that he rents primarily through the program. In one building, he rents out two identical units, with the third-floor voucher holder unit going for $250 more a month than the market-rate unit on the fourth floor. This premium creates perverse incentives for landlords to recruit poor voucher holders to properties in disadvantaged neighborhoods.

I met with one local landlord, Jake, on a spring morning. When I pulled up to the quiet block, he and a friend were on the other side of the street in a vacant lot, cleaning out trash and cutting back the weeds. Jake, an African American man in his early thirties, is a small-time local landlord. He grew up in the neighborhood, and in the past ten years has saved enough to invest in a few properties locally. He now owns four single-family homes in the area and rents three of them to families with vouchers. He tries to concentrate his properties near his mom's house so that he does not have to travel too far when they need to be inspected and to make repairs.

We went into the house, which was crowded with sheets of drywall leaning against the walls and tools strewn across the floor. He was working on the four-bedroom home on a street largely populated by older homeowners. The block was quiet, but had a new reputation for petty crime and break-ins. As was his usual practice, Jake was doing all the renovations himself.

Jake had wanted to rent the home for $1,500 per month, but he knew he couldn't get this much from a market-rate tenant—not on this block. "I mean, you can't go ask a person for $1,500 knowing they have a regular job . . . something like this house, you have to stay within the budget that somebody can afford. Now most [market-rate tenants] . . . can afford anywhere from like 700 to 900. That's what they're willing to pay for rent." But that morning Jake had some good news. He had recently found a voucher holder tenant and negotiated the rent to his crucial price point, $1,500. He had expected the housing authority to ask him to lower it a bit, perhaps to $1,200 or $1,300. But instead, they accepted his $1,500. Now everyone just needed to sign the HAP contract, the agreement between landlord, tenant, and housing authority.

Similar situations unfold every day in poor neighborhoods across Baltimore. So as long as housing voucher rents are tied to the Fair Market Rent across a metropolitan area, and these metropolitan-area average rents are higher than in certain poor neighborhoods, landlords in poorer neighborhoods are especially motivated to find tenants with housing vouchers.[16] This financial incentive, in turn, creates a market for landlords to make money in disadvantaged neighborhoods, motivating them to purchase more properties in such areas.

ALEX: THE VOUCHER COMPLEX

Alex is from a family of Russian immigrants in the Bronx. He got his start in real estate at seventeen, working for the family plumbing business. He picked up side hustles fixing up properties, and by the time he turned twenty-one he had saved enough to buy his first property, a three-family home in the Bronx. Ten years ago, he sold off his New York portfolio to move to Baltimore: "You get more for your money here," he told me, then quickly qualified, "Well, you get more units, but less profit."

Alex's strategy was to invest in a big complex, renovate it just enough to make it more suitable for today's lower-income renter, and find some voucher tenants to ensure a steady rental income to cover the mortgage.

Oakland Terrace fit the bill. At the time he purchased it, the Terrace was an aging low-rise complex, with 120 apartments spread out over ten buildings. Each building has three floors with four units per floor. The buildings are organized around a small concrete courtyard with a few trees and several picnic tables where residents like to pass the long, hot summer afternoons.

When the complex opened in 1968, the property straddled two neighborhoods: one a fairly middle-class neighborhood, filled with homeowners, and the other, fairly poor. By the time Alex purchased it in 2007, both surrounding neighborhoods were in deep economic decline.

Alex refinanced two other properties to purchase Oakland Terrace. He invested $1.7 million in renovations, ripping out the dark faux-wood paneling lining the walls of all the apartments and replacing them with clean white sheetrock. "I had it lead-free certified. So, this building is lead-free which is awesome." The floors are still covered with the original gray-flecked linoleum: "That old stuff holds up," he told me. "No point on replacing that." He upgraded the kitchens with new wooden cabinets, and one-by-one, he's been replacing the refrigerators and stoves, often with fixer uppers from his other properties or from junk yards.

There are 115 rentable units, with another five used for storage, office space, and laundry. There's no central air, as the complex was built with wall units, though most of them no longer work, and some have been removed. Alex tries to keep up minimal standards, but his expectations are low. "We try to keep the place clean. I mean right now even the people they don't really take care of the property. I gotta have two guys here every morning for like two hours cleaning up the grounds. You know like sweeping up potato chip bags and empty beer cans and stuff like that."

Before Alex bought it, the previous landlord had let things fall into disarray. "They used to rent it to drug dealers," Alex told me. He explained that the previous owner didn't keep up with the maintenance. "He paid very little for it, and he had so much real estate he was using this as a write-off. So, he wasn't even collecting any money out of here. He had a real estate guy who would rent it for him and just tell him to pay all the bills, 'I don't want no money.'"

When he took over the lease, Alex tried to remove as many of the original tenants as he could. He wanted a new group of residents that he would select himself. "Only about 15 percent of the original tenants are still living here," he told me. Alex asked the previous landlord for as much paperwork on the existing tenants as he had, "because I told him I want as many people out [as possible]. You have no rights to redemption when they are late four times or a fifth time, you can get them out automatically."[17]

But despite all his efforts, Alex feels the purchase was his "biggest mistake." Many of the new tenants have just as much trouble paying the rent as the old ones. On some days, he thinks it's a money pit. Every time someone is evicted, he has to rehab the apartment, turn it over, and find a new tenant. "So," he explained, "you're always putting money in because of people always getting evicted. People can't pay rent, get evicted, so I'm constantly fixing the same apartments." He told me about a unit that he had to have cleaned and repainted four times in a single year due to turnover.

In part, Alex has trouble attracting tenants to Oakland Terrace because it still has a reputation problem. Its moniker, "The Pool," comes not just from its old swimming pool—decommissioned soon after the building opened—but from its reputed past as a lively drug area where dealers and buyers came to exchange goods. Like the Ranch, the complex had no shortage of derogatory nicknames: "the Jungle," "the Death Trap," or, according to some, the "One way in, one way out." Alex confronts this every time a tenant comes to look at an apartment. "They've heard about it. They know what it is. And we're still having a hard time shaking the name Oakland Terrace."

Alex knows that the best thing he can do to attract tenants is to maintain the property. He battles with the city to get help keeping up the area around the Terrace. But when it comes to the street outside the complex, he said:

The city does absolutely nothing to help. I mean if you look at the street on the side here, I've been trying to get that thing paved for five years and the previous owner was trying to get that place paved for ten years before me. They said it's in the "alley" and it doesn't belong to them. . . . One, it has a name. Two, it has a sign that says 25 miles an hour. . . . They're just not doing it. They just don't want to come just to any neighborhood looks like [this]. The neighborhood looks abandoned.

His biggest challenge is collecting enough rent to cover the mortgage, taxes, and expenses. Some months, the numbers simply don't add up. He owes $59,000 in taxes a year. Alex explained:

> You gotta take into consideration that the average rent here is $650. So you're not making that back any time soon. And good luck collecting that. The mortgage is $28,000 a month, and then you got a water bill about $50,000 a year; then you got insurance around $22,000 or $23,000 a year. Then you got payroll. Then you got material. It's hard staying in business here, I don't know how much longer I can do it.

Alex sometimes keeps Oakland Terrace afloat by using proceeds from his other, more profitable, properties. He owns two other large buildings that he rents predominantly to voucher holders. To make extra cash, he also routinely buys and sells properties from one of Baltimore's "ground-rent seizers." These are people who buy ground rents, betting on low-income homeowners failing to pay up, and then seize the property when they don't. Under Maryland law, in properties with ground rent, the owner owns the home, but pays a small yearly sum (usually $50 to $150) to lease the land underneath the home to the ground-rent lien holder. If ground rent is not paid on time, the ground-owner can go to court and have a lien placed against the house. This allows the ground-owner to seize the property for very low sums of money. According to property records, Alex has bought and sold over twenty of these.[18]

His main strategy for staying liquid, however, is to fill Oakland Terrace with as many voucher holders as possible. Like David and some of the other voucher specialists, he regularly drives down to HABC to recruit tenants from the voucher office. Since most of a voucher tenant's rent is paid directly by the housing authority, Alex doesn't have to evict voucher tenants nearly as often as market tenants for not paying.[19] Alex especially likes what he calls the "specialty" voucher programs—those that offer vouchers to populations in need, such as the elderly, people with disabilities, homeless persons, or families who have experienced domestic violence. These programs not only pay reliably like the regular voucher program, but also often offer extra support to landlords. "I tell you, they take care of properties very nice now. They do, they have to, especially the programs that I got that I'm working with now. The case-worker shows up once or twice a week, three times a week," giving the landlords someone to air grievances to. For example, if the tenant is not taking out their trash or is getting noise complaints, this is something the caseworker can help the tenant to address.

The surrounding blight limits Alex's options somewhat. Some special-ized housing programs will not allow recipients to use their subsidies in distressed areas, for example on blocks with more than a certain number of vacant or boarded-up homes. The idea is that the programs want recipi-ents to use their vouchers in safe, healthy areas. Alex explained what this means for him, "The immediate neighborhood across the alley here—all abandoned houses—they're falling, overgrown shrubbery. I could get programs in here who would take all of my vacancies, as I kick people out. But they won't do it." Still, his units are more than good enough to satisfy most of the housing authority's requirements for standard vouchers.

In an effort to attract new tenants to Oakland Terrace, Alex made a significant investment to make the complex safer when he bought it. He installed a $50,000 security system, which he credits with reducing crime on the property. This, he said, changed daily life at the Terrace in a meaningful way. "If you look back at this property five years ago, if you can get police records of how many calls and how much stuff was going on in this property and now look at it a year later, I mean it's a phenom-enal turnover." He has thirty-two cameras around the complex, on the outside of the buildings, in the alleyways, and in the courtyards. Resi-dents I spoke to confirmed that the Terrace had undergone a complete transformation.

When he took over the Terrace, Alex thought that if he could get co-operation from the police, he could clean the whole place up in no time.

He convinced his father-in-law—a retired cop—to drive over to the Northwest Precinct with him and elicit their help installing the cameras. He offered the video surveillance to crack down on drugs sales in the complex. The police were extremely receptive to this plan, because until then, as Alex tells it, "They didn't have any way to actually catch them." He credits this sting operation as "100 percent [the reason it got better]. When we first took it over people were still hanging out here selling drugs. Within a month they all got arrested and the other ones ran off."

Without assuring some basic safety for his tenants, Alex would be unable to attract voucher tenants, whom he needs to attempt to make his business model work. Now, 50 out of the 115 units are occupied by voucher holders. And he can get more for these units than he would with private market tenants. Based on the payment standard, he could ask up to $1,200 for a two-bedroom with a voucher if he were to trick the units out with modern amenities. Instead, he usually settles for around $600, paid on-time, which is still better than the patchy $600 to $650 a month he gets for comparable, market-rate apartments.

VOUCHER SPECIALISTS: "NOTHING GOOD HAPPENS IN THE BASEMENT"

Once landlords learn the intricacies of the voucher rules and regulations, some become voucher "specialists," maximizing their investments by converting their properties to cater to the voucher market. They mainly follow one of two business models. Some go above and beyond what's required to pass inspection, installing luxury features to attract the most desirable tenants to some of the least desirable neighborhoods. More commonly, they do the bare minimum to pass inspection, removing any high-maintenance features of the apartment in order to cut costs and maximize profits.

Landlords who aspire to become voucher specialists typically reorient their business in specific ways. They acquire units in clusters, renovate them at the same time, advertise in the same way, and even set up inspections for the same day when possible. It may be in the landlords' best interest to acquire properties within a limited geographic area to minimize the amount of time they spend traveling across the city for frequent inspections, maintenance calls, and rent collection.

For example, David's company used to buy houses primarily to resell them, but in the past several years with the economic downturn, the firm has transitioned to renting instead. David has been working in the real estate business, either as an owner or a property manager, for the past ten years. Before 2008, he and his colleagues "were mostly doing flips. . . . When the market was high and everything, people were paying a lot of money for properties so there was a lot to be made in the rehab side of things, and then as the market started going down, the rentals started becoming more stable. . . . So we started building up a rental portfolio." David soon realized that there was money to be made in vouchers. Of the eighty-five properties David owns and manages, thirty of them are located in just one neighborhood in Baltimore's Belair-Edison area. This type of clustering is common among the voucher-friendly landlords in the sample and impacts where voucher holders live.

Once purchased, rental properties need to be renovated with the specific needs of voucher holders and exigencies of inspectors in mind. Inspections are, on the whole, a benefit of the housing voucher program— inspections mean that properties rented through the program tend to be in better shape than those that are not. Inspections also mean that the worst properties simply will not—or at least *should* not—qualify, thereby ensuring that the government is not subsidizing rent in substandard homes.

Landlords familiar with the housing authority's inspection rules sometimes make renovation decisions that might seem strange or even perverse to those unfamiliar with the system. A large portion of Baltimore homes were built before the 1970s and therefore typically have layer upon layer of lead paint. Making a home lead-free can be done with a gut renovation, but this is time-consuming and costly. Ryan, a voucher specialist, opts for an easier route: he drywalls a second wall six inches in front of the contaminated one. This reduces the room's footprint by several square feet, but it avoids the costly and risky process of deleading. While his homes aren't "lead-free," they are "lead-safe," which offers him protection from lawsuits.

Ryan targets the lower end of the voucher market, and as a voucher specialist, his business plan hinges on renovating to create low-cost, low-maintenance apartments. He explained how he accomplishes this: "I put in one bathroom. That's it. If you put in two bathrooms, then you've got to maintain two bathrooms. . . . When they clog the first one, they'll go clog the second one." Ryan even removes bathrooms during the renovation process to reduce maintenance costs: "95 percent of the time that second bath comes out. It's gone. It does not exist. Bathrooms are nightmares."

On another visit with Ryan, I arrived just after he had finished a cost-reducing project. He proudly showed me a bedroom with just one small window, where he had drywalled over the other. "[I cut it down to] one window per room. Why would I want to put in all those windows? Extra windows—they break them. Extra doors, they kick them in. Less is more. That's where my model is different." His tenants should not expect a finished basement, or even basement access. "I don't want nothing in my basement. . . . They have no reason to go down there. Nothing good happens in the basement." Ryan explained that tenants sometimes allow non–lease holding friends or relatives to sleep in the basement, or use the space for illicit activities, which he wants to avoid.

Landlords also create economies of scale by hiring tenant placement agencies and management companies experienced with rent court and other legal issues. Morgan is a thirty-five-year-old African American woman who runs a management company that contracts with several of the larger rental companies. Her job, as she puts it, is to "put out fires." She deals with a multitude of tricky problems, from rent collection, rent court, and eviction, to damage and repairs, infestations, hoarding, and more. A wide range of landlords across the city find it more efficient to outsource these specializations to companies like Morgan's with expertise in these areas. Renting to voucher holders comes with an extra set of bureaucratic steps and procedures, making the economies of scale even more important.

Some voucher specialists, like Mark at Reservoir Properties, say that they target the "higher-end" voucher holders, and they decide where to acquire properties and how to renovate them accordingly. In contrast Ryan, Jason, Larry, and Noah admit that they target the "lower end" of the voucher market, eschewing background and credit checks since they are open to tenants that are less desirable to other landlords. In some cases, these landlords may even go out of their way to attract these tenants who may be more likely to accept a unit in an undesirable neighborhood.

ENTICEMENTS

In some neighborhoods—particularly in disadvantaged, resource-poor, or high-crime neighborhoods—landlords have difficulty renting units to any type of tenant. Renting in these neighborhoods takes special effort.

Tyrone, for example, told me that he can "lock down" a tenant by showing them a property still under renovation:

> You can . . . put the tenant in a position where they are in control. So you come into a room and say, "What color do you want this room?" And they feel like now it belongs to them, so it makes them want the property even more. It makes them do the things they need to do to qualify for the property and then we rent it a lot faster.

In contrast to Ryan, who uses quick fixes to keep costs down, other landlords use upscale amenities and renovations to attract the higher end of the voucher market, even in rough neighborhoods. Mark drove me to one of his units in a poor area of East Baltimore. He gave me a tour of several of the company's homes on a single block, all of which had been gut-renovated with hardwood floors downstairs, new carpeting upstairs, new kitchens with upscale appliances, finished basements, and the tenants' choice of paint colors. He explains: "Our experience has been you have to do this to get someone to move to a neighborhood that looks like this. . . . This is towards the nicer end of what we deliver. . . . You have to do a ridiculous product in order to get a Section 8 voucher . . . to really want to live there." These measures can be selectively employed to recruit and attract voucher tenants who might otherwise use their voucher in a different neighborhood.

Alex sometimes pursues this path, though not in Oakland Terrace. He owns several single-family homes in other parts of the city. "When I redo the houses in those areas—I mean, I do really nice stuff—granite countertops on a lot of them. And then [I find a voucher tenant] before I'm even done with the Section 8 [contract]." Once Alex "cracks" a housing program by making contact with someone who works there and establishing a relationship, he uses his contact in the program to steer new tenants toward his less-desirable properties. He continues, "You find out what program they're with, who their caseworker is and then try to get their email and you start bombarding them with emails telling them 'I got properties here.' So you've gotta get creative because there's nobody coming and knocking on your door here saying, well, 'Please let me in this complex.'"

For Oakland Terrace, Alex offers move-in incentives. One afternoon in the rental office, I saw him speak with a young woman, Malia. In her midtwenties with an infant in tow, Malia had a two-bedroom voucher and was considering moving into the building. She was still on the fence after visiting the two-bedroom apartment, which would rent for $600 a month. Her voucher allowed up to $900 per month, so it was unclear why she was even considering this relatively small apartment, technically a one-bedroom with a den. But Alex had experience with this sort of situation: he asked her if she was working and had money for the security deposit. When she said she was still receiving WIC (Special Supplemental Nutrition Program for Women, Infants, and Children) for the baby and that her only additional income was a few hundred dollars in TANF, he nodded knowingly and offered to waive the $600 security deposit. She looked relieved, and a few hours later she signed on the dotted line.

Alex told me that he often has to take special measures to attract voucher tenants: "I bend over backwards for these programs and these tenants. I mean that's why my other two buildings are full of Section 8." Housing voucher subsidies do not usually offer extra funds for security

FIGURE 12: Discarded Furniture, Oakland Terrace.

FIGURE 13: Refrigerators in Pool Area, Oakland Terrace.

deposits—which typically run as much a month's rent—so waiving the deposit acts as a particularly compelling enticement to voucher holders and other cash-poor tenants.[20]

One of the largest voucher specialists, Premier Rentals, offers cash bonuses to voucher tenants after they complete their first month of occupancy. Alex can't offer cash, but he does offer other types of incentives that are especially enticing to voucher holders low on resources. He stores discarded furniture from evicted tenants underneath a tarp in the weed-filled empty lot that used to hold the water in Oakland Terrace's pool. In a pinch, Alex can always offer someone a couch, a kitchen table, or if they're lucky, a working TV.

"BUILDING A BETTER MOUSETRAP"

Even with these enticements, neighborhoods like Park Heights can be a hard sell. Several of the larger companies contract with tenant placement agencies who target and recruit voucher tenants for hard-to-rent units. Jim Lewis is an African American man who runs a large tenant placement agency. At fifty-five, Lewis is clean-shaven, wears wide-rimmed tortoise-shell glasses, and often dresses in brightly colored, checked button-down shirts. He is passionate about his work and prides himself on his ability to place tenants in difficult-to-rent units faster than anyone he knows. A key part of his strategy, I learned, is to chauffeur tenants directly from their current homes to the doorstep of the available property. "My tenant placement service is built upon this," he told me.

Lewis explained, "It depends on where their property is. If the property is in Park Heights—I'm just trying to find somebody. I don't care who that body is. . . . Park Heights, Cherry Hill, and Brooklyn all have the worst reputation in Baltimore City. So, it's not easy necessarily placing tenants in those areas." Park Heights is a particularly stigmatized neighborhood, where people are often reluctant to rent: "People call me and they say, 'What you got?' I say, 'I got this gorgeous house in Park Heights.' [They say,] 'What else you got?'"

Tenant placement agents like Jim Lewis have an arsenal of strategies to fill these hard-to-rent properties. Lewis often explains the virtues of enticements to landlords who may not be as familiar with the needs of the market: "I tell owners, 'Look, you want to get your place rented. Okay. All right, now, this girl is on Section 8, okay? Her annual income is $6,000 a year. For real. You want a $1,000 security deposit? You want one-sixth of her annual income.'" Lewis understands voucher holders' financial precarity, which allows him to make tenants offers that are too good to refuse. For example, he knows, like Alex, that waiving the security deposit on an apartment in an unattractive neighborhood can help it to rent more quickly.

On more than one occasion I watched Lewis work his magic, often with single moms, whom he calls his "Section 8 girls." One property he rented was especially tricky because there had been a recent shooting nearby. "The landlord did a beautiful $74,000 rehab," but, he explained, the home was "on the worst block . . . awful, awful, awful . . . a bunch of board-ups." The landlord had given the home to another property manager, who had been unable to get it rented. Then "the guy called me," Lewis said, "and I got it rented in about three days."

He explained how he did it. "I showed the girl the *inside* of the house. At first, she didn't want to go. I said look, 'I'll show you other houses, but the owner wants me to show this house . . . after that I'll take you to any other house that you want to see.' She said, 'Well, okay.' So, she agreed to go in and see the house." Lewis drove right up to the house, whisked the young woman quickly up the steps and opened the door to reveal a sparkling new kitchen, refreshed with upscale amenities— glossy granite countertops, stainless steel appliances. The images of the run-down block, cracked pavement, and trash lining the sidewalks quickly receded from her mind. Lewis explained: "The house, it look like anything that you might walk in on in the suburbs—on the *inside* of the house. It was beautiful. It's like, if you build a better mousetrap, you know how they say that?"

By focusing her attention on the inside of the newly renovated home, Lewis distracted the potential tenant from the surrounding block. By picking her up and driving her right up to the door, he left her little time to get a feel for the neighborhood. And once he had her in the door, it was much easier to negotiate. Lewis means no malice, but he knows exactly what he is doing. He uses the sparkling renovations as a way to lure tenants in, and before they know what they've gotten themselves into, the lease is signed.

These "mousetraps"—picking up potential tenants at their homes and driving to potential properties, recruiting tenants from outside the voucher office, enticements and cash bonuses—constantly evolve. All of these practices target families with less financial resources, less information, and fewer housing alternatives, who are therefore more susceptible to landlord manipulations. These tactics wrest control and choice away from tenants. And, like all traps, they are difficult to escape.

THE TEETH OF THE VOUCHER PROGRAM

For a landlord, acquiring tenants is only the first step of achieving cash flow. One reason so many landlords prefer Section 8 tenants is that the rules of the housing voucher program give them an unusual amount of leverage over their tenants' behavior. These "teeth" are rooted in some of the newer rules and regulations embedded in the HCV program.

Ryan explained the power of the voucher, from the landlord's perspective:

> There's only one [way to hold tenants accountable]. . . . The thing about Section 8 is that you have to be in compliance to have your voucher. If you're not in compliance, you can set up a hearing and lose your voucher. So that means you've got to pay your rent. You've got to have utilities. You've got to pass your inspections.

In Baltimore, a vouchered family cannot simply walk away from an existing lease without experiencing consequences, including the loss of their voucher.[21] The threat of voucher loss can weigh heavily on a family. As Alex explains, "It's a big threat. If there's 16,000 people that are waiting for a voucher in Baltimore . . . that's a pretty big incentive . . . I would be scared." If tenants try to move while indebted to the landlord, for example, they will lose their voucher. This gives the landlord some leverage.

The voucher program's so-called "teeth" can help landlords maintain control over their tenants. Alex explains how he has trained one of his employees, who does maintenance in tenants' homes, to observe the home and look for leverage:

> One of my workers, he's trained to look to see how these people are living and let me know. Then, I go in the house and I tell them: "You can't live like this, you gotta go. You better straighten out your act because you could lose your voucher." You can get people's behavior in line by threatening to put them out. Sometimes there's actual cause, other times you don't need it, you can just threaten. [My worker] has never actually called Section 8 to complain, he doesn't feel like he needs to.

Landlords exploit the intricacies of the voucher rules to limit the movement of voucher holders out of their properties. One of these rules, for instance, states that a tenant cannot be issued a new voucher to move if the tenant owes their landlord any money. Alex explains how the system has changed in recent years to give landlords more recourse:

> Now Section 8 is a little more refined . . . because if you have a problem with a tenant, you have somebody to go speak to. There's a lady—Miss Watkins—at Section 8, sweetheart, works with you. If these people try to even decide to move out, they have to be caught up. In other words they can't owe a water bill, they can't owe back rent or they don't give them a new voucher—they can't go. So they worked it out, and if they wreck the apartment and you file against them like a lawsuit or something, and they can't get another voucher until they settle up with you.

Alex is not alone in finding it helpful to have someone at the HABC voucher office to turn to. Several landlords reported that they had personal relationships with administrators at the voucher office whom they could call for help in dealing with a tenant.

The threat of voucher loss can be used to affect tenants' behavior. One of Oscar's tenants, a thirty-year-old woman named Marie, lives in one of his single-family homes with her mother and two children. This home is located on a stable street with a lot of homeowners who have lived there for over forty years. Oscar likes Marie, but he's had some complaints from neighbors in recent months, and he feels her lifestyle is putting him at risk of getting in trouble with the police.

On the way to her house one day, he briefed me on the situation: "The city called me up and said, 'Do you own a property on Georgia Ave.?' I said, 'Yes.' They said, 'Well, we have a concern from a lot of homeowners over there that this is a nuisance house.' They said, 'Take care of it before we take care of it.'" Oscar was torn because he knows Marie is a single mom, and by and large she has been a good tenant, paying her portion of the rent on time. He explained, "It's not so much her, it's the people that she associates with. She got a lot of guys that may be up to no good selling drugs that know her, that's always sitting on the steps. She may not be doing anything but you get it by association."

Just as Oscar had predicted, as we approached the home, Marie was sitting on the front stoop with a young woman and three men. There was music playing, and they were talking and fishing crabs out of a bucket. Oscar approached the group and said, "Look, you can't sit here." He pulled Marie aside and said in a low voice: "We got to straighten this out. I could find another tenant, but then you'll have to get another voucher. . . . If you could just settle down." On the way back to his office, he explained to me what was actually at stake: "That's the stipulations. You can't have any drug activity in your house. You can't be hanging around. It's one of those things where she could lose her voucher."

Oscar did not kick Marie out. Had he done so, she would have lost her voucher. But his threat worked: Marie knew that if she did not change her behavior, Oscar could report her to the voucher office. Unable to pay her rent on her own, she would most likely be evicted. After that Oscar told me things quieted down at Marie's place, and he didn't get any more complaints. This incident resonates with what we know about how landlords use the threat of eviction to control tenant behavior.[22]

For landlords, eviction is a powerful tool, but it comes at a cost. In fact, much of the time, landlords are not scheming of ways to rid themselves of tenants, but rather of ways to *hold on* to tenants. One of the biggest challenges landlords face is tenant turnover. In Ryan's words: "Every tenant wants to move all the time. That is the one bad thing about Section 8. . . . Got mad at the neighbor, mad at the boyfriend. Wants to move because she wants a new house. Just—there's no reason for it. . . . They all want to move, all the time." Ryan's claim may be true for his properties, but it is not the case for voucher holders overall, who move at lower rates than tenants without vouchers.

The average tenant's length of stay varies between landlords, but turnover unquestionably incurs significant costs. Every time a tenant moves, a landlord loses valuable time and money fixing up the unit and looking for a new tenant. Depending on what happened in the unit or how long the last tenant stayed, the landlord might need to invest in repainting, recarpeting, or making other repairs. Turning over a unit costs anywhere from $300 to $3,000, and sometimes more.

Many landlords describe the challenge of reducing turnover as a constant "battle" against tenants who seem to always want to move. Ryan is particularly passionate about this problem:

> Some tenants will abuse the system to get that voucher to move. When they're ready to go, they don't care what they owe, what they signed, they're ready to go, and they're going to go to every venue they can. Call every office, do this, do that. And we don't back down, bottom line. We're standing our ground, we're not giving in. We will fight you tooth and nail.

Both landlords and tenants use inspections as a tool in this battle. A failed inspection presents an opportunity for a tenant to move; it can give the tenant the right to break the lease and be issued a new voucher. Tenants can request a spot inspection from the PHA at any time. If violations are found and the landlord doesn't fix them in a timely fashion, the tenant may be able to make a case for requesting a voucher to move. If the inspector determines that there are no code violations, the tenant cannot be issued a voucher to move and the landlord "wins." Landlords know this and develop strategies to deal with the inspectors, including in the courts.

Ryan, for instance, uses surveillance to establish in court that tenants, not the property management, are responsible for failed inspections. On his wall, he has a framed copy of a court decision he was involved in establishing precedence that landlords are not responsible for rodent in-festations under certain conditions: "[The rules] used to be gray. . . . I'm making them right. . . . I'm done playing that game. The rat used to be a big go-to [for tenants trying to break a lease]. You don't hear about it anymore, because they know that it's been put to the test and won." With this legal precedent of holding tenants responsible for new vermin infesta-tions in place, tenants have a much harder time using an infestation as the basis to break a lease. Landlords like Ryan meticulously record service calls and visits with photographs and written documentation.

"Anything we do, anything that gets done, anything that happens: photographs. You can't deny photographs, so when somebody wants to say 'rats,' no problem! I guarantee you I've got six or eight pictures from prior that show the process of how this tenant is." Ryan's employees take pictures every time they visit a house in order to document any history of leaving food or trash in the kitchen. If the landlord can document that 1) he exterminated before the tenant moved in, and 2) the tenant has a history of leaving food in the kitchen, failing to remove trash, or not mowing the lawn, then the landlord is not responsible for any future rat infestation.

Landlords, like tenants, can call for a spot inspection. They may se-lectively use these inspections as a way to bring their tenants' suspected violations of voucher rules to the housing authority's attention, for in-stance, when they want a problem tenant evicted. But the financial bur-dens associated with eviction mean that landlords have a vested interest in dealing with mild "behavioral" issues themselves. Instead of calling the housing authority to report small-scale damage to their property, landlords bill the tenant for repairs. The tenants, of course, rarely have the money and end up indebted to their landlords. This debt then means that the tenant cannot move without losing their voucher. Ryan spelled out the process:

If they owe money for damages, they can't move until they make good on it. The old way, they used to be able to just pack up, move, and be irresponsible. . . . Essentially, it's not really that you're holding them . . . [it's] that they're accountable . . . that glitch got fixed. So now a tenant has to be 100 percent current before they move.

Both the tenants and the landlords use the inspection process and legal system as tools in the "struggle" over who can leave and when, but it's not a fair fight. Landlords do this for a living. They know the rules of the game and have far more resources than their low-income tenants: they play to win.[23]

The most common reason for a tenant to end up owing a landlord money, of course, is failure to pay their portion of the rent. Some landlords take their tenants to rent court every month, even for small sums. Even when tenants are ordered to pay, landlords rarely recoup the money, and even then, the court fees often outweigh the amount they recoup. Landlords like Mark say they do this on *principle*, not necessarily for the small sum owed, but to establish an expectation of payment:[24]

> It's a training issue for us . . . so we're just playing chicken. We're just letting you know how we're going to play ball, and we know we have . . . the really nice house, and it's in a nice area, so we just say, no, you have to pay your $100 portion. I'm not going to let it slide. I know I'm getting $1,200 from Section 8 but I'm getting your $100 just 'cause that's how we're going to run this ship, like it's going to be tight, I don't want to hear any stories. . . . They just think we're bluffing. . . . That's fine, we'll do this every month if you want . . . you [don't want] to lose your voucher, and so I'm going to win this game of chicken.

Other landlords have a different strategy, allowing these small sums to build up over time to keep a tenant trapped in an otherwise unrentable unit. Ryan, for instance, does not file a claim in rent court until a tenant owes him at least $500 or $600. He says it costs him $50 just to get the paperwork, and tenants so often pay late that it's better to wait. But more to the point, a tenant cannot leave if they owe him money.

Ryan didn't speak to that directly. Instead, he told me a story that demonstrated considerable ambivalence toward the whole system:

> Four months ago [a tenant] just stopped paying her portion. She has a $400-a- month portion. Hasn't paid in the last four months, so I went to rent court, got the judgment. What's going on? Going through a tough time, but she's been with me seven years. So, it's not like I'm

going to evict her over four bad months. Section 8 pays a larger portion, $800 or $900 or something like that. . . . Look, sometimes they get in jams, and at tax time, they'll make right on it. . . . Do I evict somebody over $400, $800, $1,200, go fix up the house, rerent the house, get a new tenant? . . . How long do you wait? You still are getting something. You're getting $900 out of $1,300, and you've been getting $1,300 for the last seven years, and she's been golden, a great tenant. . . . I just think it's a bad business model to evict somebody for $1,200 and destroy her whole life, because when I evict her she loses her voucher. Then her kids are homeless. I'm not going to do that as a human being, and I'm not going to do it as a businessperson. Because it's bad business.

The story that Ryan told me included several interwoven rationales. On the one hand, "as a human being," he claims he does not want to be responsible for putting the tenant and her family out on the street.[25] It is additionally clear that Ryan likes this "model" tenant and has had a positive experience with her over the seven years she has rented from him. But Ryan also acknowledges that, from a business perspective, evicting a good tenant whose rent is mostly paid by the housing authority is not a profitable business strategy in the long term. It is in his financial interest to keep tenants in place as long as possible.

Ryan's tenant does not appear to want to leave, but others clearly do. Another landlord, Mark, more directly addressed the practice of trapping tenants through unpaid rent:

[Certain landlords] game the Section 8 system back to the tenant because . . . they'll take the low-rate tenant, but then they'll keep them there because if they bang up the house they'll threaten them out. They are just very aggressive. . . . If someone owes them money or if someone doesn't pay their $100 portion . . . [they] would let them not pay and then hold that over their head so when they say, "I want to leave," "No, you owe me $1,500," and . . . they are never coming up with $1,500. They've never seen $1,500, I mean they barely have any income. . . . He just lets them [not pay] and then uses it against them so that they can't move.

This practice of allowing debt to accrue as a means of retaining tenants serves as a broader mechanism that prevents voucher tenants from leaving undesirable living situations. It also has the effect of holding the most disadvantaged voucher holders—those behind on their rent—in some of the worst quality units in the poorest neighborhoods.

THE MATCHING PROCESS:
A REVERSE SELECTION

Even within the voucher population, certain tenants are more vulnerable to landlords' targeted recruitment and retention tactics. They may lack the education or resources to use the website to make an informed choice, or lack the transportation resources to visit multiple homes before making a decision. Or, they may be in dire residential circumstances and have limited time to conduct a full housing search. Landlord tactics therefore result in a process of reverse selection: rather than tenants selecting homes and neighborhoods, landlords are selecting tenants.

Landlords make strategic decisions about which tenants will most likely settle for a unit in a rough area, and how best to attract them. As I watched landlords receive calls and visits from prospective tenants and carefully pick which properties to show them, the meaning of Oscar's statement, "there's a tenant for every home," became apparent: Landlords have an array of properties and a list of prospective tenants. They are trying to satisfy renters by finding them a home they will be interested in; at the same time, they want to fill as many of their units as possible with tenants who are likely to stay over the long term. In Baltimore, a city with a loose rental market that features high vacancies, landlords have an opportunity to shift residents around within their properties. They engage in a matching game, sorting residents into optimal units to minimize vacancies and turnover and maximize profit.

Tenants who have bad credit histories, unfavorable residential references, or criminal records have fewer options about where to live and are more likely to accept the first unit a landlord offers them. Voucher holders who have little money saved up for a security deposit are more likely to accept a unit if the landlord offers to waive it. Those who have only lived in rental units with rodent infestations, dysfunctional kitchens, or persistent water leaks might be more susceptible to the allure of a newly renovated kitchen or the landlord's offer of a dishwasher. Tenants with few resources to learn about new and different neighborhoods are more likely to be swayed by the physical features of the unit than by the less easily observable characteristics of the neighborhood. Landlords capitalize on these vulnerabilities to attract the tenants they want for their hardest-to-rent units. Not infrequently, these units are located in neighborhoods already on a downward trajectory.

Race plays a role in this. Regardless of their own racial background, landlords reserve units in more affluent areas for whites and preemptively place blacks in more disadvantaged neighborhoods.[26] It is not entirely possible here to separate whether and when landlords make explicit distinctions according to race versus socioeconomic factors that correlate to race, but the effect is the same.[27] In Baltimore, race matters in how landlords match tenants to properties.

Landlords place black voucher holders in particular types of neighborhoods, those where whites do not want to live. For example, Lewis admits that he does not even attempt to place white renters in poor, predominantly black, high-crime neighborhoods. Given that few of these landlords' units are located in majority-white neighborhoods to begin with, prioritizing the placement of white voucher holders in those neighborhoods means that tenant placement agents are de facto unable to place black tenants in those properties. This could help explain why black and white voucher holders live in different neighborhoods.

In some cases, landlords are racist, in the classic sense of the word. In other words, they subscribe to an "ideology of racial domination" that presumes the biological or cultural superiority of whiteness.[28] This type of racism is evident in some landlords' descriptions of their belief that black tenants are inherently inferior to white tenants—"noisier," "messier," "bad with money," or more likely to be "living off the system."

In Baltimore, where 94 percent of voucher tenants are African American, this type of blatant racism based on supposed inherent racial hierarchies was rare—although it is also possible that landlords were not willing to share these thoughts out loud with me. But even when they did express such views, they mostly didn't keep them from renting to African American tenants, given the financial benefits they stood to gain. More commonly, landlords justified their behavior not in attitudes of racial hierarchy and inherent racial differences, but in their perceived understandings of their *tenants'* preferences: they made assumptions that black tenants wanted to live near other black residents, and white tenants wanted to live near other white residents. This most often manifested itself in *where* they would show homes to a potential tenant, or behaviors of racial steering.

Jim Lewis admitted to this type of steering. He said:

> Now, I know this may be discrimination—and I must openly admit that I may discriminate. But, I won't take a white client and put her right down in the middle of Park Heights. When we have whites on Section 8—and we do get whites—I'll try to place them in a more safer type neighborhood. I won't place a white down in the middle of the war zone. You can call it discrimination, but to me, it just wouldn't be right.

Lewis's attitude is consistent with much of the literature on racial steering. Landlords rationalize this type of discrimination as a practical approach to renting a property as quickly as possible to the tenant most likely to sign a lease and stay put. On the flip side, some landlords with properties in more affluent white neighborhoods are averse to placing voucher tenants in such neighborhoods out of fear of flipping the neighborhood. Together, these practices result in a powerful and overt racial sorting process that reinforces segregation across neighborhoods.

Racial steering in real estate is widely viewed as discriminatory, if not outright racist. When people in power make assumptions about what others want based on their racial background, this is racism. Especially when it results in unequal outcomes, such as disproportionately sending black families to disadvantaged neighborhoods.

Racial steering and racial sorting are the ways that race plays out visibly, on the ground, in Baltimore's housing voucher market. But landlords are operating and making their living within a racist blueprint laid long before they began their work renting to low-income tenants.

Housing segregation in U.S. cities today reflects a centuries' long, systemic legacy of racist housing practices: federal home loans, racial covenants, redlining, "urban renewal," and policies associated with the construction of public housing have had an enduring legacy on the geography of housing today. Landlords sit at an important nexus between these two forms of racism—individual and structural—by operating within a housing landscape in which renters are already sorted according to race.

———

The turn to vouchers is an important new development in federal housing policy, requiring us to rethink how concentrated poverty and racial segregation may operate in new ways under this system of housing assistance. Rather than providing low-income families with the opportunity to make informed decisions about which neighborhood would be best for them, the system has been turned on its head. Instead of tenants selecting neighborhoods, landlords are selecting and recruiting tenants.

Taken together, the landlords in this sample own or manage a significant portion—over 14 percent—of the voucher units in Baltimore City. It is clear from the stories in this chapter that property owners shape where voucher holders end up in important ways. Landlord tactics serve as a powerful instrument that sorts and sometimes traps voucher holders—through the threat of voucher loss—in neighborhoods where they can be most profitable to landlords. These happen to be the very places policymakers hoped to provide voucher holders the opportunity to escape.

Landlords don't act alone: they are embedded within a market structure that shapes and supports their behavior. Because of the way rent ceilings are set, only the bottom half of the distribution of homes are available for tenants to rent at all.[29] The available homes tend to be in higher-poverty neighborhoods. When landlords with affordable homes in affluent neighborhoods opt out of the program and those in disadvantaged neighborhoods opt in, they compound the problems that limited supply of affordable housing causes, further circumscribing voucher tenants' options.

Landlords are, more or less, salesmen aiming to persuade potential renters, underplaying a property's flaws and exaggerating its strengths—this happens everywhere. But the way it happens in Baltimore's voucher market is important, because it has disparate effects on vulnerable populations. In extreme cases, landlords' efforts to match tenants to properties constitute a complete reversal of the housing choice that vouchers were meant to provide. Instead of offering choice, landlords lure renters to disadvantaged neighborhoods, limit social mobility, and perpetuate spatial inequality. By artificially drawing voucher holders into communities like Park Heights, these practices also have a significant impact on the neighborhoods that receive these voucher holders.

Chapter 6

THE RECEIVING NEIGHBORHOOD: "NOT IN MY FRONT YARD"

Bob Marshall was very concerned with the upkeep and maintenance of the homes on his block. In particular, he worried about the house on the end of his street, which has turned over quite a bit since the long-time owners sold. "The house that's down here on the corner, people moved in there about a month ago and they gone already. They were evicted. I haven't seen the inside of the house for years because the original people that used to own the house have been gone for a long time."

Bob was engaged in what he felt was a Sisyphean battle with trash pickup on the block, and these new neighbors were not helping. "They throw garbage and trash all over the place in the tall grass, which rats love hanging in," Bob complained.

> The trash cans–if they have them—they don't put the trash in them, or the kids kick the trashcans over. On trash day, the trash truck can come up this alley, so we put our trash out the back. But they can't quite come down the alley on the other side of the street, so the people across the street bring all their trashcans and all the bags down here on this corner out front. So that it smells, especially when the cats and dogs and whatever get into them. And then when trash man comes they don't clean the street or all the stuff that's laying on the ground, and we have the smell and everything, and we have the rats coming out the alley. And my neighbor and I, we go out and we clean the streets.

Bob pointed out that the trash is not just unsightly, it attracts rats, cats, raccoons, and other feral animals. Rats are a pervasive problem in Baltimore's aging housing stock, but Bob's block in particular has a serious rat infestation that has gotten worse in recent years: "Right now we have a rat population. We got the rat patrol, and we filling in holes and everything, but since *they* moved down there, I mean we see rats quite often now."

When Bob says "they," he means voucher holders. In his mind, it's no accident that the newcomers—who, he says, don't work, and are living off of government money—also have poor trash etiquette. For Bob, stray trash is a visual indicator that a neighbor is lazy or does not care about the neighborhood. To him, it suggests that a renter—and probably a voucher holder—has moved in.

We took a stroll around the block and he pointed out each "problem" house to me. When we approached the house at the end of his block, about five houses down from his own, a pit-bull resting on the front steps arose and barked a raw, hungry bark. He lunged toward us but was stopped by the chain around his neck. He whimpered for attention. "You know, he should be in the back—you want to have a dog out, you supposed to have a dog house and all, things for it. They don't have none of that." Bob was particularly concerned with this house and its upkeep. "I don't know if you notice it now, it looks a little better now that they just recently cut their grass, it was so high. . . . But if you look out at their back, they didn't cut their back [lawn], I mean they got wild trees and everything growing out there."

Bob's apprehensions about the appearance of the homes on his block do not stem from cosmetic concerns alone, and also go beyond sanitary issues related to vermin infestations. Many residents express fears that unkempt lawns, dogs chained out front, and trash strewn about signal to outsiders that the residents of the block are not paying attention and do not care what happens on the block. He is worried that such visual cues will increase drug trafficking on the corner, as the Broken Windows Theory of crime would predict.[1] According to that now controversial idea, a broken window—or any other sign of disorder and neglect—leads to more crime.[2] And what's more, Bob is worried that physical decline and crime might affect his property value:

You know people used to care about it, but now we have cars that drive up the street and just throw trash bags right out the street out the windows of the cars and keep on going. People will clear their car out. Fast food bags and half eaten food, right out in the gutter. . . . It's not good for the neighborhood. People see the trash and think no one cares about this place.

Longtime residents of Park Heights find ways to distinguish themselves from renters—and especially those they perceive to be voucher holders—particularly when it comes to maintaining order in the neighborhood. Residents obsess over lawns, gardens, trash, and upkeep of vacant lots, meticulously grooming space in the neighborhood in order to differentiate themselves from their more transient neighbors. Rather than reaching out to the newcomers to bridge the perceived differences in lawn manicuring and waste disposal, many homeowners withdraw, instead making stark moral distinctions—what sociologists call "symbolic boundaries"—about the nature of their new neighbors' character. These moral judgments reflect larger fears that trash and tall grass are signs of disorder that threaten to damage the neighborhood.

In her ethnographic study of one of the few white, working class neighborhoods in Chicago, Maria Kefalas likens this imaginary boundary drawn by residents to the "Maginot Line," originally referring to the fortifications built in France to prevent and deter German invasion in the 1930s.[3] In Kefalas's "Beltway" neighborhood, residents are defending a racial boundary, while in Park Heights they see themselves as defending a class boundary. Many longtime residents equate newcomers, and especially voucher holders, with poverty, disorder, and decline in the neighborhood.

Sociological research has documented the ways in which homeowners project racial and class prejudices onto the physical landscape of the neighborhood, and especially onto the issue of litter and the people who are presumed to do the littering.[4] Alexandra Murphy studied a suburban Pittsburgh neighborhood whose homeowners scapegoat housing voucher recipients as the litter culprits, despite rarely having actually seen anyone litter. Like Bob, these homeowners imagine "litterers" to be "disreputable" people who "don't care" about the neighborhood and even have "different values."

Like Murphy's suburbanites and Kefalas's Beltway residents, the homeowners of Park Heights share a collective understanding of what they want their neighborhood to look like and how they think their neighbors should act.[5] Many residents engage in neighborhood order maintenance, displaying an almost "fetishistic" striving for order and cleanliness. They enforce a set of aesthetic rules governing what sociologists call "disorder," including trash, unkempt lawns, and other visual cues.[6] Homeowners are concerned with keeping the neighborhood looking clean and orderly, often performing tasks that the city public works do poorly or not at all. This order maintenance is meant to regulate social behavior as well. Bob's actions are geared toward curbing drug dealing and other kinds of "unruly" activities near his home.

Most research on voucher mobility focuses on the socioeconomic status and racial make-up of the neighborhood, arguing that poor, segregated neighborhoods have less to offer voucher holders than affluent, diverse ones. However, a neighborhood like Park Heights—despite its poverty and crime—has much to offer residents in the form of social resources, due to its stable, homeowning population.

But the imaginary dividing line that is created between homeowners and newcomers has very real consequences: these boundaries serve to stigmatize voucher holders, preventing them from being fully integrated into the neighborhood and accessing what it has to offer. What's more, these social processes of stigma and social control operate differently according to where a resident lives—in a homeowner haven, a transitional area, or a voucher enclave—and depending on whether they are a homeowner, unassisted renter, or voucher holder. Homeowners are often buffered from crime in the neighborhood because of the protective power of social resources, their social standing which allows them to exercise social control, their access to social brokers, their participation in neighborhood watch groups and local community organizations, and their personal relationships with police and local officials they've known for years. However, voucher holders and often renters are excluded—both by homeowners, as well as sometimes by community organizations and local officials—and therefore cannot access these social resources. In other cases, their efforts to build such social resources are crushed by law enforcement. These social processes and the way they operate differentially across neighborhood spaces undermine a central premise of vouchers: that offering people a chance to live in new neighborhoods may give them access to more resources.

NEIGHBORHOOD CONTEXT AND THE TRANSMISSION OF SOCIAL CAPITAL

When the federal government and local housing authorities began tearing down large-scale, high-rise public housing in favor of mixed income and housing voucher solutions, they were motivated in part by new sociological theories of the detrimental effects of concentrated poverty. In his influential 1987 book *The Truly Disadvantaged*, William Julius Wilson proposed that living in a poor neighborhood had negative effects on a person's life trajectory, above and beyond their own poverty level. He traced how in the 1970s, the middle class had fled newly jobless inner-city neighborhoods in Rust Belt cities across the country, leaving behind a group that faced higher levels of *concentrated poverty* than had ever been seen in American cities, and leading to *social isolation*, where remaining residents were isolated from resources, jobs, and education.[7]

Wilson's work and the research it inspired demonstrates a key lesson: the neighborhood you live in matters.[8] Specifically, the poverty level in the neighborhood where you live impacts your future above and beyond how poor you are yourself, with important consequences for your life chances in terms of education, earnings, family life, criminal involvement, and more.[9] Neighborhood poverty is associated with a number of other traits, as well. Studies show that high-poverty neighborhoods tend to experience higher crime rates, and it is harder for residents in such neighborhoods to work together to achieve common goals—what sociologist Robert Sampson calls "collective efficacy."[10] Residents in these neighborhoods also tend to have weaker institutional ties to the city at large.

These social ties, both within the neighborhood and beyond, allow people to access social capital.[11] Social capital—like financial capital (money and financial investments) and human capital (educational investments)—is a set of resources that people can draw upon to get ahead in life. Social capital includes the informal and reciprocal obligations attached to social relationships, and the resources that people derive from these relationships, such as information, job opportunities, housing, and more.[12] This could mean a neighbor connecting another neighbor to a job opportunity mowing lawns, a homeowner showing a newcomer where to put the trash to make sure the truck picks it up properly, or a longtime resident telling a new renter where they can get their laundry done cheaply. It is through these same relationships and reciprocal obligations that neighborhood residents have the ability to socialize youth and regulate each other's behavior, what sociologists call *informal social control*.[13]

By transitioning to vouchers, it was thought, recipients of housing aid might be able to access new forms of social capital that were less available in public housing. But focusing on the amount of social capital ignores the question of access: how do existing residents receive voucher holders and what consequences does this have for voucher holders' ability to access neighborhood resources?[14]

Social capital is more effectively transmitted in neighborhoods with high social organization, where residents regularly interact with one another and regulate each other's behavior, both informally and through neighborhood organizations and other kinds of community groups.[15] Accessing social capital requires not only that residents *bond* with one another,[16] but also that they *bridge* gaps between existing groups. This is the power of so-called "weak" ties between people who may not know each other well, but are more likely to pass along *new* information or resources that may lead to advantages, such as employment opportunities.[17] Activities that bring together different churches, neighborhood associations, and community groups, potentially connecting people of different racial, religious, and socioeconomic backgrounds, are opportunities to create bridging social capital.

Housing vouchers give recipients the opportunity to move to neighborhoods with different types of social capital. In order for vouchers to work as a path out of poverty, however, voucher holders have to be able to access the social capital that homeowners and long-term residents possess. Sociologist and urban planner Xavier De Sousa Briggs, who studies social capital in the MTO experiment, calls this type of social capital *leverage*, allowing a person to use it to "get ahead" or accomplish goals they would otherwise be unable to.[18]

Yet, simply plopping a low-income family into a new environment may not be enough to access these social resources. On the one hand, there may not be much social capital in the neighborhood for the taking, or newcomers might not engage with the neighborhoods in ways that expose them to it.[19] Research has also shown that families' strong ties to old neighborhoods may hinder their integration into new ones.[20] What's more, social ties are not always positive: strong bonding ties may carry certain kinds of risk, straining social resources rather than providing them.[21]

Furthermore, existing research casts doubt on the idea that mere proximity to higher-income neighbors will automatically result in the transfer of social capital. For example, Sociologist Mario Small's study of a Boston housing project that was redeveloped to create a mixed income environment where poor, subsidized renters lived alongside more affluent neighbors, found that the transfer of social capital was not automatic.[22] Laura Tach finds that residents' varying perceptions and interpretations of their surroundings helped explain why higher income neighbors did not provide the key social benefits predicted.[23] In a study of gentrification in Washington, D.C., Derek Hyra finds evidence of what he calls "diversity segregation," where diverse groups occupy the same geographic space but do not interact. Hyra demonstrates how in one park in a gentrifying neighborhood, young white residents occupied the dog park while longtime Latino residents used the soccer field, with little interaction between the two adjacent groups.[24]

Less attention has been paid to how resistance from residents in the receiving neighborhood may impede the transmission of social capital.[25] Simply moving a family into a new community does little to foster new social ties or connect that person to local resources. This is especially true when communities experience a lot of residential instability— such as with highly mobile renter populations. They may not know each other well, meaning there is less ability to work together to achieve common goals. The situation is further complicated when a neighborhood is on a downward economic trajectory, or when landlords concentrate their voucher properties in particular microneighborhoods. Given these important social dynamics within receiving neighborhoods, understanding how voucher holders are received and how this affects their access to neighborhood social resources is key.

Longtime black homeowners in Park Heights remember all too well the legacy of redlining and the process of blockbusting that followed and allowed them to move into the neighborhood in the 1960s. Along with massive white flight, the neighborhood has experienced the large-scale disappearance of jobs and the costs of the drug epidemic and the war that was waged against it—all which has left an indelible mark on residents. Alternative forms of "off the books" employment abound and crime is high.[26] Nonetheless, there has been relative residential stability until recently, and a number of community institutions and organizations flourish. Protective of what little they feel they have left, homeowners exclude newcomers and attempt to enforce neighborhood "standards" in an effort to keep up their property values. Incoming voucher holders are not uniformly accepted or welcomed into this space, which has important implications for social capital.[27]

Two neighborhood characteristics make Park Heights a particularly interesting case for understanding the transmission of social capital: heterogeneity and residential instability.[28] Bonding social capital is thought to thrive in more ethnically homogenous and residentially stable environments, and bridging capital in more heterogeneous ones. At 94 percent black, Park Heights is fairly uniform when it comes to race. But with the recent influx of a renter population, the neighborhood has a fair bit of heterogeneity when it comes to residential status and income.[29] While median household income in the neighborhood is $29,062, median income in one of the tracts is as low as $11,570, and much higher in some of the homeowner areas.[30]

According to social capital theory, while Park Heights might once have fostered high bonding social capital because residents were of similar socioeconomic and ethnic backgrounds, newer residential instability and income heterogeneity could make this type of social capital inaccessible to newcomers. I wanted to understand how old-timers—mostly homeowners who were tapped into various neighborhood resources including jobs, social services, and community organizations—received newcomers who were mostly renters. Was there evidence of *bridging* social capital—i.e., were older residents interacting and sharing resources with newer residents—or were there divisions between residents? How did differences in socioeconomic background, age, race, and residential status shape social interactions within the neighborhood to affect the flow of social capital?

Social capital is often thought of as a neighborhood-level trait: either a neighborhood has it, or not. In Park Heights, however, social capital operates differently in different parts of the neighborhood. In 1968, Gerald Suttles's *The Social Order of the Slum* became a template for understanding how social and cultural differences patterned interaction within a neighborhood. For Suttles, who lived in the multiethnic immigrant neighborhood of Chicago's West Side, traits such as age, gender, and ethnicity clustered together to structure social interactions and separate residents—what he called "ordered segmentation."[31] Like Suttles, I found divisions along these lines. However, while sex, age, and ethnic background structured interactions, they did not do so in the determinative way that Suttles proposed. Longtime homeowners stigmatized incoming renters, which manifested itself in the way they interacted. However, this stigma was not all-encompassing—rather, it was patterned by where one lived in the neighborhood, how long they had lived there, and whether they owned, rented, or used a voucher.

In chapter 1, I identified three distinct ecological zones that shape newcomers' ability to access community resources. Mechanisms of social control operate differently in each of these three zones, with important implications for the transmission of social capital: microneighborhoods represent different social networks, varying access to job opportunities, and differential access to community resources.

Homeowner havens are areas dominated by homeowners, sheltered from the rest of the neighborhood. They display strong mechanisms of informal social control, and homeowners enforce strict norms around trash collection, litter, loitering, and drug selling.[32] Inclusive social behavior is widely evident, as neighbors plant community gardens, organize group trash collection, check in on elderly neighbors or help them carry in groceries, watch the neighbors' children, and so much more. In these areas there is strong evidence of bonding social capital.

In *transitional areas*, there are fewer and fewer homeowners, renters are moving in, and many homes are left vacant. In these areas, the ways in which residents maintain order and regulate behavior also often serve to reinforce divisions between groups. Here, homeowners' attempts to maintain order—for example by discouraging kids from hanging out on the corner, reporting neighbors who keep dogs chained up outside, ordering drug dealers away from their front stoops, and reporting "suspicious behavior"—end up stigmatizing, excluding, and surveilling newcomers, especially voucher holders. We see the negative side of social control here without the positive benefits of social capital.

In *voucher enclaves* like Oakland Terrace, apartment complexes and their immediate environs are inhabited by a significant number of voucher holders. Behavior within these often-enclosed environments is highly regulated through more "formal" means of social control, such as strict rules set by the property management that imposes curfews, noise ordinances, loitering rules, visitor restrictions, trash regulations, etc. These rules may be enforced by an onsite property manager. Cameras may also be in place for surveillance. For example, in Oakland Terrace, cameras capture much of what the residents do throughout the complex.

In Park Heights, social position is determined in large part by residential status (owner, voucher holder, or market renter), as well as where one lives in the neighborhood. These factors shape the way people experience the neighborhood: what kinds of social control they can exercise, what level of surveillance they are subject to, how they are treated at community meetings, how they perceive their role in the neighborhood, how they exercise voice, and more. Neighborhood organizations in Park Heights—which could be operating to integrate newcomers—often fail to recognize and welcome voucher holders. In some cases, they actively resist the presence of voucher holders in their midst. Certain neighborhood institutions—such as the police, churches, and community groups—tend to reinforce and reify the often-false differences between homeowners, renters, and especially voucher holders.

SEEING "SECTION 8": HOW HOMEOWNERS
DRAW SYMBOLIC BOUNDARIES

The way that longtime homeowners perceive voucher holders varies across neighborhood spaces, and has important consequences for the way in which they are received in the neighborhood. Longtime home-owners in homeowner havens are sheltered from the change that has come to the neighborhood. They know and associate predominantly with other homeowners like themselves, having fostered strong social connections with each other over decades of walking down the same streets and sharing the same corner stores.

Patty, a seventy-six-year-old longtime homeowner, has just one very close friend, her neighbor Darlene, whom she has known for years. "Some people go visit from house to house," Patty told me, but "that has never been me. I like to know my neighbors but it's not an in-and-out of their house thing." She and her next-door neighbor Darlene go to church together every week. They do their grocery shopping and take walks together. The two women "call each other each and every day, we talk on the phone the first thing in the morning, and before we go to bed, we talk on the phone again." As Patty and Darlene get older and it is more and more difficult to move around the neighborhood, they have become more isolated from local goings-on. They rarely venture beyond their block and are largely unaware that voucher holders have moved in a few blocks away. With their children and grandchildren grown, they no longer spend time at the playground, daycare, or on the sidewalks outside of schools.

Mr. Green also lives in a homeowner haven, where he is similarly insulated from the transitions occurring throughout most of the rest of the neighborhood. He thinks very highly of his neighbors: "Beautiful neighbors. I wouldn't trade them for nothing in the world. Just nice people." He says they don't spend too much time together socially, but they do check in on each other. "We just speak and holler and make sure we're okay and if they see my car don't move for a day or so, they'll knock on my door or they'll call me." Since Mr. Green doesn't know or associate with any voucher holders, none of these neighborly behaviors extend to them. However, his son Terrance Jr., who lives down the street from his father, certainly knows about the voucher holders' arrival: "Those vouchers are inching closer," he told me, "One of these days they gonna be next door."

Age plays a role in social separation too. Since many homeowners tend to be older, while voucher families tend to be younger, there is little mixing between these groups unless they are in direct physical proximity. But beyond the social distance created by age and length of tenure in the neighborhood, residents who live in different microneighborhoods perceive the presence of voucher holders differently. While in homeowner havens, voucher holders are merely a hypothetical threat, residents who live in transitional areas—where homeowners live alongside voucher holders—are directly confronted with the new group of neighbors. Some residents, like Terrance Jr., express deep fear about the changing population, stigmatizing voucher holders and blaming them. Only some exhibit bridging behavior, reaching out to newcomers to welcome them and socialize them in the ways of the neighborhood.

The ways in which residents talk about their neighbors reflect the moral and "symbolic boundaries" they draw around other residential groups.[33] Sociologists use these terms to describe how people decide who and what behaviors belong and who and what should be excluded.[34] Moral evaluations reveal distinctions people make about those from other social backgrounds. People often rationalize these distinctions to themselves in terms of moral worth, justifying their own financial or cultural superiority above other groups.[35] In the case of voucher holders, homeowners draw moral evaluations around "section eighters," judging them to be less worthy because they rely on government help to pay their rent. They make assumptions about voucher recipients' laziness, the selfishness of "living off the system," and their general moral turpitude. People apply these symbolic boundaries in matters both large and small, whether it's whom to invite to a barbeque, how to interact with your neighbor, or whether to call someone back for a job interview. Symbolic boundaries are imprinted on the social world, visible in key processes such as residential segregation and labor market inequality.[36]

In transitional areas, the symbolic boundaries that homeowners draw around voucher recipients are even more readily visible. The direct proximity to vouchers poses a more tangible threat in these residents' minds, hardening their moral stance. Shelley—a homeowner who recently bought a small row home on a transitional block with voucher holders, market renters, and homeowners—draws stark symbolic boundaries around her neighbors. She says that she can recognize voucher holders because they have a lot of kids. She claims that these "Section eights" are responsible for trashing the homes on her street and she worries that this will affect her property value. "It's different now that I'm a homeowner," she told me. "It makes you think about things differently."

Beverly also lives in a transitional area that contains an assortment of older homeowners, newer homeowners like herself, newer renters, and some vacant properties. Beverly participated in a residential drug rehabilitation program in Park Heights ten years ago, and then joined a "rent-to-own" program to purchase her home. Having herself been a renter in the area, she is sensitive to the differences she sees between homeowners and renters and the differences between microneighborhoods:

> The neighborhood can change from block to block. You can have a great homeowners block, and then the next block can be wild and crazy. When people aren't homeowners, some people don't respect the property, the neighborhood, or the neighbors in a way that homeowners would like them to. They may be loud; they may have the most visitors on a daily basis; they may stay out later, you know just more activity, more activity going on than homeowners may have. Homeowners are usually folks that work and spend time fixing up the neighborhood.

Beverly hopes the neighborhood is on the upswing, but worries that some of the renters are less invested in the area.

Beverly is not alone in noticing these correlations between homeownership and neighborhood behavior. A large body of scholarly literature is devoted to examining the benefits of homeownership, demonstrating that owning a home confers a number of advantages not just to the homeowner, but also to the community.[37]

Yet there is a more sinister side to homeownership. Sociologist Brian McCabe argues that while homeowners may be more likely to invest in upkeep in and around their home benefitting the surrounding area, they do so with a single goal in mind: protecting their property value. For example, McCabe finds that while homeowners participate in activities related to their homes, such as public meetings and community projects, at *higher* rates than renters, they participate in other groups such as labor unions, political groups, and civil rights organizations at a *lower* rate, similar to renters.[38] In other words, they participate in community groups, but less in the spirit of promoting community and more to protect their property values and fight for their own needs.

Similarly, in his book *The Homevoter Hypothesis,* William Fischel argues that homeowners participate actively in local politics because they understand that things like school quality, crime, and vacancies all affect home values.[39] Likewise, Robert Chaskin and Mark Joseph, in their book about a mixed-income development in Chicago, find that homeowners attempt to reduce the visual presence of subsidized renters and enforce practices that they believe will increase property values.[40]

For most Americans, the majority of their wealth resides in their home.[41] Yet for black Americans, homeownership is not the wealth building machine that it is for whites. And for homeowners in neighborhoods like Park Heights, the situation is even more pressured. Since home values have bottomed out in this neighborhood, residents have few options to sell without losing a lifetime's investment. Even though homeowners in Park Heights are unlikely to actually raise their property values by policing their new neighbors, they still feel they must stand guard over what little they have left. This singular goal of protecting one's property can often come at the expense of inclusive neighboring behavior.[42] In this way, homeownership and the desire to protect one's property values reinforces symbolic boundaries between homeowners and renters, making it harder for voucher holders to integrate into the community.

Bob has lived in a transitional zone since the eighties. He knows many of his neighbors because he does landscaping in the neighborhood for extra money, and he is able to point to many homes on the block and identify who lives there and what they do: "My neighbor on my left here has been there before I moved here and the people on the other side of them, they were here before we moved here, and they have been the greatest. Neighbors on the right house has changed over a couple times but they are good neighbors. I know just about everybody in the block."

Bob's block has become more transitional in recent years; many of the original homeowners have passed away or moved to other places, and many of the new owners have bought these houses to rent them out. The way Bob sees it:

> The first thing they do is they try to sell them for half price when they're vacant at auction. Then when eventually they can't get that money for them, nobody can afford to buy them then they decide to try to rent them out. And usually they rent them out to a family that has a bunch of children that are not disciplined, a little rowdy, you know.

The renters don't hire Bob to do landscaping the way many of the homeowners did, and so he does not know them as well. He feels that with the influx of new renters, there have been significant changes in the neighborhood. "It's not as quiet here anymore. Now you have to really be careful about locking your doors and everything or locking your gate, which you should never have to do. Because I mean the kids come right in your private property and just destroy."

Bob showed me how his meticulously planted flowers beds had been torn up and stomped on, strewn with cigarette butts and beer cans from the night before. He said that the kids come through the gate from the back alley and run between the houses to the front street, knocking down whatever is in their path, with no regard for his property. He sees these families as different from the ones who used to live in the neighborhood, and blames the parents: "It's mostly the parents' faults because the parents don't watch them. Some of the parents may work. Okay fine, but they not disciplining their kids, they be running up and down the street all hours of the night."

Bob claims he can tell if a family has a voucher. "It's not like they look shabby or anything like that," he says. He believes he can tell by the way the children behave: "The [parents] don't discipline their children. They're never around, they always elsewhere. The kids are raising themselves and you can sense it, you can tell by the respect that those children have for other people, elderly people, you know."

It's not entirely clear that Bob *can* tell, though. His criteria for recognizing a voucher family describe many different families in the area. The house Bob pointed out to me across the street as occupied by voucher holders turned out not to be, and his neighbors a few doors down with whom he said he got on very well, in fact do have a voucher. While Bob has strong feelings about voucher holders and their role in the demise of the neighborhood, he doesn't seem to actually know any.[43]

It became apparent that the less contact a homeowner had with voucher holders, the more likely they were to stigmatize them.[44] The Chaskin and Joseph study corroborates the finding that homeowners frequently espouse stereotypical views of their neighbors who receive housing assistance.[45] Furthermore, their case suggests that homeowners assume anyone displaying "noisy" or "troublesome" behavior is a subsidized renter.[46] In this way, voucher status—or the perception of it—becomes a symbolic boundary that serves as a moral distinction. These distinctions operate to exclude voucher holders and reify inequality in the neighborhood.[47]

NOT IN MY COMMUNITY

One of the key sites at which social capital can be spread is through social organizations. Park Heights has an active set of neighborhood organizations. As Mario Small has argued, organizations shape social capital. Everyday routines, like where you drop your kids off for daycare, the bus you take to work, the line you wait in at the grocery store to buy milk and eggs, have formal and informal rules that govern them. They shape who you know, how you build relationships with them (or don't), and what resources or information you may share with each other.[48] On the one hand, Park Heights features the kinds of community organizations that should allow residents to cross social boundaries; on the other, the resources that neighborhood institutions provide vary substantially, depending on what social group you are part of.

Despite the pervasive assumption that poor segregated neighborhoods lack social organizations, scholars have repeatedly shown that this is not necessarily the case.[49] While Park Heights has lost many businesses and organizations in the years following white flight, the neighborhood today has over twenty-seven community and social service organizations meant to serve its residents and promote well-being in the neighborhood.[50] Many of them have popped up in recent years, while others have been around for a long time. The three health clinics, a family support center, a Head Start program, and twelve churches address a multitude of community needs. Other organizations, such as three drug rehabilitation centers and four halfway homes for people exiting prison, serve many local residents, but are also reviled by longtime homeowners who fear they attract unwanted newcomers to the neighborhood. The Delphi Center, a new senior center built in 2009, serves as a gathering place for the neighborhood's older residents and also houses monthly community meetings.

Patty explains that though she remembers the neighborhood going through some rough patches, she has seen things improving in recent years. She and her neighbor watched from her back porch as the Delphi Center was built.

> You just have to learn how to adjust to different things. Like before the Delphi building was built, we would always say "Lord, I hope they put something on that corner down there." Because the young people used to be around it. They just hung around that corner. We prayed about it. We said "Lord, just send something that they can put something on that block now. That will keep the kids from down that way and it will be something that we could be involved in." I sat in my back porch right back there. I looked down that street and I saw them building [the Delphi] from the ground to the roof. . . . Everyday I'd sit on my back porch and I would watch it.

Now, Patty goes to the Delphi Center twice a week, on Mondays and Wednesdays. She rides the stationary bike to stay fit, and she also takes a Zumba class. For many senior residents of Park Heights, many of whom are homeowners, the senior center represents a central location around which social life is organized. Another longtime resident, Arnold, comes every single day to the center to play pool with his friends. They have joined the Baltimore Senior League, a citywide billiards league for seniors that competes in tournaments all over Baltimore.

The Delphi Center hosts monthly community meetings, which I attended regularly. Fifty to one hundred people usually attend, most of them homeowners and older residents of the neighborhood. Before each meeting, the agenda is set by board members. The community organization has a number of committees—including the Health Committee, the Public Safety Committee, the Sanitation Committee, the Home Energy Committee, the Seniors Committee, and the Youth Committee—and each month a representative from each committee presents on current issues.[51] I spoke to attendees each week before and after the meeting, getting to know many of them and asking them to participate in my research.

In April, Sue, a forty-five-year-old African American resident of Oakland Terrace, told me that she wanted to go with me to one of the community meetings. She had not been aware that such a meeting existed in Park Heights, but when I mentioned it to her, she was very excited. Sue had been looking for a way to get more involved in the community, and the meeting seemed like a perfect opportunity.

When we walked into the Delphi Center, Sue looked around, taking in the scene. We took two seats near the back, and she leaned in and whispered in my ear, "These here are middle-class folk. They stick to themselves." Sue looked nervous and fidgeted, adjusting her shirt and checking her make-up in a small mirror from her bag. Just before the meeting started, she opened her phone and made a quick call to her sixteen-year-old daughter: "Hi baby, do me a favor? Can you call me right back? I won't answer, I just wanna make sure the sound is off." It was. In this crowd of "middle-class folk," Sue wanted to make sure that she was fitting in and following the rules. In our first interview, Sue had told me that she thinks of herself as different than many of her neighbors in Oakland Terrace because she is from a "middle-class" background, grew up in a stable two-parent family, and attended two years of college. But it was clear during and after the meeting that Sue did not quite feel at home here either. As the meeting got going, she settled into her seat.

One issue in particular stirred up strong feelings amongst the attendees that day. A representative from the Maryland House of Delegates stood up to discuss a recently proposed bill that would limit the number of establishments selling alcohol in Baltimore City. Southern Park Heights has more liquor stores in a mile radius than any other place in the state, the delegate explained. With some disappointment, she announced the news that a bill to limit the sale of alcohol in the neighborhood had failed in committee, despite widespread support.[52] "Less Liquor, Less Crime" was the supporters' slogan. The delegate lamented the opposition from the liquor store owners. The crowd murmured mm-hmms and yeses in agreement.

The delegate was convinced enough of why the bill had failed that she filed a letter to the committee chair and provided everyone in the crowd with a copy, which she read out loud: "It boggles my mind," she said, that a bill with strong support from the Baltimore City delegation, police officers, and local residents would be voted down in committee. Furthermore, she blamed the Korean liquor store owners, saying that a number of businesses in the area were not in support of the bill, and that they were all owned by Korean families. "Korean merchants came back and played the 'race card,' arguing that limiting the sale of alcohol was discriminatory and would hurt their businesses and livelihood."[53] The delegate went on to accuse the Korean residents of Park Heights of being unfriendly: when she was canvassing houses to get support for the bill, she said, "Not once did a Korean family answer the door. The children don't socialize in the neighborhood. Tell me if I'm wrong?" Again, the crowd murmured mm-hmms.

Jennifer Lee, studying merchant-customer relationships, argues that while most conflict between Korean store owners and residents of predominantly black neighborhoods is exaggerated by stereotypes, there are isolated moments when real conflict erupts.[54] In particular, she argues that under conditions of inequality, small events can trigger racially motivated anger and actions. In this incident in Park Heights, some residents hold Korean store owners to be responsible for the moral future of the neighborhood—in much the same way they hold voucher holders to be responsible for neighborhood changes at other moments. In both cases, racial, ethnic, class, and cultural difference all of a sudden become salient, and this stigma and prejudice get in the way of residents working together to solve community problems.

After the meeting, Sue and I walked back to my car through the dark parking lot. It was just a short walk back to Oakland Terrace, but I offered to drive her since it was late. When we got in the car, I asked her what she thought of it all. She told me: "Since I come from a middle-class background, I had some of the same concerns as them, because I want things for my kids and stuff like that." Sue looked pensive. "But also, on the other," she continued, "they all have they houses." Sue meant that most of the people at the meeting owned their own homes. "I felt a little alienated about that," she said.

These "community" meetings are in fact only attended by a very particular segment of the community. Not only were they older. Not only where they largely homeowners. They were homeowners who lived in homeowner havens and transitional areas. Oakland Terrace, where Sue lives, is only two blocks from the Delphi House, if you take the split, a pathway through the woods leading to Forest Avenue. But few home-owners even know that the complex exists. And fewer renters know about the community meeting. Thus, although low- and middle-class blacks live in close proximity, this does not lead to the creation of bridging social capital.

Although Sue is an unassisted renter in Oakland Terrace, she grew up in a family with a similar class background as many of the meeting attendees. Yet she felt alienated at the meeting because she was one of the few renters, and her concerns and needs were different from those of the residents at the meeting. For example, in one of the previous meetings I attended, the "energy" committee passed out weathering strips and held a mini-workshop on how to make your home more energy efficient. Sue doesn't own a house, so she doesn't need to think about issues like weatherizing it—in Oakland Terrace, you are not allowed to make modifications to your unit, even to save money on your electric bill. None of the meetings discussed energy programs for residents who don't own their home. None of the meetings ever talked about some of the topics that might have been more relevant to Sue, such as food stamps, public transportation, or child care.

In another meeting we spent nearly forty minutes discussing the re-development of the Park Circle intersection, and how to make it more efficient for cars, while also creating an attractive new statue in the middle (one older resident was worried that a statue might distract drivers enough to cause accidents). Sue doesn't own a car, so she is not too concerned with the traffic patterns at Park Circle. The community meeting was missing a chance to bring renters in by focusing primarily on issues that affect homeowners and by raising contentious issues such as the alcohol sale bill from only one point of view. The delegate had reported that residents in Park Heights were in unanimous support of the bill limiting the sale of alcohol. While I wasn't sure that was true for the whole neighborhood, it certainly seemed to be largely the case in that room.

I asked Sue what she thought about the liquor store bill. She found the idea that it would be desirable to close liquor stores in the neighbor-hood patently absurd. Sue drinks often. She makes her daily trip through the split to the liquor store on the other side, usually returning with a large paper bag filled with orders of beer and liquor that her neighbors request her to bring back for them. Sue told me that she has struggled with an addiction for most of her life, but closing down the liquor stores isn't going to change that. There are, of course, well-documented links between poverty, housing instability, and alcoholism, but it is also the case that middle-class residents with cars are in a better position to dis-guise their drinking than their low-income neighbors.[55] Whereas the homeowners at the meeting (and, apparently the delegate) see alcohol as a sign of disorder to be eliminated, Sue and her friends see it as part of their daily life.

The "community" meeting was only geared toward a certain seg-ment of the community.[56] It's an example of *bonding* social capital, where people with things in common—in this case homeowners—can share information and skills and gain access to resources such as the energy grant. But the community meeting fails to build bridges across groups—even though it could do so in theory—because its agenda is constructed by a single group of people, that is, homeowners. Without the involvement of residents from voucher enclaves, their concerns are not likely to be addressed, and it's not clear how they might get involved in the first place.

Park Heights' residents have a wide array of needs, but its neighborhood institutions often serve only one group at a time, and there are very few opportunities for social mixing through formal community organization. The community meeting is not the only neighborhood institution that serves just one segment of the population. Head Start is for children of families who can't afford preschool. The Jai Medical Center is a health care clinic for those who don't have the money or transportation to go down the road to the fancier Sinai Hospital. Of the three health clinics, one is specifically for seniors, and one is targeted toward a low-income population, accepting patients with no health insurance. "I Can, We Can," is a low-cost alcohol and drug rehabilitation and counseling center. Other rehab centers also cater to lower-income residents, and though many stay in the area after completing treatment, they are not welcomed by local residents. Despite a density of community organizations in Park Heights, they are often better suited to serve very specific populations with varying needs, rather than bringing residents of different backgrounds together. In this way, community organizations often fail to help newcomers access the social capital that exists in the neighborhood.

BRIDGING BEHAVIOR AND SOCIAL BROKERS

In contrast to those who stigmatize and exclude voucher holders, there are a few longtime residents who know voucher recipients in the neighborhood well. Not surprisingly, this social familiarity and contact can go a long way toward destigmatizing voucher holders and breaking down the boundary between owners and renters. For example, Barbie, whom we met in chapter 2, grew up in Park Heights and now lives in her childhood home on a small street in a transitional area. She goes out of her way to befriend and welcome voucher holders.

Barbie has had a circuitous housing trajectory: she grew up in a homeowning family, then briefly owned her own home and lost it, and even had a voucher before losing that. Beyond the fact that she can connect and empathize with voucher holders based on her own experience, she is also deeply invested in the local community. Barbie firmly believes that getting to know one's neighbors is good for community life. She enacts this every day in the work that she does as a home care worker—both formally and informally.

Barbie's activities in the neighborhood bring people together. One of her passions is litter and recycling. She and her father used to take walks down the street to pick up stray bits of trash and litter. Now that her father is gone, she and her boyfriend Roman continue the tradition.

> Me and Roman and we start on the other side of the street and bag up trash. I try to recycle too. I got Miss June recycling. I got the guy on the corner recycling. The girl next door, she had been doing it when she moved there. She asked me about the recycling days and I told her. I got Andrea recycling across the street. I been trying to get them all to recycle. We have to get our own bins. When they guys don't come to collect it, I call. . . . I call for everything.

The City of Baltimore does not require residents to recycle, but Barbie encourages her neighbors to participate in the recycling program.[57] She provides them with bins that the city does not supply,[58] and teaches them how and when to use them.

But Barbie's campaign is not just about trash and recycling. She sees trash collection as an opportunity to connect with her neighbors, "get to know 'em, you know?" and to promote neighborly behavior. Just as dealing with trash can be a divisive moment in other parts of the neighborhood, here it is an opportunity for neighbors to come together. As she picks up trash in the neighborhood, Barbie develops the kinds of social ties—with renters like herself, homeowners nearby, as well as with newer voucher holders—that promote the sharing of social capital.

Like Barbie, there is another community member who manages to cross social boundaries in the neighborhood and promote the transmission of

FIGURE 14: "No Trash."

social resources across different groups in the neighborhood. I learned about him early on in my fieldwork, when I had noticed a group of haphazard and dilapidated structures protruding from the wooded area behind Oakland Terrace. They looked out of place on a city street. One afternoon I asked Sue, "What are those buildings out behind the Terrace?"

She looked incredulous that I was not familiar with this neighborhood institution: "Oh, that's the Catman's place. Wait, you haven't met Bill yet?" It sounded like a joke.

"The Cat Man?" I asked, with a quizzical smile. "Yeah!" Sue answered, sighing. "You know, the one who feeds the cats? He's been here for years, he knows everyone around this way. Let's go find him."

We exited Oakland Terrace through the back and walked through the split. There, we came upon a now-vacant home that Bill (aka "The Catman") used to live in. From the front it looked like a typical narrow, double-window, two-story row house. Plywood covered the windows and doors. Sue told me that even though Bill doesn't live there anymore, the cats remember him, and they still swarm around the house and wait for him show up to feed them each day, which he does faithfully.

To my surprise, when Bill came around, he recognized me: "Yeah, I seen you around here last week talking to Ms. Edie. I was wondering when you'd come find me," he said with a smile.

I sat with Bill on his old porch for the next few hours, while the cats meandered around us and meowed for our attention. Bill explained to me that every day he walks a three-mile stretch from South Baltimore to Park Heights. Along the way, he pushes a grocery cart stocked with several large bags of cat food—most of them donated by a local animal shelter and by residents who have come to know him well over the years he has been walking his daily trek. He walks from Smallwood, past Mondawmin, though Reisterstown Road and up Park Heights Avenue. Along the way, he feeds all the stray cats he can find.

When Bill first began defining his route, he found more and more hungry cats every day. "I kept adding until now I have a total of about thirty stops with approximately 200 cats. I feed cats all along the way. I'm able to find homes for them and with the help of others, I've been taking them to the doctor to get them fixed." Bill knows all the cats individually and has names for many of them.

When our legs got cramped from sitting on the rough wooden planks of the porch, Bill showed me the series of sheds attached to the back of the house. Years ago, with the help of friends and neighbors, he had built a kennel to house stray dogs, and another shelter for the cats. "It was a progression, adding on, adding on, and adding on to it until it reached this size."

When Bill lived here, he liked to sleep out back with the dogs to be close to the outdoors. There was no heat in the shed, but "I would try to keep warm and I tried to improvise—and not depend too much on what's not readily available. It might not conform with the building codes, but it's just something I did."

In addition to the animals, Bill took in people as well. He explained it to me this way: "You heard about the old white lady who feeds 100 cats? I'm the old black man who feeds cats and dogs and rescues human beings." Back when he lived in the house in Park Heights, he offered his spare room to people he found on the street.

FIGURE 15: Bill's shack.

One day I saw this boy and this girl that were in the freezing cold. They were covered up under one blanket so I stopped and I said, "Do you guys have a place to go?" They said, "No." I said, "Come on." I invited them into the house, I gave them a place to stay. At the time I was working at a convenience store, and every day I'd give them $10, and I told them the only one thing I ask is please don't bring any drugs in the house.

Bill made a sign and hung it above his front door that reads "NO DRUGS," spelled from cut-out letters of varying sizes—the kind of lettering you might buy from the hardware store to spell out a name on the side of a mailbox. The sign still hangs there today. But, "Lo and behold," he said, "one day, I went home on lunch break, the house got raided by the police—I was locked up. The two of them were locked up too."

The police were convinced that the drugs his houseguests had brought in belonged to Bill because the house was in his name. "But eventually they realized in the end that I didn't have anything to do with it. . . . When I came out [of jail], everything I had of value was stolen and taken. My place was ransacked and I had to start all over again." But this did not make Bill want to stop helping people, "Because I remember the days when I didn't have anything and I would hope for someone to open their doors for me."

Bill says his passion for looking after homeless people and animals stems from his experience as a child, abandoned first by his biological parents at nine months, and then by his adoptive parents at fourteen years old: "It was just like—they left me like an old pair of shoes and you tossed it out and you get a new pair," he told me. From fourteen to seventeen Bill lived on the street with the cats and dogs, "eating out of a garbage can and sleeping wherever I could find." Now Bill says he is "on the other side of the fence. . . . I've had zero and I've had plenty. . . . I've been to places people would only dream of . . . and I've also been in the gutter. I've come a full circle with my life and I think that it's prepared me for the type of person that I am today." These experiences enable him to see how renters, and especially voucher holders, are stigmatized and in many ways excluded from neighborhood life, and he seeks to remedy this however he can.

Bill's work extends far beyond feeding and rescuing cats. He serves as a bridge in the neighborhood. He has done all sorts of odd jobs for people including providing a dog walking service, a pet care and stray animal placement program, lawn work, home repairs, and a laundry business.

Like others, Bill has noticed more and more voucher holders in the area. He welcomes them. "People gotta live somewhere," he remarked, "Why not here?" He often had voucher holders who did not have a washer and dryer in their units patronize the laundry business he used to run.[59] "I would go to people's house and pick up their dirty clothes and wash it and hang on the line or put some to dry." Bill would accept whatever people offered for this service, and was happy as long as he could afford to buy food for the cats. He made between $500 and $700 a week from his business. While it may seem costly for poor tenants to pay for a laundry service, for the renters who don't have in-unit washers and dryers, the local laundromat is even more expensive. Plus, Bill would do pickup and delivery with his donated electric cart that he also used to shuttle around the cat food: "I had one woman with four kids, so she loved it." And he would offer lower rates when someone needed it: "I don't have a fixed fee, so whatever's comfortable with the person. We work it out."

In his daily treks, Bill has befriended residents throughout Park Heights and also across the entire west side of Baltimore. Beyond the services he provides directly, Bill routinely connects people to others that he knows for jobs that they may offer or desire. It started with placing dogs and cats who needed homes. Then, residents from across the neighborhood began coming to Bill for help finding someone to mow the lawn, shovel the snow, or clean the gutters. When he didn't have time to do it himself, he would refer someone he knew who had mentioned they were looking for work.

In this way, Bill is a bridge, linking people in different parts of the neighborhood in various ways. Beyond the individuals he helps, Bill's walks and his work in the neighborhood promote an important social function: connecting people throughout the neighborhood, helping them through times of need. "Some of the people I've helped, they wanted to own their own houses or be gainfully employed; I helped them. I told them my story and I spent time with them, and resources, and helped them so they can get on their feet." The help Bill provides isn't just a one-time transaction: the role he plays connecting people with jobs and resources in the neighborhood can be thought of as a social capital transfer. In many ways though, Bill is an exception.

"NOT IN FRONT OF MY HOUSE"

Who gets to exercise social control, and where, varies across the neighborhood. I saw this play out one afternoon in August, when I sat with Bob on his covered front porch to catch some breeze and escape the late-summer sun. We had exhausted topics of conversation for the day and were sitting quietly when two young neighborhood men walking down the street paused in front of the gate. They did not appear to see us sitting there as we were camouflaged in the shade of the house. A third man approached—this one appeared to be in his late teens—and the three began talking quietly, negotiating. Bob's voice rang out suddenly next to me, in a tone I had never heard from him before—sharp and authoritative, but avuncular, not hostile: "Hey. Not in front of my house, young man," he directed at the tallest of the youth. He looked up suddenly, a bit startled to see us there, nodded his head in Bob's direction in a gesture of understanding, and they made their way down the block.

Bob tilted his head toward me as he watched them walk away and said, "They listen because most of them I have known basically ever since they was children." Longtime homeowners who live in stable areas are able to exercise this sort of informal social control with neighborhood youth. They function much like the important figures that sociologist Elijah Anderson wrote about: the "old head" was a man of "stable means who believed in hard work, family life and the church. His acknowledged role was to teach, support, encourage and, in effect, socialize young men to meet their responsibilities regarding work, family life, the law and common decency."[60] The young people that Bob is able to relate to in this way are embedded in the same social networks as the older residents, and mechanisms of behavior regulation have developed over a long period of time.

While Anderson suggests that these old heads are disappearing from neighborhoods,[61] I still found some. However, they were not able to exercise their authority equally in all areas and with all types of residents. Bob made it clear that these three young men had listened to him because he has known them since they were in diapers, he knows where they live, and is friendly with their parents. But this wouldn't be true for some of the newcomers, who don't know him and aren't embedded in his social network, in part because he excludes them. Of course, many of the newcomers are not voucher holders; however, in Bob's mind they are conflated. In this way, voucher holders are less likely to benefit from the old heads in Park Heights.

Many older residents in the neighborhood live in single-family homes with covered front porches, where, like Bob, they often sit to escape the stifling heat of their un-air-conditioned homes. This provides much needed "eyes on the street," monitoring activity and serving as both an informal mechanism of social control, as well as a conduit for alerting the formal law enforcement of unusual behavior such as cars left sitting on the street or strangers lurking near the playground. Mr. Green takes it upon himself to call the police if he sees anyone suspicious or unknown in the neighborhood. "That's my job, 'cause especially in the summertime, I sit on the porch in my rocking chair . . . and if I see somebody here that shouldn't be here, [or] if I see a car sitting here for two days, I call 911 and they check it out. Every time I've called so far, [the car] has been stolen." Because they have been around longer, homeowners are much more likely to develop relationships and long-term strategies with the police.

Barbie says she does her best to make the neighborhood a better place to live. One day, she happened to glance out her window when she saw two men loading toilets, sinks, and copper piping into a truck in front of the old house where Mrs. Cohen used to live. She called the police as usual, but it took them two hours to arrive, which was not before the house had been stripped of all its copper piping and any other items of value. She worries that when homes are stripped in this way, they remain vacant for longer, attracting rats and drug dealers, and ultimately depressing the value of other homes in the neighborhood.

Barbie commonly calls the city's hotline for other matters as well, for example to ask them to board up empty homes on her street to prevent further stripping.

> I call the city, 311. They connect you to the city office and you just make your report there. They give you a claim number and tell you you got fifteen days or thirty days for them to come out. But when they don't come, I keep calling them. I got my name down there a hundred times because I call for everything. I call when that play-ground over there get dirty.

The city workers and police are not always responsive, but Barbie has a special method to get their attention, she "use[s] several names, different addresses of empty houses. I didn't want to be the same person calling. I wasn't afraid, but thought it would be more effective to be someone else." Also, she tells her neighbors "to call, call, call." Barbie thinks that calling really does make a difference, she hears fewer gunshots than she used to:

It's been I guess about five years now. They don't even shoot on New Year's no more. When they used to shoot on New Year's, I say, "get on the floor." I say, "Everybody get down." . . . You know, shoot up in the air. But they don't even do that anymore. I'm glad they don't, 'cause that used to scare me. But other than that, everything sort of calm in our neighborhood. The drug dealers, I think I done chased them away. . . . I called the police on them. They used to hang in front of my door. . . . You know, at the gate, you know, and I started calling and they would come.

While many longtime residents report that they call the police commonly for this type of behavior regulation and order maintenance, newcomers are often reticent about engaging with the police. This is especially so when it comes to issues that do not directly affect them. Raven would rather rely on her older neighbors who have lived there for a long time; "I love my old lady neighbors," she told me. "They always call." She only considers calling the cops when her family is in danger, but not for things like drug dealing that are not directly hurting her, since reporting them could create problems for her. Newcomers in the neighborhood, who are less likely to know the local police personally, risk more by calling the cops. This reticence is especially relevant for voucher holders, whose subsidy could be jeopardized if they are thought to be involved with drug activity.

As uncomfortable as it may be for newcomers to engage with agents of formal social control, such as the police, attempting to enact informal social control is also difficult—it just doesn't work as well for new residents of the neighborhood. When Bill first rented a house in the neighborhood, when no one knew him yet as "Catman" and he was just "Bill," he asked the teenagers who liked to sell drugs in front of his house to move on down the street. He did not have much luck:

You can ask them to leave. I've asked them to leave but, me asking them is like I'm telling them to stay, because they're not going to pay me no mind. They feel that they were selling drugs before I came here. One day, I had this man put up a fence for me, fence around the property. They told me, "Why are you putting a fence up? That's not going to stop me. I'm going to do what I want to do anyway."

As Bill lived in the neighborhood longer and got to know residents better, things changed. Now, he knows all the dealers, and they update him on important goings-on in the neighborhood.

There is a hierarchy of respect between longtime residents and the dealers, which helps to regulate behavior. But newcomers have a very hard time asserting informal social control—not because they don't have a "stake" in the neighborhood through property ownership, but because they simply have not been around long enough to have earned the authority and respect. The informal controls wielded by the longtime residents seem to work much better on the children of homeowners than on recently arrived children of renters, and it's largely for the same reasons: the social networks of the longtime residents are not as intertwined with those of the incoming renters. Newly arrived children have not been there long enough to know who is who in the neighborhood and form relationships with them, and so they are less likely to exhibit context-appropriate forms of respect.

This unwritten expectation of respect and protection, especially among longtime residents, was never more apparent than after a rape occurred in the neighborhood, several months before I moved in. The event was extensively covered in local news, and people were still talking about it months later when I arrived. The victim was a young mother of four who had grown up in the neighborhood and whose parents had been homeowners. She had recently moved back, renting an apartment near her childhood home. Thus, she was well connected to her neighbors and known in the community. Neighborhood residents saw the crime as a transgression of a set of unwritten rules because this woman minded her own business and stayed away from trouble. Raven explained:

> She a single mother, she have a daughter, she got three sons, she stayed to herself. . . . Even in the hood certain things is recognized and certain people are off limits. Even if you a bad guy—like, I know bad guys—and bad guys be like, "No, I don't do this, but I *will* do this." . . . In the hood, you hurt a child, or somebody's mom, you're wrong. I can say that.

Longtime residents feared that with the influx of vouchers, the tacit but well understood code that Raven speaks of would be broken more and more often. While there was a consensus among neighborhood residents that the perpetrators were two men involved in the local drug trade, this may or may not have been communicated to the police, and the men were not arrested. Raven explained that there are consequences for breaking the code and involving, in her words, "decent folk" in a violent incident: a "public justice" was meted out. She told me that the perpetrators "had the shit kicked out of them" by a group of neighborhood men who were longtime residents.

There weren't many incidents of vigilante justice during my time in the neighborhood, but when formal justice fails to operate, at least some of the time Park Heights' informal mechanisms spring into gear. But since these informal mechanisms are typically wielded by the longtime residents, their biases—especially against newcomers and voucher holders—color their actions. Since voucher holders are inappropriately blamed for a whole range of problems in the neighborhood, informal solutions to neighborhood problems are often enacted at their expense.

SURVEILLANCE AND FORMAL
SOCIAL CONTROL

For those who live outside areas where mechanisms of longstanding informal social control thrive, residents have to lean on means of formal social control. In attempt to manage blocks that have high crime, the city of Baltimore installed surveillance cameras on certain street corners throughout the city. Residents refer to the cameras as the "blue lights" because there is a blue flashing light attached to each camera to indicate to residents that they are being filmed, with the presumption that this will deter crime.[62] Residents who lived near cameras tended to take notice of what happened. Some reported that the installation of the camera really did seem to deter criminal activity such as drug sales in the near vicinity. But others noted that the installation just pushed the activity to outside the camera's range. And some residents did not notice any change at all: a number of residents told me they noticed drug sales directly underneath a blue light camera, with no immediate response from law enforcement.

Many residents think that the whole campaign is a sham, and wondered if perhaps there are no cameras at all, just blue flashing lights to make people think they are being watched.[63] A camera was put in few years ago on the corner near Bob's house when residents on his block requested one: "After they put the camera up there, the activity moved somewhere else, went to the playground back there." But after a short time it came back. "I seen drug dealing and all, I seen fights, I seen people get stabbed out there. . . . I have seen things go on out here right underneath the camera and no police comes or anything. . . . I'm not even sure they have film in there . . . you just wonder."

Not only do the cameras fail to deter crime, some residents told me they paradoxically serve as an indicator that the block is a dangerous one. When I asked Michelle what her block was like, she used the presence of the "blue lights" to give me a metric for how dangerous it was. "Right here in this area, it had got really bad. . . . They had the [blue] lights at the top [end] of our block. Because about four summers ago, people was getting choked off around here left and right. . . . You know, it's scary. You see the lights flashing. You wondering what in the world happened." Ironically, then, the cameras themselves have come to stigmatize certain areas as dangerous rather than signal safety. Residents avoid hanging out on corners with blue flashing lights, making these spaces empty and rendering them even better spots for illicit activity.

Video surveillance plays a different role for those who reside in voucher enclave areas. In Oakland Terrace, the closed-circuit cameras transmit and record a live feed into the rental office where Jill, the building manager, sits six days a week. I spent many hours with her in the office, where video feeds were displayed on a giant TV on one of the walls of the office. Residents would filter in and out of the office all day; they enjoyed peering over the desk to watch the activity on the screen and would comment on who was doing what, and where. It was commonly known among residents that these cameras existed and were monitored not only by Jill, but by other residents who might be in the office taking a peek at the screens, or staffing the desk for her while she was out dealing with a tenant on the grounds.

One afternoon I was sitting with Jill chatting as residents drifted in and out to pay rent, make a maintenance request, or just to chat. Alex, the property owner, stopped by and we began talking about crime in the complex. "Oh, you have to see this," he told me, like a kid excited for show-and-tell. "Jill, can you pull up Leon and what's his name—you know, that fight out in the courtyard."

Jill clicked through the menu and the video popped up on the wide screen. Alex, Jill, and the resident sitting with us grew quiet. We watched the screen as two men, visibly inebriated and teetering on unsteady feet, stood in the courtyard outside and swung wild punches in the air toward each other, mostly missing. A small crowd of residents was standing on the sidelines, laughing and cheering at times. No one stepped in to stop the fight. The two men fighting were so drunk they seemed to be moving in slow motion. Jill remarked: "Just keep watching the movement of the bodies . . . the science of the knock-out," she sighed. At the end, one of the residents finally landed a punch. It was one of those disturbing scenes you couldn't seem to take your eyes off of. It took a minute for what we were doing to sink in: we were watching saved video surveillance of a fight between two drunk Terrace residents, as if it were a spectator sport.

Later, I asked Jill, "What do you do if you see a fight like that *live* on camera?" It seemed to me that the whole point of these cameras was to intervene in such incidents, not *watch* them.

Jill explained that she hadn't been in the office at the time, and neither had anyone else. "Plus, they was so drunk they wasn't going to hurt much." Jill has called the cops before, but usually she tries to go out and intervene herself, since the residents know and trust her.

While the cameras didn't deter a fight in that instance, they do seem to deter open-air drug selling. Residents who have lived in Oakland Terrace for a long time report that the cameras have completely changed the housing complex, curbing the violence, crime, and drug activity.

In the renter complexes that make up voucher enclaves like Oakland Terrace, upkeep is centralized, and tenants are not responsible for trash maintenance and keeping common spaces orderly. The landlord and property manager take active steps to maintain safety and order, and are even heavy handed at times in the way they get involved in regulating everyday life in the community.

On Mother's Day, Alex heard music blasting from the inner courtyard. Two speakers were delicately balanced in the second-story windowsill of Tony's apartment, and music drifted through the unscreened windows, the sound ricocheting across the small courtyard. Sue and her friend Ronette were sitting at the picnic table with what was left of a six pack of Natty Bo between them, practically shouting to each other over the music in order to have a conversation. Paul was walking around offering roses to all the women, "For the mothers!" he yelled. "Those flowers ain't worth no $3 each," Sue shot back with some repugnance in her voice. Alex heard the ruckus from his office and sighed. He made the walk around the corner and up the two flights to Tony's apartment.

Alex was wary after the last time he paid Antoine ("Tony") a visit. Tony had called Jill, the property manager, to say he needed help. Jill was usually the one to deal with these sorts of problems, but she was out on another house call so Alex went himself. He was happy to go, since he liked to take care of his tenants. When Alex got there, he immediately saw the problem—Tony had cut himself shaving with his razor and there was blood everywhere. "Tony has full-blown AIDS," Alex explained. He was scared, he said, but he helped Tony find a bandage and clean up. "We know that if it stays out there the virus is not going to live on the razor for too long, but it will be there. You know timing is everything. It could be one of my maintenance guys' lives. It's scary." Tony also has some intellectual disabilities and he calls the office often for helping doing different tasks. "It's hard when they're not very brilliant," Alex remarked about his tenants more generally. He sees his role as one of a father figure and caretaker—he helps when he can to keep peace and order in the complex.[64]

When Alex entered the apartment on Mother's Day, everything was in order, except of course for the deafening music blasting out the window. Alex told Tony to shut it down. "But it's Mother's Day, and my mother passed," Tony pleaded to keep the music going. Alex was out of patience. "Listen that music ain't gonna bring her back to life. You're disturbing other people. Next time you do that you are out of here." He had warned Tony before that if he gets kicked out, he could lose his voucher. Alex knew Tony would probably turn it back up in a few minutes, but showing the other tenants he had made the effort was worth something.

It's not just noise that is vigilantly policed in voucher complexes. When it comes to regulating the sale of drugs, common spaces in voucher enclaves are policed through formal surveillance methods including security guards and cameras, methods that don't really exist in homeowner havens, where homeowners regulate the space informally. In voucher enclaves, residents report that formal surveillance techniques work well: everyone I spoke with in Oakland Terrace said they rarely, if ever, saw drug deals in the shared outdoor space of the complex. Last year the cameras caught one of the maintenance men being robbed after he got paid on a Friday—the cameras captured it and the police were able to use the tape to catch the perpetrator.

But what happens behind closed doors, and in the unmonitored stairwells of the buildings, is another story. Alex explained that a few years back there was a rape accusation. "A girl that was supposedly raped. We caught it on camera, where, she kissed a guy goodbye after he 'raped' her. Nah, she didn't get raped. I'm just saying." In these instances, the role of the camera is more limited, and what the camera captures (or doesn't) is sometimes disputed. What's more, due to the overly formalized social control in voucher enclaves, residents engage in *less* informal social regulatory behavior and have less of a sense of ownership over the space.[65]

THE PARADOX OF FORMAL CONTROL

Social control across different neighborhood spaces is also affected by the role of police. While police are meant to promote social control, they can paradoxically impede more informal manifestations of social organization.[66] They operate in this manner especially in transitional areas where homeowners live alongside voucher holders, as well as in voucher enclaves. What happened to Bill is a good illustration of how this can work. When Bill lived in the neighborhood, he served an important function, connecting people to goods, services, and jobs, and serving as a social capital bridge between newcomers and old timers. But when Bill's house was raided a second time, this all changed. "They didn't find any drugs," he told me, but they ransacked the house in their search. "The police had torn up the house so bad, they tore the walls down, even my doghouse." They busted into the dog shelter—where Bill often slept with the animals—with guns in hand.

Bill had three dogs staying with him at the time, two German Shepherd mixes and one Pitbull mix. Abandoned rescues, they were gentle with him but had lived on the street for years, foraging for meals in dumpsters and fighting other street dogs for scraps. Underground dog fighting circles in cities like Baltimore mean that trained fight-dogs are frequently abandoned on the street when they are injured or no longer useful for fighting.

"After breaking down the dogs' house," Bill continued, "The police drew their guns, yelling at the dogs," provoking them. Bill was handcuffed, so he couldn't do anything to restrain the dogs. He was terrified—he knew they might attack the police in an effort to protect him. They were barking and scared. Bill shouted to the dog he was most afraid might lash out in his defense: "Little Albert, sit down, don't move." Bill explained to me, "I never spoke to the dogs in dog language before. That was the first time. And the dog obeyed my command." The dog locked eyes with Bill and growled through his teeth quietly, but miraculously, he sat. The police lowered their weapons and backed out of the collapsed shack to call Animal Control: the dogs were unlicensed and Bill couldn't find their vaccination records.

When Animal Control arrived, two women in uniform hopped out of the vehicle. "They came and they put all three dogs in the paddy wagon, the dog paddy wagon." From there, Bill knew the dogs would probably go to a kill shelter. "So, I begged, I cried, I prayed and I spoke to both ladies who were driving the paddy wagon. I told them, 'Please. My dogs—they're all the family I have. You take them, you're going to take everything I have.'"

The women who worked for animal control saw scenes like this every day, so they were hardened to emotional pleas. "Life is tough," one of the women told him.

"True," Bill acknowledged, "But if I done anything wrong, I would have been locked up," pointing to the fact that the police had removed the handcuffs and let him go. "I'm begging you, please, please."

The night before the raid, Bill had watched a DVD that a friend had lent him. It was called *Eight Below*, about a man who is forced to leave his sled dogs in the frozen tundra of Antarctica to survive the winter. Bill rarely watches movies, but that night he watched the film two and half times in a row before falling asleep.

Standing in front of the Animal Control workers the next morning, looking at his dogs chained in the wagon, the film came rushing back to him. Before he knew what he was saying he was telling them all about the film. "And they said they'd seen the movie, too. I said, 'Well, I'm that man who wants to come back to get the dogs. . . . Please, I'm begging you.' She said, 'You keep talking, I'm going to cry.' Then she opened the door to the paddy wagon and told me to take the dogs out. But, if she come back the next day and find them there, she'd have to take them," she told Bill. "So, I took them to safety." Bill sought refuge at a friend's place in West Baltimore. He took a few of the cats too, but he couldn't take them all.

The cats he left behind are the ones he treks miles across the city every day to feed, many of whom sat with us that day on the porch as we talked. They were technically feral, but they acted like house cats who remembered their previous owner—swirling in between our legs, sitting on our laps, purring and meowing for food.

Not finding any drugs, the police called the building inspector. By the time he showed up, the house was in terrible condition, and he condemned it. Bill was evicted, and he no longer has a permanent residence in Park Heights, but everyone in the neighborhood still thinks of the boarded-up row house as "Catman's house," even though all that's left of his life there are the cats and the dilapidated shacks out back. He now has a few different places where he "stays" in Park Heights, but he does not have a lease of his own.

Bill thinks that part of why the raid happened the way it did was because the cops who came to his place didn't know him:

> The police in *my* community know who I am. But when the house was raided, there were about five sections of police. Not just one police department. There were about five different entities and the rest of the police—three of them didn't know who I am. And the ones who knew me didn't do anything to protect me or to share with them that "Bill doesn't have anything to do with it." So pretty much, I was on my own.

Bill wasn't sure if they were police from other districts or if they were "narcos," the cops who deal with drug-related crime in the city and are notorious for their harsher tactics. But when they raided his home, they destroyed more than just the shack. Bill lost his laundry business that had sustained his ad hoc animal shelter, as well as most of his possessions:

> The police destroyed the washing machines, the dryers. I had just bought a laptop. They busted the laptop all up. Everything of value—I had a refrigerator with icemaker, double door. They broke everything. My good clothes. Everything of value, they destroyed. Maybe they thought I was selling drugs but using the laundry as a disguise.

Bill was *not* using his laundry business as a disguise for a drug racket, but it didn't matter. His belongings trashed, his machines broken, his animals prohibited, and his trust broken, Bill moved away from the neighborhood after this incident. With his departure, the neighborhood lost a number of resources: the laundry business, which provided a much-needed service to those in the community without washers and dryers; the animal shelter, which kept stray animals off the street and found homes for them; and the landscaping business, which provided jobs as much as it did lawnmowing. In effort to establish "order" the police shattered an important neighborhood institution.[67]

The police play a particular role in transitional areas like where Bill lived, responding to the complaints of the remaining homeowners about the changes they see around them. While a longtime homeowner might have been understood and treated differently by the police, they saw Bill's rental home as a threat to the neighborhood, rather than the shelter and job hub that it was. Bill's story demonstrates how formal controls destroyed his very organic role as a broker in the neighborhood, connecting homeowners, renters, and voucher holders alike to services and resources that they needed. In this way, formal social controls operate differently for residents of different statuses in different microneighborhoods—for example, police commonly raid residents' homes in search of drugs in transitional areas, but they do so less often in homeowner havens, even those where some of the homeowners sell drugs too—in this way, police sometimes go beyond the positive social function of crime prevention they are intended to serve, and instead break down beneficial informal organization. Bill was one of the few bridges that voucher holders had to the rest of the neighborhood.

————

While previous literature has focused much attention on whether or not voucher holders move to higher-income neighborhoods, here I focus on how voucher holders are received into the neighborhood and how they access neighborhood social resources. I found that the transmission of social capital was determined by the way in which the receiving community understood voucher holders, the way social resources were used to integrate or exclude them, and the roles of social brokers and community organizations. These processes were patterned by residential status and by space in the neighborhood. In many spaces voucher holders were largely stigmatized and excluded.[68] In a few cases where residents had more contact with voucher holders, they were more sympathetic and welcoming to them. Barbie and "Catman" Bill, for example, reached across the divide and fostered strong "bridging" social capital with their neighbors of all types. But this limited bridging behavior is not enough to integrate voucher holders across the neighborhood. When residents like Bob, who didn't actually know any voucher holders personally (but claimed to know how to recognize them) reified boundaries, they built a symbolic wall around themselves, excluding and stigmatizing newcomers, and especially voucher holders.

Anderson warned that with the departure of the black middle class, poor neighborhoods are losing the once-influential "old heads" of the community who were so influential as role models and agents of social control for the behavior of young men in the neighborhood. I find that old heads operate differently throughout the neighborhood. In the transitional zones, there are longtime residents like Bob who bear a good deal of resemblance to Anderson's old heads. But their influence carries more weight with the children of homeowners and longtime renters than it does with newcomers. Longtime residents seem to be better able to draw on their social capital to enforce behavioral norms. Social control theory would predict that those more embedded in the social network would be more capable of effectively extracting reciprocal obligations; they would have more "capital" to trade, so to speak.

But this case also reveals the key role of stigma. Importantly, it's not that voucher holders don't want to or don't care to exercise social control. It's that they aren't allowed to. Their efforts to do so are sometimes ignored and other times shut down. This is the negative role that stigma plays in the neighborhood. If voucher holders are less able to benefit from the informal mechanisms that operate in areas with longtime homeowners due to stigma and exclusion, then areas with voucher holders may increasingly rely on formal mechanisms of control, such as landlord regulation and surveillance, to the detriment of informal, ground-up forms of social control that have great benefits for residents.

Social control operates through different mechanisms across the neighborhood and among different types of residents. While Mr. Green has a cooperative relationship with his homeowner neighbors who help him carry in his groceries and report unknown vehicles in the neighborhood, voucher holders are excluded from these networks. In transitional areas such as Bob's, he can tell some groups of young people not to traffic drugs in front of his home—the ones whose parents he knows—but he has less control over the newcomers. He associates newcomers with voucher holders, even though many of them aren't. In voucher enclaves, where there are very few longtime residents or homeowners, older residents have very little control over young people. Instead, the renters in complexes like Oakland Terrace rely mainly on camera surveillance and formal security measures to regulate behavior and control drug traffic in the complex. Crime control is centrally orchestrated by the management, and while residents report that cameras have made the complex safer overall, they have not promoted a sense of trust among residents. This makes individual residents even less empowered to exercise informal social control in order to influence their neighbors' behavior. The less individuals invest informally, the more they must rely upon formal mechanisms.

These interactions reveal a shift in the neighborhood dynamic with important implications for voucher holders. The older homeowners rely on tight-knit social networks forged and refined over many years of living together to keep the neighborhood safe and running smoothly. But the newer renters are somewhat disconnected from these resources, often sequestered in large apartment complexes. Although both homeowners and renters attempt to maintain order and get things done in the neighborhood, stigma can impede interaction between the two groups. In this way, the stigma that comes with the voucher makes social resources in the community more difficult to access.

Neighborhood social organizations also play a role in how voucher holders are received and integrated into the neighborhood. Urban sociologists have argued that formal social organization is the glue that can hold neighborhoods together,[69] and that a primary function of local organizations is to contribute to neighborhood integration, stability, and even violence reduction.[70] However, the organizational infrastructure of the neighborhood can also work to impede certain types of collective action.[71] Despite a density of community organizations in Park Heights, they are better suited to serve very specific populations with varying needs, and therefore do not operate to bring residents together. Thus, not only are voucher holders stigmatized by many neighborhood residents, but they are also sometimes left out from institutional benefits and resources. In this sense, division within the neighborhood is reinforced from the top down by neighborhood institutions and organizations.

Sociological theories might predict that in an ideal scenario a range of social processes could help integrate voucher holders into receiving neighborhoods. Scholars of social capital and neighborhood effects might argue that the poor would benefit from being around more affluent, resourced neighbors, and that these same poor neighbors do not negatively affect the outcomes of their affluent neighbors.[72] Formal social organizations could bridge the gap between newcomers and old-timers, providing spaces and opportunities for groups to get to know one another.[73] Collective efficacy, or the ability of community members to act together to achieve common goals, would be a key mechanism though which to achieve positive social change.[74] Social capital would be leveraged, allowing residents to draw upon local social networks and rely upon one another for help in a range of situations ranging from everyday life, to crime control, to natural disasters.[75]

But, in fact, as this case makes clear, living in proximity to neighbors with social capital is not enough to enable newcomers to access these resources. A number of research studies have shown that despite its quasi-mythical status in the policy world, social capital doesn't seem to be a cure-all in reality. Put simply: "Proximity does not a neighbor make."[76] In order to understand why voucher holders aren't accessing these neighborhood resources, we must consider how social control operates differently across the neighborhood and how it is shaped by stigma: while there are some residents such as Barbie and Bill who bridge the divide, most longtime residents in homeowner havens see voucher holders as a hypothetical threat, while those in transitional areas often take a more confrontational approach with new neighbors. The tension between old-timers and newcomers could be a phase out of which the neighborhood will transition. But if formal social organizations reify these differences rather than help to overcome them, transitional neighborhoods will be unable to integrate voucher holders.

Chapter 7

MOVING ON

On a hot summer day on our way to the housing office in West Baltimore, Vivian and I drove through the stately neighborhood of Roland Park. Lush, green, manicured lawns sloped up to the large, elegant homes around us. There was not a piece of trash in sight, no bus stops or storefronts for people to loiter at, no children playing in the street. "I've never been through this area." Vivian's voice trailed off in disbelief. "These houses sure is . . . big. What, what do they do with all this space?" Vivian wondered out loud and then added, tongue in cheek, "They must have a little extra room in there for someone like me to stay in."

We exchanged a look and both chuckled. Of course, Vivian would be unlikely to ever live in a neighborhood like this one. Not just because wealthy residents of Roland Park rarely rent out rooms, or because there are so few rental units in the neighborhood at all. Not just because if she did find a rental unit her voucher would not cover the rent in this part of town, and not simply because even if she could find a place that met the former criteria, any landlord in Roland Park would be likely to turn her away due to her voucher. All those reasons are true—but also, Vivian would likely never live here because she had literally never been to the neighborhood and didn't know it existed until that day.[1]

When I first met Vivian, she told me she was content in her neighborhood and had no plans to leave. But a dramatic event in her life changed everything, and moving felt like the only solution. While Vivian wasn't likely to end up in a neighborhood like Roland Park, the voucher did afford her the option to move. Without the voucher, she would have been stuck in her current home, with even more severely limited options. Even when residents don't manage to move to fancy neighborhoods like Roland Park—and they rarely do—the voucher can offer them the chance to make a change. In particular, this becomes relevant in response to a moment of crisis: neighborhood violence, landlord troubles, personal trauma, problems at school, or a new job are common events in the lives of the poor.

Contrary to how designers of housing programs may imagine the moving process, poor families are frequently moving *away from* something, rather than *to* somewhere. Poor families face high rates of eviction and move frequently in response to housing quality issues, landlord problems, job changes, and neighborhood violence.[2] While some literature has theorized these moves as negative because of the instability they create, sometimes staying can be worse. Vouchers allow low-income families to respond to crises by moving, solving problems that—for cash-poor families—may have no other solution.[3]

MOVING FROM, NOT TO

Why do people stay in disadvantaged neighborhoods, and when and why do they decide to move? When they do leave, where do they go and what role does the voucher play? Understanding residential decisions from the perspective of the residents themselves is key to unlocking how housing vouchers can help low-income renters.

A long line of research suggests that the reasons families move are motivated by a perpetual desire to move "up" to the "best" homes and neighborhoods they can afford.[4] But there are so many barriers that get in the way of these kinds of moves. Those without vouchers—the low-income homeowners of Park Heights whose property values have dropped, and the renters who receive no housing assistance—are stuck with few options to leave. The voucher—in theory—provides such options: a chance to move to a home in a neighborhood they might not have dreamed possible. In practice, though, few make these kinds of moves, for all the reasons that residential decisions are constrained: time pressure, limited housing supply, landlord persuasion, and discrimination.[5]

In fact, while vouchers may facilitate moving, most commonly they don't facilitate much "upward" mobility, that is, movement to a neighborhood with a higher socioeconomic status. Given all that this book has shown so far about the barriers to mobility, it is no surprise that without measures to provide voucher holders with the tools—other than the voucher itself—to access new kinds of neighborhoods, they don't.

What does it mean then to move, if not "up"? Sociologists typically think residential instability has negative effects on people. Much of the current scholarship focuses on the ways in which being forced to move (what some call "involuntary mobility") can be detrimental, setting off a chain of instability and other negative consequences.[6] Others call attention to the process of "reactive mobility," where families aren't strictly forced to move, but do so in response to problems with a landlord or housing issues.[7] However, moving can offer certain benefits. In particular, some recent work has suggested that moving may allow families to improve their perceived safety, even when they don't move to higher income neighborhoods.[8]

The voucher eases the financial burden associated with moving, making the move a possibility. Moving can solve problems that have no other immediate solutions. This could mean getting your child out of a bullying situation at school, moving closer to a job, getting away from a neglectful landlord, escaping a dangerous neighborhood environment or a block where drugs are sold, or leaving a space that is laden with emotional trauma related to a violent incident. For those residents who had one, the voucher allowed them the option to move in response to such incidents in their personal lives and in the neighborhood. They were deeply grateful for the ability to try to solve these problems by moving away from them. Those who didn't have vouchers had far fewer options when it came to relocating.

COPING STRATEGIES: NAVIGATING NEIGHBORHOOD VIOLENCE

While voucher designers imagine that when families move they are moving *to* something—a bigger house, a safer neighborhood, a new job—in fact, much of the time, families understand their moves as moves *away* from something. One of the most common catalysts for moving was violence in the neighborhood. But people endure violent conditions for long periods of time before deciding to move. In order to do so, they develop a set of strategies to understand their neighborhood and cope with the challenges it presents.

Violence and its aftermath are a significant part of life in Baltimore's poorest neighborhoods. It is true that even in high-crime neighborhoods, violent events are relatively rare occurrences.[9] But the longer one lives in a neighborhood with high rates of violent crime, the more likely a person is to witness or experience it over the course of living there. And, of course, just once is enough to mark someone for life.[10] The residents I got to know in Park Heights bore indelible markers of the physical and symbolic violence they witnessed and were victims of over their years in high-crime neighborhoods. The nature of neighborhood violence is that it is punctuated, rather than consistent. A community might go days, weeks, or even months in peace and quiet, and then one violent event erupts and shakes things up.

Violent crime in Baltimore is high. While Baltimore's homicide rate reached a historic low in 2011 with only 197 homicides in the city, it quickly jumped back to 219 in 2012, defying national trends where violent crime has dramatically declined in recent years, and as of 2017, the number of homicides in the city was 342, topping the most recent high in 1993, when the city was home to 100,000 more people than it is today.[11] Park Heights sees a disproportionate number of these homicides. As for violent crime (including homicide, rape, aggravated assault, and robbery), the rate in Southern Park Heights was 18 per 1,000 residents in 2011, which was elevated compared to the city as a whole at 15.[12]

Even though residents don't witness violent events every day, violence plays an outsized role in the way people think about and talk about their neighborhood. Residents I got to know reported feeling like they lived in a war zone, and many have scars marking the violence they have encountered. When I met Shawn, who is twenty-three and lives in Oakland Terrace with his mother and stepfather, I asked him about his experience in the neighborhood. The first thing he told me was: "I have a bullet in my brain." When you look at Shawn from straight on and his hair is cut short, you can see that the left side of his head is misshapen from the incident, and there is a large scar where the bullet entered his head.

There are more indirect forms of violence that wreak havoc on the body as well. Patty's daughter Michelle is a recovering heroin addict. She has been clean for thirteen years, but at forty-five, has no teeth left and lost part of her calf due to an infection at an injection site, neither an uncommon problem among heroin users. "I have a mark from here to here," she told me pointing to her leg, "You can see clean down to my bone. I have five skin grafts. Three of my own and two cadavers. It took almost ten years for my leg to fully heal." Michelle, with some effort, rolled up the leg of her acid washed jeans to show me a gaping gash. A chunk the size of an avocado had been excised. The skin now had darkened bluish scar lines running through it like spider webs. "They were going to cut my leg off and they told me I wasn't going to walk. [But] I'm walking. I'm here."

Michelle was a teen when her mother moved the family to the neighborhood, and it was a rough transition. She fell in with the "wrong crowd," she said, and while this gave her a place in the neighborhood, it led to drug use and to the health problems she deals with now. But, Michelle added, "I don't feel ashamed, these are my battle wounds." As Michelle explained it, her scars are the physical reminder that she survived this neighborhood.

Other Park Heights residents recounted more direct and immediate encounters with neighborhood violence. Sometimes they were involved as bystanders, other times as participants. Bob told me the story of how his brother was shot dead on his own front porch. Bob thinks it was by a gang member who mistook his brother for someone else, though the shooter was never caught, so it's impossible to know for sure. Bob lives with the weight of this uncertainty.

Marlena, too, spoke often of violence in the neighborhood. She told me that she hears gunshots often: "I confuse firecrackers with gunshots. Derrick can tell the difference." He always reassures Marlena, "'I'll tell you when you hear gunshots.'" "He grabbed me when he heard the six gunshots outside. We grabbed the baby and we all got down. That was the first time I've ever heard anybody that close shooting a gun." This constant stress—wondering whether the popping sound outside is a firecracker, maybe a car backfiring, or a gunshot—weighs on Marlena.

And research shows that proximity to violent crime has all kinds of detrimental effects on mental health, school performance, and job performance.[13]

I saw frustrated residents—renters, voucher holders, and owners alike—confront daily violence in their community. The police are not always there when needed, and when they are there their presence often makes things worse. The police are known to unreasonably harass African American residents, like David, a twenty-three-year-old renter in Park Heights who, after being stopped by the cops three times on the way to work, quit his fast-food job in a predominantly white area of Baltimore to avoid the encounters. The police regularly stopped Ricky, a recovering addict, on his trips to support-group meetings. Once, they insisted on a strip search in broad daylight on his front steps.

In this context of high crime and violence, it's understandable that some people want to leave. Others, though, actively want to *stay*. For some the neighborhood holds fond memories, or they have close friends or family in the neighborhood; they may have family members who are engaged in crime themselves.[14] For others, it just feels like home. For many, living in a neighborhood you know is safer than one you don't. Some believe their lived understanding of the neighborhood keeps them safe in a city full of dangers. How then do those who stay navigate their environment?

The perception of the threat of crime and violence permeates daily existence for residents, who develop strategies to explain, understand, and feel safe in their neighborhood.[15] For example, some—especially those who are familiar with the community—move around the neighborhood and social scene strategically to avoid conflict. Others reach out to develop social connections to safeguard against trouble. In contrast, other residents feel that the best way to protect themselves is to avoid social encounters altogether by hunkering down indoors.

These strategies are linked to stories, or "narratives," that residents craft about how to stay safe, to live and survive in their communities despite the perils they face. These understandings are critical to making their living situations sustainable, enabling households to make sense of staying put when they have few options. These malleable narratives adapt and expand to accommodate new information and experiences, but crime and violent events strain their coherence. People live with violent events and neighborhood challenges, until one day they just can't. At times, a dissonant event contrasts so sharply with one's neighborhood narrative that the story ruptures, inciting a resident to action, such as a move.

———

Vivian recognizes there is some crime in the neighborhood, but she feels it is manageable, and she stays safe by strategically navigating the neighborhood's social and physical landscape. Vivian's words, "The more you stick to yourself, the more better it be," encapsulate a narrative of social disengagement that is well documented in recent research.[16] Vivian explained the strategy she thinks works best with her neighbors: "They fine, you just don't hang out there with them, 'cause they all in your business. They in everybody's business, so I just don't sit around and carry gossip. They don't come in my house I don't go in theirs." Vivian sees most crime, such as robberies and muggings, as attached to certain kinds of people:

> It's the crowd that you're with, the activity that you do. If you go to work every day and pay your bills and living right, you're not going to have all that kind of drama. But when you're out there getting high, going to the drug spots and hanging with that, then you're setting yourself to get robbed. . . . It's not random robbery. You put yourself there.

That said, Vivian allows that some incidents are unpredictable: "Don't get me wrong it *can* be a random robbery. It could be one day I'm walking home from work and coming through the crack [the alleyway] and someone could be coming through and try to stick me up." But Vivian tries not to worry too much: "We have cameras in the complex. Once you get out you got the police lights there too. When I go out, I just say the blood of Jesus, Lord watch over me and I just put it in his hands and pray that nothing like that happen to me." Beyond prayer, Vivian also takes some practical precautions to protect herself when she is out and about:

> I always call my husband so when I'm coming home on the bus, I say, "Alright, meet me at the bus stop." And he's right there. . . . I take a little caution. I don't try to put myself in harm's way because I am aware of the surroundings, and it *can* happen. What I do is, I won't get off at the Forest Ave. stop and walk through that gap. I get off at Tulane, and I will walk around where the police lights is, where there's more light.

Compared to many of the other residents I knew, Vivian was comfortable moving around the neighborhood, and she felt fairly confident that her strategies kept her, her boys, and her husband Roland safe. I would only later learn another side to this story.

Roland has lived in many more cities than Vivian has. Curious to hear about these experiences, I asked him to tell me more. He looked at me askance, squinting one eye. "Baltimore is the worst. . . . In most places nowadays it's a battle zone. Because this is every day, not once a year, every day in this town. We had eight people got shot the other day, it's a battle zone. . . . I think political and social structures are basically the same everywhere you go. But the violence is outrageous [here]. It's in the schools, it's on the streets. They take it from the streets to your school, and back into the streets."

That said, Roland likes Oakland Terrace better than other places he has lived for a simple reason: each building has its own entrance. Although the Terrace is a bit noisier than he would like, he told me, "It doesn't matter to me because I live in here, I don't live out there." This, too, is a coping mechanism—what sociologists Stefanie DeLuca and Peter Rosenblatt call "telescoping."[17] By defining his home not as the whole neighborhood, but as a smaller more immediate area, it feels easier to manage safety. Roland does not think there is much crime or violence inside the complex: "You might not believe it, but crime is basically nonexistent in here. You are going to have little kids out there fussing and fighting. . . . Just kids, young kids, no knives, guns or nothing like that."

Roland is well aware of Oakland Terrace's reputation. Like others, he told me about its history: "I heard it used to be a hell hole. . . . There are bad stories. You know drugs, violence. It's under new management now. Maybe that's the difference: you have cameras everywhere now. That's a good thing too. For real. They have a big monitor in the manager office. Yeah say if something did happen they could always go in and look at the camera. . . . Some hallways, not all of them. Some of them. But they definitely have them in every building, back and front. So maybe that's a deterrent. Definitely working."[18] While Baltimore may be a "battlezone," he doesn't worry too much about crime in Park Heights. "Most everyone that's out here knows who I am. They see me every day going or coming."

In one conversation I pressed Roland to tell me more about which kinds of neighborhood situations he feels safe in. I asked him, "What if your wife wanted to go out and get a pack of cigarettes or something?"

"I would go with her, or I would go get them myself."

"What if she wanted to go out alone, would you feel okay about that?"

"Yeah, because there is nothing—" Roland paused. "It's not that treacherous out there."[19] Neither of us knew that just a few months later a situation nearly identical to this one would present itself, revealing the limits of Roland's strategy.

Whereas Vivian navigates her neighborhood with specific strategies to stay safe, and Roland trusts that people know who he is, Tina (the unassisted renter from chapter 3, who, unable to afford the upkeep, lost her grandmother's home and moved into Oakland Terrace) employs a different strategy: she relies on a more complete social *and* physical withdrawal from the neighborhood. Tina and her daughter venture outdoors only during the light of day, "but at night neither one of us walks. When it turn nightfall, we in the house around here. It's not a good place to walk." For Tina and others, keeping to herself and staying close to home are key methods of protection.

On one of my visits, Tina told me that a friend had recently informed her of a registered sex offender living in the complex. We sat down on the couch and she brought up the website on my laptop. We scrolled through pages and pages of names and mug shots, and just as I thought maybe her friend had been mistaken, Tina shuddered. I recognized him too: We had stumbled on a picture of her neighbor.

Tina advises her daughter to stay away from public areas in Oakland Terrace and to avoid other kids. But this neighbor lives in her building, just one floor down. She passes by his apartment every day on her way up the stairs. Tina's generalized fear of her neighbors, which gives her a strong inclination to stay close to home to protect herself and her daughter, has a tremendous impact on the family's ability to live normally in the neighborhood, to see friends, engage with the community, run errands, and spend time in the fresh air. And yet for the time being, Tina felt it was the best strategy.

In contrast, some residents deal with the instability and crime in the neighborhood by reaching out and investing in social relationships to protect themselves. A conversation between Ray and Sandra exemplifies the tension between the competing strategies of minding your own business, retreating entirely, and reaching out. Sandra recounted a recent incident:

> I was sitting on the porch yesterday and a Caucasian lady came down here. She came because she was looking to buy something [drugs] and stuff. We saw her transaction right there. But, see the thing about it is, you see and you don't see. You've got to mind your business. You have to live in the neighborhood, you know what I mean?

Ray responded to his wife, countering:

> No, no if it's done in front of me and I don't get the respect that I think that's necessary, I'm going to say something. But, we don't have no problems here because I know all the young guys. Just like with that transaction that transpired, the [neighbor] said, "Get on, take that over there somewhere." Didn't he? Because we was sitting on the porch. We get respect. We give everybody in our community

respect. . . . And thus far we get respect around here. Ain't had no problems, have we?

Sandra added:

> We mind our business. You know sometimes when you move into a neighborhood, until you know what's up with your neighborhood you've got to mind your business. You can't get too friendly with the neighbors because then that's when trouble comes because there will be a whole bunch of he say, she say, we say stuff, because half the people in your neighborhood they got idle time. They ain't got nothing going on. So then they conjure up stuff and that's when drama comes in the neighborhood.

Whereas Sandra employs a strategy of keeping to herself to avoid "drama" that, in her experience, comes with socializing, Ray relies on a strategy of reciprocal respect that comes with "knowing" his neighbors well.

Raven took an approach more like Ray's. Instead of isolating herself from her neighbors, Raven tried to develop social connections to safeguard against trouble. At the time that I met her, Raven was squatting in the home she and her family used to rent. She grew up in Lafayette Courts, one of Baltimore's high-rise public housing complexes that has since been demolished. In all our discussions of what makes a good neighborhood, Raven implicitly and explicitly made comparisons to her childhood home. The cement structure of the high-rise buildings—and the violence she witnessed there—have marked her indelibly, shaping the way she thinks about neighborhoods and housing even now.

Before moving to Park Heights, Raven and her family had lived in the suburbs in Baltimore County. Although some families might covet a quiet suburban lifestyle, for Raven it was a nightmare. In the "County," Raven said, she did not know anyone, and so she was more afraid of crime than she had been in public housing. Like Roland, she finds comfort in the fact that people know her in Park Heights: "If something happens around *here*, everybody's gonna know. For me, I was more scared out there [in the County] than I ever was walking around the projects. . . . But now, I can go to the gas station three, four o'clock in the morning, true that, any one of us can. And I'm not going to say nothing's ever gonna happen, but I'll tell you, we all know each other."

Raven has cycled through several strategies during her time in the neighborhood. When she arrived, she was wary of her neighbors and kept to herself to stay out of trouble. But when one day Raven fainted on the street a few blocks from her house, three local men who sell cigarettes on the corner picked her up and carried her home. She was shocked that they knew who she was and where she lived. It was at this moment that she realized the protective value in getting to know people in the neighborhood. Since then she has begun actively reaching out to make friends with her neighbors, especially two of the older women who live on her block.

Raven has had several formative experiences with violence in Park Heights. A few years ago, she was sexually and physically assaulted on her way to work, just a block from her house. After the incident, Raven went through a period of deep fear about the neighborhood. She was afraid to walk to the bus, and she would spend ten minutes before leaving the house trying to decide which route to take and how she could protect herself. But recently, knowing that her neighbors have an eye out for her, she has come to think differently about how to interact with the neighborhood. She considers the rape "an act of violence" that has the potential to fuel her fear and maintain enduring power over her. But, "if you don't be afraid of it" she said, it cannot control you. Raven now walks unencumbered and fearlessly in the neighborhood, with the confidence that her neighbors are watching out for her.

In the past few years of living in Park Heights, Raven has realized it is a happy medium between the close-knit but dangerous projects where she grew up and the anonymous suburbs. Although Park Heights has a lot of crime and her home has severe structural problems, the neighborhood has some key advantages over the other places she and her family have lived. Unlike her time in Lafayette Courts, living in Park Heights feels like a choice to her, and unlike in the suburbs, Raven feels protected by her neighbors. In the first few months I knew Raven, it was clear that even though she and her family were living in their home precariously, she had finally found a place that felt tenable. She had no plans to leave unless absolutely necessary. This was good, because with no voucher and not much money in the bank, she had few options for moving elsewhere.

DECIDING TO MOVE

As time went on and I watched events in residents' lives unfold, their narratives and coping strategies "worked" much of the time, accommodating all sorts of new events and allowing them to remain and survive in the neighborhood. But these stories were regularly challenged by violent neighborhood incidents. In many cases, the narratives had breaking points or "ruptures." In these moments, people were unable to continue telling themselves that the neighborhood was "safe enough," or that they could protect themselves simply by "minding their own business" or by "knowing the right people." No longer under the protection of an illusory sense of safety, these moments of rupture often prompted a decision to move.

Over the time I knew her, Raven attempted to refine the delicate balancing act of self-preservation by reaching out to her neighbors in strategic ways. One afternoon as we sat at the table, Raven made a cryptic statement about her neighbors: they are "nosy when they shouldn't be, and not enough nosy when they should be." I asked her what she meant, and Raven recounted what had happened the previous weekend.

Unbeknownst to her, someone had left the front door unlocked— with nine children in the house this happened from time to time. Early Saturday morning, Raven's six-year-old daughter Carla tip-toed into the room Raven shares with her husband and tugged at the sheets: "Mom, somebody's downstairs in our house." Carla is always telling stories, jokes, even lies—anything to get her mother's attention. So, Raven did not take her seriously and turned over sleepily. But Carla came around to the other side of the bed and, as Raven explained, "she gave me this look, and she didn't have to say no more. So, we gets up and I got a bat. And I'm coming down the steps, and—there's literally a guy in my house, in my kitchen!"

Raven watched him for a few minutes, incredulous, trying to decide what he was doing. He "knows where I keep the glasses because wasn't none of the other cabinets was open. He went straight to the cabinet. . . . Like he's been here before!" Raven could not believe her eyes. He was meandering around the kitchen, "getting a glass and sippin'. . . . So, I make like this sigh noise, because I'm saying to myself 'What the . . . ?' I'm having this personal conversation with myself, like 'Raven did you just see this?'" The intruder was an older man and did not seem to be doing anything illicit, other than trespassing in the home and helping himself to the kitchen.

Less angry than confused at this point, Raven summoned the courage to speak to him:

> I'm like, "what in the bleep, bleep, bleep are you doing?" He's real nonchalant: "I'm having a glass of water." Like I was almost inconveniencing him, like intruding on *him*?! So, I go back inside myself and say, "Raven, you know what needs to be done." I look at Carla: "Get your brother, go upstairs." And I said to the man, "You got such and such a time to get to the door." He says "Phew," puts the cup down. . . . So, he takes the chair, the same chair you're sitting in, and he takes it, and he sits it outside my door.

Raven went on to call the police, and they identified the intruder as a man who lived just a few blocks away. He had Alzheimer's and often wandered off and into other people's homes. But Raven was livid that her neighbors did not notice or say anything: "Now I'm mad, I am so heated. So I'm cursing, so all the neighbors come outside. They like, 'Raven what's wrong, calm down.' I said, 'No you calm down! You see him in my chair. Who IS this?' So, they like, 'Well Raven we thought that was probably your father because we seen him come there earlier.'"

Raven's friend, who lived across the street, had noticed the old man hanging out on the porch and going in and out of the house on several occasions. Raven was surprised to find that the problem was not that her neighbors had neglected to look out for her. Rather, they did not know her well enough to understand that the man was in fact an intruder.

When I stopped by Raven's house a few weeks later she opened the door just enough to ask if we could talk the following day instead. She said the family "had to leave" and was scrambling to figure out where they would go. I returned the next day to see how things were going. No one answered. I tried Raven's cell phone several times. When I finally got through to her, I learned that she and her youngest kids were staying with a friend in the suburbs, and her four older children were spread around staying with various friends and relatives. I asked her if she had been evicted. She said no. I asked her if she had received a notice. She said she had not. "But why did you leave then?" I queried.

Raven told me that the incident with the intruder had got her thinking. Even though she had been building relationships with the older women on the block and with the men on the corner of whom she was very fond, she had realized something important: there were some things her neighbors could help her with, and others they could not. The fact that Raven's family was technically squatting put them in a precarious position. The day the sheriff comes to serve eviction papers, or the city comes to claim the house, she said, "There ain't nothing they can do for me then." And with such a large family, Raven did not want to be rushed out in a dramatic scene with the sheriff. But more importantly, Raven wanted to live in a place where she could feel that her relationships with her neighbors would protect her.

———

On an early spring day, I paid a visit to Tina. This time, when I arrived she was not waiting for me. The front door to the building was ajar, as usual, so I let myself in and climbed the stairs. When I reached the second floor, I noticed a spattering of dark stains on the walls and railings. Some of it looked streaked, as if it had been wiped down but not very thoroughly. Tina opened the door hurriedly, grabbing my shoulder to pull me inside the apartment. "I need to tell you something," she said nervously as she pulled out a chair for me at the table.

Just a few days before, Tina explained, she heard a commotion in the stairway. She opened her door a crack, enough to see her neighbor from downstairs—the one we found online on the list of registered sex of-fenders. He was banging on the front door to his own apartment, yelling and begging his wife to let him in. Tina peered down the stairwell and saw three women come in the unlocked front door to the building, run up the stairs, and proceed to beat him up, kicking him in the stomach and ribs, smashing his head against the iron banister:

> He was busted open, in a puddle of blood. . . . The man was at the door saying, "Help me! Let me in, let me in," she wouldn't. And three women beat his head, beat him . . . his wife, she didn't open that door. She was scared to death. They probably would have stomped her head in. . . . When she threw the first punch and his head hit the step, I shut my door.

Tina was shocked and terrified. The police came, but she did not feel she could rely on them to keep her daughter safe. Even if they were able to subdue the violent altercation, this would not address the more mun-dane dangers represented by the blood on the walls: "Every time you turn around there is blood in that hallway." The management company sent one of the tenants, who often performs odd jobs for pay, to clean up the blood. He has "full-blown AIDS," Tina said, which is why they send him to do jobs like that. But Tina remarked with dismay, "He don't even clean it all the way like he supposed to."

In the following weeks, Tina's fear of her neighbors transmuted into a metaphorical fear of contracting a communicable disease like HIV. She began to warn me obsessively about the neighborhood hazards of catching an illness: "This area code has the highest AIDS rate there is in Baltimore City. I didn't know that until I moved here. . . . I know one thing, you just have to be careful. Be very careful." Tina was especially worried that her daughter would contract HIV from the neighbors since they share an entryway; she warned her daughter not to touch the door or the railings when she walks into the building, she fastidiously washed her hands, and she placed a bottle of hand sanitizer on the shelf right next to the door.

In the time that I knew Tina before the violent altercation in the hallway, she had a stable understanding of how to keep herself and her daughter safe: avoid social encounters and stay near home. When Tina learned about the sex offender in the complex, she became reluctant to stray too far from the apartment building. But when Tina saw blood spilled in her own hallway, she realized that none of these strategies would be enough. Now Tina was afraid to leave the apartment. She wanted to move, but she did not have the money. Moved to action by this incident, but unable to physically move, Tina instead altered her strategy, circumscribing her use of space even more severely. Tina now stays inside and keeps her daughter there too; she leaves just twice a day, to walk her daughter to and from school.

———

One day I put a question to Roland the way it seems to appear over and over in the research, curious to hear if the distinction between "good" neighborhoods and "bad" ones made any sense to him. I asked him: "So what makes a neighborhood a good neighborhood versus a bad neighborhood?"

He didn't skip a beat: "People," Roland told me.

"People?"

"People do good things, people do bad things."

"What would you call this neighborhood?"

"In between."

"How come?"

"People are undereducated. A lot of people come from different parts of the city, where the projects were built and the violence was built, and they were misplaced and put into areas like this. So, a lot of them bring that old stuff with them, whatever they were into, they didn't have anywhere where to put it. People that were here moved out. This actually started in 1968. They started building the boulevards and the highway, basically doing nothing but separating downtown from the inner city."

For Roland, Park Heights was "in between." I took that to mean that if you know a neighborhood well, it can't be all "good" or all "bad." There are the people, there is what the people do, and then there's the structure—education, the economy, even urban planning, and broader forces of inequality—that allow certain things to happen and not others.

That summer, I received a call from Vivian. She asked if I could come over to her place. Before I could answer, she blurted out: "Roland is dead." Her words seemed incommensurate with the reality of their meaning. I had spent many hours with her husband Roland at Oakland Terrace. I immediately drove over to the apartment. When I arrived, Vivian explained in a daze that she had been out at a friend's a few blocks away until around 10 p.m. the night before, and she called to see if Roland would come over to walk home with her since it was late. On the short walk home, she told me:

> A guy followed us. He just pulled out a gun and started waving the gun around, "Give me the money, give me the money." Roland was trying to stop him from hitting me in the head with the gun. So he shot in the air one time, and the second time he just pointed to his head and shot him. I was screaming and running, and screaming for help. I ran back to him, and he was laying there . . . and blood was running down the street.

Vivian stopped and took a long pause as she struggled to find her words. "I just really lost it. It seemed the police took so long to get there. And then they came and then the ambulance, and they took him. And I had to sit in the police car and wait on Homicide for about forty-five minutes. And I just said, Oh my god."

Vivian, who had never seemed to mind Oakland Terrace—whose strategies made it feel manageable and even safe—had a new story. She now said, understandably, that she was frightened and felt she had to leave: "I just want a new place to live, you know. I just wanna feel safe."

The narrative she had told me over the previous months about how she protected herself by strategically navigating the neighborhood seemed to have completely burst, revealing a divergent one lying dormant underneath. In this new version, Vivian and her family had had numerous encounters with violence that she had previously left out of her stories. One of her boys had been mugged last year and hit over the head with the barrel of a gun. She told me about a robbery in a local take-out restaurant where she had witnessed someone getting shot. Although we had had numerous conversations about violent incidents in the neighborhood, personal experiences with crime, and strategies she used to protect herself and her family, she had not mentioned these confrontations. It was as if she was now describing a different neighborhood. It was not that Vivian had been lying to me, but her recent experience with intense violence and loss had rendered these past experiences more salient. Her narrative of a neighborhood that was manageable if you "stick to yourself" and "take a little caution" enabled her to deal with the regular violence she was subjected to around her home. That is, until she was confronted with it in a way that changed her life undeniably and irrevocably.

I spent a good deal of time with Vivian that summer observing her take steps to move. The first step was to add her sons—who had recently moved back home—to her voucher, so she could get a bigger home. In Oakland Terrace, she was able to get a two-bedroom unit even though she had a one-bedroom voucher, because one of the bedrooms counted as a den. But if she were to move, it might be hard to find a similar situation.

First, we went to the housing voucher office to discuss the process for getting a new voucher. It was 107 degrees that day, and so we drove down to the HABC office in my car rather than taking the bus. We sat in silence for a few moments, watching the neighborhood fly by. "These are some bad streets in Baltimore." A few minutes later she added, "I just wanna move. You know, the whole apartment just reminds me of him. I have to get rid of things, you know throw 'em out, give 'em away. I still got things under the bed I haven't cleaned out. I gave some of his stuff to the lady underneath me. But I just want a new place to live." Vivian sighed and kept thinking out loud. "It's like there some days I feel like I'm waiting on him to walk up, on his way in the house. There's so many memories that I just wanna leave back there. And move on."

"Are there other places you've lived in the past that you'd go back to?" I asked her, wondering where she would go next.

"No, they were rooms more so [where I used to live], living with somebody. . . . I don't know what to do. I just wanna feel safe. Now I'm by myself, I'm not used to that. . . . I thank god for my kids. I'm glad they are with me, cause I'd be really alone right now."

"They still need you."

"Yeah, and that's why I can't show them any fear. 'Cause I don't want them to get that in they mind to be fearful. . . . They've had it pretty good, they so strong, I tell 'em all the time how proud I am of them for being so strong about things. . . . They seeing what we're going through now, and that makes them strong too, 'cause they used to things being so easy. And I told them they can learn something from our struggles that we're having right now. I told them, I said 'I don't have the extra money to give you. Roland's not here. We gotta keep food in the house.'"

Vivian continued thinking out loud about what kind of place she wanted to live in. "See, I have a bedroom set that's on layaway for the boys. So, I pay on that 263 a month. I usually put the whole 263 but I only put 240 this month, I try not to miss a payment. I should only have two more payments on that set. It was supposed to have been three when I first got it, but it looks like it's more like five or six now." She paused to think. "See that's why I gotta get the two-bedroom apartment." We planned to go check in on the payment plan, the furniture store was around the corner from HABC.

We passed a food cart with a bright blue awning selling "snowballs." In the summer Baltimore has snowball stands littered around the city like New York has hot dog stands. "Maybe we can get us a snowball!" Vivian remarked, smiling for the first time that day.

Later, when we sat down in front of the agent—a white man who looked to be in his early twenties—Vivian made an impassioned plea to be issued a two-bedroom voucher, to accommodate her sons. She explained that her husband had recently been killed, that she had watched him die, and that now she was afraid for herself and her kids in their own neighborhood, and she needed a new voucher to move.

He stared back blankly as the weight of the story hung in the air. I wondered how he would translate this emotional onslaught into concrete bureaucratic steps. He paused and took a deep breath. Then suddenly he lifted his keyboard off his desk and slammed it back down to squash a roach that had crawled out from under. Vivian and I both started, and then burst into laughter, releasing the tension in the room.

With a sigh, the young man explained that there were two separate issues to deal with. First, adding Vivian's boys to the voucher would depend on how old they were. To get them added, Vivian would need a copy of their birth certificates. Second, once Vivian initiated the process to get a new voucher, she would have only sixty days in which to find a new home. Getting the timing right would be tricky. The agent advised her to find the new place first, and then initiate the voucher process. For the next several weeks, I accompanied Vivian around the city in the summer heat as she took the steps to get new copies of the birth certificates, return to the housing office to add the boys to the voucher, speak to her landlord, and begin the process of thinking about where she would like to move.

MOVING ON, NOT UP

I left the field before Vivian moved, and since she did not have a phone, it was hard to keep in touch. When we caught up, she explained that when she had informed her landlord she was planning to move, he proposed that she relocate to one of his other buildings about a mile away. Although she had some doubts about whether the new apartment would be safer, she had bigger doubts about moving somewhere completely unknown: she made the move.

Vivian is armed with a powerful narrative to deal with a neighborhood like Park Heights. Moving to a new home, she had hoped, would allow her to resolve the dissonance that emerged with her husband's death. But when she actually went to go look for a new place, she still had the same set of tools—tools she has used her entire life to get by in tough neighborhoods. Her courage and confidence in her ability to navigate the neighborhood had failed her in Park Heights, but maybe they would work in a new place. Under enormous constraint, reconstructing the old narrative of safety in a different space was far more feasible than staying in the old neighborhood. The fact that Vivian had a voucher enabled her to move and to reset her narrative about how to stay safe; it just didn't get her very far geographically.

The families I got to know crafted narratives and adopted strategies delicately balanced between social engagement and withdrawal (i.e., "if I do this, I will be safe") to manage their neighborhood environments. For some of them, this worked. Others, however, encountered moments in which their narratives stopped working and revealed themselves for the stories they were—both to me as an observer and to the participants themselves. This breakdown is what I call narrative rupture.[20] Raven, who reached out to her neighbors and believed this social safety net would protect her, learned the limits of this approach when her home was invaded by a stranger and her neighbors didn't notice. Tina, who withdrew from social interaction to protect herself and her daughter, found that when danger came right to her doorstep she did not have the means to escape without literally shutting herself within the confines of her apartment. And Vivian, who believed that violence in the neighborhood was rare if she played her cards right, was confronted with an undeniable moment of truth in her husband's death. In these instants of narrative rupture, families were faced with irrefutable evidence that contradicted the stories that had heretofore explained their daily existence in the neighborhood. In light of these contradictions, residents' narratives about the neighborhood and their place within it changed before my eyes, and they were motivated to action when they had previously been inert.

———

People endure all sorts of uncomfortable conditions as long as they have a working understanding of how to manage them. But when the safety narrative ruptures, residents see moving as one of the solutions to the problem. For those without vouchers, this solution is fraught.

Raven and her family lived in semi-squalid conditions with no electricity and the imminent threat of eviction for months, but because Raven believed the neighborhood provided safety through community, the family had no plans to leave. The break-in unveiled the mirage of safety as an illusion. Remaining in the precarious housing situation no longer made sense. Raven preempted the inevitable eviction by moving out. She found a temporary solution staying with family, but this kind of move comes with problems: she will likely have to relocate again soon. If Raven had a voucher she would be protected from this kind of instability.

Tina's story shows how—without a voucher—she had few options when violence came to her doorstep. She was alarmed to learn that a sex offender lived on the floor below her, and when she witnessed his violent beating in the stairwell, Tina decided she desperately wanted to move. But without a voucher, she did not have the means to do so. In lieu of a physical change, Tina completely withdrew from the neighborhood.

Vivian is the only one of the three who has a voucher, and therefore the option to move with some planning and choice. Her story illustrates a similar stasis right up until the moment of rupture. For Vivian, her narrative about sticking to herself to stay safe in the neighborhood was shattered when her husband was killed on the street in front of her. She was faced with the undeniable reality that she in fact could *not* deal with the neighborhood, that she was no longer in control of the situation, and worse, that perhaps she never had been. The rupture that Vivian experienced necessitated some kind of change to restore a sense of safety. Her voucher did ultimately allow her to move to a new home, but not to a more advantaged neighborhood. The ability to move away from the problems she wants to flee is powerful, but while the voucher facilitates a move, it does little in and of itself to substantially change the type of neighborhood in which she lives. Vivian's case highlights the insight that removing financial constraints to make room for choice is not always enough to allow people to take full advantage of the available options.

Existing theories of spatial assimilation and residential choice—the theories on which housing vouchers are based—assume that when people move out, they do so in order to move "up."[21] They suggest that people use their resources to move to the "best" neighborhood possible. However, these ways of thinking about moving cannot fully explain when, why, and where families move. In fact, residential *movement* is not always *upward mobility*.

Previous research shows that significant structural forces—including financial limitations, the logistics of moving, housing discrimination, and landlord practices—constrain residential options for the poor.[22] But how families think about their options matters too, even when these options are significantly constrained. And the families I got to know felt they were making important choices about where to live. What appears to researchers as involuntary moves may in fact have elements of calculated strategy. Even in cases where moves don't get families to higher-income or lower-crime neighborhoods, we can understand these moves as attempts to solve problems rather than attempts to achieve what researchers narrowly define as "upward" mobility.

Families also use moves to solve other sorts of problems beyond violence: for example, to get a child out of a school setting where they were not learning, or where they were being bullied, or to move somewhere closer to work. Middle- and high-income families do not necessarily face the same challenges in their environments—their neighborhoods are more likely to readily meet basic needs such as safety and high-performing schools. And when they do not meet these needs, higher-income families have the social and financial capital to solve the problem in other ways: hire a tutor, send their child to a different school, or move.

Housing vouchers provide some of the flexibility that middle-class families don't think twice about. And yet, as we have seen, voucher holders like Vivian don't necessarily move to neighborhoods that look better on paper. Their resulting moves are often horizontal, largely due to structural factors related to landlords and the housing market, and also in part because past residential experiences shape how residents imagine what is possible in ways that preclude more ambitious moves.[23] The dominant model of residential "choice" thus ignores how residents' narratives give rise to residential decisions that are neither purely forced nor entirely in line with normative aspirations of upward mobility. Even when residents do not move far, the act of moving after a narrative rupture allows them to restore a narrative of safety.

For both Raven and Vivian, making a choice to be in control of their own fates and do something for their families was better than doing nothing. In this way, families use residential moves—even if lateral in terms of neighborhood poverty—as a strategy to repair a broken narrative, recreating a sense of safety at least temporarily. A new address—even if it's not a "better" one—can solve problems that some people do not have the resources to solve by any other means. A move can be a pragmatic solution to the pressing problem of high crime for which they have no other tools to address.

————

Months earlier, I had asked Roland what he thought about people moving to Park Heights. "If you're gonna move to Park Heights, move to Park Heights, but move further out, near the county line," Roland reflected. "I am not going to say they shouldn't move here, I am going to say move here until maybe your situation gets better and then move on. . . . The thing is you don't want to stay stuck."

Toward the end of one of our interviews, I asked him, "Where will you be in five or ten years?"

"Living in Baltimore County, sitting in a rocking chair." Roland would have been sixty-five that August. I asked him—as I do everyone—if there was anything else he thought I should know. He told me: "Only that I will move on."

There is a power in *fluidity*, the ability to "move on," even without "moving up." Researchers who study housing sometimes underestimate this power. In its current form, the voucher doesn't seem to provide families with the upward mobility that many policymakers hoped it would. But it does provide something else: flexibility. Vouchers of course, are one of the few tools the poor have that allow them to move on. Within this context, the voucher offers poor renters like Vivian a chance that neither Raven nor Tina had: the chance to pick up and start fresh.

Chapter 8

CONCLUSION

Tina watched the storm from her second-story window. She could see the large picture window flexing with the force of the wind outside. She peered out cautiously and saw the trees bending at unnatural angles, a tall skinny one arched over so far it nearly touched the ground. Through the sideways rain she could just make out what looked like a trash can flying through the air. "It was like that movie *Twister*," she told me later.

It started out as the hottest summer day in 2012. Summers in Baltimore are always hot, but that summer we had a heat wave. While temperatures in July and August usually hover in the 90s, with unrelenting sunny days, this week it was well over 100 during the day. The thick humidity layered on top slows everything down to a slow ooze. The heat felt unbearable. At ten o'clock at night, it was still 91 degrees.

When the storm came, the weather service called it a "derecho" rather than a tornado: basically, an extended series of fast-moving, intense thunderstorms accompanied by driving, direct winds. In this case, the derecho moved from Chicago to Maryland, dropping sheets of drenching rain across eleven states in all. The winds, topping 87 mph, caused twenty-two deaths. The power went out, plunging much of the city into darkness. Governor O'Malley declared a state of emergency in Maryland. With over 1.6 million Maryland households out of power, with downed trees and power lines everywhere, some areas waited ten days for power to be restored.

After the storm, the heat returned with force. Without power, food began to warm in the fridge. The first day, you keep the door closed, hoping the power would come back on. By the first night you use the melting ice cubes to cool off your body—they would soon evaporate in the freezer anyway. The second day you start eating everything you can before it rots.

A few days out from the storm, I was on my way to Oakland Terrace for a community cook-out. I approached an intersection where the stoplight hung in the hot, thick air. It was neither red, nor green or yellow, just black. The power was still out. While the other three-quarters of the city had their ACs buzzing overtime, the northwest section of the grid was still dead. Every light for a mile in either direction was out. Some cars sped through honking, while others slowed to a crawl, the drivers looking two or three times before stepping on the gas and zooming through. This particular intersection brought six streets together. It would have been a mess if it weren't mostly empty.

I was looking for ice. Earlier I had asked Jill, the property manager at Oakland Terrace, what I could bring to the party. "Ice! You got some Miss Eve?" I didn't—the ice in my freezer had long since melted. But I had promised Jill I would find some. This proved harder than I expected. I stopped at three gas stations. One was closed. The other two had no ice. The outdoor bins were empty, save for the deflated, empty plastic bags, their hard chunks of ice liquified and evaporated into the hot summer air. I drove around looking for another gas station, before I eventually realized that as long as the street lights were out, there would be no ice.

Still, I didn't want to show up empty-handed. Then I saw a man and woman unloading from a truck. They were running a small storefront restaurant. In what seemed like a miracle, they were lifting huge bags of ice from the back of the truck—they had been to some other part of the city where the power had already been restored. I pulled up and asked, "What will you take for two bags of ice?" They exchanged a glance, "Whatever its worth to you hon, a few bucks?" I handed them a ten and hauled the bags into my car.

When I got to Oakland Terrace, to my surprise, everything was as normal. No one seemed fazed by several days without power. People had emptied their fridges and brought down what they had to share. Few residents had cars, so they hadn't even noticed that the street lights were out. Kids were running around. A five-year old zipped by on his tricycle and teenagers yelled to each other across the terrace. Alex was flipping burgers and passing out sodas to the kids to keep them hydrated.

"Miss Eve, where you been?" Jill called out to me. The older women were sitting in the shade of the buildings, gossiping and fanning themselves, seemingly oblivious to the smoky heat of the grill just a few feet from their circle. No one was talking about the power outage, or even the heatwave. They weren't comparing notes on which traffic lights were out or whether anyone had found a supermarket with food. If they knew that the electric company had restored power days ago to virtually every neighborhood except theirs, that wasn't on the day's agenda. People were eating, talking, laughing, and enjoying the sun. It was just another summer day at Oakland Terrace, where people have been living with limited resources and unexpected setbacks for a long time.

RESILIENCE AND FRAGILITY

This book is an ethnography of a key policy shaping American urban life—housing vouchers—and how that policy operates within a particular social context. Over the course of my efforts to learn about this policy, I found that the story of vouchers and the people who receive them is inextricable from that of the neighborhoods to which voucher holders move. While some voucher holders have moved to more affluent, integrated neighborhoods with jobs and good schools, many others have not. What does it mean for some of America's poorest renters to move to a neighborhood like Park Heights—an area lacking city resources, neglected by the electric company, and simultaneously under-policed but over-surveilled?

The community of Park Heights is home to several sets of populations who have experienced different kinds of socioeconomic and racial exclusion and wealth extraction. These cycles of exclusion and extraction have come in waves. The federal government—unable (or unwilling) to fund public housing at a level sufficient to maintain its upkeep[1]—outsourced the problem of housing the poor to private landlords through housing vouchers. When public housing residents were "vouchered out" of public housing, the moves disrupted their stability, their social networks, their habits of daily living. And when they arrived in their new homes, they were often stigmatized and shut out by existing homeowners. These existing residents have, in turn, been excluded in their own way: historically barred from living and owning homes in many neighborhoods through redlining, these homeowners now feel that their property values—their largest source of wealth—are threatened by the arrival of voucher holders. Meanwhile, unassisted renters are excluded from the voucher program altogether, unable to access its benefits. Even the neighborhood is marginalized. It is left to bear the brunt of the shift in housing policy; it is left, largely unequipped, to shelter and integrate these newcomers.

Neighborhoods like Park Heights are both incredibly resilient and deeply fragile all at once. Park Heights, formerly a middle-class neighborhood, experienced profound racial upheaval in the 1960s, but has since stabilized as a black homeowning community with a newer renter population. Residents display a tremendous sense of history and of community, but also of change, division, and insecurity.

The neighborhood of Park Heights as it stands today was built by the longtime homeowners who form the bedrock of the community. When most of these African American homeowners moved to the area in the late 1960s and early 1970s, it was their first opportunity to own a home. Many were children of migrants from the south, and most of these original settlers are still there. These were mostly working-class households whose members hoped that buying a home would give them access to greater resources and better opportunities. Through a process of "predatory inclusion," homeowning opportunities that had been previously barred to blacks opened up, but at a higher cost.[2] And as black families moved in, the white population moved out. The resources soon left, too. Homeownership did not confer the same benefits to black households as it had to the whites who had left.[3]

For the homeowners of Park Heights, the neighborhood represents their family and social networks as well as their most significant financial investment: their homes. They have a lot invested in their neighborhood and many are reluctant to leave for reasons both sentimental and financial: their homes are not worth much. In Mr. Green's words, "We all stuck with homes that ain't worth nothing."

These homeowners have been in the neighborhood for years, developing and relying on a network of stable social relations. This network could be a valuable resource to incoming renters. But homeowners—still reeling from the social and financial upheaval of the changes in their neighborhood decades ago—aren't always ready to support and welcome newcomers. The homeowners' position is precarious: their financial worth is vested entirely in one asset, their homes. And it is this very home that they feel is most threatened by the influx of renters to the neighborhood. As the neighborhood has declined with aging housing stock, drugs, and disinvestment, many homeowners in Park Heights have experienced downward mobility. Some have even lost their homes and joined the renter class. They fear and stigmatize voucher holders as the newest in a long line of threats to neighborhood stability.

Unassisted renters—like voucher holders—have recently been moving to the neighborhood in larger numbers. Their story offers an important counterpoint to the voucher story. Since only one in four qualified renters receives housing assistance, unassisted renters are often even worse off than voucher holders. And as we saw in chapter 2, without the subsidy, their position is even more precarious.

The stigma associated with vouchers structures the social relations of housing in ways that limit interaction between homeowners and renters. Banal everyday interactions between longtime homeowners and incoming renters who share the same space reveal the tension and turmoil brewing as the social order is created, maintained, and contested. Residents organize in myriad ways to fill the gaps left by the absence of formal social services, ranging from trash collection and cleanup in vacant lots, to managing adolescents in the neighborhood, curbing drug sales, and meting out community justice. Barbie shows her new neighbors how to recycle, and Bob fights his never-ending war against improper trash collection, eyeing his new neighbors suspiciously as he organizes the waste in such a way that the Baltimore Public Works trucks will actually collect it, rather than leaving behind scraps that attract rats and other animals. "Catman" Bill walks a three-mile stretch from South Baltimore to Liberty Heights every day, pushing a grocery cart stocked with several large bags of cat food, feeding all the stray cats he can find along his way. Through his daily treks, Bill has befriended residents across the entire west side of Baltimore. These relationships made him a vital resource for connecting residents with available jobs or services.

There are limits to the power of these informal mechanisms, though. Bob's effort to clean up the trash on his block floundered when a group of teenagers taunted him by leaving a pile of garbage on his front lawn late one night. His suspicion of the renters on his block—some of whom he incorrectly assumes to be voucher holders—doesn't do much for community building. Bill's laundry and dog care operations were shut down by the city for code violations. Tracey, who succeeded in getting a surveillance camera installed outside Oakland Terrace, found that residents were subsequently less likely to intervene in altercations because they believed that the police were monitoring the cameras when, in fact, many of the cameras were not being monitored at all. Raven learned she could not depend on her neighbors for protection when no one questioned a stranger who entered her home and made himself comfortable in the kitchen. And Vivian was confronted with the undeniable violence in the neighborhood when her husband was shot in the street.

Residents are, for the most part, stuck, each group in their own way. Homeowners like Mr. Green and Bob cannot sell because their home values are so low. Unassisted renters like Raven and Tina cannot afford to move, though they want to. For Raven, this means doubling up with relatives. For Tina, it means she stays indoors as much as possible. Vivian, who has a voucher, is the only one with a ticket to find a new place to live, though she doesn't get far.

In fact, voucher holders are the only group with the ability—in theory, at least—to get unstuck. Vouchers provide families with the flexibility to respond to life events and crises for which they have no other means to respond. While they don't fully provide households with the *upward* mobility that some policymakers hoped it would, they do provide freedom of mobility or the sense of flexibility. The voucher is one of the few tools the poor have to respond to personal and community-level crises.

For everyone else, this feeling of being "stuck" goes hand in hand with exclusion. African American homeowners, who were excluded for so many years from ownership in neighborhoods like Park Heights, are now protective of what little they have to the point of excluding renters, and especially voucher holders, from much of their social activity. The homeowners rely on tight-knit social networks forged and refined over many years of living together to ward off crime and keep things running smoothly. But the newer renters—and especially voucher holders, who are stigmatized—aren't always connected to these social resources. They are often sequestered in large apartment complexes, where the stigma they face from longtime residents keeps them at a social distance. Although both homeowners and renters attempt to maintain order and get things done in the neighborhood, their modes are often at odds, and community institutions do not always facilitate interaction between the two groups.

The social relations of housing shape neighborly interaction in keys ways. But these social relations aren't born out of a vacuum. Rather, they are shaped by historical events and processes. Like so many neighborhoods in America, Parks Heights experienced dramatic job loss through deindustrialization. Real estate agents made things worse by blockbusting, preying on limited opportunities for black homeownership, inflating home prices to unsuspecting black buyers, and exacerbating white flight to the suburbs. Decades of disinvestment have left the neighborhood with one of the highest vacancy rates in the city. This made it susceptible to prospecting landlords who see a way to turn a profit. It is no coincidence that vouchers have flocked here. This confluence of historical and present forces makes for a vulnerable neighborhood.

As Roland explained to me, the neighborhood is fragile: "People are undereducated. A lot of people come from different parts of the city, where the projects were built and the violence was built, and they were misplaced and put into areas like this." Neighborhoods like this one—already the victims of earlier waves of predation, discrimination, segregation, and underinvestment—are commonly recipients of voucher holders.

This set of historical forces has created a social environment in which homeowners feel protective of what little they have left. It also has contributed to an environment of financial risk in which landlords feel they have to charge more to protect their risky real estate investment.[4] The voucher program offers landlords a safe way to invest in the neighborhood. But landlords' motives are aligned with *their* bottom line, not necessarily with the greater good. As housing programs increasingly rely on the private market to house the poor, we see how the scaffolding of the private market stratifies housing voucher recipients, mirroring decades-old patterns of racial segregation.

As a result, the "choice" of where to live that policymakers hoped to provide to voucher holders is largely an illusion. The primary goal of the voucher program has always been to make housing more affordable for those who receive a voucher, and it has done so. But increasingly the program has also embraced a secondary goal of providing the poor with more options and choice about where to live. This secondary goal is based on an underlying assumption that historical patterns of racial and class segregation can be solved by providing people, particularly low-income people of color, with more options. This assumption evokes the notion of *choice* that comes to mind when we think of middle-class people's housing options (the kind of home searches we see on TV shows like HGTV's *House Hunters*). Yet, given the spatial distribution of the existing supply of homes, the lack of legal protections for voucher holders, the persistence of racial discrimination, and the role of landlords, "choice" among voucher holders remains largely fictional. The potential is there, but it is unrealized.

STIGMA AND SCAPEGOATING

The scapegoating of voucher holders reaches well beyond the homeowners of Park Heights. In 2015, at a pool in McKinney, Texas, cell phone video captured a white woman telling an African American teenager to, "Go back to your Section 8 Homes," ultimately culminating in a shocking scene of police brutality against the teenage girl. In many areas of the United States today, "Section 8" is nearly synonymous with a racial slur. Its popular usage denotes areas that are poor and segregated, and carries much of the stigma that used to be associated only with public housing. There is a widely pervasive myth that voucher holders bring with them crime and disorderliness.

The stigma and myth surrounding housing vouchers is woven through our popular and even intellectual discourse. In 2008, a well-respected journalist, Hanna Rosin, fell prey to just this myth. Rosin wrote about a spike in violent crime in certain Memphis neighborhoods. She suggested—contrary to the interpretation of the many housing experts with whom she consulted—that the explanation lay in voucher holders who had moved into new neighborhoods and brought "their problems," including violent crime, with them: "The match was near-perfect," Rosin reported. "Dense violent-crime areas are shaded dark blue, and Section 8 addresses are represented by little red dots. All of the dark-blue areas are covered in little red dots, like bursts of gunfire. The rest of the city has almost no dots."[5]

Anyone who knows the classic maxim, that the presence of fire trucks doesn't *cause* fires, knows that correlation doesn't equal causation. And while there were correlations between where voucher holders lived in Memphis and rising rates of violent crime, there was no evidence to suggest that voucher holders were responsible for this rise in crime. "All Rosin offers are the fears—some would say stereotypes—of police officers who believe that the families relocated out of demolished housing projects are the culprits," wrote a team of housing experts who penned a critique of the article.[6] Rosin misread the data and misled a vast audience of *Atlantic* readers into thinking that vouchers increase crime, what Briggs and Dreier deemed the "ghetto-migration hypothesis," which was "part investigative reporting, part misleading caricature."[7] There was no evidence for it then, and there's little now.[8]

A much more likely explanation is that voucher holders were moving to neighborhoods that were *already* on the decline, including places where crime rates were already rising, for all the reasons outlined in this book. The real story hidden in Rosin's article is that voucher holders *end up* in disproportionately high-crime neighborhoods—not because they commit crimes at higher rates, but because they have trouble using their vouchers to move to neighborhoods on an upward trajectory. This is where researchers and policymakers should be focusing their attention. Numerous studies since the 2008 article have refuted the hypothesis that voucher holders introduce crime into neighborhoods (and Rosin herself has recanted).[9] A study by Susan Popkin and colleagues suggests that, contrary to popular thought, public housing demolition and redevelopment in cities like Chicago and Atlanta may actually have lowered these cities' overall crime rates.[10]

When it comes to scapegoating voucher holders, race is not accidental. Stereotypes of voucher holders are intimately tied up with racial stigma. Nationwide, 64 percent of voucher holders are racial minorities.[11] Stereotypes of welfare queens living off the system run deep in this country and have been transferred to housing assistance programs. Studies have found that black and Latino voucher holders moving into white neighborhoods across the country encounter virulent and racially motivated hostility.[12] The racial imbalance of the voucher program is less visible in Baltimore, where the general population is 66 percent black and the voucher population is 93 percent black, but it is no less salient.

Just as vouchers were not responsible for the crime wave in Memphis, neither are they responsible for the physical and economic decline of Park Heights, which began long before voucher holders arrived on the scene. Redlining and racial covenants kept potential black residents out of the neighborhood until the 1960s, when realtors began blockbusting, driving out whites and reselling to black families at higher prices. All to make a quick buck. In the 1970s manufacturing jobs began to leave Baltimore City. Low-income residents in neighborhoods like Park Heights were hit especially hard. In the years after the Vietnam War, drugs hit the neighborhood in full force, and then the War on Drugs landed people in prison.[13] Disinvestment by the city kept the neighborhood isolated and precipitated its decline, leaving it vulnerable in more ways than one.

The blaming of voucher holders is scapegoating, pure and simple. It's not all that different from the way in which Park Heights homeowners scapegoat voucher holders. Vouchers trigger fears and stereotypes across a range of domains: crime, neighborhood change, racial and class divisions. In Rosin's *Atlantic* piece, voucher holders were blamed for an inexplicable rise in crime. There are other examples too: in Baltimore, the second phase of MTO was called off due to racially motivated resistance from white Baltimore communities who didn't want poor, African American MTO participants moving into their neighborhoods.[14] HUD even changed the name of the program in 1998 from "Section 8" to rebrand it the "Housing Choice Voucher Program" (HCVP) in an effort to shed some of the stigma associated with the program.[15]

In the Bible, a "scapegoat" is an animal ritually burdened with the suffering and sins of others, and then driven away. Finding someone to blame for a problem that seems to have no other explanation provides an emotional catharsis. Like most scapegoating, blaming voucher holders for crime and disorder makes sense to the people who do it: it's an obvious, seemingly visible answer. But it doesn't make it true. Larger forces are sometimes hard to see, hard to label, hard to understand. But this historical series of exclusions and extractions sets the stage for the current situation in the neighborhood.

The shift in American housing policy in the last two decades toward individual subsidies—touted as a way to let the private market solve housing affordability—created space for private landlords to enter into the world of subsidized housing. Landlords enter onto the scene and are able to extract capital from neighborhoods like Park Heights, which provides both cheap single-families homes, as well as affordable multi-unit complexes. Both types of properties are easily renovated to attract a voucher tenant. Because of their role, a program that is meant to provide a safety net for tenants is perverted to also become one for landlords.

Landlords are important mediators of the program, responsible for key decisions regarding where the supply of housing for vouchers is available and who is successful finding a home. Rather than tenants choosing homes and neighborhoods, landlords are choosing tenants, and sorting them into the properties where they will be most profitable.

Despite its potential to facilitate the mobility of low-income households, the HCV program has mirrored outcomes in the private market. In this process of reverse selection, supply actually *shapes* demand, as landlords' actions shape and constrain residents' choices. This reversal illuminates a mechanism in processes of residential sorting and selection that urban sociologists have long studied. The voucher case demonstrates the ways in which landlord practices intervene to pervert the process of residential choice, revealing the limits of a market-based solution to a complicated and entrenched social process. The set of landlord practices described here becomes a powerful sorting instrument that channels the most disadvantaged voucher holders into some of the worst neighborhoods, thus reproducing spatial inequality and concentrated poverty.

Yet, it is also important to remember that landlords are part of a bigger system. Though at times they operate in discriminatory ways, landlords themselves are not solely responsible for the patterns of racial and economic segregation that persist in this country. They operate within a social map of the city laid long before their arrival. Turning attention to the broader risk environment in Park Heights and the structural forces that created it does not absolve individual owners of their responsibility, but does refocus attention toward large-scale policy solutions.

Racial discrimination in housing markets, residential preferences, and structural forces operate in concert to produce and reproduce these patterns of "durable inequality" across time and place.[16] As Chester Hartman pointed out when he called housing vouchers the "grand delusion," the idea that we can rely solely on forces of the free market to address inequality is intrinsically flawed.[17] Without explicit intervention, it is likely that the same forces that sorted and marginalized low-income minority renters across the city in the first place will continue to operate.

Public housing was created with the intent to alleviate slum conditions of overcrowding and hazardous housing. But by the 1990s, much of it was falling apart due to lack of funding and poor maintenance. Troubled developments became notorious for concentrating poor families in segregated, disadvantaged neighborhoods with high unemployment, high crime, and failing schools. In the 1990s, HUD began shifting away from the high-rise towers of public housing to housing vouchers.

In his book, *New Deal Ruins*, Edward Goetz argues that public housing failed "catastrophically and almost willfully."[18] But even as it came to be seen as a failure in both the public eye and the policy world, Goetz points out that, in most places, public housing *worked*. Yet we've transitioned away from this system, insisting that it failed residents and communities. In one city after another, high-rises have been torn down or blown up, the land has been redeveloped, and the poor have been pushed out and relocated. Goetz draws parallels between public housing demolition and redevelopment and the now-maligned process of urban renewal in the 1950s, highlighting how the redevelopment of public housing has ended up serving the gentrifying communities in which it is now located, rather than the residents who were pushed out and bore the brunt of the social costs related to redevelopment.

Public housing—much like vouchers—has been scapegoated for the larger forces that in fact pushed people into public housing in the first place: racism in the job market that excluded African Americans from much of the employment sector, racist zoning policies that created and solidified the urban ghetto, and discriminatory and predatory lending practices that prevented black families from accumulating wealth.[19] In fact, it wasn't public housing itself that caused its own demise, but rather the government's failure to adequately fund and maintain it.[20] Today, we risk making the same mistakes in evaluating the voucher program. The housing voucher program as it currently exists is flawed—there aren't enough vouchers, they don't promote as much choice and mobility as policymakers hoped, and landlords pervert the program for their own ends. But, in and of themselves, vouchers are not the problem, and they have an important role to play as part of the solution.[21]

HOUSING SOLUTIONS: MAKING A GOOD PROGRAM BETTER, NOT JUST BIGGER

How can we create national housing policy that addresses the needs of poor Americans, that is flexible enough to adapt to local demands, and durable enough to do more than simply put a Band-Aid on poverty and housing instability?

In her agenda-setting article "Housing: Commodity versus Right," sociologist Mary Pattillo argues that the precarious housing conditions endemic to the lives of the poor—eviction, homelessness, and severe housing cost burden—result from the fact that we treat housing as a commodity, that is, a good that can be bought and sold, rather than a right.[22] Indeed, there is no *right* to housing in this country. In fact, many forms of homelessness—such as living in a car, sleeping in public, and camping in a city—are criminalized,[23] eviction records act as marks on one's residential history and credit report,[24] and receiving housing assistance can carry tremendous stigma.

The clamor of voices calling for housing to be treated as a right rather than a commodity is growing louder. The voucher system, which makes housing affordable for those lucky enough to take part, is a step in this direction. In his book *Evicted*, Desmond suggests a sweeping solution to the problem of housing instability in this country by creating a universal voucher program in which every American who needs housing aid would receive it.[25] Such a program, he argued, would cost less than many of the alternatives, in that it could rely on existing housing rather than new construction. The Bipartisan Policy Center estimates that a voucher program available to every American who needed it would cost an additional $22.5 billion, increasing total spending on housing assistance to about $60 billion.[26]

Vouchers offer a powerful potential solution to the affordable housing crisis. In the program's current formulation, vouchers are especially geared toward helping those most in need, in particular the extremely low-income, families with children, the elderly, and the disabled.[27] The voucher system has a number of key advantages over other forms of housing assistance. Because vouchers change with families' needs, responding to fluctuations in income, family size, and job location, they allow recipients the flexibility (at least in theory) to move to new neighborhoods as they choose. Unlike public housing, vouchers also provide families the potential to live outside of areas of concentrated poverty,[28] and do so more effectively than other forms of housing assistance.[29] This flexibility is a hallmark strength of vouchers.

There is no question that the United States needs to invest more in housing the poor. And a universal voucher program certainly sounds within reach financially, at least in theory. However, achieving this goal would, of course, be politically challenging if not impossible without a dramatic reorientation in the U.S. political landscape.[30] Experts have argued that an expanded program is politically unpopular, and therefore simply infeasible. What's more, scaling up vouchers in their current form is not enough; if we are to even entertain the notion of using housing vouchers to address the problems of poverty and housing instability, we must directly confront the program's limitations.

All of the strengths of the voucher program discussed above are more *potential* fortes than actualized ones. Voucher experts emphasize the need for reform to make the voucher program more efficient and effective. Indeed, scaling up the program as is would come with some risk. In their current form, based as they are on the logic of the private housing market, vouchers mirror many of the same discriminatory processes that produce unequal outcomes for poor, nonwhite Americans. Thus, when it comes to scaling up, "the devil is in the details," as some experts argue.[31] *How* we scale up could produce very different kinds of outcomes for recipients and neighborhoods.

A number of fixes would make the voucher program work better for recipients and, ultimately, do more to address housing insecurity. These include such practical tweaks to the system as consolidating PHAs, more flexibility in setting rent ceilings, and offering more services to tenants, as well as stauncher protections against discrimination.[32] Most of these interventions would simultaneously work to reduce barriers that prevent families from using their voucher in low-poverty, integrated neighborhoods.

But where would available homes come from in an expanded voucher program?[33] We cannot address the limitations of the voucher program without confronting the shortage of affordable housing in this country. As Edie's story shows, landlord discrimination is a huge problem, and mandating that landlords participate isn't enough—under the current system it's too easy for them to price out voucher holders or rely on other criteria to screen them out. Increasing supply by incentivizing more landlords to participate is key. Below, I detail three key areas that will need to be addressed if housing vouchers are to fulfill their potential as a tool that can unmake patterns of racial segregation and inequality rather than reproduce them.

Reforming PHA Practices

The findings in this book are supported by a wealth of research documenting the ways in which PHAs could better support voucher families in their search for housing. PHAs can empower voucher recipients to make more informed decisions by, for example, providing housing information, counseling, transportation to help families explore new neighborhoods, and offering security deposit assistance, which is hard for cash-poor families to pay, especially in neighborhoods with higher rent.[34] These sorts of actions would not only help tenants enact the flexibility promised by the program, but would also counteract landlords' attempts to attract and trap vulnerable voucher holders.

Providing counseling would help families learn about neighborhood resources such as schools, jobs, and crime when considering a move. Families must also be informed of their rights as tenants so that they know the circumstances under which they can break their lease and feel empowered to report necessary repairs or request to move without fear of losing their voucher. Extending the period of time voucher holders have to use their voucher would reduce pressure on renters to take housing that fails to meet their needs. This is a simple but important fix. We know from mobility programs such as the Baltimore Regional Housing Program (BRHP) and the Mobility Assistance Program in Dallas that these kinds of interventions both help families find homes and help them move to neighborhoods with more resources.[35] Yet we haven't implemented them more broadly.

The stories in this book provide even more evidence to support the implementation of such programs. Recently, HUD and Congress took a small step in this direction. The Voucher Mobility Demonstration Act, passed by Congress in 2019 with bipartisan support, includes $28 million to fund housing mobility support services such as counseling and landlord outreach to help voucher families find homes in new kinds of neighborhoods, as well as to evaluate these supports in order to determine the most cost-effective components. This act is a step in the right direction, however a larger implementation of such services would require HUD and Congress to authorize additional funding.

Beyond providing more services to families, important reforms would improve the way PHAs operate. Currently, the HCV program is administered by over 2,200 separate PHAs across the country, nearly 1,500 of which are also busy administering a public housing program.[36] What's more, an analysis by the Center for Budget and Policy Priorities (CBPP) reports that most large metropolitan areas—where 71 percent of HCV households live—have multiple PHAs. Typically, there is one housing authority for the central city, and one or more for surrounding suburban areas, but 35 percent of large metro areas have at least ten separate PHAs.[37]

This fragmented system makes it difficult for families to move across PHA jurisdictional boundaries with their voucher, even when they're staying within the same metropolitan area. For example, it was much easier for Vivian to move just a mile away than it would have been for her to consider moving out to Baltimore County, which is serviced by a separate PHA. This would have meant "porting" her voucher, or transferring it from the Housing Authority of Baltimore City to the Housing Authority of Baltimore County. Research shows that PHAs discourage portability to other PHAs because it adds to their administrative burden.[38]

This unnecessary administrative fragmentation and complexity, as Vice President for Housing Policy at the CBPP Barbara Sard argues, hinders families' ability to use their voucher as a tool for mobility.[39] But it doesn't have to be this way. The program's administration could be modified to reduce these service boundaries, create incentives for PHAs to encourage voucher portability, making the flow of vouchers across space more fluid. HUD could do this, Sard and others propose, by encouraging PHAs within the same metropolitan area to consolidate and unify their services on a regional scale. They could strictly enforce the performance standards and dissolve those agencies that don't meet them.[40] A more regional approach to administering housing vouchers would not only improve mobility outcomes for families,[41] it would make the voucher program run more efficiently saving costs both in local administration as well as federal oversight, according to an analysis from the Government Accountability Office (GAO) and a recent HUD study.[42]

Landlord Incentives and Discrimination

As the gatekeepers to every rental home, landlords have enormous power to shape residential outcomes for voucher tenants. Designing policy that considers how landlords think about and use the voucher program is key for maximizing their participation in a way that benefits tenants.[43] It is therefore important to note that Baltimore, and Park Heights in particular, are at one end of a spectrum in terms of the types of places to which voucher holders move. Landlords who become "voucher specialists" thrive in neighborhoods like this one. While all cities likely have "voucher specialists," some undoubtedly have fewer than others.

Landlords have incentives to rent to voucher holders in areas where they cannot find reliable market-rate tenants. In Baltimore, this situation applies in most of the city, and especially in Park Heights. Landlords have much less incentive to rent to voucher holders in more affluent, white neighborhoods like Canton or Federal Hill. In cities with less affordable housing stock, landlords are motivated to rent to voucher holders only in certain types of neighborhoods where they can make a profit, and in particular, in certain types of properties.[44] In these cities, vouchers become profitable as part of a real estate "filtering" process. Landlords use them to fill units in large complexes until the owner is ready to renovate and attract a more affluent tenant population. In cities with less of a discrepancy between average rents across a metropolitan area there is less profit to be made through the voucher program, but landlords still use it as a last resort to fill vacant units when they cannot find anyone else to rent them.[45]

There are a number of fixes that take account of the important role that landlords play in the voucher program. One important action would be to pass national legislation making it illegal to discriminate against someone who pays their rent with a voucher. Currently, such Source of Income (SOI) legislation exists in a handful of cities and states, but there is no federal statute banning such discrimination.[46] For many years, Baltimore City has discussed passing legislation to ban this type of discrimination. In the spring of 2019, the city council finally did.

While Baltimore's SOI law is a step in the right direction, the ruling has a few quirks that limit its scope. First, it has a sunset provision, meaning that the law will expire unless the city council votes to uphold it in four years. Second, the law exempts buildings in which 20 percent of units are already occupied by voucher holders. From a civil rights perspective, the cap exemption is alarming: it's hard to imagine a cap of

20 percent on members of a particular religious group in a building, or say, a gender cap, both of which are protected classes under the Fair Housing Act. Access to housing is an essential human need, and yet even those laws specifically designed to counteract discrimination pull back from offering full protections.

In Baltimore, where the bigger problem is that a subgroup of voucher specialists actively *seek* voucher holders and sort them into poorer neighborhoods, the 20 percent exemption may not prove much of a barrier to access. The legislation covers only Baltimore City, not Baltimore County, which contains many more neighborhoods where landlords are likely to discriminate against voucher holders since they have viable market tenants lined up to rent their units. As with voucher portability, an SOI law that extends across the region would do more to open up new kinds of neighborhoods to voucher recipients. In late 2019, Baltimore County passed the HOME Act, approving legislation to ban SOI discrimination against voucher holders, exempting landlords who own three or fewer properties if those properties have four or fewer units each.

As with all civil rights protections, the effectiveness of SOI laws depends on their enforcement. It is clear that landlords who don't want to accept vouchers have plenty of ways to avoid them. A landlord who disqualifies a voucher tenant on the basis of credit history (which may not be as strong as for more affluent market tenants), for example, has not technically violated SOI laws. Nevertheless, the data show that that implementing these laws does have tangible and significant, if modest, results.[47]

In and of themselves, SOI laws are no silver bullet. In order for them to work well, they need to be implemented alongside another type of intervention. Mandating landlords to participate in the program without raising the payment standard to include properties located in higher-rent areas would mean that voucher holders would still be confined to a limited number of properties in lower-rent neighborhoods. While implementing a federal SOI law is not currently on the agenda at HUD, the agency has been reconsidering its approach to calculating rent ceilings. In 2016, HUD introduced a policy called Small

Area Fair Market Rent (SAFMR).[48] In the twenty-four metropolitan areas in which the policy was eventually implemented in 2018, the formula that calculates FMR was reformed to use numbers for smaller areas, rather than citywide averages. SAMFR is an important tool to help eliminate the incentive structure that rewards landlords who convince voucher holders to live in their properties in the most disadvantaged neighborhoods.

When the FMR is defined at the zip-code level rather than at the metropolitan level, voucher holders have more money to spend in more affluent neighborhoods, allowing them to move to such communities with no additional net costs.[49] Lowering rental payments in disadvantaged neighborhoods eliminates the voucher "premium," removing the financial incentive for landlords to disproportionately recruit voucher holders to disadvantaged neighborhoods. And by raising rental payments in higher income neighborhoods, SAFMR can, in theory, recruit new landlords in new neighborhoods, as well as provide voucher households with more choice and access to those neighborhoods.[50] This has important implications for both the cost-effectiveness of voucher administration as well as for mobility outcomes.[51] In areas where housing authorities spend less on rent, they could help a larger number of families, or alternatively, they could divert these funds to provide voucher recipients with higher allotments for neighborhoods with more resources. When funds are limited, this is a tradeoff that may be best decided by local housing authorities acting on local needs.

Expanding the supply of units to voucher holders could also be achieved to some degree by attracting and keeping more landlords in the voucher program. Previous research shows that many landlords who have affordable units but don't rent through the voucher program, have in fact participated in the program at some point in the past. The majority of them had a negative experience with the PHA that drove them away from the program.[52] Reforms could focus on reducing the bureaucratic red tape for landlords, lessening the frequency of inspections for landlords who demonstrate a record of repeatedly passing them, providing holding fees to compensate landlords for lost rent during the time it takes to approve a new unit, and even providing them with damage insurance to assuage fears about voucher tenants that may be stopping landlords from participating in the program.

Beyond Vouchers

But even with these tweaks, vouchers can't solve everything. This is, in part, because of the role of landlords. Any reforms to the housing voucher program must wrestle with the fact that vouchers allow landlords to extract profit from poor tenants—and in some cases, as in Park Heights, even more profit than they would otherwise get in the open market.[53] In places like Park Heights, where vouchers are especially profitable, this system that was meant to be a safety net for tenants has also become one for landlords. In sociologist Michael Burawoy's words, "Exploitation becomes super exploitation."[54] This is not true everywhere and for all landlords, but it is true for a certain group of landlords in disadvantaged neighborhoods like Park Heights. Meanwhile, in places where vouchers are less profitable, landlords have viable alternatives and are motivated to find their way around laws that require them to accept vouchers.[55]

This is why some have advocated for housing solutions that go beyond vouchers. Vouchers are a stopgap measure for the underlying problem: lack of affordable housing. We cannot fix vouchers without finding a way to increase the supply of homes to which they have access. This could happen through a numbers of tools: incentivizing new construction, expanding inclusionary zoning laws, combatting exclusionary zoning, developing community land trusts to protect affordable housing in gentrifying and higher income areas, reforming the Community Reinvestment Act to bring more mortgage capital into low-income neighborhoods and to support mixed-income developments, and using Community Development Block Grants to help revitalize neighborhoods and preserve affordable housing stock.[56]

Zoning laws, especially, could be reformed to open up more types of neighborhoods to low-income renters. Zoning laws exist to regulate land use within urban areas. In practice, though, they have been found to be motivated by class exclusions and racism.[57] Research documents a number of detrimental effects from zoning regulations such as the exclusion of rentals units from homeowner areas, racial segregation, and racial concentration.[58] These laws could be changed, for example, to eliminate rules that impede the development of affordable housing in more affluent areas.[59]

The Low-Income Housing Tax Credit (LIHTC) is the single largest supply side program of U.S. housing assistance. Together, vouchers and LIHTC form the two sides of a dual housing strategy: demand and supply, complementing each other in important ways. Where there are plentiful units but not enough affordability, vouchers can bridge the gap to get low-income tenants into these units, and they have the unique ability to offer mobility. But in areas where there aren't enough rental units in range, LIHTC can help provide them. Urban Planner Kirk McClure has argued for the importance of fungibility between the two programs.[60] If jurisdictions could exchange LIHTC for vouchers, they would be better able to respond to local needs. It is also important that we locate LIHTC developments near areas of opportunity whenever possible, to avoid their concentration in high-poverty segregated neighborhoods, were they tend to cluster. In a landmark case in 2016, the Supreme Court addressed this issue, ruling that housing discrimination need not be intentional to have the harmful effect of segregation. This is the first time the legal concept of "disparate impact"—the idea that a policy may disproportionately affect certain groups even absent injurious intent—was applied to federal housing policy.

Despite all these tools, the private market has historically been either unable or unwilling to meet the housing needs of Americans living in poverty. While we should continue to move away from high-rise public housing—which dangerously concentrates the poor even more than other types of housing and gives them little flexibility in where to live— there remains a need for some form of public housing in the United States, which continues to shelter 1.5 million households, including some of the neediest Americans: very large households, the elderly, and the disabled. Vouchers, which require that individuals locate housing units that suit their needs in the private market, do not always work for these families. Often, this population needs extra help in finding a place to live. These families need us to invest more in maintaining and improving existing public housing infrastructure.

In Baltimore, previous budget cuts have resulted in a public housing stock plagued with maintenance backlogs, cockroach and bedbug infestations, rampant rodent problems, mold, lead paint, and broken elevators that leave elderly and disabled residents with long waits just to go to the grocery store or the doctor. These problems pose real health dangers for residents. Cutting budgets for routine maintenance ends up costing more in the long run. The historical failure of public housing has always been an external problem of lack of funding. If we choose to invest in this infrastructure, and think creatively about how to avoid some of the pitfalls of the past (for example, by avoiding concentrated poverty by using scattered site and mixed-income developments),[61] public housing could be a vital resource for vulnerable households who need it.

MOBILITY AND PLACE-BASED PARADIGMS: HOW DO NEIGHBORHOODS MATTER?

Many of the policy fixes targeted at improving the voucher program mentioned above would work not just to open up opportunities for voucher holders to live *somewhere*, but specifically for them to move somewhere *else*. This is the idea of *mobility*, that is, that households could use their vouchers to move to higher-income neighborhoods. The conversation about housing vouchers as an anti-poverty policy, however, is a slightly different one from the conversation about housing vouchers as a mobility solution.

I recommend the above fixes less to create *mobility*, and more to create the *freedom of mobility*.[62] Thinking about the voucher program purely as a chance to move poor people out of disadvantaged environments is a missed opportunity. By keeping people housed, vouchers act as an anti-poverty program no matter where residents choose to live. Additionally, as we saw in chapter 7, vouchers create important flexibility that helps low-income families respond to crises in their lives and in their neighborhoods. Given this, we should recognize that the vouchers have important value even when they don't create "opportunity" moves to lower-poverty neighborhoods.

At the same time, using the voucher program to move poor people out of poor neighborhoods is a Band-Aid solution to the problem of deeply entrenched urban poverty. It does nothing to address the fact that poor neighborhoods exist. Unless and until the country as a whole commits itself to addressing the affordable housing crisis, we need housing vouchers. And yet, they are not nearly enough.

Furthermore, we may not know enough about how to engineer mobility. Economist Raj Chetty's work has laid bare the huge advantages to mobility for certain groups in certain places.[63] But while the press has largely focused on the success story, Chetty's work also offers a clear admonition to policymakers: while moving before the age of 13 is hugely beneficial to children, moving *after* the age of 13 may be detrimental for children's long-term outcomes. We simply don't know enough to know under what circumstances mobility helps or harms people.[64] Scaling up a mobility program without careful evaluation built in could be risky, with effects on both the sending and receiving neighborhoods.[65] In the absence of clear data, it is especially important to enhance households' ability to make the decision that best suits their needs.

There are two main ways in which housing experts think about creating policy related to poor households in poor neighborhoods: on the one hand, moving people out of disadvantaged environments, and on the other, improving these environments around the people who live in them to improve housing conditions, crime, job opportunities, and schools. The debate between "mobility-based" policies and "place-based" policies is a long-standing one. But any successful solution to deeply entrenched concentrated disadvantage will require elements of both.

Sociologist Patrick Sharkey's research adds a startling layer of complexity to our understating of concentrated poverty and racial segregation: In his book *Stuck in Place*, he shows how the families who live in today's most disadvantaged neighborhoods are the children and grandchildren of those who lived in the urban ghettos of the 1970s. Despite a major change in the way government houses the poor, neighborhood disadvantages have been passed down to the next generation, with important implications for inequality.[66] Sharkey and others encourage us to look at *place* as a key stratifier of inequality in the United States. This would suggest using policy to improve neighborhoods in place, rather than simply moving families out of disadvantaged environments.

Moving the poorest of the poor out of poverty-stricken neighborhoods is not enough to address the challenges of economic disadvantage and racial segregation. It is imperative that we address the root causes of poverty and inequality by implementing change at the level of the neighborhood itself, improving the environments around poor families by investing in schools, institutions, and the economy. Sharkey puts forth a "durable" policy agenda: investment that makes lasting changes in individual lives, as well as that which can withstand economic fluctuations and political reshuffling to create change that persists over generations within neighborhood spaces.[67] The voucher program has the capacity to be just this, if part of a larger approach as outlined above rather than an individual, piecemeal one.

I would argue that we need to pay attention not just to how policy can shape neighborhood environments, but also to how neighborhood context shapes the effectiveness and implementation of policy. On the ground, ethnographic work with residents and community organizations reveals how this might work for the study of vouchers: we need to think about how place shapes the way vouchers work for those who receive them. Park Heights teaches us that investing in the whole neighborhood—for example in community organizations that foster relations between homeowners and renters—may improve the experiences of voucher holders by reducing stigma and improving social interaction between groups.

Vouchers provide homes for (some) people who need them. But we might question whether vouchers are the right tool to address poverty in this country. Is it enough to simply move the poor out of poverty-stricken neighborhoods? Or should we be addressing the root causes of poverty and inequality, implementing change at the level of the neighborhood itself, improving the environments around poor families by investing in schools, neighborhood institutions, and the economy?

When voucher holders choose a home, they also choose a neighborhood. The way the housing subsidy works for them (or doesn't) is inextricable from *where* they use it. As this book shows, we cannot fully understand how vouchers work and why without taking the neighborhood environment into consideration.

Typically, researchers think about the "where" component in a narrow way: that is, they think about how we can use voucher policy to get people to healthier neighborhoods. Indeed, vouchers offer households the chance to move out of some of the nations most distressed buildings and communities. But vouchers don't have to operate purely based on a "mobility" strategy. (And, of course, most public housing authorities don't think of them as one.) Recipients are moving into neighborhoods that need support. When we ignore these communities, we do everyone a disservice. In particular, vouchers face tremendous stigma and exclusion in new neighborhoods.

Vouchers offer a perfect case to highlight the benefits of both mobility-based and place-based anti-poverty measures. Housing vouchers are a powerful instrument to remedy the indelible dangers of living in a poor environment for families of all backgrounds, but we can (and should) create policy that invests in the places to which voucher holders move. This would do several things. It would take seriously the choices and preferences of voucher holders themselves. As we saw in chapter 7, voucher holders like Vivian sometimes make residential decisions that don't entirely make sense to policymakers, but solve important problems for the voucher holder. These receiving communities are often in great need of help themselves. We should target policies that bolster these neighborhoods, providing support to community groups that serve homeowners as well as renters and voucher holders. We need policies that serve an integrating function and generate bridging social capital in receiving neighborhoods.[68]

While thinking about vouchers primarily as an anti-poverty tool to provide affordable shelter for the poor—what they are best at doing—we can simultaneously support voucher holders' ability to make informed choices about where to live, and provide resources to communities that receive vouchers by investing local community organizations that serve integrative functions. In this way, vouchers could be a "durable" policy tool.

This book demonstrates the ways in which a market-based solution is inherently limited for solving housing inequality. However, the will for place-based solutions does not appear to be on the immediate political horizon. In the meantime, housing vouchers provide a valuable tool for addressing housing affordability problems, as well as the enduring dangers of living in a poor environment.

Housing vouchers help over two million families find and afford homes every year. They represent one of the nation's most important anti-poverty programs. By so many measures, voucher holders experience better outcomes than similarly poor Americans who haven't been lucky enough to receive this key subsidy. Housing vouchers could be a powerful instrument to remedy the indelible dangers of living in a poor environment for families of all backgrounds.

But, voucher holders still don't do as well as they could. And perhaps more importantly, they don't do as well as they would if we made some strategic reforms to the program. Without explicit countermeasures, the housing voucher program risks reproducing the same entrenched patterns of racial and economic disparity that have long marginalized the poorest members of our society. Reform is within our reach. Investing in the housing voucher program in a durable way while simultaneously addressing housing discrimination, poverty, and other forms of structural oppression is key to the future of so many poor Americans.

METHODOLOGICAL
APPENDIX

On the day I began my fieldwork, I stared down Park Heights Avenue, and felt paralyzed. Where to start? The books I had read and the seasoned ethnographers I had talked to as I formulated a research plan told me that ethnography was like playing catch. You start by throwing the ball and you see who bounces it back. But what did that mean for me? I wasn't studying street life, or homelessness, or the informal economy, or any of the things you can see by standing on the street and observing. I wasn't a man, who might have easily joined a pick-up game of basketball, or become a member of a local boxing gym, or stood on a street corner to bum a cigarette. What's more, I wasn't studying the *neighborhood*, the way many traditional ethnographers do. I was studying a policy. A policy *in* a neighborhood. Where do you go to find a policy?

When I teach qualitative methods, I often tell my students to start with a map. Maps tell their own story, and they can provide hints about where to start. After the summer I spent doing fieldwork on the Baltimore MTO project, I wanted to check to see whether my hunch was right. Was Park Heights in fact home for a disproportionate number of voucher holders? And if so, why? I looked up statistics on the Department of Housing and Urban Development's website, and I made some maps.

I did some simple math and estimated the voucher rate by dividing the total number of vouchers in the neighborhood, which was 841, by the total number of occupied rental units which was 4,751.[1] Across the neighborhood has a whole, voucher holders occupied 17 percent of the occupied rental stock, but the percentage in individual census tracts ranged from about 8 percent in some to as high as 29 percent in others. In contrast, the average rate across the city of Baltimore is around 14 percent. Park Heights is not the only area in Baltimore with an above-average voucher rate, nor is it the highest. But the maps told me that, indeed, many of the homes in Park Heights were occupied by voucher holders. What they didn't tell me was which ones. Finding this answer to this question proved harder than I anticipated.

I decided that my best approach was to just start knocking on doors. I started out by walking down a small quiet street where I spoke to a few people who were sitting out on their front lawns. Then I began knocking on doors. People were sometimes skeptical and wary of opening their doors at first—I often had to yell through the door to explain why I was there, that I was a student studying the neighborhood, and I was interested in hearing about what it was like to live there. Once they heard me out, most opened their doors. They were surprisingly welcoming and even eager to share their stories across the kitchen table.

The problem was, as I continued knocking on doors, I wasn't finding that many voucher holders. As it turns out, even in a neighborhood with an above-average number of subsidized renters, it takes some work to find them. Plus, I wanted to be systematic about finding voucher holders in different parts of the neighborhood, living in different types of units—some single family, some in big complexes—and with different types of neighbors.

I had heard that the Section 8 office kept a big three-ring binder of all the properties for rent through the program. I thought maybe if they had the old binders full of previous listings, I could use those to find the addresses of current voucher holders. I drove down to the voucher office on Pratt Street and asked the receptionist if I could look at the binder. She met my eyes with a blank stare. "Binder? Honey we don't have no binders no more. Have you been on gosection8.com?" I had not. "W-W-W DOT GO SECTION EIGHT DOT COM." She sounded it out like she did this many times a day. "It's where we tell all the landlords and voucher holders to go for listings." She chuckled to herself and added, "Binders, ha." It dawned on me that of course there was no "master list" of all the properties available for rent through the voucher program. This is exactly what makes finding a home tricky for tenants.

So, I did what tenants do. I went to www.gosection8.com. I collected all of the addresses listed over a period of three months, which totaled 169 listings in Park Heights. I randomized the order of the list and started making my way down it. Many doors I knocked on were vacant, or it turned out that the family residing there did not have a voucher. But eventually I started finding some voucher holders. I also learned that if I wanted to understand how the policy worked in this neighborhood, I needed to talk to a range of residents, not just the voucher holders. So, I also knocked on neighbors' doors. If the household was not a voucher household, I asked them to participate as either a homeowner or an unassisted renter.

In order to understand more about the neighborhood, I decided I needed to door-knock on blocks where I had no addresses from the list—I wanted to learn not just about streets where units were frequently listed on gosection8.com, but also about the streets that had no such listings. I returned to knocking on doors that were not on my list of voucher addresses, this time purposefully seeking homeowners and unassisted renters. Additionally, for the homeowners, I went to the local senior center (where many members were homeowners) and introduced myself to residents at lunch. I got calls from people for months afterwards wanting to tell me their stories.

Finally, I posted flyers around the neighborhood at churches, community centers, the Head Start, the drug store, and several health clinics. This is what sociologists call "sampling for range." The process doesn't necessarily produce a sample that is "representative" in a statistical sense—since it is still relatively small compared to the large samples used in quantitative research—but it produces one that includes the kinds of variation that are of theoretical interest to the research topic.[2]

While I got to know hundreds of people in the neighborhood over the time that I spent there living and observing, I sat down for an interview with 82 residents. Twenty-seven were voucher holders, 37 were unassisted renters, and 18 were homeowners. About half were men ($n = 39$) and half women ($n = 43$). Two participants died during the course of fieldwork. All of the respondents were African American, except for one female voucher holder who was white. There is considerable variation in age among the respondent sample: the homeowners tended to be older, while the voucher holders and unassisted renters tended to be younger. This age difference reflects a similar age distribution in the neighborhood as a whole. The "unassisted" group is comprised of low-income renters, 90 percent of whom earn less than 80 percent of area median rent, and therefore would qualify for a housing voucher, though they do not receive one. This group also included several residents who were homeless or "staying" with a friend or relative, but who were not on the lease. I also conducted informal key informant interviews with community members.

For a fifteen-month period from 2011 to 2012, I conducted intensive ethnographic fieldwork in the neighborhood. I lived there for eleven months of this, and continued visiting the area and some of the respondents for years afterward. I used a combination of ethnographic observations and in-depth interviews to provide a multi-faceted window into both lived experience and interactional events. In addition to the daily observations I made while living in the neighborhood, my participant observation included a range of structured and unstructured activities. In order to understand how people experienced their neighborhoods, I participated in their daily activities, both in the home to capture elements of family life, as well as outside of the home to gain an understanding of how they interacted with the world around them. In particular, I accompanied residents on their daily routines to school and work, as well as on such errands as going to the housing authority, shopping, and picking up children. I shared meals with families in their homes. Additionally, I attended monthly neighborhood community meetings held by the local neighborhood development organization in order to learn about residents' concerns regarding their neighborhood.

Interviews were semi-structured and focused on topics surrounding residential history, past and present housing and neighborhood experiences, moving decisions, and future plans. Interviews lasted between two and five hours. Most of the interviews took place in the respondent's home, where they were comfortable and where I could learn a lot more about them than just what they said.

TALKING TO LANDLORDS

After some time in the field, I realized that I couldn't understand how vouchers worked in the neighborhood without talking to another set of key actors in this story: landlords. I designed the sampling strategy for the landlord sample to incorporate as much heterogeneity as possible, with an effort to include both small, self-employed landlords holding a handful of properties, as well as the biggest companies in the Baltimore rental market. I recruited a portion of the landlord sample through contacts I made in my ethnographic work. I identified most through a more formal method: I drew a random selection of landlords from all online listings for units in Park Heights, posted from June to September 2011 on the website www.gosection8.com.

For those I recruited through the random draw, I contacted the individual associated with each listing by phone, using the telephone number listed in the advertisement. If this person was the landlord or property manager in charge of that property, I invited him or her to participate in a study regarding the experiences of landlords in Baltimore City. I arranged an interview, assured confidentiality,[3] and offered compensation.[4] This technique generated a high degree of cooperation: over 80 percent agreed to meet with me.

The targeted-random sampling method produced a sample of twenty landlords that spans the range of types of landlords who rent to voucher holders. The sample also represents the ownership of a significant portion of the units rented through the HCV program in Baltimore. Together, these individuals and companies own and manage over 3,000 units in Baltimore City, over 1,600 of which are rented to voucher holders, meaning they controlled over 14 percent of the units rented through the Baltimore City HCV program at the time of the study.[5]

All landlord respondents own one or more rental units, though some are also property managers, and I observed them in this capacity as well. The sample includes high-level management personnel at three of the largest rental agencies in the city, several large tenant placement agencies that also own property, and two well-known local landlords who have played a role shaping policy and legislation related to the HCV program in Baltimore. Sixteen out of twenty landlords in the sample are open to, or prefer renting through, the HCV program; four landlords no longer accept *new* voucher holders as a policy. Thirteen landlords rent 50 percent or more of their units through the HCV program. Nineteen landlords rent at least one property in Park Heights. Of these, eight rent the majority of their properties in Park Heights. The other twelve have properties spread throughout Baltimore City. Two of the landlords are female. Eight are non-Hispanic black, and twelve are non-Hispanic white. Five landlords have small businesses, owning or managing between one and thirty properties; seven have midsized businesses, with between thirty-one and one hundred properties; and eight landlords have large businesses, owning or managing over one hundred properties.

Through a series of visits and unstructured observations, these landlords came to willingly let me into their world and trust me as a confidant with whom they could share the frustrations, joys, and daily struggles of their work. In each of these visits, I observed landlords conduct daily business. I accompanied them on property tours with prospective tenants, tours of properties under renovation, and maintenance calls, and I was present for evictions. On all these visits I observed firsthand the physical conditions and neighborhood contexts of the units themselves. I also accompanied landlords on visits to the HABC for lease-signings and other official meetings with tenants. These formal and informal interactions provided opportunities to discuss a number of open-ended topics related to their business, as well as to observe how events played out on the ground. Some landlords volunteered access to records of various kinds, such as rental applications, logs of maintenance requests and rent payments, evictions, and inspection reports.

I also conducted at least one interview with each landlord. Initial interviews lasted between one and three hours, with the average interview being two hours long. These interviews took place in the landlords' offices, in empty rental units, or while riding around on a visit. In the initial interview, we covered a set of predetermined topics, although the exact wording, order, and additional topics followed the flow of the conversation. I asked each landlord to tell me the whole story of how he or she became a landlord, to describe all aspects of the job, and to address a range of topics pertaining to tenant selection, property acquisition, the HCV program, and more.

All interviews were recorded and transcribed, and after each day in the field I spent several hours every night recording detailed field notes describing the interactions and activities in which I participated and observed.[6] These data were loaded into the qualitative data analysis software Atlas.ti, and coded both inductively and deductively, with thematic coding schema related to my research questions. In this way, I was able to allow hypotheses to emerge inductively from the data, while also systematically identifying and revealing the prevalence of various practices hypothesized to be important. Qualitative data software was enormously helpful in organizing interview data for a sample of 102 respondents and linking it to thousands of pages of field notes and observations, in order to identify and assess the scope of a hypothesis or finding. I also relied heavily on my experiences from the field as an ethnographer and my own knowledge of how people and places were connected. Some of the most important insights were revealed during an interaction I witnessed or was a part of that illuminated a process that had been obscured in the interview.

ENTRÉE, SOCIAL DISTANCE, AND POSITIONALITY

Urban ethnographers have all kinds of ways of gaining "entrée," becoming accepted in the communities they study, and establishing trust with their respondents. Forrest Stuart, who writes about initially having trouble being accepted and was constantly mistaken for a cop, eventually joined the men he was studying in Los Angeles in their outdoor gym routine. As he "hung from pull up bars alongside other shirtless park users sweating in the sun," he knew he had found his point of entry.[7] When I jogged by similar outdoor gyms ("pocket parks") in Baltimore, I was frequently cat-called and (jokingly) offered marriage proposals. Sudhir Venkatesh arbitrated basketball games in the public housing complex he studied, Rob Vargas played basketball with young men as a way to break the ice, and Mitch Duneier sold books on the street.[8] As an outsider across multiple dimensions—race, gender, age, and education, varying depending on whether I was talking to a voucher holder, an older homeowner, or a landlord—how would I gain entrée?

It would be important to establish trust for both fieldwork and interviews, but in my case, I found it helpful to use the interviews to establish trust *for* the fieldwork. In the first few months of fieldwork, I conducted interviews with new respondents *prior* to spending time with them doing observation. Interviews were a concrete way of introducing myself and my purpose. An in-depth interview can be a highly effective way to establish trust and rapport. In this way, interviews can offer a way into a neighborhood and a house where one otherwise has no legitimate place. They can be used, ultimately, to gain entrée. It is much harder to knock on someone's door and ask to begin "following" them around than it is to first ask to discuss their experience in the neighborhood at the kitchen table. Once getting to know them, it was not difficult to ask if I could observe them and participate in their daily lives. Later on in the fieldwork, as I got to know more people in the neighborhood, I met people more organically and spent time with them casually before setting up an interview.

In some ways, my status as a woman allowed me entrée that may not have been as easy for a man. I may have been seen as less threatening, less likely to be a cop. It was easy to join daily life activities in the home.

Overall, families were interested in my research and eager to talk to me. Some were reticent at first, though once people in the neighborhood got to know me and saw me around, many of them let me know they were interested in participating. I spent time with residents on their front porches, walking around the neighborhood, participating in community events. As a white woman, I stood out in the neighborhood. While it certainly closed some doors, in other ways, my very visibility turned out to be beneficial. Within a few weeks of beginning fieldwork, people whom I had not yet met knew who I was. More than once when I knocked on a stranger's door, I was greeted with "I've been waiting for you to come by."

When people were reticent to talk, it was often related to a fear that I might use their personal information against them, misrepresent them, or exploit them in some way. And they weren't wrong to be afraid. Residents were well-versed in the history of medical research in Baltimore and beyond. The famous case of Henrietta Lacks—the Baltimore cancer patient whose cells were used without her family's permission and became the basis of an entire industry and field of research—stood in for long histories of exploitation and mistreatment.[9] There was a general distrust of what someone in a position of power could do with personal information; perhaps something they couldn't even imagine. Respondents also feared that they might divulge information about someone else that could get them in trouble, such as information about a crime that someone they knew committed.

To my surprise, explaining that I was a student from Harvard University seemed to help people feel more comfortable talking to me. In contrast, when I mentioned I was visiting Johns Hopkins for the year, doors shut in my face. To them, Harvard was just a good, respectable school, with none of the negative associations that Hopkins has in the city among poor, black residents. Coming all the way from Massachusetts, I was repeatedly reminded, "It's cold up there!" or "I once had a friend from Boston!" It felt like the northern part of the country was a different world to people in Park Heights. Even if they started out skeptical, people noticed that I cared enough to stay and listen to their story for as long as they felt like sharing it. They noticed that I came back to hear and see more. This went a long way toward establishing trust.

In the style of interviewing that I use, the goal is for the fieldworker to speak as little as possible.[10] This allows the respondent to define much of the structure and content of the interview. Even so, I did ask prompting questions, and I followed up when things were unclear or large topics had not been covered. Depending on the respondent, this can take a bit of practice. But even when respondents initially assumed it would be a short survey, they quickly opened up. Interviews generally lasted as long as they did because respondents did not want to stop talking. There is something powerful about being asked to talk about one's past and daily life experiences. The fact that I was a stranger and an outsider was palpable to both parties in the early part of the interview, but in most cases, this seemed to fade into the background over the course of the interview.

By the end of these interviews, something had shifted in the room. Respondents often marveled at how much they had shared, sometimes with genuine, warm, trusting feelings, and occasionally with suspicion. This was a delicate moment. If I left too quickly or did not return, it could lead to feelings of resentment or distrust. By following up to spend more time with the person, I was able to establish a trusting relationship over time.

White people were few and far between in Park Heights. After I got to know residents, I often asked them what they thought of me when they first saw me. Most commonly, people told me they had thought I was a social worker or inspector; of course there was also always the possibility that I was there to buy drugs. I dressed casually in an effort to not stand out in any particular way. But I also tried to be myself, since there wasn't really any way not to be.[11] I was kindly chastised by respondents for going out alone, for leaving things in the car that people might see and try to steal, for abandoning my bag on the couch or kitchen chair when I went to use the bathroom. Respondents frequently walked me home or to my car on occasions when it was getting dark by the time I left.

Two things dramatically changed my reception in the neighborhood for the better. The first occurred by accident. After getting to know a resident, I would often ask him or her to introduce me to friends or neighbors to learn about the people that lived nearby. I quickly learned the power of this introduction. The third party took the introduction very seriously. There seemed to be a tacit assumption that if a neighbor introduced me, that person was somehow vouching for me. I found the relationships with people to whom I was introduced by others to be more open more quickly.

The second change happened when I moved into the neighborhood, which I did after the first few months of living near, but not in, Park Heights. Once I could introduce myself as someone who "lived down the street" and could talk in detail about goings on in the community, which corners to avoid, where to get the best produce, and started bumping into respondents on the street, people interacted with me very differently. I was also able to observe events as they unfolded. As I gained a more stable position in the field, I met people organically—for example, walking down the street, in the supermarket, or at church— and spent time with them in their daily lives as a participant observer *before* conducting an interview. I did not, however, find that relationships with these respondents were significantly different from those with whom I conducted the interview before the observation.

As I became more embedded in the field, these webs of relations provided two forms of validity checks. One, people began being more "truthful," or at least more open with me. They were less concerned with how they wanted to portray themselves to me (a white woman, an academic, a northerner, an outsider) in a short interview. Second, as they became aware that I was embedded in the community and had access to multiple sources of information (other people in the neighborhood, my own experience as a resident of the neighborhood), it became more complicated to dissimulate.

One of the biggest dilemmas I faced was how to deal with the ways in which my presence might have been changing the course of events. For example, once people realized I had a car, they frequently asked me for rides. Carol Stack, in *All Our Kin*, lamented having a car because she ended up spending so much time driving people around.[12] I was warned about this, and did some thinking about how to approach it. Ultimately, I drove the car sometimes, and other times left it at home. For example, the experience of taking an hour-plus bus trip to get to the voucher office is part of the data. Sometimes we took a "hack," an unmarked, unofficial taxi (i.e., any person with a car who wanted to make a few bucks in the days before Uber and Lyft). We would stand on the side of the road and Vivian would wave her hand in an up and down motion until a car pulled over and offered us a ride for a small sum. But when Vivian needed to get to the voucher office in 110-degree heat to request a move after she lost her husband, I decided to drive us.

One day Vivian asked me to pick up some laundry detergent for her. When I handed her a distinctive white and red Target bag she laughed and said "white people love to shop at Target." To me it seemed trivial at first: detergent cost a few bucks at Target just like it did at the Shop & Save. And actually, when I went to the Target in Mondawmin Mall, there were very few white shoppers there. In fact, most of the white Baltimoreans I knew wouldn't even go to Mondawmin; they would instead trek out to the Target in suburban Towson. But Vivian had a point. For one, you needed a car to get to Target. And two, most household items were indeed far cheaper at the Shop & Save down the street.

There were other little moments. Vivian thought it was funny that I was always snapping pictures of everything to keep track of what we did and saw. One day after lunch at McDonald's (Vivian had a craving for a chocolate shake), she handed me the receipt and said, "You wanna take a picture of this too?" laughing. I laughed too, and then realized that's how it must have seemed to her. She didn't mind most of the time, but she did think I was odd.

These moments were important because they revealed something about the social distance between us and how she navigated it. Vivian thought it was silly that I went to Target for the detergent and that I took pictures of all sorts of random things that didn't seem important, but at the same time she was able to laugh at our differences. The fact that she poked fun at me—rather than putting up walls around our differences— suggested to me that she felt comfortable telling me what she really thought, at least some of the time. The social distance between me and the people I was getting to know was ever present—more in some moments than in others. Even once people got to know me, I was still an outsider—ever visible—a curiosity. But I was not unwelcome. And honesty and laughter were often a way to bridge the divide.

ACKNOWLEDGMENTS

I am indebted to a great many people who have supported me and made this research possible. Above all, I would like to thank the residents of Park Heights, who opened their world to me, shared their daily lives and experiences, triumphs, and tragedies, and trusted me with their stories.

I owe deep gratitude to a small group of people who read the manuscript cover to cover, some of them multiple times: Brian McCabe read multiple drafts and generously rolled up his sleeves to help me rewrite over and over. Ann Owens, who gave me the eye of a housing expert as well as a friend who has read every serious thing I've written since the beginning of grad school. Kristin Perkins, Raphael Calel, and Dustin Andres all provided invaluable comments on the manuscript. Phil Garboden, who read this draft and so many others, and is a collaborator for life. Many thanks to Meagan Levinson, who was a tremendous support all the way through. Lisa Adams helped me structure this project from the beginning, was always ready to lend an ear, read a draft, or talk though a title or question, no matter the size.

In the years since finishing the research for my dissertation, my PhD advisors have only become more important. Over the years Mary Waters has listened to my half-formed ideas and repeated them back to me in a way that made them sound brilliant. She is a voice of wisdom and reason, and has been the best role model—both academic and personal—that I could ever imagine. I am deeply grateful to Michèle Lamont for always reminding me not to forget theory, for pushing me to do the best work possible. To William Julius Wilson, who has been unwaveringly supportive and who never failed to remind me how the research mattered. I want to thank Matt Desmond, who set a high bar for what ethnography can teach the world, and provided insightful and indispensable guidance.

I owe deep gratitude to Kathy Edin, who taught me how to do fieldwork, how to talk to people, and how to let them teach me. She inspired me to do this project not just from the work we did together in Baltimore

in 2010, but dating back to when I read *Making Ends Meet* before applying to graduate school. She has believed in me, supported me, cheered
me on, and is always game to talk at 7 a.m. on a Saturday morning.
Thank you to Stefanie DeLuca, who has been an inspiration since the
day I met her in the James Coleman room on the fourth floor of Mer-
genthaler at JHU. Stefanie is a true inspiration and a dear friend. And I
am indebted to Sudhir Venkatesh, who showed me the great American
city that is Chicago, and taught me so much about sociology and how
it was created there. I could not have done this work without this group
of truly incredible mentors.

At Johns Hopkins, the participants of the PIRL lunch, including
Emily Warren, Anna Rhodes, Christine Jang-Trettien, Allison Young,
and Meredith Greif, listened and provided feedback to drafts of many
pieces of this book. The 21st Century Cities Initiative and Ben Siegel
generously supported my research as a postdoctoral fellow. Nora Gor-
don, Pam Herd, and George Ackerlof have offered tremendous mentor-
ship since I joined the faculty at the McCourt School at Georgetown.

Perhaps more than anyone else, this book was made possible through
the support of my friends and peers in graduate school, where I began
this research. They taught me how to do research, how to write, how to
laugh, and how to survive seven years of a doctoral program. Alex Murphy has long been a friend. Kim Pernell-Gallagher and Eleni Arzoglou
kept me sane through the most difficult times, personal and professional.
Kevin Lewis provided invaluable feedback throughout this process.
Francois Bonnet, for endless hours of conversation in the basement of
SIPA, and the years of friendship since. The members of Urban Writing
Workshop, Monica Bell, Jackie Hwang, Jeremy Levine, and Robert Vargas read early chapters back when this was a dissertation, and provided
thoughtful feedback and conversation. Jasmin Sandelson read excerpts
and was always there to talk ethnography.

Thank you to all the anonymous reviewers who read parts of this
book. And thanks to the four inspiring scholars who read an early draft
as part of a book workshop, lending their time and advice: Xavier De
Sousa Briggs, Maria Krysan, Karyn Lacy, and Waverly Duck.

Many thanks to my research assistants, who provided invaluable background research, proofreading, and moral support: Alyvia Walters, Natasha Camhi, and Isaiah Fleming-Klink.

A number of people had a hand in showing me the ins and outs of Baltimore: Josh Greenfeld, for helping me to decipher Baltimore politics; Ben Frock, who provided invaluable inside Baltimore history; and Brian Adams, who showed me parts of the city I never would have found on my own.

This research has been generously supported by numerous sources: the National Science Foundation, the U.S. Department of Housing and Urban Development, the Harvard Joint Center for Housing, the Taubman Center for Urban Policy, the Horowitz Foundation for Social Policy, the Harvard Kennedy School Malcolm Weiner Center, the Harvard Multidisciplinary Program in Inequality & Social Policy, the Harvard Real Estate Academic Initiative, and the Barnard College Alumnae Association.

And finally, I would like to thank my family: my mom, who finished her PhD while raising three kids and, I am told, sometimes brought me into class in a backpack to woo her professors into giving her extensions. I don't know how she did it. My dad, who works harder than anyone I know, and, along with Anne, taught me that it is indeed possible to love your job. To my sisters Hayley and Nyla, who have always believed in me. These family members, friends, and mentors have supported me through every choice I made, loved me unconditionally, and had an unflagging faith in me that allowed me to tell this story.

NOTES

PREFACE

1. Life expectancy in Southern Park Heights is 69 years; in Pimlico/Arlington/Hilltop, it's 67.7, compared to Greater Roland Park, where it is 83.6 (Baltimore Neighborhood Indicators Alliance, Jacob France Institute, *Vital Signs 17*).

2. In the years since beginning this fieldwork, crime in Baltimore has spiked.

3. Rothstein, *The Color of Law*; Fischel, *The Homevoter Hypothesis*; Rothwell and Massey, "The Effect of Density Zoning on Racial Segregation in U.S. Urban Areas"; Pendall, "Local Land Use Regulation and the Chain of Exclusion."

4. Taylor, *Race for Profit*.

INTRODUCTION

1. Names, streets, and identifying details of individuals have been changed to protect the confidentiality of participants.

2. In 2010 Baltimore had a population of 620,961 residents, as compared to 939,024 in 1960 (U.S. Census Bureau 1960, "Total Population"; U.S. Census Bureau 2010, "Total Population").

3. American Community Survey, 2008–2012: B02001: "Race"; American Community Survey, 2008–2012: B03003: "Hispanic or Latino Origin."

4. Thirty-one percent of Park Heights residents lived below poverty line in 2011 (American Community Survey, 2007–2011: B17001 "Poverty Status in the Past 12 Months by Sex by Age").

5. In Park Heights, the unemployment rate (those who are unemployed, divided by those in the labor force) is 21.8 percent. A full 45 percent of the population over sixteen years old in Park Heights is not in the labor force, compared to 37 percent citywide (American Community Survey, 2007-2011: B23025 "Employment Status for the Population 16 Years and Over").

6. This is the true name of the neighborhood. All names of people, places, and streets within the neighborhood are pseudonyms in order to maintain confidentiality. In some instances, additional personal details are changed in order to protect participants' identities.

7. Freeman, "The Impact of Source of Income Laws on Voucher Utilization and Locational Outcomes"; Newman and Schnare, "'. . . And a Suitable Living Environment'"; McClure, "The Prospects for Guiding Housing Choice Voucher Households to High-Opportunity Neighborhoods"; Goering, "Expanding Choice and Integrating Neighborhoods."

8. See Pattillo, "Housing."

9. Rainwater, *Behind Ghetto Walls*; Gans, *The Urban Villagers*.

10. Sampson, *Great American City*; Sharkey, *Stuck in Place*.

11. Wilson, *The Truly Disadvantaged*.

12. Anderson, *Code of the Street*; Pattillo, *Black Picket Fences*; Venkatesh, *American Project*; Desmond, *Evicted*; Edin and Shaefer, *Two Dollars a Day*.

13. Rothstein, *The Color of Law*; Massey and Denton, *American Apartheid.*

14. Gotham, "Urban Space, Restrictive Covenants and the Origins of Racial Residential Segregation in a US City, 1900–50"; Jones-Correa, "The Origins and Diffusion of Racial Restrictive Covenants"; Rothstein, *The Color of Law.*

15. Rothstein, *The Color of Law.*

16. Rothstein, *The Color of Law.*

17. Oliver and Shapiro, *Black Wealth / White Wealth*; Baradaran, *The Color of Money.*

18. Korver-Glenn, "Compounding Inequalities"; Turner and Ross, "How Racial Discrimination Affects the Search for Housing"; Yinger, *Closed Doors, Opportunities Lost*; Boehm, Thistle, and Schlottmann, "Rates and Race"; Williams, Nesiba, and Mcconnell, "The Changing Face of Inequality in Home Mortgage Lending."

19. Massey and Denton, *American Apartheid*; Rothstein, *The Color of Law.*

20. Turner and Kingsley, "Federal Programs for Addressing Low-Income Housing Needs"; A new estimate suggests the number is as low as one-fifth (Kingsley, "Trends in Housing Problems and Federal Housing Assistance").

21. Riis, *How the Other Half Lives.*

22. Kotlowitz, *There Are No Children Here*; Newman, "Defensible Space."

23. It is now widely accepted that the presence of housing projects in predominantly black neighborhoods substantially increased the concentration of poverty in these areas in later years (Massey and Kanaiaupuni, "Public Housing and the Concentration of Poverty").

24. Park and Burgess, *The City*; Sampson, Morenoff, and Gannon-Rowley, "Assessing Neighborhood Effects"; Wilson, *The Truly Disadvantaged.*

25. Wilson, *The Truly Disadvantaged*; Wilson, *When Work Disappears.*

26. Massey and Kanaiaupuni, "Public Housing and the Concentration of Poverty."

27. This proportion was originally capped at 25 percent, and it has since been raised to 30 percent of *net* income, taking into account additional social service benefits.

28. Edin and Lein, *Making Ends Meet.*

29. Department of Housing and Urban Development v. Rucker.

30. Jacobs et al., "Guide to Federal Housing Programs." This would change again in 1998 with the Quality Housing and Work Responsibility Act (QHWRA) in an effort to deconcentrate poverty in public housing.

31. See Bloom, *Public Housing That Worked* for an account of how the New York City Housing Authority operated differently from other housing authorities, with an emphasis on avoiding a preponderance of nonworking poor residents.

32. Vale, *From the Puritans to the Projects.*

33. Massey and Kanaiaupuni, "Public Housing and the Concentration of Poverty"; Goetz, *New Deal Ruins*; Vale, *From the Puritans to the Projects*; Hirsch, *Making the Second Ghetto.*

34. These estimates are for the year 2000 (Schwartz, *Housing Policy in the United States*).

35. Turner, Popkin, and Rawlings, *Public Housing and the Legacy of Segregation*; Hirsch, *Making the Second Ghetto*; Vale, *From the Puritans to the Projects*; Goetz, *New Deal Ruins.*

36. Bickford and Massey, "Segregation in the Second Ghetto"; Hirsch, *Making the Second Ghetto.*

37. Jackson, *Crabgrass Frontier*; Massey and Denton, *American Apartheid*.

38. For a detailed description of the Thompson case, see Darrah and DeLuca, "'Living Here Has Changed My Whole Perspective'"; Engdahl, "New Homes, New Neighborhoods, New Schools." In 2005, a consent decree created the Baltimore Housing Mobility Program, which provides vouchers for families to move to racially and economically integrated neighborhoods in Baltimore and neighboring counties.

39. Vale, *Purging the Poorest*; Goetz, *New Deal Ruins*.

40. Commission on Severely Distressed Public Housing, "Final Report to Congress and the Secretary of Housing and Urban Development."

41. Popkin et al., *The Hidden War*.

42. "Severe distress" was defined by four factors: 1) physical disrepair of the buildings, 2) impediments to management such as high vacancy and turnover, 3) high crime rates, and 4) family distress, such as high unemployment, low incomes, and low educational attainment (Commission on Severely Distressed Public Housing, "Final Report to Congress and the Secretary of Housing and Urban Development").

43. Zhang and Weismann, "Public Housing's Cinderella"

44. HUD, "Public Housing in a Competitive Market."

45. This $5 billion redevelopment program called HOPE VI, or "Housing Opportunities for People Everywhere," launched in 1992. The program's objectives were to demolish, rehabilitate, or replace severely distressed housing projects in order to improve living conditions for residents and lower the concentration of very-low-income families, the addition of market-rate units to create mixed-income communities, and the revitalization surrounding communities, making them more "sustainable" for all residents (Popkin et al., "A Decade of HOPE VI"). HOPE VI created less-poor, often safer communities, and provided better housing to residents (Cunningham, *An Improved Living Environment?*). However, these new neighborhoods were built to house mixed-income communities, and thus provided only enough units for a fraction of the original residents to return. It is estimated that about 19 percent of tenants in HOPE VI projects moved back to their original sites (Popkin et al., "A Decade of HOPE IV"). Many residents who were left without homes due to demolition received vouchers for use in the private housing market.

46. Importantly, it was the elimination of the "one-for-one replacement" law requiring housing authorities to replace any demolished units with the same number of units in "nonimpacted" areas that allowed this transformation to take place (Salama, "The Redevelopment of Distressed Public Housing").

47. See Lowry, "Housing Assistance for Low-Income Urban Families"; Orlebeke, "The Evolution of Low-Income Housing Policy, 1949 to 1999."

48. Khadduri and Struyk, "Housing Vouchers for the Poor."

49. Khadduri, "Deconcentration."

50. While the deconcentration of poverty in and of itself is not an explicit, comprehensive goal of the HCV program, the consent decrees related to public housing lawsuits do have neighborhood poverty level requirements, e.g., Gautreaux in Chicago, the Thompson Program in Baltimore (Darrah and DeLuca, "'Living Here Has Changed My Whole Perspective'"), and the

Walker program in Dallas. See Popkin et al., "Obstacles to Desegregating Public Housing," for more on these cases. Furthermore, an emphasis on helping families attain low-poverty neighborhoods and a desire to demonstrate that an increasing proportion of HCV households are moving to low-poverty census tracts is reflected in various HUD documents (HUD, "Housing Choice Voucher Program Guidebook"; see also Wang, Varady, and Wang, "Measuring the Deconcentration of Housing Choice Voucher Program Recipients in Eight U.S. Metropolitan Areas Using Hot Spot Analysis").

51. Schwartz, *Housing Policy in the United States*.

52. HUD suspended the one-for-one replacement rule in 1995 and officially repealed it in 1998 with the Quality Housing and Work Responsibility Act (QHWRA). The repeal allowed HUD greater flexibility to demolish distressed public housing without immediately replacing it (Solomon, "Public Housing Reform and Voucher Success").

53. Between 1981 and 2000, Baltimore City reduced its number of "family" public housing units from 12,016 to 6,854. Rosenblatt, *The Renaissance Comes to the Projects*.

54. Newman, "Low-End Rental Housing."

55. HUD, "Picture of Subsidized Households, 2011."

56. Author's calculations, based on HUD's "Picture of Subsidized Households, 2011," and American Community Survey, 2007-2011: B25003: "Tenure." There were 17,042 vouchers in Baltimore City and 120,636 renter households in 2011.

57. Newman, "Low-End Rental Housing."

58. CBPP, "Fact Sheet," 2012.

59. Schwartz, *Housing Policy in the United States*; Turner and Kingsley, "Federal Programs for Addressing Low-Income Housing Needs."

60. CBPP, "United States Federal Rental Assistance Fact Sheet."

61. HUD, "FY 2012 Budget Summary"; CBPP, "Fact Sheet," 2012.

62. Turner and Kingsley, "Federal Programs for Addressing Low-Income Housing Needs." Anyone earning up to 80 percent of the area median income qualifies to receive a voucher, although not everyone who qualifies applies, and most who apply do not receive one, as there aren't enough vouchers to meet the need.

63. There is some regional variation in the details. In 2001, the FMR was raised to the 50th percentile in the 39 most expensive housing markets in the country including Baltimore. It was lowered back down to the 40th percentile in 2017. The QHWRA allows housing authorities to set payment standards between 90 and 110 percent of FMR, and even heigher under certain circumstances. *Moving to Work* (MTW) provides housing authorities further flexibility to set payment standards above the FMR. For example, in D.C., the payment standard goes to 175 percent of the FMR in some high-cost neighborhoods.

64. Since the QHWRA in 1998, if a voucher holder chooses to live in a unit that rents above the payment standard, he or she must independently pay for the extra rent. The rent cannot exceed 40 percent of the resident's income (Schwartz, *Housing Policy in the United States*).

65. Park Heights had 841 vouchers in 2011 (HUD, "Picture of Subsidized Households, 2011").

66. See Rothstein, *The Color of Law*.

67. Briggs, Popkin, and Goering, *Moving to Opportunity*; Briggs, "Housing Opportunity, Desegregation Strategy, and Policy Research."

68. "Place-based" mobility interventions, such as the scattered site public housing units built in Yonkers, New York, featured in the HBO miniseries *Show Me A Hero* have been around for decades.

69. Polikoff, *Waiting for Gautreaux*.

70. Gautreaux was designed to move families to less residentially segregated neighborhoods (under 30 percent black), although this requirement was relaxed in 1981 when families were allowed to move to neighborhoods that were above 30 percent black if they were deemed "revitalizing" (Duncan and Zuberi, "Mobility Lessons from Gautreaux and Moving to Opportunity"). Although evidence suggested favorable effects on high school dropout rates, college enrollment, employment outcomes, and mortality rates (Rosenbaum, "Changing the Geography of Opportunity by Expanding Residential Choice"). The data must be interpreted carefully because there is no control group. Researchers have compared subgroups of those who moved, in particular, comparing those who moved to the white suburbs to those who moved within Chicago (Rubinowitz and Rosenbaum, *Crossing the Class and Color Lines*). Subsequent research (Mendenhall, DeLuca, and Duncan, "Neighborhood Resources, Racial Segregation, and Economic Mobility,") found that Rosenbaum's work was methodologically flawed: in fact, with a longer-term look at the data, there were no employment, earnings, or self-sufficiency effects. Additionally, despite controlling for neighborhood characteristics, there is still some concern that there may be issues of selection bias (Duncan and Zuberi, "Mobility Lessons from Gautreaux and Moving to Opportunity." A second wave of Gautreaux—"Gautreaux Two"—took place in 2002. Gautreaux Two emphasized moving to more affluent neighborhoods, in addition to those that were less segregated (Boyd et al., "The Durability of Gains from the Gautreaux Two Residential Mobility Program"; Pashup et al., "Participation in a Residential Mobility Program from the Client's Perspective").

71. Briggs, Popkin, and Goering, *Moving to Opportunity*.

72. Kling, Liebman, and Katz, "Experimental Analysis of Neighborhood Effects"; Clampet-Lundquist and Massey, "Neighborhood Effects on Economic Self-Sufficiency"; Ludwig et al., "Long-Term Neighborhood Effects on Low-Income Families."

73. Clampet-Lundquist et al., "Moving Teenagers Out of High-Risk Neighborhoods"; Kessler, Duncan, and Gennetian, "Associations of Housing Mobility Interventions for Children in High-Poverty Neighborhoods with Subsequent Mental Disorders during Adolescence"; Kling, Ludwig, and Katz, "Neighborhood Effects on Crime for Female and Male Youth"; Popkin, Leventhal, and Weismann, "Girls in the 'Hood"; Kling, Liebman, and Katz, "Experimental Analysis of Neighborhood Effects."

74. Chetty, Hendren, and Katz, "The Effects of Exposure to Better Neighborhoods on Children."

75. See for example Ludwig et al., "What Can We Learn about Neighborhood Effects from the Moving to Opportunity Experiment," and Sampson, "Moving to Inequality."

76. Gubitz et al., "Family Options Study."

77. Fisher, "Research Shows Housing Vouchers Reduce Hardship and Provide Platform for Long-Term Gains Among Children."

78. Briggs, Comey, and Weismann, "Struggling to Stay out of High-Poverty Neighborhoods." Briggs et al. argue that there are four main ways in which expectations for locational outcomes

have been pursued: the shift from project-based to tenant-based subsidies, tweaks that have made the voucher program more mobility friendly, a series of desegregation consent decrees, and the launch of MTO.

79. For a review of how vouchers affect a range of outcomes, see Owens, "How Do People-Based Housing Policies Affect People (and Place)?"

80. Galvez ("What Do We Know about Housing Choice Voucher Program Location Outcomes?") and Finkel and Buron ("Study on Section 8 Voucher Success Rates") estimate 21 percent of successful voucher users lease in place. Feins and Patterson ("Geographic Mobility in the Housing Choice Voucher Program") estimate 25 percent of familes with children lease in place.

81. Newman and Schnare, "'. . . And a Suitable Living Environment'"; Pendall, "Why Voucher and Certificate Users Live in Distressed Neighborhoods"; Turner, "Moving out of Poverty."

82. 40 percent is commonly used as a threshold for extremely high poverty (Kneebone, et al., *The Re-Emergence of Concentrated Poverty*).

83. NLIHC, "Who Lives in Federally Assisted Housing?"

84. Turner, "Moving out of Poverty"; Devine, "Housing Choice Voucher Location Patterns"; McClure, "Deconcentrating Poverty with Housing Programs"; Schwartz, *Housing Policy in the United States*.

85. More broadly, there is important evidence of the deconcentration of the poor in the 1990s. During this decade, there was an overall decrease in concentrated poverty for all racial and ethnic groups in the U.S. The number of people living in high-poverty neighborhoods (above 40 percent) declined by 24 percent in the 1990s, a dramatic departure from the doubling of people in concentrated poverty that had occurred in the preceding twenty years (Jargowsky, *Stunning Progress, Hidden Problems*). During the same period, there was also an increase in the proportion of low-income neighborhoods that experienced gains in economic status. This is true even with the rollback in poverty deconcentration of the 2000s, which occurred in the Midwest, and to some degree in the South, and predominantly in the suburbs and in smaller metropolitan areas (Jargowsky, *Concentration of Poverty in the New Millennium*; Kneebone, Nadeau, and Berube, "The Re-Emergence of Concentrated Poverty"). Shifts in housing policy have been posited as part of the explanation for these changes (Ellen and O'Regan, "Reversal of Fortunes?"; Kingsley and Pettit, "Concentrated Poverty"); however, others argue that such policy shifts are unlikely to have had such large effects on poverty given the small proportion of the poor whom they affected (Briggs and Dreier, "Memphis Murder Mystery?"). Also, the loss of subsidized units in a neighborhood has not been found to be associated with a deconcentration of poverty in that area (Owens, *The New Geography of Subsidized Housing*). It is clear that subsided housing is less concentrated in poor areas than it used to be. Assisted housing in general, and housing vouchers in particular, are now located in the vast majority of census tracts across the nation. Today there are vouchers in about 85 percent of census tracts across the country, compared to only 10 percent of tracts in 1977 (Devine, "Housing Choice Voucher Location Patterns"; Owens, *The New Geography of Subsidized Housing*). However, the HCV program takes advantage of only 6 percent of all affordable rental housing in the largest fifty metropolitan statistical areas (Devine, "Housing Choice Voucher Location Patterns").

86. Chetty, Hendren, and Katz, "The Effects of Exposure to Better Neighborhoods on Children."

87. Devine, "Housing Choice Voucher Location Patterns"; Galster, "Consequences from the Redistribution of Urban Poverty During the 1990s"; Hartung and Henig, "Housing Vouchers and Certificates as a Vehicle for Deconcentrating the Poor."

88. Only one-quarter (26 percent) of HCV holders reside in census tracts with less than 10 percent poverty; and only 17 percent of blacks and 19 percent of Hispanic voucher holders reside in such low-poverty neighborhoods (McClure, "Deconcentrating Poverty with Housing Programs"). White voucher holder families are about twice as likely as black and Hispanic families to live in low-poverty neighborhoods (Devine, "Housing Choice Voucher Location Patterns"). An interesting paradox is that compared to their unsubsidized counterparts, the voucher offers black families with children more of a leg up than white families with children (for whom receiving a voucher is associated with a decline in neighborhood poverty (https://www.cbpp.org/research/housing/realizing-the-housing-voucher-programs-potential-to-enable-families-to-move-to).

89. Wang and Varady, "Using Hot-Spot Analysis to Study the Clustering of Section 8 Housing Voucher Families"; Wang, Varady, and Wang, "Measuring the Deconcentration of Housing Choice Voucher Program Recipients in Eight U.S. Metropolitan Areas Using Hot Spot Analysis."

90. Boyd, "The Role of Social Networks in Making Housing Choices"; Rosen, "Rigging the Rules of the Game"; DeLuca, Garboden, and Rosenblatt, "Segregating Shelter"; Pendall, "Why Voucher and Certificate Users Live in Distressed Neighborhoods."

91. Chetty, Hendren, and Katz, "The Effects of Exposure to Better Neighborhoods on Children."

92. Despite some early research on landlords (Sternlieb, *The Urban Housing Dilemma*; Sternlieb, *The Tenement Landlord*; Stegman, *Housing Investment in the Inner City*) that pointed to the possible role landlords play, few academics have directly studied landlords until very recently. Since beginning my research, a number of papers doing just this have been published (Korver-Glenn, "Compounding Inequalities"; Garboden and Rosen, "Serial Filing"; Garboden et al., "Taking Stock"; Garboden et al., "Urban Landlords and the Housing Choice Voucher Program"; Greif, "Regulating Landlords"; Greenlee, "More Than Meets the Market?"; Rosen and Garboden, "Landlord Paternalism"; Rosen, "Rigging the Rules of the Game"; Varady, Jaroscak, and Kleinhans, "How to Attract More Landlords to the Housing Choice Voucher Program"; Zuberi, "The Other Side of the Story").

CHAPTER 1. PARK HEIGHTS: "A GHOST TOWN"

1. Pietila, *Not in My Neighborhood*; Jackson, *Crabgrass Frontier*.

2. Keeanga-Yamahtta Taylor calls this "predatory inclusion" (Taylor, *Race for Profit*).

3. Pietila, *Not in My Neighborhood*.

4. Orser, *Blockbusting in Baltimore*, 4.

5. American Community Survey, 2007–2011: B17001: "Poverty Status in the past 12 Months by Age by Sex."

6. In Park Heights, 46.7 percent of the occupied homes are owner-occupied (American Community Survey, 2007–2011: B25003: "Tenure").

7. The extra cash that a voucher frees up is very unlikely to provide enough money to allow a poor family to buy a Lexus. I got to know this family later in my fieldwork. As it turned out, Bob was incorrect—they weren't voucher holders. The older brother of the leaseholder was involved in selling drugs, but it wasn't his Lexus, he told me; he had inherited it from a friend who passed away.

8. Note: quotes are edited for length and clarity.

9. American Community Survey, 2006–2010. Central and Southern Park Heights are comprised of six census tracts and two community statistical areas (CSAs). I exclude Northern Park Heights in my study, which has a very different demographic profile and is socially quite distinct from Southern and Central Park Heights.

10. American Community Survey, 2007–2011: B25034: "Year Structure Built."

11. Jones, Brent. "Troublesome Pall Mall Apartments Come Down."

12. Http://darkroom.baltimoresun.com/2014/08/exploring-baltimores-neighborhoods -park-heights/#1.

13. For more on RAD, see Econometrica, *Evaluation of HUD's Rental Assistance Demonstration (RAD)*.

14. Fritze, John, "New Police, Fire Training Facility Opens."

15. Orser, *Blockbusting in Baltimore*.

16. Goldstein and Weiner, *Middle Ground*, reports that the Roland Park Company pioneered a method of excluding Jews that was then adapted for use by other real estate companies: they would screen potential buyers, then exclude Jews. They did so not through deed covenants which were primarily used against African Americans, but rather through advertising, signage, and a "gentleman's agreement" with the city's real estate board.

17. See Wilson, *The Truly Disadvantaged*; Massey and Denton, *American Apartheid*.

18. American Community Survey, 2007–2011: B17001. "Poverty Status in the Past 12 Months by Sex by Age." Neighborhood level statistics sometimes hide the heterogeneity that may exist within neighborhoods. Park Heights would be classified as "moderately poor" as it has a poverty rate between 20 and 30 percent. However, it is not comprised of a monolithic group of "moderately" poor, but by an array of populations including homeowners, unassisted renters, and voucher holders, each with a unique set of financial and social circumstances and challenges.

19. American Community Survey, 2007–2011: B19013: "Median Household Income in the Past 12 Months (in 2011 Inflation-Adjusted Dollars)."

20. Author's calculations using unemployed / total in labor force, American Community Survey, 2007–2011, B23025: "Employment Status for the Population 16 Years and Over."

21. American Community Survey, 2007–2011: B25002: "Occupancy Status."

22. DeLuca, Garboden, and Rosenblatt, "Segregating Shelter."

23. Indeed, in many cities landlords can get more rent through the voucher program than they could from a market tenant. New research demonstrates that in cities like Milwaukee, landlords may be getting around $50 more on average for a unit rented to a voucher holder (Desmond and Perkins, "Are Landlords Overcharging Housing Voucher Holders?"). In

neighborhoods like Park Heights, though, this "premium" is substantially higher (Rosen, "Rigging the Rules of the Game"; Garboden et al., "Taking Stock").

24. See https://explore.baltimoreheritage.org/items/show/500 and https://grahamprojects.com/2014/01/memorial-pool/ for more on this history.

25. Park Heights has a significant population of homeowners, who make up 46.7 percent of all occupied units, just below the Baltimore average of 49.5 percent (American Community Survey, 2007–2001: B25003: "Tenure"). Over the past thirty years, the homeownership population has stayed relatively stable, while the renter population has declined slightly, resulting in an overall decline in population.

26. The majority (54 percent) of current homeowners in Park Heights moved into the neighborhood before 1990, and only 29 percent of current homeowners have arrived since 2000. In contrast, a mere 7 percent of the current renters in Park Heights arrived before 1990, and a full 83 percent of all renters arrived just since the year 2000 (American Community Survey, 2007–2011: B25038: "Tenure by Year Householder Moved into Unit").

27. Though these data are not publicly available at the block group level, the uneven distribution of vouchers across the neighborhood at the tract level suggests that vouchers tend to cluster in groups within the neighborhood. In 2012, there were above-average concentrations of voucher holders in three of Park Heights' six census tracts as compared to Baltimore City, while the other three were just below average.

28. HUD, "Picture of Subsidized Households, 2011"; American Community Survey, 2007–2011: B25003: "Tenure."

CHAPTER 2: HOUSING INSECURITY AND SURVIVAL STRATEGIES

1. Cox et al., "Roadmap to a Unified Measure of Housing Insecurity."

2. Turner and Kingsley, "Federal Programs for Addressing Low-Income Housing Needs." Kingsley, "Trends in Housing Problems and Federal Housing Assistance."

3. Aurand et al., "The Gap."

4. Pelletiere, "Getting to the Heart of Housing's Fundamental Question."

5. Garboden, "The Double Crisis."

6. Garboden, "The Double Crisis."

7. American Community Survey, 2007–2011: B25064: "Median Gross Rent (Dollars)." Gross rent is the amount of the contract rent plus the average monthly cost of utilities, if paid by renter.

8. American Community Survey, 2007–2011: B25070: "Gross Rent as a Percentage of Household Income in the Past 12 Months."

9. Five residents in my sample were involved in these programs, or had participated in one in the past, and found housing locally once they completed treatment.

10. For more research on doubling up, see Harvey, "When Mothers Can't 'Pay the Cost to Be the Boss.'"

11. Rosen, "Rigging the Rules of the Game."

12. For more on how landlords charge a voucher premium, see Rosen, "Rigging the Rules of the Game"; Desmond and Perkins, "Are Landlords Overcharging Housing Voucher

Holders?" For how they profit in poor neighborhoods more generally, see Desmond and Wilmers, "Do the Poor Pay More for Housing?"

13. For more on squatting, see Herbert, "Squatting for Survival."

14. It has not been independently verified whether or not Marlena and Derrick's landlord was in fact "Little Melvin" Williams.

15. Schwartz, *Housing Policy in the United States.*

16. For more on the informal economy, see Bourgois, *In Search of Respect*; Venkatesh, *Off the Books.*

CHAPTER 3: "A PLACE TO CALL HOME": THE PROMISE OF HOUSING VOUCHERS

1. Wood, Turnham, and Mills, "Housing Affordability and Family Well-Being"; Mills et al., "Effects of Housing Vouchers on Welfare Families."

2. Public Housing provides around 1.1 million households with a home, and vouchers house 2.2 million households (Schwartz, *Housing Policy in the United States*). Additionally, 1.3 million households live in project-based Section 8 units, and 140,000 households live in homes subsidized through the Section 202 and Section 811 programs, which provide housing for the elderly and those with disabilities.

3. Schwartz, *Housing Policy in the United States*; NLIHC, "Who Lives in Federally Assisted Housing?"

4. Approximately 4 percent of all households in the United States and 12 percent of all U.S. renter households receive federal housing assistance. Steffan et al., "Worst Case Housing Needs 2009"; Turner and Kingsley, "Federal Programs for Addressing Low-Income Housing Needs."

5. NLIHC, "Who Lives in Federally Assisted Housing?" For more on how housing authorities set preferences, see also Moore, "Lists and Lotteries"; McCabe and Moore, "Waitlists and Preferences."

6. HUD regulations require that 75 percent of Housing Choice Vouchers are issued to households below 30 percent of median income, so in practice most families receiving vouchers earn far less than this upper income limit (http://static.baltimorehousing.org/pdf/hcvp_faqs_onthelist.pdf).

7. CBPP, "Fact Sheet," 2016. Although another estimate looking at earned incomes puts this figure at 48 percent (Lens, McClure, and Mast, "Does Jobs Proximity Matter in the Housing Choice Voucher Program?").

8. NLIHC, "Who Lives in Federally Assisted Housing?"

9. This represents a slightly higher proportion of white tenants than in public housing, and slightly lower proportion of Hispanic tenants (NLIHC, "Who Lives in Federally Assisted Housing?").

10. HUD, "Housing Choice Voucher Program Guidebook."

11. Baltimore has since passed a Source of Income (SOI) discrimination protection law, prohibiting landlords from turning down a voucher holder solely on the basis of their voucher.

12. Tighe and Ganning, "Do Shrinking Cities Allow Redevelopment without Displacement?"; Hunt, Shulhof, and Holmquist, "Summary of the Quality Housing and Work Responsibility Act of 1998 (Title V of P.L. 105–276)."

13. McCabe and Moore, "Waitlists and Preferences"; Moore, "Lists and Lotteries."

14. Jacobson, "The Dismantling of Baltimore's Public Housing."

15. Wenger, Yvonne. "Thousands sign up as city's Section 8 wait list opens for first time in a decade." *Baltimore Sun,* Oct. 27, 2014.

16. It remained open until 2008 for those with disabilities.

17. Wenger, Yvonne. "Thousands sign up as city's Section 8 wait list opens for first time in a decade." *Baltimore Sun,* Oct. 27, 2014.

18. Aurand et al., "Housing Spotlight."

19. Based on a nationally representative sample of HCV recipients in large metropolitan PHAs in 2000 (Finkel and Buron, "Study on Section 8 Voucher Success Rates").

20. Tighe and Ganning, "Do Shrinking Cities Allow Redevelopment without Displacement?"

21. McCabe and Moore, "Waitlists and Preferences."

22. From 2000 to 2004, "The Effects of Housing Vouchers on Welfare Families Study" followed over 8,000 families from six study sites who were poor enough to receive TANF (Temporary Assistance to Needy Families). See Mills et al., "Effects of Housing Vouchers on Welfare Families"; Wood, Turnham, and Mills, "Housing Affordability and Family Well-Being."

23. Wood, Turnham, and Mills, "Housing Affordability and Family Well-Being."

24. Other studies similarly find that housing assistance reduces doubling up and overcrowding (Ellen and O'Flaherty, "Social Programs and Household Size"). At the same time, while vouchers significantly reduced homelessness, crowding, and doubling up, no effects were found on marriage, cohabitation, or fertility (Wood et al., "Housing Affordability and Family Well-Being").

25. The Family Options Study involved an experiment across twelve sites, with over 2,000 families enrolled in emergency shelters. Families were randomly assigned into one of four treatments: 1) "subsidy"—usually a housing voucher, 2) "project-based transitional housing" with supportive services, 3) "community-based rapid rehousing"—temporary rental assistance with limited housing services, and 4) "usual care"—whatever the family accessed without immediate referral to other services. Families were assigned from 2010 to 2012 and surveyed for three years after assignment to assess outcomes including housing stability and homelessness, and also family preservation, adult well-being, child well-being, and self-sufficiency (Gubitz et al., "Family Options Study").

26. Fisher, "Research Shows Housing Vouchers Reduce Hardship and Provide Platform for Long-Term Gains Among Children." Other forms of federal housing assistance that play a role are the Low-Income Housing Tax Credit, public housing, and place-based vouchers.

27. Wood, Turnham, and Mills, "Housing Affordability and Family Well-Being." While voucher assistance did not affect cash-income poverty, it did affect poverty once "near-cash" income was taken into account.

28. Bania, Coulton, and Leete, "Public Housing Assistance, Public Transportation, and the Welfare-to-Work Transition"; Harkness and Newman, "Recipients of Housing Assistance under Welfare Reform"; Shroder, "Does Housing Assistance Perversely Affect Self-Sufficiency?"

29. Gubitz et al., "Family Options Study"; Jacob and Ludwig, "The Effects of Housing Assistance on Labor Supply"; Olsen et al., "The Effects of Different Types of Housing Assistance on Earnings and Employment"; Susin, "Longitudinal Outcomes of Subsidized Housing Recipients in Matched Survey and Administrative Data." The Family Options Study found a small negative effect on work. Compared to the control group, receiving the voucher reduced the proportion of household heads who were working at twenty months from 30 to 24 percent, and those who had worked between follow-up surveys from 64 to 58 percent. See also Newman, Holupka, and Harkness, "The Long-Term Effects of Housing Assistance on Work and Welfare"; and Lubell, "Rental Assistance."

30. Carlson et al., "Long-Term Earnings and Employment Effects of Housing Voucher Receipt."

31. Patterson et al., "Evaluation of the Welfare to Work Voucher Program." Gautreaux suggests that voucher families who moved to the suburbs were more likely to be employed, but because of the nonexperimental design of the study, this may be due to selection effects (Popkin, Rosenbaum, and Meaden, "Labor Market Experiences of Low-Income Black Women in Middle-Class Suburbs"). MTO provides one of the rare experimental opportunities to examine the voucher's effect on employment.

32. Wood, Turnham, and Mills, "Housing Affordability and Family Well-Being."

33. Andersson et al., "Childhood Housing and Adult Earnings."

CHAPTER 4: "NO VOUCHERS HERE": THE CHALLENGES OF USING THE VOUCHER

1. In most jurisdictions, voucher holders can apply for a thirty-day extension, sometimes longer.

2. I later spoke to David (the landlord) and visited the house and street to gather details.

3. The payment standard is set at between 90 and 110 percent of the FMR, which in Baltimore in 2011 was $1263 for a two bedroom, set at the 50th percentile of area rent (but has since moved to the 40th percentile).

4. For more on the process of porting a voucher, see HUD, "Housing Choice Voucher Handbook"; Schwartz, *Housing Policy in the United States.*

5. Turner et al., "Discrimination in Metropolitan Housing Markets"; Yinger, "Housing Discrimination Is Still Worth Worrying About."

6. In April 2019 a law was passed banning Source of Income discrimination in Baltimore City.

7. See Tighe, Hatch, and Mead, "Source of Income Discrimination and Fair Housing Policy," for a detailed discussion of SOI discrimination laws. See PRRAC, "Expanding Choice," Appendix B, for an updated list of all jurisdictions with SOI laws.

8. The Urban Institute and HUD conducted a recent study on voucher denial by landlords across five cities (Cunningham et al., *A Pilot Study of Landlord Acceptance of Housing Choice Vouchers*).

9. The Housing Assistance Payment (HAP) contract is a HUD document to which local PHAs can add certain stipulations—setting the terms of the lease, the contact rent, the responsibility for utilities, etc.

10. Nationwide, black households make up 45 percent of voucher households (NLIHC, "Who Lives in Federally Assisted Housing?").

11. See also Garboden and Rosen, "Taking Stock," for a larger sample of landlords across the city of Baltimore and that attitudes about voucher holders.

12. See DeLuca, Garboden, and Rosenblatt, "Segregating Shelter," and Rosen, "Segregating Shelter," for more on how the housing voucher search is circumscribed.

13. Finkel and Buron, "Study on Section 8 Voucher Success Rates." Furthermore, the "take-up rate" for the MTO experimental group was 58 percent in Baltimore and 48 percent across all five cities (Shroder, "Moving to Opportunity"), and 66 percent for the Section 8 group (Chetty et al., "The Effects of Exposure to Better Neighborhoods on Children").

14. Finkel and Buron, "Study on Section 8 Voucher Success Rates."

15. Finkel and Buron, "Study on Section 8 Voucher Success Rates."

16. Pendall, "Why Voucher and Certificate Users Live in Distressed Neighborhoods."

17. Vandenbroucke, "Is There Enough Housing to Go Around?" Also see Owens "How Do People-Based Housing Policies Affect People (and Place)?" for a review of the literature on affordable housing supply.

18. Williamson, Smith, and Strambi-Kramer, "Housing Choice Vouchers, the Low-Income Housing Tax Credit, and the Federal Poverty Deconcentration Goal."

19. Mayer and Jencks, "Growing Up in Poor Neighborhoods"; Brooks-Gunn et al., "Do Neighborhoods Influence Child and Adolescent Development?"; Cutler and Glaeser, "Are Ghettos Good or Bad?"; Sampson, Morenoff, and Gannon-Rowley, "Assessing Neighborhood Effects"; Chetty, Hendren, and Katz, "The Effects of Exposure to Better Neighborhoods on Children."

20. Schwartz, *Housing Policy in the United States*, 240.

21. Sard and Rice, "Realizing the Housing Voucher Program's Potential to Enable Families to Move to Better Neighborhoods."

22. Schwartz, *Housing Policy in the United States*.

23. The paradox here is that vouchers help black recipients more than they do white recipients. But even given this, they are far more likely to live in high-poverty neighborhoods than white recipients.

24. Pendall, "Why Voucher and Certificate Users Live in Distressed Neighborhoods"; Newman and Schnare, "'. . . And a Suitable Living Environment'"; NLIHC, "Who Lives in Federally Assisted Housing?"

25. NLIHC, "Who Lives in Federally Assisted Housing?"

26. NLIHC, "Who Lives in Federally Assisted Housing?"

27. Wang, Varady, and Wang, "Measuring the Deconcentration of Housing Choice Voucher Program Recipients in Eight U.S. Metropolitan Areas Using Hot Spot Analysis."

28. Turner, Popkin, and Cunningham, "Section 8 Mobility and Neighborhood Health."

29. Author's calculations using HUD's "Picture of Subsidized Households, 2011" and the American Community Survey, 2007–2011.

30. Author's calculations using HUD's "Picture of Subsidized Households, 2011" and the American Community Survey, 2007–2011.

31. Previous research suggests that transportation is an important factor in residential decisions (Rosenblatt and Deluca, "Walking Away From the Wire").

32. Wood, "When Only a House Makes a Home," finds that voucher holders feel they can get better units with more space and more amenities in less advantaged, predominantly African American neighborhoods.

33. DeLuca, Garboden, and Rosenblatt, "Segregating Shelter"; Boyd et al., "The Durability of Gains from the Gautreaux Two Residential Mobility Program"; Pashup et al., "Participation in a Residential Mobility Program from the Client's Perspective"; Boyd, "The Role of Social Networks in Making Housing Choices."

34. Finkel and Buron, "Study on Section 8 Voucher Success Rates."

CHAPTER 5: "A TENANT FOR EVERY HOUSE": THE ROLE OF LANDLORDS

1. Moynihan, "The Negro Family."

2. Some portions of this chapter were first published in *City & Community* (Rosen, "Rigging the Rules of the Game").

3. Specifically, the HABC now requires all tenants to be current on their rental payments before they can request a voucher to move.

4. In practice, of course, this is not always the case. For a good example of this, see Greif, "Regulating Landlords."

5. While these homes are often in some of the most disadvantaged neighborhoods, the homes themselves aren't always the worst quality, since at a minimum homes must pass a yearly quality inspection. However, in the course of my fieldwork I saw a good many homes that I had trouble believing had passed inspection.

6. Garboden et al., "Taking Stock."

7. U.S. Census Bureau, *American Housing Survey for the United States: 2007*.

8. American Community Survey, 2007–2011: B25064: "Median Gross Rent (Dollars)." Gross rent is the amount of the contract rent plus the average monthly cost of utilities, if paid by renter.

9. Garboden et al., "Taking Stock"; Rosen, "Rigging the Rules of the Game."

10. Indeed, Desmond found that higher eviction rates among women were driven by the fact that they were more likely to have children (Desmond, *Evicted*).

11. NLIHC, "Who Lives in Federally Assisted Housing?"

12. In in many jurisdictions, including Baltimore, the FMR was raised from the 40th to the 50th percentile of Area Rent in 1998 but was lowered back to the 40 percentile in 2016. The payment standard is then typically set at between 90 and 110 percent of the FMR.

13. Recent evidence suggests that this premium averaged around $60 above market rent in cities such as Milwaukee (Desmond and Perkins, "Are Landlords Overcharging Housing Voucher Holders?").

14. Using data published by HUD, voucher rent ceilings would go down by as much as $300 a month for a two-bedroom apartment if the FMR were to be recalculated at the zip code level.

15. Criteria for comparison include location, quality, size, unit type, and age of the unit, amenities, housing services, maintenance, and utilities the owner must provide under the lease (HUD, "Housing Choice Voucher Program Guidebook").

16. An alternative is to calculate the FMR for a smaller area ("Small Area FMR"), such as zip code, as HUD proposed in certain jurisdictions in 2016, and eventually implemented.

17. It is true in Maryland that after a tenant has been late on rent three times in a row and the landlord has filed for eviction each of those times, the "right to redemption"—the law that allows a tenant to stop an eviction by paying the amount owed—is waived, and the landlord can proceed with eviction even if the tenant settles up.

18. The practice of collecting "ground rent" dates back to the feudal seventeenth century. When purchasing a home on a plot of land subject to ground rent, the homeowner may be able purchase the land, but many homebuyers do not know this, and many have inherited property from family without rights to the land. The practice of ground-rent seizing occurred over 4,000 times in Baltimore City from 2000 to 2006 (as reported by Shulte and Arney, "On Shaky Ground").

19. See Garboden and Rosen, "Serial Filing," for more on how landlords think about eviction.

20. See Rosenblatt and Cossyleon, "Pushing the Boundaries."

21. This is not the case everywhere. HABC only recently instated this rule.

22. Desmond and Valdez, "Unpolicing the Urban Poor"; Garboden and Rosen, "Serial Filing."

23. Rosen, "Rigging the Rules of the Game."

24. See Rosen and Garboden "Landlord Paternalism," for more on landlord training techniques.

25. Other research finds that landlords talk about the "human" side of landlording, and the emotional toll that eviction takes on landlords too (Greenlee, "More Than Meets the Market?"). It is also possible that landlords exaggerate this emotional toll in an interview setting. In my observations, I did not find that it seemed to exact much of an emotional toll, especially for the larger landlords.

26. See Devine, "Housing Choice Voucher Location Patterns" and Pendall, "Why Voucher and Certificate Users Live in Distressed Neighborhoods" for more on racial disparities in the voucher program.

27. Rosen, Garboden, and Cossyleon, "Discrimination without Discriminants."

28. Desmond and Emirbayer, "What Is Racial Domination?"

29. Rent ceilings are typically set at 90–110 percent of the Fair Market Rent (FMR), which is typically defined as the 40th (or in some cases 50th) percentile of area rent. This means that in most areas, only about the bottom 40 percent of homes qualify for the program. Baltimore is part of the Moving to Work (MTW) demonstration, which at the time of this research, allowed certain cities to set the FMR at 50 percent of area rent, allowing for slightly more homes to qualify. But Baltimore's FMR, like other MTW cities, has now been moved back down to the 40th percentile.

CHAPTER 6: "NOT IN MY FRONT YARD"

1. Kelling and Wilson, "Broken Windows."

2. For more on the limitations of the Broken Windows Theory see Sampson and Raudenbush, "Seeing Disorder."

3. Kefalas, *Working-Class Heroes.*

4. Murphy, "'Litterers,'" 212; Murphy, *Where the Sidewalk Ends.*

5. Kefalas, *Working-Class Heroes.*

6. Sampson, *Great American City*.

7. Concentrated poverty is also related to what is sometimes called "social disorganization": with the departure of middle-class social institutions, Wilson argued, came the decline of social organization, contributing to the community's inability to realize its collective goals and resulting in disorder and a consequent rise in crime (Wilson, *The Truly Disadvantaged*).

8. Kefalas, *Working-Class Heroes*; Sampson, *Great American City*; Sharkey, *Stuck in Place*; Venkatesh, *American Project*; Anderson, *Streetwise*; Taub, Taylor, and Dunham, *Paths of Neighborhood Change*; Pattillo McCoy, *Black Picket Fences*; Chetty, Hendren, and Katz, "The Effects of Exposure to Better Neighborhoods on Children."

9. See Sampson, Morenoff, and Gannon-Rowley, "Assessing Neighborhood Effects"; Brooks-Gunn, Duncan, and Aber, *Neighborhood Poverty*; Sharkey and Faber, "Where, When, Why, and for Whom Do Residential Contexts Matter?" for reviews. See also Chetty, Hendry and Katz, "The Effect of Exposure to Better Neighborhoods on Children" for important effects.

10. Sampson, Raudenbush, and Earls, "Neighborhoods and Violent Crime"; Sampson, Morenoff, and Earls, "Beyond Social Capital"; Sampson, *Great American City*; Bursik and Grasmick, *Neighborhoods and Crime*.

11. If poor neighborhoods have a negative effect on residents' life chances, might moving to a neighborhood with higher-income neighbors have a positive effect? This is the subject of a great many research studies. Much of this research has focused on mixed-income developments rather than vouchers, due to the fact that this was a much more explicit goal of mixed income redevelopment than vouchers. But vouchers operate under a similar logic and affect many more people than mixed-income developments. Furthermore, this assumption lies at the heart of mobility programs and interventions such as Gautreaux and MTO. Many have argued that moving to a context with less poor neighbors or creating housing with mixed-income environments might reduce social isolation. This was the impetus for a number of interventions designed to move poor families to more affluent neighborhoods (Joseph, Chaskin, and Webber, "The Theoretical Basis for Addressing Poverty Through Mixed-Income Development"). See also Briggs, "Brown Kids in White Suburbs," and Naparstek, Freis, and Kingsley, *HOPE VI*, on mixed income developments. Yet we know little about how such resources might be transmitted from neighbor to neighbor. Joseph, Chaskin, and Webber propose four pathways through which benefits may accrue from higher- to lower-income residents. This transfer could occur through 1) social capital, 2) social control, 3) culture and behavior (e.g., "rolemodeling"), and 4) the political economy of place. They suggest that the most compelling pathways are through greater informal social control and access to higher quality services.

12. Coleman, "Social Capital in the Creation of Human Capital"; Bourdieu, "The Forms of Capital"; Small, *Villa Victoria*; Briggs, "Brown Kids in White Suburbs."

13. Shaw and McKay, *Juvenile Delinquency and Urban Areas*; Kornhauser, *Social Sources of Delinquency*; Bursik and Grasmick, *Neighborhoods and Crime*.

14. This question has been explored to some degree in other contexts. For example, Chaskin and Joseph, *Integrating the Inner City*, look at how social capital is transmitted in HOPE VI redevelopments. Briggs, Popkin, and Goering, *Moving to Opportunity*, consider the transmission of social capital in MTO neighborhoods.

15. Sampson and Wilson, "Toward a Theory of Race, Crime, and Urban Inequality."

16. Bonding social capital is the kind formed by "strong," deep ties between people in the same social group over long periods of time.

17. Granovetter, "The Strength of Weak Ties"; Burt, *Structural Holes*.

18. Briggs, "Brown Kids in White Suburbs."

19. Briggs, Popkin, and Goering, *Moving to Opportunity*.

20. Briggs, Popkin, and Goering, *Moving to Opportunity*.

21. Pattillo, "Sweet Mothers and Gangbangers."

22. Small, *Villa Victoria*.

23. Tach, "More than Bricks and Mortar."

24. Hyra, *Race, Class, and Politics in the Cappuccino City*.

25. A number of studies document the way in which white communities stigmatize black residents, assuming them to be voucher holders, and mobilize against them (McCormick, Joseph, and Chaskin, "The New Stigma of Relocated Public Housing Residents"; Kurwa, "Deconcentration without Integration"). Residents draw on the power of local police and government to regulate certain groups through "third-party policing" (Buerger and Mazerolle, "Third-Party Policing"; Desmond and Valdez, "Unpolicing the Urban Poor"). Political scientist Ryan Enos finds that whites increase their voting participation in response to blacks moving into their neighborhoods (Enos, "What the Demolition of Public Housing Teaches Us about the Impact of Racial Threat on Political Behavior"). There is also evidence that local governments respond to such attitudes by using and creating policy tools to regulate and even remove minority voucher residents. But there has been little work considering how this plays out in all-black neighborhoods (but see Pattillo, *Black Picket Fences*).

26. See Bourgois, *In Search of Respect*, and Venkatesh, *Off the Books*, for detailed discussions of the informal economy.

27. In his book, *Villa Victoria*, Mario Small finds that "the influence of living in a poor neighborhood on social capital is contingent on the residents' framing of their neighborhood and the complexities of loyalties and sentiments about where they live, as well as cohort effects, ecological characteristics, and the prevalence of institutional resources, generational status, and employment." Similarly, it is clear that longtime homeowners who view voucher holders as a threat to their livelihood (usually though home value), are likely to be less welcoming.

28. Sociologists have sought to understand how social organization operates across a range of different kinds of neighborhoods. Certain neighborhood traits including ethnic heterogeneity and residential instability are thought to be associated with higher crime through their erosion of social control (Byrne and Sampson, *The Social Ecology of Crime*; Shaw and McKay, *Juvenile Delinquency and Urban Areas*). When there is a revolving door of residents and people don't get to know and trust each other, it is harder to work together to achieve common goals in the neighborhood. Robert Sampson's study of Chicago neighborhoods demonstrates the links between poverty, social organization (what he calls "collective efficacy"), and crime, showing that poverty is associated with lower collective efficacy, which is associated with higher crime. Mary Pattillo's middle-class black neighborhood of Chicago's "Groveland" is highly socially organized, but it is geographically surrounded by poor, residentially unstable neighborhoods, and its social networks are infused with what Pattillo calls a "visible criminal element."

(Pattillo, "Sweet Mothers and Gangbangers," 750). Sudhir Venkatesh's study of a public housing project in Chicago shows the rich social organization and informal economy that emerges to fill in the gaps left when a public housing community is deeply isolated—socially and economically—from the outside world (Venkatesh, *American Project*).

29. Studying a racially mixed neighborhood outside of Los Angeles, sociologist Rahim Kurwa finds that predominantly black voucher tenants experience significant social exclusion and monitoring by their new neighbors (Kurwa, "Deconcentration without Integration"). Residents label their black neighbors as voucher holders, and aggressively report them for any suspicious behavior to the housing authority and the police. Voucher tenants react to this by withdrawing from community life. While I do not find this level of aggressive oversight in Park Heights, I do find significant social exclusion.

30. American Community Survey, 2007–2011: B19013: "Median Household Income in the Past 12 Months (in 2011 Inflation-Adjusted Dollars)."

31. Scholars of neighborhood effects have only recently begun to acknowledge and examine the heterogeneity that exists between different types of residents in the neighborhood. New work highlights the ways in which residents may have vastly different experiences even within the same neighborhood (Sharkey, *Stuck in Place*; Small, *Villa Victoria*; Harding, *Living the Drama*).

32. See Murphy, "Litterers" for more on social control and littering.

33. Lamont, *The Dignity of Working Men*.

34. Lamont and Fournier, *Cultivating Differences*, 12.

35. Lamont and Small, "How Culture Matters," 84–85.

36. Lamont and Molnar, "The Study of Boundaries in the Social Sciences."

37. See McCabe, *No Place like Home*, for more on this literature.

38. McCabe, "When Property Values Rule."

39. Fischel, *The Homevoter Hypothesis*. Similarly, Ingrid Gould Ellen in her book *Sharing America's Neighborhoods* suggests that white avoidance of black neighborhoods can be explained by fears of declining property values.

40. Chaskin and Joseph, *Integrating the Inner City*.

41. McCabe, "When Property Values Rule."

42. McCabe, "Are Homeowners Better Citizens?"

43. Research by Galster, Tatian, and Smith, "The Impact of Neighbors Who Use Section 8 Certificates on Property Values," corroborates the idea that residents' perceptions of where voucher holders live are imperfect. Their research on home prices in Baltimore County in 1999 finds that the presence of housing voucher sites or units had a negative effect on home values within 2000 feet *only* in neighborhoods that had already experienced economic decline since 1990. Importantly, this operated through imperfect assumptions that vouchers units were poorly managed and maintained.

44. Berger and Luckmann explain how this operates in their seminal work *The Social Construction of Reality*, showing that the farther people are from face-to-face interaction, the more likely they are to rely on stereotypes, or "typifications" to make sense of each other.

45. Indeed, much research has shown that attitudes about subsidized renters are often based on knowledge and stereotypes of public housing, rather than on actual experiences with assisted renters, and that existing residents often judge assisted renters to be undeserving, deviant, and

undesirable neighbors (Nguyen, Basolo, and Tiwari, "Opposition to Affordable Housing in the USA"). Unlike in some neighborhoods receiving voucher holders such as Patterson Park, where many residents are white (see Churchill et al., "Strategies That Enhance Community Relations in Tenant-Based Section 8 Programs"), residents of Park Heights are almost exclusively African American. Race thus plays a different role here as it is not correlated with voucher status or housing assistance as obviously.

46. Chaskin and Joseph, *Integrating the Inner City*.

47. For more on social distinctions see Bourdieu, *Distinction*.

48. Small, *Unanticipated Gains*, makes the argument that organizations fundamentally shape inequality through our social networks.

49. Small and McDermott, "The Presence of Organizational Resources in Poor Urban Neighborhoods"; Wilson, "The Political Economy and Urban Racial Tensions."

50. Small and McDermott ("The Presence of Organizational Resources in Poor Urban Neighborhoods") have argued that theories of the deinstitutionalized ghetto apply more to the effects of black segregation and depopulation rather than those of concentrated poverty, making it highly relevant in this neighborhood. It would suggest that due to institutions, a poor black neighborhood may be especially ill-suited to support an incoming voucher population. They find that: "(1) on average, as the poverty rate of a neighborhood increases, the number of establishments increases slightly; (2) as the proportion of blacks increases, the number of establishments decreases; (3) as the proportion of foreign-born increases, so does the number of establishments. Finally (4), metropolitan context matters: poor neighborhoods have more establishments in cities with low poverty rates, and in cities in the South and West, than in other parts of the country."

51. Over the course of the year, the most often discussed topic was sanitation, it was on the agenda nearly every month. The senior committee was on the agenda in seven meetings. Health was discussed in about half of the meetings. Crime and safety, youth, energy, traffic, and local business were also discussed in about half of the meetings I attended.

52. Delegate Robinson sponsored this state bill in the 2012 State Legislative Session of the Maryland General Assembly along with the other delegates in the area. (See http://mgaleg.maryland.gov/webmga/frmMain.aspx?tab=subject3&ys=2012rs/billfile/hb0263 .htm.) It was a bill specific to the Park Heights Redevelopment area, as outlined in a 2006 master plan (see http://mgaleg.maryland.gov/2012rs/bills/hb/hb0263f.pdf). The state regulates alcohol in Maryland so all changes, even to local liquor laws in Baltimore City, have to go through the state. There have been numerous attempts to regulate alcohol more closely in the city over the years, from limiting new liquor licenses to weaponizing the zoning code to enforce alcohol matters (for example, see https://www.baltimoresun.com/business/bs -xpm-2013-01-10-bs-bz-liquor-zoning-hearing-20130110-story.html). The bill received a public hearing in the House Economic Matters Committee on February 27, 2012 and was voted down by that Committee on March 30, 2012. The voting list shows that the bill should have passed out of committee (http://mgaleg.maryland.gov/2012rs/votes_comm/hb0263_ecm .pdf), but because the identical Senate bill (http://mgaleg.maryland.gov/webmga/frmMain .aspx?ys=2012rs%2fbillfile%2fsb0363.htm) failed to pass its committee, the bill never stood a chance in the house.

53. Though research shows that heated clashes between merchants and customers are not the norm, extreme poverty coupled with the visible presence of newcomers can provide fertile ground for deep-seated conflict (Lee, *Civility in the City*).

54. Lee, "From Civil Relations to Racial Conflict."

55. Cerda et al., "The Relationship Between Neighborhood Poverty and Alcohol Use."

56. Levine, "The Privatization of Political Representation." Other work also documents how community meetings can be a place where homeowners make disparaging remarks about renters (see Chaskin and Joseph *Integrating the City*; Pattillo *Black on the Block*, "Housing").

57. Certain states require recycling by law. Baltimore has a recycling program, but does not mandate recycling.

58. At that time the city did not systematically supply recycling containers.

59. Whether a tenant has a washer and dryer depends on the business model of the landlord. As we saw in chapter 5, while voucher landlords catering to the most desired voucher tenants install upscale amenities like washers, dryers, and dishwashers, those who are trying to target the lower end of the voucher market minimize extra appliances in order to curtail extra upkeep and maintenance.

60. See Anderson, *Streetwise*.

61. Anderson argues that old heads were losing prestige and authority as legitimate employment became scarce and the drug economy rose (Anderson, *Code of the Street*).

62. A report by the Urban Institute on the impact of the cameras in Baltimore finds positive improvements in crime in four out of the five neighborhoods it evaluated. Impacts were larger in the downtown area which are saturated with cameras and are more heavily monitored. However, cameras have limited use for convictions in the courtroom due to visibility issues related to light and obstructions (La Vigne et al., "Evaluating the Use of Public Cameras for Crime Control and Prevention").

63. In reality, this may not be far from the truth. In recent years the intervention has been expanded to encourage private residents to install their own cameras, and use a blue flashing light in their window to indicate its presence. Yet these cameras are not monitored by law enforcement at all, and so there is no guarantee of police response in their presence either.

64. See Rosen and Garboden, "Landlord Paternalism" for more discussion on landlord paternalism vis-à-vis their tenants.

65. Chaskin and Joseph, *Integrating the City*, find a similar phenomenon in their study.

66. Criminologist Todd Clear has argued that "at the ecological level, the side effects of policies intended to fight crime by controlling individual behavior may exacerbate the problems they are intended to address" (Clear, *Imprisoning Communities*).

67. This highlights an interesting paradox about policing in the neighborhood: For newer residents who haven't formed relationships with the police, the police can pose a huge risk. In Bill's case, he did know his local cops, but when they sent in police from other units who didn't know him, they made assumptions about drugs that Bill doesn't think they would have made if they had known him.

68. In *The Social Order of the Slum*, Suttles argues that social group divisions shape interaction within the neighborhood, describing the ways in which age, sex, and ethnic background separated residents and structured social interactions. I, too, saw that traits like age and gender structured who interacted with whom. But stigma also played a key role.

69. Marwell, *Bargaining for Brooklyn*.

70. Sharkey, Torrats-Espinosa, and Takyar, "Community and the Crime Decline"; Sánchez-Jankowski, *Cracks in the Pavement*.

71. Sampson et al., "Civil Society Reconsidered."

72. Mayer and Jencks, "Growing Up in Poor Neighborhoods."

73. Marwell, *Bargaining for Brooklyn*.

74. Sampson, Raudenbush, and Earls, "Neighborhoods and Violent Crime."

75. Klinenberg, *Heat Wave*.

76. Briggs, "Moving up versus Moving Out."

CHAPTER 7: MOVING ON

1. See Krysan and Crowder, *Cycle of Segregation*, on how lack of information shapes residential outcomes. Also see Darrah and DeLuca, "'Living Here Has Changed My Whole Perspective.'"

2. DeLuca, Wood, and Rosenblatt, "Why Poor Families Move (And Where They Go)."

3. Some portions of this chapter are adapted from Rosen, "Horizontal Mobility," 270–296.

4. Massey and Mullan, "Processes of Hispanic and Black Spatial Assimilation"; Owens, "Inequality in Children's Contexts Income Segregation of Households with and without Children."

5. Research shows that poor households are likely to move laterally to a similarly disadvantaged place (Sharkey, *Stuck in Place*; South and Crowder, "Escaping Distressed Neighborhoods"). Research also shows that some groups experience significant barriers (Alba and Logan, "Minority Proximity to Whites in Suburbs"), highlighting the constraints that circumscribe residential choice, showing that unpredictable forces in the lives of the urban poor catalyze involuntary displacement and amplify future instability (DeLuca, Garboden, and Rosenblatt, "Segregating Shelter"; Desmond "Eviction and the Reproduction of Urban Poverty"; Pashup et al., "Participation in a Residential Mobility Program from the Client's Perspective"; Skobba and Goetz "Mobility Decisions of Very Low-Income Households").

6. DeLuca, Garboden, and Rosenblatt, "Segregating Shelter"; Desmond, "Eviction and the Reproduction of Urban Poverty"; Pashup et al., "Participation in a Residential Mobility Program from the Client's Perspective"; Skobba and Goetz, "Mobility Decisions of Very Low-Income Households."

7. DeLuca, Wood, and Rosenblatt, "Why Poor Families Move (And Where They Go)."

8. Ludwig et al., "Long-Term Neighborhood Effects on Low-Income Families."

9. Collins, *Violence*.

10. Sharkey, "The Long Reach of Violence."

11. Baltimore Police Department, 2011 and Baltimore Police Department, 2012.

12. Baltimore Neighborhood Indicators Alliance, Jacob France Institute, *Vital Signs 11*.

13. Sharkey, "The Acute Effect of Local Homicides on Children's Cognitive Performance"; Sharkey, "The Long Reach of Violence"; McCoy, Raver, and Sharkey, "Children's Cognitive Performance and Selective Attention Following Recent Community Violence"; Sharkey et al., "High Stakes in the Classroom, High Stakes on the Street."

14. See also Pattillo, "Sweet Mothers and Gangbangers"; Briggs, Popkin, and Goering, *Moving to Opportunity*; Turner, Popkin, and Rawlings, *Public Housing and the Legacy of Segregation*.

15. See also Sharkey, "Navigating Dangerous Streets."

16. Rosenblatt and DeLuca, "'We Don't Live Outside, We Live in Here'"; Murphy, *Where the Sidewalk Ends*.

17. This exact phrase is used by respondents in another Baltimore study (Rosenblatt and DeLuca, "We Don't Live Outside, We Live in Here'").

18. Other accounts of cameras in housing developments suggest that residents resent the surveillance (see Chaskin and Joseph, *Integrating the Inner City*). However, in Oakland Terrace residents nearly universally feel that the cameras have improved safety in the complex.

19. Alternately, this could be read as a case where Roland might have been trying to dispel the reputation of Park Heights as a dangerous neighborhood. Residents sometimes seemed to have an agenda to push, wanting to portray the neighborhood as an okay place to live, especially to a white outsider. And most days, most of the time, on most streets, it *was* an okay place to live. So, it is understandable that residents might not have wanted to confirm what they may have imagined to be my priors about the neighborhood. However, in this case, I don't think this is what Roland was doing. I spent a good deal of time with Vivian and Roland, and noted that Vivian sometimes went out alone at night, while other times she would ask Roland to accompany her. Their behavior suggested that they generally felt comfortable in the neighborhood, but still took precautions when possible.

20. For more on this concept of narrative rupture, see Rosen, "Horizontal Immobility."

21. Massey and Mullan, "Processes of Hispanic and Black Spatial Assimilation"; Alba and Logan, "Minority Proximity to Whites in Suburbs."

22. Desmond, Gershenson, and Kiviat, "Forced Mobility and Residential Instability among Urban Renters"; DeLuca, Rosenblatt, and Wood, "Why Poor Families Move (And Where They Go)."

23. Swidler, *Talk of Love*; Polletta, *It Was Like a Fever*.

CHAPTER 8: CONCLUSION

1. Goetz, *New Deal Ruins*; Vale, *Purging the Poorest*.

2. Taylor, *Race for Profit*.

3. Baradaran, *The Color of Money: Black Banks and the Racial Wealth Gap*; Rothstein, *The Color of Law*; Satter, *Family Properties*.

4. See Desmond and Wilmers, "Do the Poor Pay More for Housing?"

5. Rosin, "American Murder Mystery."

6. Briggs and Dreier, "Memphis Murder Mystery?"

7. Briggs and Dreier, "Memphis Murder Mystery?"

8. A study by Hendey and colleagues finds no support for the idea that growth in voucher holders leads to growth in *violent* crime rates. They do find that growth in voucher holders is positively associated with growth in *property* crime rates, though only in higher-poverty neighborhoods or exceeding a very high threshold of voucher holders, which are two rare conditions (Hendey et al., "Housing Choice Voucher Holders and Neighborhood Crime").

9. Lens, "The Impact of Housing Vouchers on Crime in US Cities and Suburbs"; Ellen, Lens, and O'Regan, "American Murder Mystery Revisited."

10. Popkin et al., "Public Housing Transformation and Crime."

11. NLIHC, "Who Lives in Federally Assisted Housing?"

12. Kurwa, "Deconcentration without Integration."

13. Western, *Punishment and Inequality in America*; Clear, *Imprisoning Communities*; Alexander, *The New Jim Crow*.

14. Briggs, Popkin, and Goering, *Moving to Opportunity*.

15. Abt Associates, "*Tools and Strategies for Improving Community Relations in the Housing Choice Voucher Program.*"

16. Tilly, *Durable Inequality*.

17. Hartman, *Housing and Social Policy*.

18. Goetz, *New Deal Ruins*. Hunt, *Blueprint for Disaster*.

19. Baradaran, *The Color of Money*; Oliver and Shapiro, *Black Wealth / White Wealth*; Rothstein, *The Color of Law*; Massey and Denton, *American Apartheid*.

20. Goetz, *New Deal Ruins*.

21. In several conversations with Martha Galvez of the Urban Institute, she framed vouchers in exactly this way: Vouchers are not perfect, but they "are part of the solution, not the problem."

22. Pattillo, "Housing."

23. Bauman, *Housing Not Handcuffs*.

24. Desmond, *Evicted*.

25. Desmond, *Evicted*. Other scholars who have suggested large expansions of vouchers include Polikoff, *Waiting for Gautreaux*. Grigsby and Bourassa, "Section 8," argue that housing vouchers should be directly integrated into the federal safety net as an entitlement program. Others (Armstrong and Basgal, "Comment on William G. Grigsby and Steven C. Bourassa's 'Section 8: The Time for Fundamental Program Change?'") disagree.

26. Bipartisan Policy Center, "Housing America's Future"; Buron, Kaul, and Khadduri, *Estimates of Voucher-Type and Emergency Rental Assistance for Unassisted Households*.

27. In order to qualify for a voucher, a family must be low-income—at or below 80 percent of the area median income. Three-quarters of vouchers are earmarked for "extremely low-income" families, or those who are at or below 30 percent of area median income.

28. Newman and Schnare, "'. . . And a Suitable Living Environment.'"

29. Sard, "Housing Vouchers Should Be a Major Component of Future Housing Policy for the Lowest Income Families."

30. Priemus, Kemp, and Varady, "Housing Vouchers in the United States, Great Britain, and the Netherlands," argue the voucher program is more palatable to many than, for example, a negative income tax, because vouchers are designed for a specific purpose and cannot be misused. They suggest that the American public might be convinced of the voucher program's value if it were reformed to have explicit self-sufficiency goals. However, adding a work requirement to the voucher program has significant disadvantages. Since such a high proportion of vouchers go to families with children, the elderly, and the disabled, a work requirement does not seem appropriate.

31. Priemus, Kemp, and Varady, "Housing Vouchers in the United States, Great Britain, and the Netherlands."

32. See Sard, "Housing Vouchers Should Be a Major Component of Future Housing Policy for the Lowest Income Families," for a comprehensive discussion of these reforms.

33. Burawoy, "On Desmond."

34. Rosenblatt and Cossyleon, "Pushing the Boundaries"; Pendall, "Driving to Opportunity"; Tighe and Ganning, "Do Shrinking Cities Allow Redevelopment without Displacement?"; DeLuca, Garboden, and Rosenblatt, "Segregating Shelter,"; Rosen, "Rigging the Rules of the Game"; Maney and Crowley, "Scarcity and Success."

35. An analysis of outcomes for the first 1,800 families participating in the BRHP found that they moved to lower-poverty, more integrated neighborhoods. DeLuca and Rosenblatt, "Walking away from the Wire"; Darrah and DeLuca, "'Living Here Has Changed My Whole Perspective'"; Berdahl-Baldwin, "Housing Mobility Programs in the U.S."

36. Sard and Thorpe, "Consolidating Rental Assistance Administration Would Increase Efficiency and Expand Opportunity."

37. Sard, "Housing Choice Voucher Program."

38. Feins et al., "State and Metropolitan Administration of Section 8"; Tegeler, Hanley, and Liben, "Transforming Section 8"; DeLuca, Garboden, and Rosenblatt, "Segregating Shelter."

39. Sard, "Housing Choice Voucher Program"; Sard and Thorpe, "Consolidating Rental Assistance Administration Would Increase Efficiency and Expand Opportunity."

40. These performance standards are established by SEMAP, "Section Eight Management Assessment Program," which measures the performance of public housing agencies across fourteen different dimensions, including income determinations, applicant selection, inspection, and rent reasonableness, among others. See https://www.hud.gov/program_offices/public _indian_housing/programs/hcv/semap/semap_FAQs.

41. Landis and McClure, "Rethinking Federal Housing Policy"; Katz and Turner, "Who Should Run the Housing Voucher Program?"

42. U.S. Government Accountability Office, "Housing Choice Vouchers"; Turnham et al., "Housing Choice Voucher Program."

43. See Garboden et al., "Taking Stock," for an in-depth discussion of what motivates landlords to participate in the voucher program in different contexts.

44. For example, in Dallas (Garboden et al., "Taking Stock").

45. For example in Cleveland (Garboden et al., "Taking Stock").

46. See PRRAC, "Expanding Choice," for a full list of jurisdictions with SOI laws.

47. Freeman, "The Impact of Source of Income Laws on Voucher Utilization and Locational Outcomes"; Tighe, Hatch, and Mead, "Source of Income Discrimination and Fair Housing Policy"; Bell, Sard, and Koepnick, "Prohibiting Discrimination against Renters Using Housing Vouchers Improves Results Lessons from Cities and States That Have Enacted Source of Income Laws."

48. See https://www.cbpp.org/research/housing/a-guide-to-small-area-fair-market-rents -safmrs. Baltimore was not one of these areas. This is for a complicated set of reasons. Because Baltimore is a poor city in a wealthy metropolitan area, recalibrating the FMR at the local level would mean reducing price ceilings in nearly every neighborhood within the city's limits. Policymakers need to think carefully about how to set rent ceilings in cities like Baltimore in order to calibrate rents to local prices, while also allowing voucher holders to stay within the city limits if they choose to.

49. Collinson and Ganong, "How Do Changes in Housing Voucher Design Affect Rent and Neighborhood Quality?" Other research finds that while SAFMRs don't affect overall move rates, they do affect locational outcomes among those who move (Dastrup, Finkel, and Gould, "The Effects of Small Area Fair Market Rents on the Neighborhood Choices of Families with Children"; Aliprantis, Martin, and Phillips, "Landlords and Access to Opportunity"). Another paper suggests that there may be significant regional variation and that more research over a longer period of time is needed to understand the effects of SAFMR (Reina, Acolin, and Bostic, "Section 8 Vouchers and Rent Limits"). See also Olsen, "Does HUD Overpay for Voucher Units, and Will SAFMRs Reduce the Overpayment?"

50. New research finds that SAFMR increases the likelihood of voucher lease-ups in new neighborhoods among those who move by 13 percentage points (although the effect of a higher payment standard on new lease-ups is not significant compared to the total number of vouchers in the tract). Notably, the data suggest that the landlords renting in these neighborhoods are not new to the program, but rather new to the neighborhood. Their results suggest that that in order to eliminate the voucher penalty among landlords in the sample, we would have to dramatically increase voucher payment amounts (Aliprantis, Martin, and Phillips, "Landlords and Access to Opportunity").

51. Some have also cautioned that given persistent racial discrimination in housing, SAFMR could reduce opportunities for minority voucher holders to find housing in the kinds of neighborhoods they tend to rent in (see McClure and Schwartz, "Small Area Fair Market Rents, Race, and Neighborhood Opportunity).

52. Garboden et al., "Taking Stock."

53. See Desmond and Perkins, "Are Landlords Overcharging Voucher Holders?" who find that in Milwaukee landlords charge on average $60 more per month for properties rented to voucher holders. See also Olsen, "Does HUD Overpay for Voucher Units, and Will SAFMRs Reduce the Overpayment?" and Desmond and Wilmers, "Do the Poor Pay More for Housing?"

54. Burawoy, "On Desmond."

55. Rosen, Garboden, and Cossyleon, "Discrimination without Discriminants."

56. Pastor, Benner, and Matsuoka, *This Could Be the Start of Something Big*; Pastor and Turner, "Reducing Poverty and Economic Distress after ARRA"; Rose, "Beyond Gentrification"; Burchell et al., *Inclusionary Zoning*; Landis and McClure, "Rethinking Federal Housing Policy"; Schwartz, *Housing Policy in the United States*; Metzger and Webber, *Facing Segregation*; Galster, *Making Our Neighborhoods, Making Our Selves*.

57. Fischel, "An Economic History of Zoning and a Cure for Its Exclusionary Effects"; Fogelson, *Bourgeois Nightmares*.

58. Rothwell and Massey, "The Effect of Density Zoning on Racial Segregation in U.S. Urban Areas"; Pendall, "Local Land Use Regulation and the Chain of Exclusion."

59. Metzger and Webber, *Facing Segregation*.

60. McClure, "The Future of Housing Policy."

61. Santiago, Galster, and Tatian, "Assessing the Property Value Impacts of the Dispersed Subsidy Housing Program in Denver."

62. See Sharkey, *Stuck in Place*.

63. Chetty, Hendren, and Katz, "The Effects of Exposure to Better Neighborhoods on Children."

64. Sharkey, *Stuck in Place.*

65. See Sharkey, *Stuck in Place*, for an in-depth discussion of these different scenarios.

66. Sharkey, *Stuck in Place*, 166.

67. See the conclusion of Sharkey, *Stuck in Place*, for an in-depth discussion of a range of place-based policy solutions concerning joblessness in disadvantaged communities, investments in children and local education, and approaches to mobility. See also the concluding chapter of Sampson, *Great American City*, for a complementary discussion of these types of policies.

68. For ideas around generating social capital, see Sampson, *Great American City.*

METHODOLOGICAL APPENDIX

1. American Community Survey, 2007–2011: B250003: "Tenure"; HUD, "Picture of Subsidized Households, 2011."

2. See Small, "'How Many Cases Do I Need?'" for a discussion of how to think about sampling in ethnographic work. See Waters, *Black Identities*, Appendix, for an example of sampling for range.

3. All names, company names, and addresses are pseudonyms to protect the identity of participants.

4. About one-third of the landlords initially did not want to accept payment, though I remunerated every participant with $50 and suggested that if they did not feel comfortable accepting the money they could use it in some way for the benefit of their tenants. For example, one landlord used the money to buy snacks and soda for all the children in the building.

5. In 2009 there were 11,834 units rented to voucher holders in Baltimore City (HUD, "Picture of Subsidized Housing, 2009"). By compiling the total number of units that the landlords in my sample control, which is 1,634 (units that they own, combined with units that they manage, subtracting duplicates), I calculated that they control approximately 14.2% of all units rented to voucher holders in Baltimore City.

6. One landlord requested not to be recorded, but agreed to be directly quoted. Extensive notes were taken on this interview instead. A list of the forty codes that were used for analysis is available upon request.

7. Stuart, *Down, Out, and Under Arrest*, 285.

8. Venkatesh, "'Doin' the Hustle'"; Vargas, *Wounded City*; Duneier, *Sidewalk.*

9. Skloot, *The Immortal Life of Henrietta Lacks.*

10. For more on ethnographic interviewing, see Boyd and DeLuca, "Fieldwork with In-Depth Interviews"; Garboden and Rosen, "Talking to Landlords"; Spradley, *The Ethnographic Interview.*

11. See Duneier, *Sidewalk*, for a discussion of how he dresses as an ethnographer.

12. Stack, *All Our Kin.*

WORKS CITED

Abt Associates. *Tools and Strategies for Improving Community Relations in the Housing Choice Voucher Program*. Washington, D.C.: Department of Housing and Urban Development, Office of Policy Development and Research, 2001.

Alba, Richard, and John Logan. "Minority Proximity to Whites in Suburbs: An Individual-Level Analysis of Segregation." *American Journal of Sociology* 98, no. 6 (1993): 1388–1427.

Alexander, Michelle. *The New Jim Crow: Mass Incarceration in the Age of Colorblindness*. New York: The New Press, 2012.

Aliprantis, Dionissi, Hal Martin, and David Phillips. "Landlords and Access to Opportunity." Cleveland: Federal Reserve Bank of Cleveland, 2019.

American Community Survey, 2007–2011: B01003: "Total Population." U.S. Census Bureau.

American Community Survey, 2007–2011: B17001: "Poverty Status in the Past 12 Months by Sex by Age." U.S. Census Bureau.

American Community Survey, 2007–2011: B19013: "Median Household Income in the Past 12 Months (in 2011 Inflation-Adjusted Dollars)." U.S. Census Bureau.

American Community Survey, 2007–2011: B23025: "Employment Status for the Population 16 Years and Over." U.S. Census Bureau.

American Community Survey, 2007–2011: B25003: "Tenure." U.S. Census Bureau.

American Community Survey, 2007–2011: B25002: "Occupancy Status." U.S. Census Bureau.

American Community Survey, 2007–2011: B25034: "Year Structure Built." U.S. Census Bureau.

American Community Survey, 2007–2011: B25038: "Tenure by Year Householder Moved into Unit." U.S. Census Bureau.

American Community Survey, 2007–2011: B25064: "Median Gross Rent (Dollars)." U.S. Census Bureau.

American Community Survey, 2007–2011: B25070: "Gross Rent as a Percentage of Household Income in the Past 12 Months." U.S. Census Bureau.

American Community Survey, 2008–2012: B02001: "Race." U.S. Census Bureau.

American Community Survey, 2008–2012: B03003: "Hispanic or Latino Origin." U.S. Census Bureau.

Anderson, Elijah. *Streetwise: Race, Class, and Change in an Urban Community*. Chicago: University of Chicago Press, 1992.

Anderson, Elijah. *Code of the Street: Decency, Violence, and the Moral Life of the Inner City*. New York: W. W. Norton & Company.

Andersson, Fredrik, John C. Haltiwanger, Mark J. Kutzbach, Giordano E. Palloni, Henry O. Pollakowski, and Daniel H. Weinberg. "Childhood Housing and Adult Earnings: A Between-Siblings Analysis of Housing Vouchers and Public Housing." Working Paper. National Bureau of Economic Research, October 2018.

Armstrong, James P., and Ophelia B. Basgal. "Comment on William G. Grigsby and Steven C. Bourassa's 'Section 8: The Time for Fundamental Program Change?'" *Housing Policy Debate* 15, no. 4 (2004.): 851–63.

Aurand, Andrew, Dan Emmanuel, Diane Yentel, and Ellen Errico. *The Gap: A Shortage of Affordable Homes*. Washington, D.C.: The National Low Income Housing Coalition, 2017.

Aurand, Andrew, Dan Emmanuel, Diane Yentel, Ellen Errico, Zoe Chapin, Gar Meng Leong, and Kate Rodrigues. *Housing Spotlight: The Long Wait for a Home*. Washington, D.C.: The National Low Income Housing Coalition, 2016.

Baltimore Neighborhood Indicators Alliance. *Vital Signs 11*. Baltimore: Jacob France Institute, 2013.

Baltimore Neighborhood Indicators Alliance. *Vital Signs 17*. Baltimore: Jacob France Institute, 2019.

Baltimore Police Department. Homicide Data. 2011. https://www.baltimorepolice.org.

Baltimore Police Department. Homicide Data. 2012. https://www.baltimorepolice.org.

Bania, Neil, Claudia Coulton, and Laura Leete. "Public Housing Assistance, Public Transportation, and the Welfare-to-Work Transition." *Cityscape* 6, no. 2 (2003): 7–44.

Baradaran, Mehrsa. *The Color of Money: Black Banks and the Racial Wealth Gap*. Cambridge, MA: Harvard University Press, 2019.

Bauman, Tristia. *Housing Not Handcuffs: Ending the Criminalization of Homelessness in US Cities*. Washington, D.C.: National Law Center on Homelessness and Poverty, 2019.

Bell, Alison, Barbara Sard, and Becky Koepnick. "Prohibiting Discrimination against Renters Using Housing Vouchers Improves Results Lessons from Cities and States That Have Enacted Source of Income Laws." Washington, D.C.: Center on Budget and Policy Priorities, 2018.

Berdahl-Baldwin, Audrey. "Housing Mobility Programs in the U.S." Sixth National Conference on Housing Mobility, Washington, D.C., 2015.

Berger, Peter L., and Thomas Luckmann. *The Social Construction of Reality: A Treatise in the Sociology of Knowledge*. Garden City, NY: Anchor, 1967.

Bickford, Adam, and Douglas S. Massey. "Segregation in the Second Ghetto: Racial and Ethnic Segregation in American Public Housing, 1977." *Social Forces* 69, no. 4 (1991): 1011–36.

Bipartisan Policy Center. *Housing America's Future: New Directions for National Policy*. Washington, D.C.: Bipartisan Policy Center Housing Commission, 2013.

Bloom, Nicholas Dagen. *Public Housing That Worked: New York in the Twentieth Century*. Philadelphia: University of Pennsylvania Press, 2008.

Boehm, Thomas P., Paul D. Thistle, and Alan Schlottmann. "Rates and Race: An Analysis of Racial Disparities in Mortgage Rates." *Housing Policy Debate* 17, no. 1 (2006): 109–49.

Bourdieu, Pierre. *Distinction: A Social Critique of the Judgement of Taste*. Cambridge, MA: Harvard University Press, 1984.

Bourdieu, Pierre. "The Forms of Capital." In *Handbook of Theory and Research for the Sociology of Education*, edited by J. Richardson, 241–58. New York: Greenwood, 1986.

Bourgois, Philippe I. *In Search of Respect: Selling Crack in El Barrio*. Cambridge University Press, 2003.

Boyd, Melody. "The Role of Social Networks in Making Housing Choices: The Experience of the Gautreaux Two Residential Mobility Program." *Cityscape* 10, no. 1 (2008): 41–63.

Boyd, Melody, and Stefanie DeLuca. "Fieldwork with In-Depth Interviews: How to Get Strangers in the City to Tell You Their Stories." In *Methods in Social Epidemiology*, edited by J. S. Kaufman, 239–307. San Francisco: Jossey-Bass, 2018.

Boyd, Melody, Kathryn Edin, Susan Clampet-Lundquist, and Greg Duncan. "The Durability of Gains from the Gautreaux Two Residential Mobility Program." *Housing Policy Debate* 20, no. 1 (2010): 119–46.

Briggs, Xavier De Souza. "Moving up versus Moving Out: Neighborhood Effects in Housing Mobility Programs." *Housing Policy Debate* 8, no. 1 (1997): 195–234.

Briggs, Xavier De Souza. "Brown Kids in White Suburbs: Housing Mobility and the Many Faces of Social Capital." *Housing Policy Debate* 9, no. 1 (1998): 177–221.

Briggs, Xavier De Souza. "Housing Opportunity, Desegregation Strategy, and Policy Research." *Journal of Policy Analysis and Management* 22, no. 2 (2003): 201-06.

Briggs, Xavier de Souza, Jennifer Comey, and Gretchen Weismann. "Struggling to Stay out of High-Poverty Neighborhoods: Housing Choice and Locations in Moving to Opportunity's First Decade." *Housing Policy Debate* 20, no. 3 (2010): 383–427.

Briggs, Xavier De Souza, and Peter Dreier. "Memphis Murder Mystery? No, Just Mistaken Identity." *Shelterforce*, July 2008.

Briggs, Xavier De Souza, Susan J. Popkin, and John Goering. *Moving to Opportunity: The Story of an American Experiment to Fight Ghetto Poverty*. New York: Oxford University Press, 2010.

Brooks-Gunn, Jeanne, Greg J. Duncan, and J. Lawrence Aber. *Neighborhood Poverty: Context and Consequences for Children*. New York: Russell Sage Foundation, 1997.

Brooks-Gunn, Jeanne, Greg J. Duncan, Pamela Kato Klebanov, and Naomi Sealand. "Do Neighborhoods Influence Child and Adolescent Development?" *American Journal of Sociology* 99, no. 2 (1993): 353–95.

Buerger, Michael E., and Lorraine Green Mazerolle. "Third-Party Policing: A Theoretical Analysis of an Emerging Trend." *Justice Quarterly* 15, no. 2 (1998): 301–27.

Burawoy, Michael. "On Desmond: The Limits of Spontaneous Sociology." *Theory and Society* 46, no. 4 (2017): 261–284.

Burchell, Robert C., Conine Kent, Richard Dubin, David Flanagan, Catherine C. Galley, Eric Larsen, David Rusk, Ann B. Schnare, Bernard Tetreault, and Richard Tustian. *Inclusionary Zoning: A Viable Solution to the Affordable Housing Crisis?* Volume 1, Issue 2. Washington, D.C.: The Center for Housing Policy, 2000.

Buron, Larry, Bulbul Kaul, and Jill Khadduri. *Estimates of Voucher-Type and Emergency Rental Assistance for Unassisted Households*. Bethesda, MD: Abt Associates, 2012.

Bursik, Robert, and Harold G. Grasmick. *Neighborhoods and Crime: The Dimensions of Effective Community Control*. Lanham, MD: Lexington Books, 1993.

Byrne, James, and Robert J. Sampson (eds.). *The Social Ecology of Crime*. New York: Springer-Verlag, 1986.

Burt, Ronald S. *Structural Holes: The Social Structure of Competition*. Cambridge, MA: Harvard University Press, 1992.

Carlson, Deven, Robert Haveman, Tom Kaplan, and Barbara Wolfe. "Long-Term Earnings and Employment Effects of Housing Voucher Receipt." *Journal of Urban Economics* 71, no. 1 (2012): 128–50.

Center on Budget and Policy Priorities (CBPP). "Fact Sheet: The Housing Choice Voucher Program." Washington, D.C.: CBPP, 2012. http://www.cbpp.org/files/3-10-14hous-factsheets/US.pdf.

Center on Budget and Policy Priorities (CBPP). "Fact Sheet: The Housing Choice Voucher Program." Washington, D.C.: CBPP, 2016. http://www.cbpp.org/files/3-10-14hous-factsheets /US.pdf.

Center on Budget and Policy Priorities (CBPP). "United States Federal Rental Assistance Fact Sheet." Washington, D.C.: CBPP, 2019.

Cerda, Magdalena, Ana V. Diez-Roux, Eric Tchetgen, Penny Gordon-Larsen, and Catarina Kiefe. "The Relationship Between Neighborhood Poverty and Alcohol Use: Estimation by Marginal Structural Models." *Epidemiology* 21, no. 4 (2010): 482–89.

Charles, Camille Zubrinsky. "The Dynamics of Racial Residential Segregation." *Annual Review of Sociology* 29 (2003): 167–207.

Chaskin, Robert J., and Mark L. Joseph. *Integrating the Inner City: The Promise and Perils of Mixed Income Public Housing Transformation.* University of Chicago Press, 2015.

Chetty, Raj, Nathaniel Hendren, and Lawrence F. Katz. "The Effects of Exposure to Better Neighborhoods on Children: New Evidence from the Moving to Opportunity Experiment." *American Economic Review* 106, no. 4 (2016): 855–902.

Churchill, Sarah, Mary Joel Holin, Jill Khadduri, and Jennifer Turnham. "Strategies That Enhance Community Relations in Tenant-Based Section 8 Programs." Washington, D.C.: Department of Housing and Urban Development, 2011.

Clampet-Lundquist, Susan, Kathryn Edin, Jeffrey R. Kling, and Greg J. Duncan. "Moving Teenagers Out of High-Risk Neighborhoods: How Girls Fare Better than Boys." *American Journal of Sociology* 116, no. 4 (2011): 1154–89.

Clampet-Lundquist, Susan, and Douglas S. Massey. "Neighborhood Effects on Economic Self-Sufficiency: A Reconsideration of the Moving to Opportunity Experiment." *American Journal of Sociology* 114, no. 1 (2008): 107–43.

Clear, Todd. *Imprisoning Communities: How Mass Incarceration Makes Disadvantaged Neighborhoods Worse.* Oxford: Oxford University Press, 2009.

Coleman, James S. "Social Capital in the Creation of Human Capital." *American Journal of Sociology* 94 (1988): S95–120.

Collins, Randall. *Violence: A Micro-Sociological Theory.* Princeton, N.J.: Princeton University Press, 2009.

Collinson, Robert, Ingrid Gould Ellen, and Jens Ludwig. "Reforming Housing Assistance." *The ANNALS of the American Academy of Political and Social Science* 686, no. 1 (2019): 250–85.

Collinson, Robert, and Peter Ganong. "How Do Changes in Housing Voucher Design Affect Rent and Neighborhood Quality?" *American Economic Journal: Economic Policy* 10, no. 2 (2018): 62–89.

Commission on Severely Distressed Public Housing. "Final Report to Congress and the Secretary of Housing and Urban Development." Washington, D.C.: U.S. Government Printing Office, 1992.

Cox, R., B. Henwood, S. Rodnyansky, S. Wenzel, and E. Rice. "Roadmap to a Unified Measure of Housing Insecurity." Working Paper, Washington D.C.: Washington Center for Equitable Growth, 2017.

Cunningham, Mary K., Martha Galvez, Claudia Aranda, Robert Santos, Doug Wissoker, Alyse Oneto, Rob Pitingolo, and James Crawford. *A Pilot Study of Landlord Acceptance of Housing Choice Vouchers.* Washington, D.C.: Department of Housing and Urban Development, Office of Policy Development & Research, 2018.

Cunningham, Mary K. *An Improved Living Environment? Relocation Outcomes for HOPE VI Relocatees.* Urban Institute, Center on Metropolitan Housing and Communities, Washington, D.C., 2004.

Cutler, David M., and Edward L. Glaeser. "Are Ghettos Good or Bad?" *Quarterly Journal of Economics* 112, no. 3 (1997): 827–72.

Darrah, Jennifer, and Stefanie DeLuca. "'Living Here Has Changed My Whole Perspective': How Escaping Inner-City Poverty Shapes Neighborhood and Housing Choice." *Journal of Policy Analysis and Management* 33, no. 2 (2014): 350–84.

Dastrup, Samuel, Meryl Finkel, and Ingrid Gould Ellen, "The Effects of Small Area Fair Market Rents on the Neighborhood Choices of Families with Children." *Cityscape* 21, no. 3 (2019): 19–48.

DeLuca, Stefanie, Philip Garboden, and Peter Rosenblatt. "Segregating Shelter: How Housing Policies Shape the Residential Locations of Low-Income Minority Families." *Annals of the American Academy of Political and Social Science* 647, no. 1 (2013): 268–99.

DeLuca, Stefanie, and Peter Rosenblatt. "Walking Away from the Wire: Housing Mobility and Neighborhood Opportunity in Baltimore." *Housing Policy Debate* 27, no. 4 (2017): 519–46.

DeLuca, Stefanie, Holly Wood, and Peter Rosenblatt. "Why Poor Families Move (and Where They Go): Reactive Mobility and Residential Decisions." *City & Community* 18, no. 2 (2019): 556–93.

Department of Housing and Urban Development (HUD). "A Picture of Subsidized Households, 2009." Washington, D.C.: HUD, 2009.

Department of Housing and Urban Development (HUD). "A Picture of Subsidized Households, 2011." Washington, D.C.: HUD, 2011.

Department of Housing and Urban Development (HUD). "FY 2012 Budget Summary." Washington, D.C.: HUD, 2011. https://www.hud.gov/sites/documents/2012BUDGETFINAL_03_07_WEB.PDF

Department of Housing and Urban Development (HUD). "Housing Choice Voucher Program Guidebook." Washington, D.C.: HUD, 2001. http://portal.hud.gov/hudportal/HUD?src=/program_offices/public_indian_housing/programs/hcv/forms/guidebook.

Department of Housing and Urban Development (HUD). "Public Housing in a Competitive Market: An Example of How It Would Fare." Washington, D.C.: HUD, Office of Policy Development and Research, 1996. https://www.huduser.gov/portal/publications/pubasst/compmrkt.html.

Department of Housing and Urban Development v. Rucker, 535 U.S. 125 (2002).

Desmond, Matthew. "Eviction and the Reproduction of Urban Poverty." *American Journal of Sociology* 118, no. 1 (2012): 88–133.

Desmond, Matthew. *Evicted: Poverty and Profit in the American City.* New York: Crown, 2016.

Desmond, Matthew, and Mustafa Emirbayer. "What Is Racial Domination?" *Du Bois Review: Social Science Research on Race* 6, no. 2 (2009): 335–55.

Desmond, Matthew, Carl Gershenson, and Barbara Kiviat. "Forced Mobility and Residential Instability among Urban Renters." *Social Service Review* 89, no. 2 (2015): 227–62.

Desmond, Matthew, and Kristin L. Perkins. "Are Landlords Overcharging Housing Voucher Holders?" *City & Community* 15, no. 2 (2016): 137–62.

Desmond, Matthew, and Nicol Valdez. "Unpolicing the Urban Poor: Consequences of Third-Party Policing for Inner-City Women." *American Sociological Review* 78, no. 1 (2012): 117–41.

Desmond, Matthew, and Nathan Wilmers. "Do the Poor Pay More for Housing? Exploitation, Profit, and Risk in Rental Markets." *American Journal of Sociology* 124, no. 4 (2019): 1090–1124.

Devine, Deborah J. "Housing Choice Voucher Location Patterns: Implications for Participant and Neighborhood Welfare." Washington, D.C.: Department of Housing and Urban Development, Office of Policy Development and Research, 2003.

Duncan, Greg J., and Anita Zuberi. "Mobility Lessons from Gautreaux and Moving to Opportunity." *Northwestern Journal of Law and Social Policy* 1 (2006): 110.

Duneier, Mitchell. *Sidewalk*. New York: Farrar Straus & Giroux, 2001.

Econometrica. *Evaluation of HUD's Rental Assistance Demonstration (RAD): Interim Report*. Washington, D.C.: Department of Housing and Urban Development, 2016.

Edin, Kathryn, and Maria Kefalas. *Promises I Can Keep: Why Poor Women Put Motherhood Before Marriage*. Berkeley: University of California Press, 2005.

Edin, Kathryn, and Laura Lein. *Making Ends Meet: How Single Mothers Survive Welfare and Low-Wage Work*. New York: Russell Sage Foundation, 1997.

Edin, Kathryn, and Luke Shaefer. *Two Dollars a Day: Living on Almost Nothing in America*. New York: First Mariner Books, 2015.

Ellen, Ingrid Gould. *Sharing America's Neighborhoods: The Prospects for Stable Racial Integration*. Cambridge, MA: Harvard University Press, 2001.

Ellen, Ingrid Gould, Michael C. Lens, and Katherine O'Regan. "American Murder Mystery Revisited: Do Housing Voucher Households Cause Crime?" *Housing Policy Debate* 22, no. 4 (2012): 551–72.

Ellen, Ingrid Gould, and Brendan O'Flaherty. "Social Programs and Household Size: Evidence from New York City." *Population Research and Policy Review* 26, no. 4 (2007): 387–409.

Ellen, Ingrid Gould, and Katherine M. O'Regan. "Reversal of Fortunes? Lower-Income Urban Neighbourhoods in the US in the 1990s." *Urban Studies* 45, no. 4 (2008): 845–69.

Engdahl, Lora. "New Homes, New Neighborhoods, New Schools: A Progress Report on the Baltimore Housing Mobility Program." Poverty & Race Research Action Council, Washington, D.C., 2009.

Enos, Ryan D. "What the Demolition of Public Housing Teaches Us about the Impact of Racial Threat on Political Behavior." *American Journal of Political Science* 60, no. 1 (2016): 123–42.

Feins, Judith D., and Rhiannon Patterson. "Geographic Mobility in the Housing Choice Voucher Program: A Study of Families Entering the Program, 1995–2002." *Cityscape* 8, no. 2 (2005): 21–47.

Feins, Judith D., W. Eugene Rizor, Paul Elwood, and Linda Noel. "State and Metropolitan Administration of Section 8: Current Models and Potential Resources: Final Report." Washington, D.C.: Department of Housing and Urban Development, Office of Policy Development and Research, 1997.

Finkel, Meryl, and Larry Buron. "Study on Section 8 Voucher Success Rates: Quantitative Study of Success Rates in Metropolitan Areas." Department of Housing and Urban Development, Office of Policy Development and Research (2001): 1–134.

Fischel, William A. "An Economic History of Zoning and a Cure for Its Exclusionary Effects." *Urban Studies* 41, no. 2 (2004): 317–40.

Fischel, William A. *The Homevoter Hypothesis: How Home Values Influence Local Government Taxation, School Finance, and Land-Use Policies.* Cambridge, MA: Harvard University Press, 2005.

Fisher, Will. "Research Shows Housing Vouchers Reduce Hardship and Provide Platform for Long-Term Gains Among Children." Washington, D.C.: Center on Budget and Policy Priorities, 2015. http://www.cbpp.org/sites/default/files/atoms/files/3-10-14hous.pdf.

Fogelson, Robert M. *Bourgeois Nightmares: Suburbia, 1870-1930.* New Haven, CT: Yale University Press, 2007.

Freeman, Lance. "The Impact of Source of Income Laws on Voucher Utilization and Locational Outcomes." Assisted Housing Research Cadre Report. Washington, D.C.: Department of Housing and Urban Development, Office of Policy Development and Research, 2011.

Fritze, John. "New Police, Fire Training Facility Opens." *Baltimore Sun*, July 31, 2008.

Galster, George C. "Consequences from the Redistribution of Urban Poverty During the 1990s: A Cautionary Tale." *Economic Development Quarterly* 19, no. 2 (2005): 119–25.

Galster, George C. *Making Our Neighborhoods, Making Our Selves.* Chicago: University of Chicago Press, 2019.

Galster, George C., P. Tatian, and R. Smith. "The Impact of Neighbors Who Use Section 8 Certificates on Property Values." *Housing Policy Debate* 10, no. 4 (1999): 879–917.

Galvez, Martha. *What Do We Know about Housing Choice Voucher Program Location Outcomes?* Washington, D.C.: The Urban Institute, 2017.

Gans, Herbert. *The Urban Villagers: Group and Class in the Life of Italian Americans.* New York: The Free Press, 1982 [1962].

Garboden, Philip M. E. *The Double Crisis: A Statistical Report on Rental Housing Costs and Affordability in Baltimore City, 2000-2013.* Volume 29, Number 1. Baltimore: The Abell Foundation, 2016.

Garboden, Philip M. E., and Eva Rosen. "Talking to Landlords." *Cityscape* 20, no. 3 (2018): 281-291.

Garboden, Philip M. E. and Eva Rosen. "Serial Filing: How Landlords Use the Threat of Eviction." *City & Community* 18, no. 2 (2019): 638–61.

Garboden, Philip M. E., Eva Rosen, Stefanie DeLuca, and Kathryn Edin. "Taking Stock: What Drives Landlord Participation in the Housing Choice Voucher Program." *Housing Policy Debate* 28, no. 6 (2018): 979–1003.

Garboden, Philip M. E., Eva Rosen, Meredith Greif, Stefanie DeLuca, and Kathryn Edin. "Urban Landlords and the Housing Choice Voucher Program: A Research Report." Washington, D.C.: Department of Housing and Urban Development, May 2018.

Goering, John. "Expanding Choice and Integrating Neighborhoods: The MTO Experiment." In *The Geography of Opportunity: Race and Housing Choice in Metropolitan America*, edited by Xavier De Souza Briggs: 127–149. Washington, D.C.: Brookings Institution Press, 2005.

Goetz, Edward G. *New Deal Ruins: Race, Economic Justice, and Public Housing Policy.* Ithaca, NY: Cornell University Press, 2013.

Goldstein, Eric L., and Deborah R. Weiner. *Middle Ground: A History of the Jews of Baltimore.* Baltimore: Johns Hopkins University Press, 2018.

Granovetter, Mark S. "The Strength of Weak Ties." *American Journal of Sociology* 78, no. 6 (1973): 1360-380.

Greenlee, Andrew J. "More Than Meets the Market? Landlord Agency in the Illinois Housing Choice Voucher Program." *Housing Policy Debate* 24, no. 3 (2014): 500–24.

Greif, Meredith. "Regulating Landlords: Unintended Consequences for Poor Tenants." *City & Community* 17 (2018): 658–74.

Grigsby, William G., and Steven C. Bourassa. "Section 8: The Time for Fundamental Program Change?" *Housing Policy Debate* 15, no. 4 (2004): 805–34.

Gubits, Daniel, Marybeth Shinn, Michelle Wood, Stephen Bell, Samuel Dastrup, Claudia D. Solari, Scott R. Brown, Debi McInnis, Tom McCall, and Utsav Kattel. "Family Options Study: 3-Year Impacts of Housing and Services Interventions for Homeless Families." Washington, D.C.: Department of Housing and Urban Development, 2016.

Hannerz, Ulf. *Soulside: Inquiries into Ghetto Culture and Community*. Chicago: University of Chicago Press, 1969.

Harding, David J. *Living the Drama: Community, Conflict, and Culture Among Inner-City Boys*. Chicago: University of Chicago Press, 2010.

Harkness, Joseph M., and Sandra J. Newman. "Recipients of Housing Assistance under Welfare Reform: Trends in Employment and Welfare Participation." *Housing Policy Debate* 17, no. 1 (2006): 81–108.

Hartman, Chester, ed. *Housing and Social Policy*. Englewood Cliffs, NJ: Prentice Hall, 1975.

Hartung, John. M., and Jeffrey. R. Henig. "Housing Vouchers and Certificates as a Vehicle for Deconcentrating the Poor: Evidence from the Washington, D.C., Metropolitan Area." *Urban Affairs Review* 32, no. 3 (1997): 403–19.

Harvey, Hope "When Mothers Can't 'Pay the Cost to Be the Boss': Roles and Identity within Doubled-up Households." *Social Problems* (forthcoming).

Hendey, Leah, George Galster, Susan J. Popkin, and Chris Hayes. "Housing Choice Voucher Holders and Neighborhood Crime: A Dynamic Panel Analysis from Chicago." *Urban Affairs Review* 52, no. 4 (2016): 471–500.

Herbert, Claire W. "Squatting for Survival: Precarious Housing in a Declining U.S. City." *Housing Policy Debate* 28, no. 5 (2018): 797–813.

Hirsch, Arnold R. *Making the Second Ghetto: Race and Housing in Chicago 1940–1960*. New York: Cambridge University Press, 1983.

Hunt, D. Bradford. *Blueprint for Disaster: The Unraveling of Chicago Public Housing*. Chicago: University of Chicago Press, 2009.

Hunt, Louise, Mary Shulhof, and Stephen Holmquist. *Summary of the Quality Housing and Work Responsibility Act of 1998 (Title V of P.L. 105-276)*. Washington, D.C.: Department of Housing and Urban Development, Office of Policy, Program and Legislative Initiatives, 1998.

Hyra, Derek S. *Race, Class, and Politics in the Cappuccino City*. Chicago: University of Chicago Press, 2017.

Jackson, Kenneth T. *Crabgrass Frontier: The Suburbanization of the United States*. New York: Oxford University Press, 1985.

Jacob, Brian A., and Jens Ludwig. "The Effects of Housing Assistance on Labor Supply: Evidence from a Voucher Lottery." *American Economic Review* 102, no. 1 (February 2012): 272–304.

Jacobs, B. G., K. R. Hareny, C. L Edson, and B.S. Lane. "Guide to Federal Housing Programs (2nd Ed.)." The Bureau of National Affairs, Inc., Washington, D.C., 1986.

Jacobson, Joan. "The Dismantling of Baltimore's Public Housing." Baltimore: The Abell Foundation, 2007. http://www.abell.org/sites/default/files/publications/arn907.pdf.

Jargowsky, Paul A. *Poverty and Place: Ghettos, Barrios, and the American City*. New York: Russell Sage Foundation, 1997.

Jargowsky, Paul A. *Stunning Progress, Hidden Problems*. Washington, D.C.: Brookings Institution Press, 2003.

Jargowsky, Paul A. *Concentration of Poverty in the New Millennium: Changes in Prevalence, Composition, and Location of High Poverty Neighborhoods*. The Century Foundation, New York, 2013.

Jones, Brent. "Troublesome Pall Mall Apartments Come Down." *Baltimore Sun*, November 21, 2008.

Joseph, Mark L., Robert J. Chaskin, and Henry S. Webber. "The Theoretical Basis for Addressing Poverty Through Mixed-Income Development." *Urban Affairs Review* 42, no. 3 (2007): 369–409.

Katz, Bruce, and Austin Turner. "Who Should Run the Housing Voucher Program? A Reform Proposal." *Housing Policy Debate* 12, no. 2 (2001): 239–262.

Kefalas, Maria J. *Working-Class Heroes: Protecting Home, Community, and Nation in a Chicago Neighborhood*. Berkeley: University of California Press, 2003.

Kelling, George L., and James Q. Wilson. "Broken Windows." *The Atlantic*, March 1982.

The Kenner Commission Report. 1968. Report of the National Advisory Commission on Civil Disorders. United States Government Printing Office.

Kessler R. C., G. J. Duncan, L. A. Gennetian, L. F. Katz, J. R. Kling, N. A. Sampson, L. Sanbonmatsu, A. M. Zaslavsky, and J. Ludwig. "Associations of Housing Mobility Interventions for Children in High-Poverty Neighborhoods with Subsequent Mental Disorders during Adolescence." *JAMA* 311, no. 9 (March 5, 2014): 937–48.

Khadduri, J. "Deconcentration: What Do We Mean? What Do We Want?" *Cityscape* 5, no. 2 (2001): 69–84.

Khadduri, Jill, and Raymond J. Struyk. "Housing Vouchers for the Poor." *Journal of Policy Analysis and Management* 1, no. 2 (1982): 196–208.

Kingsley, G. Thomas. *Trends in Housing Problems and Federal Housing Assistance*. Washington, D.C.: The Urban Institute, 2017.

Kingsley, Thomas G., and Kathryn Pettit. "Concentrated Poverty: A Change in Course. Neighborhood Change in Urban America." The Urban Institute. Washington, D.C.: May 2003. https://www.urban.org/sites/default/files/publication/58946/310790-Concentrated-Poverty-A-Change-in-Course.PDF.

Klinenberg, Eric. *Heat Wave: A Social Autopsy of Disaster in Chicago*. Chicago: University of Chicago Press, 2003.

Kling, Jeffrey R., Jeffrey B. Liebman, and Lawrence F. Katz. "Experimental Analysis of Neighborhood Effects." *Econometrica* 75, no. 1 (2007): 83–119.

Kling, Jeffrey R., Jens Ludwig, and Larry Katz. "Neighborhood Effects on Crime for Female and Male Youth: Evidence from a Randomized Housing Voucher Experiment." *Quarterly Journal of Economics* 120, no. 1 (2005): 87–130.

Kneebone, E., Cary Nadeau, and Alan Berube. *The Re-Emergence of Concentrated Poverty*. Washington, D.C.: Brookings Institution Press, November 2011.

Kornhauser, R. R. *Social Sources of Delinquency: An Appraisal of Analytic Models*. Chicago: University of Chicago Press, 1978.

Korver-Glenn, Elizabeth. "Compounding Inequalities: How Racial Stereotypes and Discrimination Accumulate across the Stages of Housing Exchange." *American Sociological Review* 83, no. 4 (2018): 627–56.

Kotlowitz, Alex. *There Are No Children Here: The Story of Two Boys Growing up in the Other America*. New York: Anchor Books, 1991.

Krysan, Maria, and Kyle Crowder. *Cycle of Segregation: Social Processes and Residential Stratification*. New York: Russell Sage Foundation, 2017.

Kurwa, Rahim. "Deconcentration without Integration: Examining the Social Outcomes of Housing Choice Voucher Movement in Los Angeles County." *City & Community* 14, no. 4 (2015): 364–91.

La Vigne, Nancy, Samanth S. Lowry, Joshua Markman, and Allison Dwyer. "Evaluating the Use of Public Cameras for Crime Control and Prevention." Washington, D.C.: The Urban Institute, 2011.

Lamont, Michèle. *The Dignity of Working Men: Morality and the Boundaries of Race, Class, and Immigration*. Cambridge, MA: Harvard University Press, 2000.

Lamont, Michèle, and M. Fournier. *Cultivating Differences: Symbolic Boundaries and the Making of Inequality*. Chicago: University of Chicago Press, 1992.

Lamont, Michèle, and V. Molnar. "The Study of Boundaries in the Social Sciences." *Annual Review of Sociology* 28 (2002): 167–95.

Lamont, Michèle, and Mario Luis Small. "How Culture Matters: Enriching Our Understanding of Poverty." In *The Colors of Poverty: Why Racial and Ethnic Disparities Persist*, edited by Ann Chih Lin and David R. Harris, 76–102. New York: Russell Sage Foundation, 2008.

Landis, John D., and Kirk McClure. "Rethinking Federal Housing Policy." *Journal of the American Planning Association* 76, no. 3 (2010): 319–48.

Lee, Jennifer. "From Civil Relations to Racial Conflict: Merchant-Customer Interactions in Urban America." *American Sociological Review* 67, no. 1 (2002): 77–98.

Lee, Jennifer. *Civility in the City: Blacks, Jews, and Koreans in Urban America*. Cambridge, MA: Harvard University Press, 2006.

Lens, Michael C. "The Impact of Housing Vouchers on Crime in US Cities and Suburbs." *Urban Studies* 51, no. 6 (2014): 1274–89.

Lens, Michael, Kirk McClure, and Brent Mast. "Does Jobs Proximity Matter in the Housing Choice Voucher Program?" *Cityscape* 21, no. 1 (2019): 145–62.

Levine, Jeremy R. "The Privatization of Political Representation: Community-Based Organizations as Nonelected Neighborhood Representatives." *American Sociological Review* 81, no. 6 (2016): 1251–75.

Lowry, Ira S. *Housing Assistance for Low-Income Urban Families: A Fresh Approach*. Santa Monica, CA: RAND Corporation, 1971.

Lubell, Jeff, "Rental Assistance: A Drag on Work or a Platform for Opportunity?" *Spotlight on Poverty and Opportunity*, December 12, 2011. http://www.spotlightonpoverty.org/ExclusiveCommentary.aspx?id=8f1764fe-5e54-4e1d-aee1-71e51f8bbc2e.

Ludwig, Jens, Greg J. Duncan, Lisa A. Gennetian, Lawrence F. Katz, Ronald C. Kessler, Jeffrey R. Kling, and Lisa Sanbonmatsu. "Long-Term Neighborhood Effects on Low-Income Families: Evidence from Moving to Opportunity." *American Economic Review* 103, no. 3 (2013): 226–31.

Ludwig, Jens, Jeffrey B. Liebman, Jeffrey R. Kling, Greg J. Duncan, Larry Katz, R. C. Kessler, and L. Sanbonmatsu. "What Can We Learn about Neighborhood Effects from the Moving to Opportunity Experiment." *American Journal of Sociology* 114, no. 1 (2008): 144–88.

Maney, Brian, and Sheila Crowley. "Scarcity and Success: Perspectives on Assisted Housing." *Journal of Affordable Housing & Community Development Law* 9, no. 4 (2000): 319–68.

Marwell, Nicole P. *Bargaining for Brooklyn: Community Organizations in the Entrepreneurial City.* Chicago: University of Chicago Press, 2007.

Massey, Douglas S., and Nancy A. Denton. *American Apartheid: Segregation and the Making of the Underclass.* Cambridge, MA: Harvard University Press, 1993.

Massey, Douglas S., and S. M. Kanaiaupuni. "Public Housing and the Concentration of Poverty." *Social Science Quarterly* 74, no. 1 (1993): 109–22.

Massey, Douglas S., and Brendan P. Mullan. "Processes of Hispanic and Black Spatial Assimilation." *American Journal of Sociology* 89, no. 4 (1984): 836–73.

Mayer, Susan E., and Christopher Jencks. "Growing Up in Poor Neighborhoods: How Much Does It Matter?" *Science* 243, no. 4897 (March 17, 1989): 1441–45.

McCabe, Brian J. "Are Homeowners Better Citizens? Homeownership and Community Participation in the United States." *Social Forces* 91, no. 3 (2013): 929–54.

McCabe, Brian J. "When Property Values Rule." *Contexts* 13, no. 1 (2014): 38–43.

McCabe, Brian J. *No Place Like Home: Wealth, Community, and the Politics of Homeownership.* New York: Oxford University Press, 2016.

McCabe, Brian J., and Kathleen M. Moore. "Waitlists and Preferences: How Public Housing Authorities Run the Housing Choice Voucher Program." Working Paper, 2017.

McClure, Kirk. "Deconcentrating Poverty with Housing Programs." *Journal of the American Planning Association* 74, no. 1 (2008): 90–99.

McClure, Kirk. "The Prospects for Guiding Housing Choice Voucher Households to High-Opportunity Neighborhoods." *Cityscape* 12 (December 1, 2010): 101–22.

McClure, Kirk. "The Future of Housing Policy: Fungibility of Rental Housing Programs to Better Fit With Market Need." *Housing Policy Debate* 27, no. 3 (2017), 486–89.

McClure, Kirk, and Alex Schwartz. "Small Area Fair Market Rents, Race, and Neighborhood Opportunity." *Cityscape* 21, no. 3 (2019): 49–70.

McCormick, Naomi, Mark L. Joseph, and Robert J. Chaskin. "The New Stigma of Relocated Public Housing Residents: Challenges to Social Identity in Mixed-Income Developments." *City & Community* 11, no. 3 (2012): 285–308.

McCoy, Dana Charles, C. Cybele Raver, and Patrick Sharkey. "Children's Cognitive Performance and Selective Attention Following Recent Community Violence." *Journal of Health and Social Behavior* 56, no. 1 (2015): 19–36.

Mendenhall, Ruby, Stefanie DeLuca, and Greg J. Duncan. "Neighborhood Resources, Racial Segregation, and Economic Mobility: Results from the Gautreaux Program." *Social Science Research* 35, no. 4 (2006): 892–923.

Metzger, Molly W., and Henry S. Webber (eds.). *Facing Segregation: Housing Policy Solutions for a Stronger Society.* New York: Oxford University Press, 2018.

Mills, Gregory, Daniel Gubits, Larry Orr, David Long, Judie Feins, Bulbul Kaul, Michelle Wood, and Amy Jones. "Effects of Housing Vouchers on Welfare Families." Washington, D.C.: Department of Housing and Urban Development, Office of Policy Development and Research, 2006.

Moore, Kathleen M. "Lists and Lotteries: Rationing in the Housing Choice Voucher Program." *Housing Policy Debate* 26, no. 3 (2015): 474–87.

Moynihan, Daniel P. *The Negro Family: The Case for National Action.* Washington, D.C.: Department of Labor, Office of Policy Planning and Research, 1965.

Murphy, Alexandra K. "'Litterers': How Objects of Physical Disorder Are Used to Construct Subjects of Social Disorder in a Suburb." *The ANNALS of the American Academy of Political and Social Science* 642, no. 1 (2012): 210–27.

Murphy, Alexandra K. *Where the Sidewalk Ends: Poverty in an American Suburb.* New York: Oxford University Press (forthcoming).

Naparstek, Arthur J., Susan R. Freis, and G. Thomas Kingsley. *HOPE VI: Community Building Makes a Difference.* Washington, D.C.: Department of Housing and Urban Development, 2000.

Newman, Oscar. "Defensible Space: A New Physical Planning Tool for Urban Revitalization." *Journal of the American Planning Association* 61, no. 2 (1995): 149–55.

Newman, Sandra. "Low-End Rental Housing: The Forgotten Story in Baltimore's Housing Boom." Washington, D.C.: The Urban Institute, August 2005.

Newman, Sandra, C. Scott Holupka, and Joseph Harkness. "The Long-Term Effects of Housing Assistance on Work and Welfare," *Journal of Policy Analysis and Management* 28, no. 1 (2009) 81–101.

Newman, Sandra J., and Ann B. Schnare. "'. . . And a Suitable Living Environment': The Failure of Housing Programs to Deliver on Neighborhood Quality." *Housing Policy Debate* 8, no. 4 (1997): 703–41.

Nguyen, Mai Thi, Victoria Basolo, and Abhishek Tiwari. "Opposition to Affordable Housing in the USA: Debate Framing and the Responses of Local Actors." *Housing, Theory and Society* 30, no. 2 (2013): 107–30.

National Low Income Housing Coalition (NLIHC). "Who Lives in Federally Assisted Housing?" *National Low Income Housing Coalition Spotlight,* Housing Spotlight, 2, no. 2 (November 2012).

Oliver, Melvin, and Thomas M. Shapiro, eds. *Black Wealth / White Wealth: A New Perspective on Racial Inequality.* 2nd ed. New York: Routledge, 1995.

Olsen, Edgar O. "Does HUD Overpay for Voucher Units, and Will SAFMRs Reduce the Overpayment?" *Cityscape* 21, no. 3 (2019): 89–102.

Olsen, Edgar O., Catherine A. Tyler, Jonathan W. King, and Paul E. Carrillo. "The Effects of Different Types of Housing Assistance on Earnings and Employment." *Cityscape* 8, no. 2 (2005): 163–87.

Orlebeke, Charles J. The Evolution of Low-Income Housing Policy, 1949 to 1999. *Housing Policy Debate* 11, no. 2 (2000), 489–520.

Orr, Larry, Judith D. Feins, Eric Beecroft, Robin D. Jacob, Lisa Sanbonmatsu, Lawrence F. Katz, Jeffrey B. Liebman, and Jeffrey R. Kling. "Moving to Opportunity for Fair Housing Demonstration: Interim Impacts Evaluation." Washington, D.C.: Department of Housing and Urban Development, Office of Policy Development and Research, September 2003.

Orser, W. Edward. *Blockbusting in Baltimore: The Edmondson Village Story*. Lexington: University Press of Kentucky, 1997.

Owens, Ann. "The New Geography of Subsidized Housing: Implications for Urban Poverty." PhD diss., Harvard University, 2012.

Owens, Ann. "Inequality in Children's Contexts Income Segregation of Households with and without Children." *American Sociological Review* 81, no. 3 (2016): 549–574.

Owens, Ann. "How Do People-Based Housing Policies Affect People (and Place)?" *Housing Policy Debate* 27, no. 2 (2017): 266–81.

Park, Robert Ezra, and Ernest Watson Burgess. *The City: Suggestions for Investigation of Human Behavior in the Urban Environment*. Chicago: University of Chicago Press, 1925.

Pashup, Jennifer, Kathryn Edin, Greg J. Duncan, and Karen Burke. "Participation in a Residential Mobility Program from the Client's Perspective: Findings from Gautreaux Two." *Housing Policy Debate* 16, no. 3–4 (2005): 361–92.

Pastor, Manuel, Chris Benner, and Martha Matsuoka. *This Could Be the Start of Something Big: How Social Movements for Regional Equity Are Reshaping Metropolitan America*. Ithaca, NY: Cornell University Press, 2009.

Pastor, Manuel, and Margery Austin Turner. "Reducing Poverty and Economic Distress after ARRA: Potential Roles for Place-Conscious Strategies." Washington, D.C.: The Urban Institute, 2010.

Patterson, Rhiannon, Michelle Wood, Ken Lam, Satyendra Patrabansh, Gregory Mills, Steven Sullivan, Hiwotte Amare, and Lily Zandinapour. "Evaluation of the Welfare to Work Voucher Program: Report to Congress." Washington, D.C.: Department of Housing and Urban Development, Office of Policy Development and Research, 2004.

Pattillo, Mary E. "Sweet Mothers and Gangbangers: Managing Crime in a Black Middle-Class Neighborhood." *Social Forces* 76, no. 3 (1998): 747–74.

Pattillo McCoy, Mary. *Black Picket Fences: Privilege and Peril among the Black Middle Class*. 1st ed. Chicago: University of Chicago Press, 1999.

Pattillo, Mary. *Black on the Block: The Politics of Race and Class in the City*. Chicago: University of Chicago Press, 2007.

Pattillo, Mary. "Housing: Commodity versus Right." *Annual Review of Sociology* 39 (2013): 509–31.

Pelletiere, Danilo. *Getting to the Heart of Housing's Fundamental Question: How Much Can a Family Afford?* Washington, D.C.: National Low Income Housing Coalition (NLIHC), 2008.

Pendall, Rolf. "Local Land Use Regulation and the Chain of Exclusion." *Journal of the American Planning Association* 66, no. 2 (2000): 125–42.

Pendall, Rolf. "Why Voucher and Certificate Users Live in Distressed Neighborhoods." *Housing Policy Debate* 11, no. 4 (2000): 881–910.

Pendall, Rolf. "Driving to Opportunity: Understanding the Links among Transportation Access, Residential Outcomes, and Economic Opportunity for Housing Voucher Recipients," 2014. https://www.urban.org/research/publication/driving-opportunity-understanding -links-among-transportation-access-residential-outcomes-and-economic-opportunity -housing-voucher-recipients.

Pietila, Antero. *Not in My Neighborhood: How Bigotry Shaped a Great American City*. 1st ed. Chicago: Ivan R. Dee, 2010.

Polikoff, Alexander. *Waiting for Gautreaux: A Story of Segregation, Housing, and the Black Ghetto.* Evanston, IL: Northwestern University Press, 2006.

Polletta, Francesca. *It Was Like a Fever: Storytelling in Protest and Politics.* Chicago: University of Chicago Press, 2006.

Popkin, Susan J., George C. Galster, Kenneth Temkin, Carla Herbig, Diane K. Levy, and Elise K. Richer. "Obstacles to Desegregating Public Housing: Lessons Learned from Implementing Eight Consent Decrees." *Journal of Policy Analysis and Management* 22, no. 2 (2003): 179–99.

Popkin, Susan J., Victoria E. Gwiasda, Lynn M. Olson, Dennis P. Rosenbaum, and Larry Buron. *The Hidden War: Crime and the Tragedy of Public Housing in Chicago.* New Brunswick, NJ: Rutgers University Press, 2000.

Popkin, Susan J., Bruce Katz, Mary Cunningham, Karen Burke, Jeremy Gustafson, and Margery A. Turner. "A Decade of HOPE VI: Research Findings and Policy Challenges." Washington, D.C.: The Urban Institute, May 2004.

Popkin, Susan J., Tama Leventhal, and Gretchen Weismann. "Girls in the 'Hood: How Safety Affects the Life Chances of Low-Income Girls." *Urban Affairs Review* 45, no. 6 (July 1, 2010): 715–44.

Popkin, Susan J., Michael J. Rich, Leah Hendey, Chris Hayes, Joe Parilla, and George Galster. "Public Housing Transformation and Crime: Making the Case for Responsible Relocation." *Cityscape* 14, no. 3 (2012): 137–60.

Popkin, Susan J., James E. Rosenbaum, and Patricia M. Meaden. "Labor Market Experiences of Low-Income Black Women in Middle-Class Suburbs: Evidence From a Survey of Gautreaux Program Participants. *Journal of Policy Analysis and Management* 12, 3 (1993): 556–573.

Poverty & Race Research Action Council (PRRAC). "Expanding Choice: Practical Strategies for Building a Successful Housing Mobility Program: Appendix B." Washington, D.C.: PRRAC, 2017. http://www.prrac.org/pdf/AppendixB.pdf.

Priemus, Hugo, Peter A. Kemp, and David P. Varady. "Housing Vouchers in the United States, Great Britain, and the Netherlands: Current Issues and Future Perspectives." *Housing Policy Debate* 16, no. 3–4 (2005): 575–609.

Rainwater, Lee. *Behind Ghetto Walls: Black Families in a Federal Slum.* Chicago: Aldine, 1970.

Reina, Vincent, Arthur Acolin, and Raphael W. Bostic. "Section 8 Vouchers and Rent Limits: Do Small Area Fair Market Rent Limits Increase Access to Opportunity Neighborhoods? An Early Evaluation." *Housing Policy Debate* 29, no. 1 (2019): 44–61.

Rose, Kalima. "Beyond Gentrification." *Shelterforce*, May 2001.

Rosen, Eva. "Horizontal Mobility: How Narratives of Neighborhood Violence Shape Housing Decisions." *American Sociological Review* 82, no. 2 (2017): 270–296.

Rosen, Eva. "Rigging the Rules of the Game: How Landlords Geographically Sort Low-Income Renters." *City & Community* 13, no. 4 (2014): 301–340.

Rosen, Eva, and Philip Garboden. "Landlord Paternalism: Housing the Poor with a Velvet Glove." *Social Problems* (forthcoming).

Rosen, Eva, Philip Garboden, and Jennifer E. Cossyleon. "Discrimination without Discriminants: Racial Logics in Tenant Screening." Working Paper, 2019.

Rosenbaum, James E. "Changing the Geography of Opportunity by Expanding Residential Choice: Lessons from the Gautreaux Program." *Housing Policy Debate* 6, no. 1 (1995): 231–69.

Rosenblatt, Peter. "The Renaissance Comes to the Projects: Public Housing, Urban Redevelopment, and Racial Inequality in Baltimore." PhD diss. Johns Hopkins University, 2011.

Rosenblatt, Peter, and Jennifer E. Cossyleon. "Pushing the Boundaries: Searching for Housing in the Most Segregated Metropolis in America." *City & Community* 17, no. 1 (2018): 87–108.

Rosenblatt, Peter, and Stefanie DeLuca. "'We Don't Live Outside, We Live in Here': Neighborhood and Residential Mobility Decisions Among Low-Income Families." *City & Community* 11, no. 3 (2012): 254–84.

Rosin, Hanna. "American Murder Mystery." *The Atlantic*, August 2008.

Rothstein, Richard. *The Color of Law: A Forgotten History of How Our Government Segregated America*. 1st ed. New York: Liveright, 2017.

Rothwell, Jonathan, and Douglas S. Massey. "The Effect of Density Zoning on Racial Segregation in U.S. Urban Areas." *Urban Affairs Review* 44, no. 6 (2009): 779–806.

Rubinowitz, Leonard S., and James E. Rosenbaum. *Crossing the Class and Color Lines: From Public Housing to White Suburbia*. Chicago: University of Chicago Press, 2000.

Salama, Jerry J. "The Redevelopment of Distressed Public Housing: Early Results from HOPE VI Projects in Atlanta, Chicago, and San Antonio." *Housing Policy Debate* 10, no. 1 (1999): 95–142.

Sampson, Robert J. *Great American City: Chicago and the Enduring Neighborhood Effect*. Chicago: University of Chicago Press, 2012.

Sampson, Robert J. "Moving to Inequality: Neighborhood Effects and Experiments Meet Social Structure." *American Journal of Sociology* 114, no. 1 (2008): 189–231.

Sampson, Robert J., D. McAdam, H. MacIndoe, and S. Weffer-Elizondo. "Civil Society Reconsidered: The Durable Nature and Community Structure of Collective Civic Action." *American Journal of Sociology* 111, no. 3 (2005): 673–714.

Sampson, Robert J., Jeffrey D. Morenoff, and Felton Earls. "Beyond Social Capital: Spatial Dynamics of Collective Efficacy for Children." *American Sociological Review* 64 (1999): 633–660.

Sampson, Robert J., Jeffrey D. Morenoff, and Thomas Gannon-Rowley. "Assessing Neighborhood Effects: Social Processes and New Directions in Research." *Annual Review of Sociology* 28 (August 2002): 443–78.

Sampson, Robert J., and Stephen W. Raudenbush. "Systematic Social Observation of Public Spaces: A New Look at Disorder in Urban Neighborhoods." *American Journal of Sociology* 105, no. 3 (1999): 603–51.

Sampson, Robert J., and Stephen W. Raudenbush. "Seeing Disorder: Neighborhood Stigma and the Social Construction of 'Broken Windows.'" *Social Psychology Quarterly* 67, no. 4 (2004): 319–42.

Sampson, Robert J., Stephen W. Raudenbush, and Felton Earls. "Neighborhoods and Violent Crime: A Multilevel Study of Collective Efficacy." *Science* 277, no. 5328 (August 15, 1997): 918–24.

Sampson, Robert J., and William Julius Wilson. "Toward a Theory of Race, Crime, and Urban Inequality." In *Crime and Inequality*, edited by J. Hagan and R. D. Peterson, 37–54. Stanford, CA: Stanford University Press, 1995.

Sanbonmatsu, Lisa, Jens Ludwig, Lisa A. Gennetian, Greg J. Duncan, Ronald L. Kessler, Emma Adam, Thomas W. McDade, and Stacey Tessler Lindau. "Moving to Opportunity For Fair

Housing Demonstration Program: Final Impacts Evaluation." Department of Housing and Urban Development, Office of Policy Development and Research, 2011. http://www.huduser .org/portal/publications/pubasst/mtofhd.html.

Sánchez-Jankowski, Martín. *Cracks in the Pavement: Social Change and Resilience in Poor Neighborhoods*. Berkeley: University of California Press, 2008.

Santiago, Anna M., George C. Galster, and Peter Tatian. "Assessing the Property Value Impacts of the Dispersed Subsidy Housing Program in Denver." *Journal of Policy Analysis and Management* 20, no. 1 (2001): 65–88.

Sard, Barbara. "Housing Vouchers Should Be a Major Component of Future Housing Policy for the Lowest Income Families." *Cityscape* 5, no. 2 (2001): 89–110.

Sard, Barbara. "Housing Choice Voucher Program: Oversight and Review of Legislative Proposals Testimony of Barbara Sard, Vice President for Housing Policy, before the House Financial Services Subcommittee on Housing and Insurance." Washington, D.C.: Center on Budget and Policy Priorities, 2018.

Sard, Barbara, and Douglas Rice. *Realizing the Housing Voucher Program's Potential to Enable Families to Move to Better Neighborhoods*. Washington, D.C.: Center on Budget and Policy Priorities, 2016.

Sard, Barbara, and Deborah Thorpe. "Consolidating Rental Assistance Administration Would Increase Efficiency and Expand Opportunity." Washington, D.C.: Center on Budget and Policy Priorities, 2016.

Satter, Beryl. *Family Properties: Race, Real Estate, and the Exploitation of Black Urban America*. New York: Metropolitan Books, 2010.

Schwartz, Alex F. *Housing Policy in the United States*. 3rd ed. New York: Routledge, 2015.

Sharkey, Patrick T. "Navigating Dangerous Streets: The Sources and Consequences of Street Efficacy." *American Sociological Review* 71, no. 5 (2006): 826–46.

Sharkey, Patrick. "The Acute Effect of Local Homicides on Children's Cognitive Performance." *Proceedings of the National Academy of Sciences* 107, no. 26 (2010): 11733–38.

Sharkey, Patrick. *Stuck in Place: Urban Neighborhoods and the End of Progress toward Racial Equality*. Chicago: University of Chicago Press, 2013.

Sharkey, Patrick. "The Long Reach of Violence: A Broader Perspective on Data, Theory, and Evidence on the Prevalence and Consequences of Exposure to Violence." *Annual Review of Criminology* 1, no. 1 (2018): 85–102.

Sharkey, Patrick T., and Jacob W. Faber. "Where, When, Why, and for Whom Do Residential Contexts Matter? Moving Away from the Dichotomous Understanding of Neighborhood Effects." *Annual Review of Sociology* 40 (2014): 559–79.

Sharkey, Patrick, Amy Ellen Schwartz, Ingrid Gould Ellen, and Johanna Lacoe. "High Stakes in the Classroom, High Stakes on the Street: The Effects of Community Violence on Student's Standardized Test Performance." *Sociological Science* 1 (2014): 199–220.

Sharkey, Patrick, Gerard Torrats-Espinosa, and Delaram Takyar. "Community and the Crime Decline: The Causal Effect of Local Nonprofits on Violent Crime." *American Sociological Review* 82, no. 6 (2017): 1214–40.

Shaw, Clifford Robe, and Henry Donald McKay. *Juvenile Delinquency and Urban Areas: A Study of Rates of Delinquency in Relation to Differential Characteristics of Local Communities in American Cities*. Chicago: University of Chicago Press, 1942.

Shroder, Mark. "Moving to Opportunity: An Experiment in Social and Geographic Mobility."
   Cityscape 5, no. 2 (2001): 57–67.

Shroder, Mark. "Does Housing Assistance Perversely Affect Self-Sufficiency? A Review Essay."
   Journal of Housing Economics 11, no. 4 (2002): 381–417.

Shulte, Fred, and June Arney. "On Shaky Ground." *The Baltimore Sun*, December 10, 2006.

Skloot, Rebecca. *The Immortal Life of Henrietta Lacks*. New York: Broadway Books, 2011.

Skobba, Kimberly, and Edward Glenn Goetz. "Mobility Decisions of Very Low-Income Households." *Cityscape* 15, no. 2 (2013): 155–71.

Small, Mario Luis. *Villa Victoria: The Transformation of Social Capital in a Boston Barrio*. 1st ed.
   Chicago: University of Chicago Press, 2004.

Small, Mario Luis. "'How Many Cases Do I Need?': On Science and the Logic of Case Selection
   in Field-Based Research." *Ethnography* 10, no. 1 (2009): 5–38.

Small, Mario Luis. *Unanticipated Gains: Origins of Network Inequality in Everyday Life*. Reprint
   ed. New York: Oxford University Press, 2010.

Small, Mario Luis, David J. Harding, and Michèle Lamont. "Reconsidering Culture and Poverty." *The ANNALS of the American Academy of Political and Social Science* 629, no. 1 (2010):
   6–27.

Small, Mario Luis, and Monica McDermott. "The Presence of Organizational Resources in Poor
   Urban Neighborhoods: An Analysis of Average and Contextual Effects." *Social Forces* 84,
   no. 3 (2006): 1697–1724.

Solomon, Rod. *Public Housing Reform and Voucher Success: Progress and Challenges*. Washington,
   D.C.: Brookings Institution Press, 2005.

South, Scott J., and Kyle D. Crowder. "Escaping Distressed Neighborhoods: Individual, Community, and Metropolitan Influences." *American Journal of Sociology* 102, no 4 (1997):
   1040–84.

Spradley, James P. *The Ethnographic Interview*. Belmont, CA: Wadsworth, 1979.

Stack, Carol B. *All Our Kin: Strategies for Survival in a Black Community*. New York: Basic Books,
   1975.

Steffan, Barry L., Keith Fudge, Marge Martin, Maria Teresa Souza, David A. Vandenbroucke,
   and David Yao Young-Gann. "Worst Case Housing Needs 2009: Report to Congress." Washington, D.C.: Department of Housing and Urban Development, Office of Policy Development and Research, 2011.

Stegman, Michael A. *Housing Investment in the Inner City*. Cambridge, MA: The MIT Press, 1972.

Sternlieb, George. *The Tenement Landlord*. 1st ed. New Brunswick, NJ: Rutgers University Press,
   1966.

Sternlieb, George. *The Urban Housing Dilemma: The Dynamics of New York City's Rent Controlled
   Housing*. New York: Housing and Development Administration, 1972.

Stuart, Forrest. *Down, Out, and Under Arrest: Policing and Everyday Life in Skid Row*. Chicago:
   University of Chicago Press, 2016.

Susin, Scott. "Longitudinal Outcomes of Subsidized Housing Recipients in Matched Survey
   and Administrative Data." *Cityscape* 8, no. 2 (2005): 189–218.

Suttles, Gerald D. *The Social Order of the Slum: Ethnicity and Territory in the Inner City*. Chicago:
   University of Chicago Press, 1968.

Swidler, Ann. *Talk of Love: How Culture Matters*. Chicago: University of Chicago Press, 2003.

Tach, Laura M. "More than Bricks and Mortar: Neighborhood Frames, Social Processes, and the Mixed-Income Redevelopment of a Public Housing Project." *City & Community* 8, no. 3 (2009): 269–99.

Taub, Richard P., D. Garth Taylor, and Jan D. D. Dunham. *Paths of Neighborhood Change: Race and Crime in Urban America*. Chicago: University of Chicago Press, 1987.

Taylor, Keeanga-Yamahtta. *Race for Profit: How Banks and the Real Estate Industry Undermined Black Homeownership*. Chapel Hill: University of North Carolina Press, 2019.

Tegeler, Philip D., Michael L. Hanley, and Judith Liben. "Transforming Section 8: Using Federal Housing Subsidies to Promote Individual Housing Choice and Desegregation." *Harvard Civil Rights–Civil Liberties Law Review* 30 (1995): 451–485

Tighe, J. Rosie, and Joanna P. Ganning. "Do Shrinking Cities Allow Redevelopment without Displacement? An Analysis of Affordability Based on Housing and Transportation Costs for Redeveloping, Declining, and Stable Neighborhoods." *Housing Policy Debate* 26, no. 4–5 (2016): 785–800.

Tighe, J. Rosie, Megan E. Hatch, and Joseph Mead. "Source of Income Discrimination and Fair Housing Policy." *Journal of Planning Literature* 32 (2017): 3–15.

Tilly, Charles. *Durable Inequality*. Berkeley: University of California Press, 1999.

Turner, Margery Austin. "Moving Out of Poverty: Expanding Mobility and Choice through Tenant-Based Housing Assistance." *Housing Policy Debate* 9, no. 2 (1998): 373–94.

Turner, Margery Austin, and Thomas Kingsley. "Federal Programs for Addressing Low-Income Housing Needs: A Policy Primer." Washington, D.C.: The Urban Institute, December 1, 2008.

Turner, Margery A., Susan J. Popkin, and Mary Cunningham. "Section 8 Mobility and Neighborhood Health: Emerging Issues and Policy Challenges." Washington, D.C.: The Urban Institute, 1999.

Turner, Margery Austin, Susan J. Popkin, and Lynette Rawlings. "Public Housing and the Legacy of Segregation." Washington, D.C.: The Urban Institute, 2009.

Turner, Margery Austin, Stephen L. Ross, George C. Galster, and John Yinger. "Discrimination in Metropolitan Housing Markets." Washington, D.C.: Department of Housing and Urban Development, 2002.

Turnham, Jennifer, Meryl Finkel, Larry Buron, Melissa Vandawalker, Bulbul Kaul, Kevin Hathaway, and Chris Kubacki. "Housing Choice Voucher Program: Administrative Fee Study Final Report." Washington, D.C.: ABT Associates for Department of Housing and Urban Development, 2015.

U.S. Census Bureau. *American Housing Survey for the United States: 2007*. Washington, D.C.: Department of Housing and Urban Development and the U.S. Census Bureau, 2008.

U.S. Census Bureau. "Census 2010, DP-1—Profile of General Population and Housing Characteristics: 2010."

U.S. Census Bureau. U.S. Census 1960: "Total Population."

U.S. Census Bureau. U.S. Census 2010: "Total Population."

U.S. Government Accountability Office. *Housing Choice Vouchers: Options Exist to Increase Program Efficiencies*. Washington, D.C., 2012.

Vale, Lawrence J. *From the Puritans to the Projects: Public Housing and Public Neighbors*. Cambridge, MA: Harvard University Press, 2000.

Vale, Lawrence J. *Purging the Poorest: Public Housing and the Design Politics of Twice Cleared Communities*. Chicago: University of Chicago Press, 2013.

Vale, Lawrence J., and Yonah Freemark. "From Public Housing to Public-Private Housing." *Journal of the American Planning Association* 78, no. 4 (2012): 379–402.

Vandenbroucke, David A. "Is There Enough Housing to Go Around?" *Cityscape* 9, no. 1 (2007).

Varady, David P., Joseph Jaroscak, and Reinout Kleinhans. "How to Attract More Landlords to the Housing Choice Voucher Program: A Case Study of Landlord Outreach Efforts." *Urban Research & Practice* 10, no. 2 (2017): 143–55.

Vargas, Robert. *Wounded City: Violent Turf Wars in a Chicago Barrio*. New York: Oxford University Press, 2016.

Venkatesh, Sudhir A. *American Project: The Rise and Fall of a Modern Ghetto*. Cambridge, MA: Harvard University Press, 2002.

Venkatesh, Sudhir A. "'Doin' the Hustle' Constructing the Ethnographer in the American Ghetto." *Ethnography* 3, no. 1 (2002): 91–111.

Venkatesh, Sudhir A. *Off the Books: The Underground Economy of the Urban Poor*. Cambridge, MA: Harvard University Press, 2006.

Wang, Xinhao, and David P. Varady. "Using Hot-Spot Analysis to Study the Clustering of Section 8 Housing Voucher Families." *Housing Studies* 20, no. 1 (2005): 29–48.

Wang, Xinhao, David Varady, and Yimei Wang. "Measuring the Deconcentration of Housing Choice Voucher Program Recipients in Eight U.S. Metropolitan Areas Using Hot Spot Analysis." *Cityscape* 10, no. 1 (2008): 65–90.

Waters, Mary C. *Black Identities: West Indian Immigrant Dreams and American Realities*. Cambridge, MA: Harvard University Press, 2001.

Western, Bruce. *Punishment and Inequality in America*. New York: Russell Sage Foundation, 2007.

Williams, Richard, Reynold Nesiba, and Eileen Diaz McConnell. "The Changing Face of Inequality in Home Mortgage Lending." *Social Problems* 52, no. 2 (2005): 181–208.

Williamson, Anne R., Marc T. Smith, and Marta Strambi-Kramer. "Housing Choice Vouchers, the Low-Income Housing Tax Credit, and the Federal Poverty Deconcentration Goal." *Urban Affairs Review* 45, no. 1 (2009): 119–32.

Wilson, William Julius. "The Political Economy and Urban Racial Tensions." *The American Economist* 39, no. 1 (1995): 3–14.

Wilson, William Julius. *The Truly Disadvantaged: The Inner City, the Underclass, and Public Policy*. Chicago: University of Chicago Press, 1987.

Wilson, William Julius. *When Work Disappears: The World of the New Urban Poor*. 1st ed. New York: Vintage, 1997.

Wilson, William Julius, and Richard P. Taub. *There Goes the Neighborhood: Racial, Ethnic, and Class Tensions in Four Chicago Neighborhoods and Their Meaning for America*. New York: Random House Digital, 2006.

Woldoff, Rachael A. *White Flight/Black Flight: The Dynamics of Racial Change in an American Neighborhood*. Ithaca, NY: Cornell University Press, 2011.

Wood, Holly. "When Only a House Makes a Home: How Home Selection Matters in the Residential Mobility Decisions of Lower-Income, Inner-City Black Families." *Social Service Review* 88, no. 2 (2014): 264–94.

Wood, Michelle, Jennifer Turnham, and Gregory Mills. "Housing Affordability and Family Well-Being: Results from the Housing Voucher Evaluation." *Housing Policy Debate* 19, no. 2 (2008): 367–412.

Yinger, John. "Housing Discrimination Is Still Worth Worrying About." *Housing Policy Debate* 9, no. 4 (1998): 893–927.

Zhang, Y., and G. Weismann. "Public Housing's Cinderella: Policy Dynamics of HOPE VI in the Mid-1990s." In *Where Are Poor People to Live? Transforming Public Housing Communities*, edited by Larry Bennett and Patricia A. Wright. Armonk, NY: M. E. Sharpe, 2006: 41–67.

Zuberi, Anita. "The Other Side of the Story: Exploring the Experiences of Landlords in Order to Improve Housing Opportunity for Low-Income Households." Working Paper, 2019: 451–485.

INDEX

Note: Page numbers in *italic* type indicate figures or tables.

AIDS, 200, 224
American Civil Liberties Union, 12
American Gangster (documentary series), 73
Anderson, Elijah, 193, 206; *Code of the
    Street*, 6
Animal Control, 202–3
Atlantic (magazine), 242, 243

background checks, 138
Baltimore: affordable housing crisis in, 61;
    crime/violence in, 212; decline of, 2; FMR
    in, 301n48; inequality in, 2–3; vouchers in,
    15–16
Baltimore Afro-American Newspaper, 28–29
Baltimore County, 52, 95, 116–18, 219, 233,
    250, 252, 294n43
Baltimore Housing Mobility Program,
    279n38
Baltimore Regional Housing Program
    (BRHP), 249, 300n35
Baltimore Sun (newspaper), 45, 103
Belair-Edison, 16, 127, 146
Bel Park Towers public housing, 44
Bipartisan Policy Center, 247
blockbusting, ix, 30–31, 46, 119, 172, 240,
    243
blue light cameras, 197–98, 296n62, 296n63
BRHP. *See* Baltimore Regional Housing
    Program
Briggs, Xavier De Sousa, 170–71, 242
Broken Windows Theory, 166
Brooke Amendment, 10
Buchanan v. Warley (1917), 7
Buprenorphine, 88
Burawoy, Michael, 254

Cabrini-Green housing project, Chicago, 8, 12
cameras, for surveillance, 197–201, 216–17,
    239, 296n62, 296n63, 298n18
Canton, 24, 119, 127, 251
Center for Budget and Policy Priorities
    (CBPP), 249
Chaskin, Robert, 178, 180
Chetty, Raj, 18, 21, 257
Chicago Housing Authority (CHA), 17
children: effects of residential mobility on,
    18, 257; effects of vouchers on, 25, 111–12;
    renter families with, viewed negatively,
    119, 132, 136–37, 179–80
choice, in housing: constraints on, xi, 4, 21,
    23–24, 26, 32, 99, 114, 121, 128, 133, 164, 210,
    232, 241, 244, 284n22 (*see also* vouchers:
    challenges of using); failures of, x, 126; as
    focus of housing voucher program, x, 2, 4,
    10, 14, 19–20, 32, 120, 126, 231, 241; portability
    of vouchers, 117, 250; value and meaning
    of, 25–26. *See also* mobility, residential;
    moving; search process, for using
    vouchers
Cisneros, Henry, 13
city services hotline, 194
Clear, Todd, 296n66
Clinton, Bill, 13
Cochran, Johnny, 108
collective efficacy. *See* social organization
Community Development Block Grants, 254
community meetings, 182–86, 295n51, 296n56
Community Reinvestment Act (1977), 7, 254
Corrigan v. Buckley (1926), 7
Craigslist, 63, 117
credit history, 137–38, 252

crime/violence: in Baltimore, 212; deterrence of, 192–98, 206–7, 217, 296n62, 296n63, 298n18; experiences with/coping strategies for, 211–30; in Oakland Terrace, 144–45, 216–17; in Park Heights, 3, 40–41, 51, 97, 128, 131, 172, 194–201, 211–21, 224–26; voucher holders associated with, 242, 299n8
criminal history, 137–38
culture of poverty, 132
Cylburn Arboretum, 37

decline, folk theories of, 47–51
DeLuca, Stefanie, 216
Desmond, Matthew, *Evicted*, 6, 132, 247
disability, and eligibility for vouchers, 99–100
discrimination: in employment, 246; gender-based, 136; housing, 5–8, 26–27, 119, 128–29, 284n16; in housing policy, ix–x, 6–10, 16, 29, 163, 243, 245, 293n25; in private market, 5–8, 26–27, 128–29; in residential race relations, 293n25; in tenant-rental matching process, 161–63; voucher holders subject to, 118–19, 128, 243, 251–52, 287n11; in zoning, 7, 246, 254–55. *See also* segregation
Dixon, Sheila, 41
dog fighting, 202
doubling up, 62–63, 90, 93
Dreier, Peter, 242
drug rehabilitation centers, 181, 186
drugs: dealing in, 54, 60, 73–74, 84–87, 101, 145, 166, 195–99, 201; families destroyed by, 47–48; in Park Heights, 26, 41, 47, 50, 124, 130, 131, 142, 145, 190, 195–96, 243; use of/addiction to, 47, 50–51, 81–85, 87–89, 213; voucher program rules against, 155, 195
Druid Hill Park, 54, 55
Du Bois, W.E.B., *The Philadelphia Negro*, 5
Duneier, Mitch, 267

Edin, Kathryn, *$2.00 a Day* (with Luke Shaefer), 6
Edmonson Village, 31, 46

Eight Below (film), 203
Ellen, Ingrid Gould, 294n39
employment: discrimination in, 246; effect of vouchers on, 111–12, 288n29, 288n31. *See also* informal economy; unemployment
entrée, into field of research, 267–70
eviction: costs of, for landlords, 142, 157; experiences of, 203; landlords' strategies concerning, 155, 157, 159, 291n17; stigma associated with, 246

Fair Housing Act (1968), 7, 12, 136, 252
Fair Market Rent (FMR), 16, 99, 138, 140, 253, 280n63, 290n12, 291n29, 301n48
Fairway Gardens apartment complex, 116
Family Options Study, 110, 287n25, 288n29
Federal Hill, 24, 119, 127, 251
Federal Housing Administration (FHA), 7
Fischel, William, *The Homevoter Hypothesis*, 178
Flag Homes public housing, Baltimore, 100
FMR. *See* Fair Market Rent
food stamps, 78, 88, 97, 104
foreclosure, 23, 65

Galvez, Martha, 299n21
Gans, Herbert, 5
Gautreaux program, 17, 281n70, 288n31, 292n11
Gautreaux v. CHA (1976), 12, 17
gender, housing discrimination based on, 136
gentrification, 245
Goetz, Edward, *New Deal Ruins*, 245
Government Accountability Office (GAO), 250
Gray, Freddie, 37
Great Depression, 8, 29
Great Migration, 6, 29
Green Acres apartment complex, 79
ground-rent seizers, 143, 291n18

HABC. *See* Housing Authority of Baltimore City

halfway houses, 181

HAP. *See* Housing Assistance Payment

Hartman, Chester, 245

Harvard University, 269

Head Start, 181, 186

heroin, 47, 73, 213

Hirsch, Arnold, 9

HOME Act, 252

home inspections: checklist for, 119; as guarantee of housing quality, 133–34, 146, 290n5; landlord strategies concerning, 118, 121, 145, 146, 156–57; landlords' use of, to deny tenants, 119; required by voucher program, 52–53, 69, 99, 102, 119, 122; tenants' use of, 156

homelessness: criminalization of, 246; experiences of, 23, 87, 88, 91, 105–6, 109; housing insecurity and, 61, 62; vouchers as means of reducing, 19, 94, 102–3, 110

homeowner havens, 57–58, 173–76, 205, 208

homeowners: access of, to social resources, 168; distinguishing of themselves from renters, 165–68, 172–80, 208, 238–40; property values as issue for, 166–67, 177–78, 237, 294n39, 294n43; social capital of, 192–94

homeownership: dream of, 1, 4, 5, 26, 29, 30, 33, 91, 113; housing insecurity associated with, 65–70; in Park Heights, 29–30, 32–33, 57–59, 165–68, 172, 175–80, 237, 284n6, 285n25; positive and negative effects of, on neighborhoods, 177–78

HOPE VI, 13, 279n45

housing: affordable, 61; availability of, 254–55; discrimination in, 5–8, 26–27, 119, 128–29, 284n16; income spent on, 61–62; inequality in, 5–12; policy proposals for, 246–60; poverty linked to, vii, 5–6; research on, 5–6; as a right, 246–47. *See also* neighborhoods; private market

Housing Act (1974), 14

Housing Assistance Payment (HAP), 118–19, 140, 289n9

housing assistance programs: cost of, 247; history of, 8–9; inadequate to meet demand, 8; percentage of population served by, 286n4; shortcomings/failures of, 1; stigma associated with, 246. *See also* vouchers

Housing Authority of Baltimore City (HABC), 1, 24, 103–4, 120, 133, 154, 227, 250, 266

Housing Authority of Baltimore County, 250

Housing Choice Voucher (HCV) program ("Section 8"), ix, 14, 33, 41, 44, 51, 52, 68, 131–32, 135, 143, 149, 152–54, 158–59, 162, 241, 243, 262, 286n2. *See also* voucher holders; vouchers

housing insecurity, 60–90; case studies in, 62–89; facets of, 60–61; and life outcomes, 90; rent burden as factor in, 61–62; renters' experience of, 62

housing policy: discrimination in, ix–x, 6–10, 16, 29, 163, 243, 245, 293n25; "race-blind," 16; segregation as unintended consequence of, 255

Housing Quality Standards (HQS), 119

HUD. *See* U.S. Department of Housing and Urban Development

Hyra, Derek, 171

informal economy, 42, 62, 89, 97, 112, 172

informal social control: defined, 170; erosion of, by formal control, 201–5, 207, 239, 296n66; length of residence as factor in, 173, 193–97; limits of, 195, 239

inspections. *See* home inspections

interviews, 264, 266–70

Jai Medical Center, 186

Jews: housing discrimination against, 284n16; in Park Heights, 29–30, 32, 34–36, 46

Johns Hopkins University, 269

Joseph, Mark, 178, 180

Kefalas, Maria, 167
Kerner, Otto, ix
Kerner Commission, ix–x, 9–10
King, Martin Luther, 74
Korean store owners, 183–84
Kurwa, Rahim, 294n29

Lacks, Henrietta, 268
Lafayette Courts housing project, 13, 65, 219
landlords: case examples of, 140–45;
    cost- and maintenance-saving strategies
    of, 146–47; discretion of, in accepting
    vouchers, 102, 117–19, 252, 287n11;
    enticements offered by, to tenants,
    148–49, 151–52; financial risk reduction
    for, 133; former residents persisting as,
    48–49; human/emotional side of, 159,
    291n25; incentives for renting to voucher
    holders, 24, 59, 131–36, 138–40, 143–44,
    248, 250–53, 285n23; recruitment and
    retention of, in voucher program, 253–54;
    recruitment of tenants by, 24, 115–16,
    130–31, 134–35, 143–44, 253; rent
    collection problems faced by, 134–36, 142,
    158; rents charged by, 52–53, 61, 63, 72,
    134, 145; as research participants, 264–66;
    role of, in voucher use, 23–24, 130–64,
    244–45, 250, 283n92; scholarship on,
    283n92; screening tactics used by, 137–38;
    tenant selection process by, 131, 133–34,
    136–38, 160–63, 244, 252; tenants'
    relations with, 153–55; turnover issues for,
    155–60
lead paint, 146
Lee, Jennifer, 183
leverage, 171
Lexington Terrace housing project, 12, 13
life chances, housing/neighborhoods linked
    to, 21, 32, 90, 126, 169–74, 257–59, 292n11
LIHEAP. See Low Income Home Energy
    Assistance Program
LIHTC. See Low-Income Housing Tax
    Credit

liquor stores, 183, 185, 295n52
locational attainment, 19–22, 281n78
Low Income Home Energy Assistance
    Program (LIHEAP), 74
Low-Income Housing Tax Credit
    (LIHTC), 15, 79, 88, 123, 255

management companies, 147
manufacturing, decline of, 48
McCabe, Brian, 178
McClure, Kirk, 255
McDermott, Monica, 295n50
memorials, for victims of violence, 40, 41
methadone, 85
methodological issues, 261–72; creating a
    sample, 260–64; entrée, 267–70;
    interviews, 264, 266–70; landlords as
    participants, 264–66; positionality,
    268–71; research methods used, 264,
    266–67; social distance, 272
mice, 78, 96–97, 137. See also rats
mobility, residential: effects on children of,
    18, 257; horizontal vs. upward, 211, 231–33;
    place-based interventions for addressing,
    257–59, 281n68; research on, 17–18;
    voucher program's failures concerning,
    126–29, 210–11, 242, 244, 246; as voucher
    program's goal, 16–19, 109, 112, 239,
    256–60, 279n38. See also choice, in
    housing; moving
Mobility Assistance Program, Dallas, 249
Mondawmin Mall, 37
mortgages, ix, 7, 29
moving: precipitating incidents for, 215,
    221–30; reasons for, 210–11, 232–33;
    vouchers as aid to, 211. See also choice, in
    housing; mobility, residential
Moving to Opportunity (MTO), vii–viii,
    17–19, 170, 243, 261, 292n11
Moving to Work (MTW), 280n63, 291n29
Moynihan report, 132
MTO. See Moving to Opportunity
Murphy, Alexandra, 167

Naloxone, 88

narrative ruptures, 215, 221, 225, 230–33

National Commission on Severely Distressed Public Housing, 12–13

neighborhoods: interventions for improving, 257–59; landlord holdings in, 133–34, 136; life chances linked to, 21, 32, 90, 126, 169–74, 257–59, 292n11; low-poverty, housing projects in, 11; poverty linked to, 10–12, 17–18; public housing erected in, 11–12; receiving, 3, 31–34; social capital in, 169–74; voucher holders' residence in, by poverty level, 18–19, 21, 126–27, 133–34, 283n88. *See also* housing

New York City Housing Authority, 278n31

Oakland Terrace apartment complex, 53–54, 56, 59, 60, 66, 95–99, 112, 141–45, 149, 150, 174, 182, 184, 188, 198–201, 206–7, 212, 216–18, 227, 235–36, 239, 298n18

old heads, 193, 206

O'Malley, Martin, 234

one-for-one replacement rule, 279n46, 280n52

Orser, Edward, 31

Oswego Mall public housing, 44, 45

Pall Mall Apartments ("The Ranch"), 40–41, 101, 124

Park Heights, 28–59; attractive features of, 128; black settlement of, 29–30; blockbusting in, 30–31; crime/violence in, 3, 40–41, 51, 97, 128, 131, 172, 194–201, 211–21, 224–26; decline of, 33–34, 36–51, 123, 172, 237–38, 243; demographics of, viii, 2–3, 22, 30, 31, 284n9; description of, 37–45; drug activity in, 26, 41, 47, 50, 124, 130, 131, 142, 145, 190, 195–96, 243; history of, ix, 26, 29–30, 32–36, 237; homeownership in, 29–30, 32–33, 57–59, 165–68, 172, 175–80, 237, 284n6, 285n25; home prices in, 58, 237; Jews living in, 29–30, 32, 34–36, 46; marginalizations and exclusions characterizing, 236–37; median household income in, 172; microneighborhoods in, 57–59, 173–74, 177, 205; photographs of, 39–41, 45; population of, 37; poverty in, 3, 22, 32, 49, 284n18; rental market in, 51–53, 62; rents in, 52–53, 61, 63, 72, 134, 138–40; reputation of, 151; social capital in, 173–74; social organizations in, 180–86, 207–8; unemployment in, 3, 49, 240, 277n5; vacancies in, 26, 38, 40, 49–51, 58, 64, 102, 115–16, 123, 131, 240; vibrancy of, in the past, 33–35, 37, 42–44; voucher holders living in, x–xi, 16, 24, 26–27, 32, 53–54, 127–28, 165–67, 240, 261–62, 285n27

Patterson Park, 295n45

Pattillo, Mary, 246, 293n28; *Black Picket Fences*, 6

Pimlico Junior/Middle School, 45

Pimlico Race Course, 37, 42–43, 43

police: calls to, for suspicious behavior, 193–95; harassment by, 214; misconduct of, 74; and Oakland Terrace, 144–45; in Park Heights, 41; raids by, 201–5; training facility for, 45

Popkin, Susan, 242

positionality, as researcher, 268–71

poverty: concentrated, x, 4–5, 10–14, 20, 31, 114, 163, 169, 244–45, 247, 255–57, 282n85, 292n7; housing/neighborhoods linked to, vii, 5–6, 10–12, 17–18; in Park Heights, 3, 22, 32, 49, 284n18; of public housing residents, 10–11, 13; root causes of, 258–59; voucher holders living in, 19–21; vouchers as means of reducing, 19, 110, 112, 114, 170

Preakness Stakes, 43

predatory inclusion, ix, 30, 237

private market: barriers to finding housing in, xi, 4; discrimination and segregation in, 5–8, 26–27, 128–29, 244–45; housing of the poor transferred to, x, 15–16, 19, 114, 129, 236, 244–45

property values, 166–67, 177–78, 237, 294n39, 294n43

Pruitt-Igoe housing project, St. Louis, 5, 8, 12

public housing: attitudes about, 241, 245–46, 295n45; availability of, 14, 15, 255, 286n2; demolition of, 5, 14, 279n46, 280n52; location of, 11–12; National Commission (1992) report on, 13; need for, 255; origins of, 8, 245; populations served by, 255–56; poverty linked to, 10–11, 13; repair of, 44; success and failure of, 8–11, 14, 100, 245–46, 256

public housing authorities (PHAs), 13, 102–3, 122, 132, 139, 156, 248–50, 253, 259

Quality Housing and Work Responsibility Act (QHWRA), 103, 278n30, 280n52, 280n63

race of voucher holders: as factor in tenant-rental matching, 161–63; neighborhood of residence by, 21, 126, 283n88; percentages of holders by, 100, 119; stigma associated with, 243. *See also* discrimination

racial covenants, ix, 6–8, 29, 243

racism, 161–63, 246, 254

Rainwater, Lee, 5

The Ranch. *See* Pall Mall Apartments

rape, 196, 201, 220

rats, 50, 60, 66, 92, 116, 123, 157, 165–66, 194, 238, 256. *See also* mice

recycling, 187, 296n57

redlining, ix, 7–8, 29, 172, 237, 243

references, tenants', 137–38

registered sex offenders, 218, 224–25

Rental Assistance Demonstration (RAD) program, 44

renters: attitudes toward, 49; burdened by rents, 61–62, 102–3, 134; case examples of, 62–89; housing insecurity faced by, 62; social networks lacking for, 58; socioeconomic circumstances of, 22–23; as source of Park Heights' decline, 48–49; unassisted (market-rate), 52, 57, 59, 60, 62, 90, 134–35, 238, 263–64. *See also* voucher holders

rent reasonableness, 139

restrictive covenants. *See* racial covenants

roaches, 96–97, 229, 256

Roland Park, 2, 46, 127, 209

Roland Park Company, 284n16

Rosenblatt, Peter, 216

Rosin, Hanna, 242, 243

SAFMR. *See* Small Area Fair Market Rent

sampling for range, 263

Sampson, Robert, 169, 293n28

Sard, Barbara, 250

scapegoating: of public housing, 246; of voucher holders, 243–44

Scott, Joyce J., Memorial Pool, 54, 55

search process, for using vouchers: bus tours provided for, 1, 95; case examples of, 114–18, 120–25; and housing availability, 122–23; landlord recruitment of tenants in, 24, 115–16, 130–31, 134–35, 143–44, 253; online, 120–21; proposals for improving, 248–50; tenant-rental matching in, 131, 133–34, 136–38, 151–52, 160–63, 244; time period allotted for, 114–15, 121–22, 288n1. *See also* choice, in housing

"Section 8." *See* Housing Choice Voucher (HCV) program; voucher holders; vouchers

Section 8 Certificate Program, 14

Section 202 program, 286n2

Section 811 program, 286n2

segregation: "diversity segregation," 171; housing policies contributing to, ix–x, 6–10, 16, 255; by neighborhood, 12, 161–63; in public housing, 12; tenant-rental matching process as factor in, 161–63. *See also* discrimination

senior centers, 181–82

sex work, 75–76

Shaefer, Luke, *$2.00 a Day* (with Kathryn Edin), 6

Sharkey, Patrick, 257–58

Shelley v. Kraemer (1948), 7

Show Me a Hero (miniseries), 281n68
Small, Mario, 180, 293n27, 295n50
Small Area Fair Market Rent (SAFMR),
    252–53, 301nn49–51
social capital: access to, 193, 205–8, 238, 240,
    293n27; benefits of, 168, 169; bonding
    mode of, 170, 172–73, 184, 293n16; bridging
    mode of, 170, 173, 184–92, 205; defined,
    169–70; of homeowners, 192–94; of
    longtime residents, 195–97, 206; in
    neighborhoods, 168–74; organizations as
    factor in, 180–86; in Park Heights, 173–74
social capital theory, 172
social control: access to, 170–72; formal,
    174, 195, 197–205, 296n66; informal, 170,
    173, 193–97, 201, 207, 239
social control theory, 206
social distance, 272
social isolation, 10, 12, 169, 292n11
social organization (collective efficacy), 59,
    169, 170, 201, 207–8, 292n7, 293n28
social organizations, 180–86, 207–8,
    295n50
Source of Income (SOI) discrimination
    protection laws, 118–19, 251–52, 287n11,
    289n6
squatting, 64–65, 219, 223
SSI. *See* Supplemental Security Income
Stack, Carol, 271
Stewart, Martha, 87
stigma, of vouchers, 4, 25, 44, 59, 168,
    173–74, 176, 180, 191, 205–8, 236, 238,
    240–46, 258, 259
Stuart, Forrest, 267
Suboxone, 88
Supplemental Security Income (SSI), 74,
    78, 97
surveillance: formal, 197–201, 216–17,
    296n62, 296n63; informal, 192–97
Suttles, Gerald, *The Social Order of the
    Slum*, 173
swimming pools, 54, 55
symbolic boundaries, 167, 176–80

Tach, Laura, 171
TANF (Temporary Assistance to Needy
    Families), 149
Temporary Cash Assistance (TCA), 104
tenant placement agencies, 147, 151
tenement housing, 8
Thompson v. HUD (1995), 12
transitional areas, in neighborhoods, 58, 174,
    177–79, 201, 204–6
Transitions, 105–6
trash, 165–68, 187, *188*
trust, 267–70

unemployment: living situation linked to,
    70–71; manufacturing decline as cause
    of, 48; in Park Heights, 3, 49, 240, 277n5.
    See also employment
urban renewal, 245
U.S. Congress, 249
U.S. Department of Housing and Urban
    Development (HUD), 9, 11, 16–18, 243,
    245, 249, 250, 252–53, 261, 286n6
U.S. Housing Act (1937), 11
U.S. Supreme Court, 255

Venkatesh, Sudhir, *American Project*, 6, 267,
    293n28
Vietnam War, 47, 108, 243
violence. *See* crime/violence
voucher enclaves, 59, 174, 197–202, 206
voucher holders: access of, to social
    resources, 168, 193, 205–8, 238, 240;
    attitudes about, 33–34, 41, 51, 59, 131, 135,
    165–68, 173–87, 191, 197, 205–8, 238, 240,
    240–46, 294n29, 295n45; buying habits
    of, 34, 111; crime associated with, 242,
    299n8; discrimination against, 118–19,
    128, 243, 251–52, 287n11; enticements
    offered by landlords to, 148–49, 151–52;
    geographic distribution of, 282n85;
    indebtedness of, to landlords, 153–54,
    157–60, 291n17; landlords' relations with,
    153–55; in low-poverty neighborhoods,

voucher holders (*continued*)
18–19, 21, 283n88; matching of, to rental
properties, 131, 133–34, 136–38, 151–52,
160–63; mobility/turnover of, 155–60;
neighborhoods of, 19–21; in Park
Heights, x–xi, 16, 24, 26–27, 32, 53–54,
59, 127–28, 165–67, 240, 261–62, 285n27;
race of, 21, 100, 119, 126, 243, 283n88;
receiving neighborhoods for, 3, 31–34;
rent payments of, 52–53; scapegoating
of, 243–44; social networks lacking for,
58; stigma associated with, 236, 238;
women-headed households, 100, 132,
136. *See also* renters
Voucher Mobility Demonstration Act, 249
vouchers: administration of, 249–50;
challenges of using, 114–29 (*see also*
choice, in housing: constraints on);
control/stability/empowerment enabled
by, xi, 26, 88–89, 91, 94–95, 107–8, 109, 113;
eligibility for, 15, 88, 99–100, 280n62,
299n27 (*see also* shortage of, for qualified
individuals); experimental research on,
17–18, 109–10, 287n25; flexibility offered
by, xi, 25–26, 232–33, 239, 247, 249, 256;
goals of, x, 1–2, 19, 114, 169, 241, 279n45;
history of, 12–19; housing available for,
254–55, 302n5; inability to use, 122;
limitations of, 248; outcomes of, 3–4, 19,
23, 109–12, 247, 260, 287n24; payment
standard of, 16, 95, 110, 116, 138–39, 145,
252–53, 288n3, 290n12; policy proposals
for, 246–60; political and popular will for,
247, 260, 299n30; populations targeted for,
99, 103, 144, 247, 2999n27; portability of,
117, 250; premium rents applicable to,
138–39, 252–53; prevalence of, x, 15, 99,
286n2; project-based, 44; rules governing, 101, 117, 133, 153–60, 286n6; shortage
of, for qualified individuals, 15–16, 61,
99, 103–4 (*see also* waiting list for);
shortcomings/failures of, 4–5, 20–21,
23–24, 26–27, 122, 245–46; specialty
programs, 144; stigma associated with, 4,
25, 44, 59, 168, 173–74, 176, 180, 191, 205–8,
240–46, 258, 259; transformative potential
of, xi, 4–5, 19–20, 23, 25–26, 94–95, 107–9,
112–13, 209–10, 233; universal program for,
246–48; work requirements linked to,
299n30. *See also* Housing Choice Voucher
(HCV) program; search process, for
using vouchers; waiting list for vouchers
voucher specialists, 139, 143, 145–48, 251

waiting list for vouchers: causes of backlog
in, 102; closing of, 103–4; length of time
spent on, 1, 22–23, 63, 94, 101–2, 104, 108;
mismanagement of, 103; numbers of
families on, 15; rules governing, 102–3
Walker case (1985), 12
War on Drugs, 172, 243
welfare queen stereotype, 50, 100, 243
white flight, 30, 45–46, 119, 172, 181, 240
WIC (Special Supplemental Nutrition
Program for Women, Infants, and
Children), 149
Williams, "Little Melvin," 73–74, 286n14
Wilson, William Julius, 21; *The Truly
Disadvantaged*, 5–6, 10, 169
Wirth, Louis, "Housing as a Field of
Sociological Research," 5
woman-headed households, 100, 132, 136

zoning, 7, 246, 254–55

A NOTE ON THE TYPE

This book has been composed in Arno, an Old-style serif typeface in the classic Venetian tradition, designed by Robert Slimbach at Adobe.